T0258256

Structured Finance Modeling with Object-Oriented VBA

Founded in 1807, John Wiley & Sons is the oldest independent publishing company in the United States. With offices in North America, Europe, Australia, and Asia, Wiley is globally committed to developing and marketing print and electronic products and services for our customers' professional and personal knowledge and understanding.

The Wiley Finance series contains books written specifically for finance and investment professionals as well as sophisticated individual investors and their financial advisors. Book topics range from portfolio management to e-commerce, risk management, financial engineering, valuation, and financial instrument analysis, as well as much more.

For a list of available titles, visit our Web site at www.WileyFinance.com.

Structured Finance Modeling with Object-Oriented VBA

EVAN TICK

BICENTENNIAL

1807

WILEY

2007

John Wiley & Sons, Inc.

Published by John Wiley & Sons, Inc., Hoboken, New Jersey
Published simultaneously in Canada

For general information on our other products and services or for technical support, please
contact our Customer Care Department within the United States at (800) 762-2974, outside
the United States at (317) 572-3993 or fax (317) 572-4002.

Wiley also publishes its books in a variety of electronic formats. Some content that appears in
print may not be available in electronic books. For more information about Wiley products,
visit our Web site at www.wiley.com

Library of Congress Cataloging-in-Publication Data

Tick, Evan, 1959–
Structured finance modeling with object-oriented VBA / Evan Tick.
    p. cm.—(Wiley finance series)
    Includes bibliographical references and index.
    ISBN-13: 978-0-470-09859-2 (cloth)
    ISBN-10: 0-470-09859-7 (cloth)
    1. Finance—Mathematical models.   2. Investment—Mathematical models.
3. Microsoft Visual Basic for applications.   I. Title.
HG106.T53 2007
332.01'13—dc22

                                                                2006032748

Printed in the United States of America

10 9 8 7 6 5 4 3 2 1

For Lisa

Contents

Preface

Using even the most conservative estimates, asset-backed securities (ABSs) and collateralized debt obligations (CDOs) have grown tremendously over the past 10 years. ABS includes asset sectors in credit card debt, auto loans, student loans, subprime mortgages, home-equity loans, and equipment loans. This doesn't even include prime mortgages, which are categorized as mortgage-backed securities (MBSs). In 2004, the U.S. ABS supply reached $617 billion, with subprime mortgages and home-equity loans around half (J. P. Morgan 2005). These assets can be held as "raw" or whole loans on bank balance sheets, or bonds created through securitization. A percentage of the ABS bonds themselves are repackaged into CDOs. In 2004, $160 billion of cash CDOs were issued (Lucas 2006) of which about $50 billion were ABS CDOs (Bear Stearns 2006). There are also corporate, high-yield, and emerging market CDOs. CDO issuance has grown exponentially over the past 10 years. Synthetic CDOs (built with credit default swaps rather than cash assets) issuance is growing significantly faster than "cash" CDOs (Tavakoli 2003).

The phenomenal growth of these asset classes, and primarily subprime mortgages, can certainly be attributed to the structure of interest rates in the recent past. Historically low interest rates after the Internet bubble and 9/11 led to the rational response of increased debt levels. Subprime home buyers could borrow at affordable rates and prime home buyers could borrow against appreciated home values (home-equity loans). In addition, efficient credit scoring techniques and information on borrowers helped supply grow to meet demand. The Housing Affordability Index, measuring the average ratio of income to housing prices in the United States, reached 144% in 2003, a 30-year high (Molony 2003). The series of Fed interest rate hikes during 2004–2006 has damped growth, and perhaps we have seen the plateau of ABS supply. The big story of the past year has been one of squeezed margins of subprime originators, leading them to relax underwriting standards to goose volume. The chickens started to come home to roost in late 2005—recent vintages appear to be the worst *ever* in terms of delinquencies and defaults (Zimmerman 2007). But the lasting innovations during these past years are the financial structures for efficiently packaging debt.

Why such explosive growth? Two things: innovative assets and financial engineering. The continual evolution of assets makes borrowing more affordable. Securitization enables unparalleled partitioning and transfer of risk. The repackaging of risk, for example, has allowed banks to buy investment-grade pieces while hedge funds buy lesser-rated (and higher-return) residuals. Issuance has grown to fill market demand among these different niches. Regulated banks, insurance companies, and other investors that could not own whole loans on their balance sheets, either by charter or by severe capital requirements, found they could economically own securitized assets.

Over the past 10 years, on the whole, these investments have fared rather well. Comparing the historical constant annual default rates and recoveries of MBS and corporates, MBS (residential and commercial) do better across the ratings (Lucas 2006). ABS did not perform as well as corporates, but averaged with MBS, the ABS/MBS market as a whole is competitive with corporates, given this metric for risk.

These products are derivatives and hence can grow faster than the underlying assets. Debt is resecuritized—loans into bonds, bonds into CDOs, even CDOs built from other CDOs. On top of this, synthetic structures allow cash assets to be resecuritized any number of times. Thus, talking about the growth of these products may not mean much. Risk is not growing at the same rate because the products are often hedged and much of the risk cancels out.

Two things loom large on the horizon: market rates and regulation. ABS/MBS assets migrate as market conditions change. For example, recently with flat forward rates and uncertain outlook for inflation, U.S. borrowers are switching from floating- to fixed-rate loans. As affordability declines, subprime borrowers increase at the expense of prime borrowers. With rates high enough in the short term, new debt creation will decrease. However, derivatives built from these fixed-income assets will not necessarily decline. Basel II regulations give low-risk tranches better capital treatment, and risky tranches get penalized more (Fitch 2005). As these regulations are adopted, banks and other investors will likely shift their appetites for securitized product. This flexibility is conducive to the long-term health of the securitization market, which is second only to equities in the United States. It is a market that cannot be ignored; it is represented in any significant fixed-income portfolio. Lastly, new products are continually being innovated. Four years ago, synthetic baskets of corporate credits (IBOXX) started trading, evolving into trading standard tranches and then bespokes. In early 2006, synthetic baskets of ABS credits (ABX) started trading, leading to standard tranches in 2007 (TABX) (Morgan Stanley 2006). TABX had birth pains due to declining home prime appreciation creating a bearish one-sided market. If history is any indicator, a more liquid market will develop once participants converge on a pricing model.

Originally, banks used securitization for balance-sheet arbitrage. Then other parties became involved in securitization, such as mortgage originators and hedge funds issuing CDOs. The growth of demand for mezzanine bonds was critical to this development. From 1998 to 2005 balance-sheet arbitrage dropped from 48% to 18% of new CDO issuance, replaced by transactions wherein the equity investor aims to arbitrage the excess spread (Mahadevan 2006a). The banks did and will continue to buy seniors, whatever the capital requirements are. High-risk investors (investment funds and hedge funds) will continue to buy the equity pieces. The weak link may very well be the mezzanine investors. Mezzanine demand comes from both "real" money investors and other securitizations. A key question is: How robust and diverse is this class of investors? How correlated are the assets due to the investor base? Should demand slow, can pricing adjust to shift investors outward to senior and equity tranches, keeping securitization as a viable business?

Modeling is essentially abstraction and simplification while producing an accurate estimate of some aspect of a complex system. If the system is physical or financial, the attributes of a good model remain the same. By modeling I am talking about a broader area than simply a mathematical representation of a system. I am also referring to the implementation of the model. Of the financial engineering innovations developed over the past 10 years of feverish ABS growth, the cash flow securitization model is key. In general, this model has three components: loss generation, collateral cash flow generation, and bond cash flow generation. Loss generation models the loss distribution of the assets. The collateral model takes the loss characteristics and produces asset cash flows. The bond model takes the asset cash flows and produces liability cash flows. Be it a vanilla securization or a CDO of CDOs, be it supported by mortgages, loans, or bonds, be it cash or synthetic, the valuation model is essentially the same.

This book introduces this model and its implementation. Illustrations of the model in action are given with empirical studies of the sensitivities of actual structures. To concretize the discussion, subprime mortgage securitization is used throughout the book as a unifying example. It was chosen because in combination with prime and commercial mortgages, mortgage assets and their securitizations make up the bulk of the securitized market. Modeling lessons learned in this sector can certainly be applied to other asset classes and sectors. Subprime is also topical because of the recent efforts to model TABX, perhaps with a combination of cash flow securitization model and market-spread-driven copula model.

The main topics covered in this book are:

- *Securitization*: asset and liability cash flow models, waterfalls, rating agency stresses, residuals, hedging, bond allocation, and sensitivity analyses. The details of the financial model are uncovered, with formal specifications given.
- *Stochastic models*: Monte Carlo, using copula to account for correlations, and credit index modeling. The previous static models are converted here to dynamically simulate (correlated) random variables. This increases accuracy and depth. For example, rather than boil loss down to a single expected value, the entire loss distribution can be used.
- *Optimization techniques*: simulated annealing, zero-one programming, search methods. Several problems arise in securitization that benefit from optimization, for example, allocating bonds and selecting collateral. Practical nonlinear methods are emphasized.
- *Object-oriented architecture*: classes, methods, and inheritance. Effective programming methodology is introduced that facilitates the implementation of these models. These techniques are popular in science, engineering, and certain areas of finance such as exotic derivatives. The same tools are leveraged here for cash flow modeling.
- *Excel and VBA*: advanced techniques, recommended style, and extensive examples. Many books introduce financial applications in Excel. Raise the level of your game with modular programming in VBA.

Various sections of offering materials are reproduced in this book for illustrative purposes only, and make no representation as to the accuracy of the information so reproduced. Readers are encouraged to contact the author with comments and corrections at evan_tick@yahoo.com.

List of Acronyms

ABCDS	Asset-Backed Credit Default Swap
ABS	Asset-Backed Security
ABX	Asset-Backed indeX
ADB	Amortized Defaulted Balance
AFC	Available Funds Cap
ARM	Adjustable-Rate Mortgage
API	Application Program Interface
BET	Binomial Expansion Technique
BEY	Bond Equivalent Yield
BRCFA	Basis Risk Carry-Forward Amount
CADR	Constant Annual Default Rate
CDI	CMO Description Information
CDO	Collateralized Debt Obligation
CDR	Constant Default Rate
CDS	Credit Default Swap
CLTV	Combined Loan-To-Value (ratio)
CMBS	Commercial Mortgage-Backed Security
CMO	Collateralized Mortgage Obligation
CMT	Constant Maturity Treasury
CPR	Constant Prepayment Rate
DLL	Dynamically Linked Library
ERFA	Excess Reserve Fund Account
FICO	Fair Isaac Company
FRM	Fixed-Rate Mortgage
GUI	Graphical User Interface
HEL	Home-Equity Loan
IC	Interest Coverage (test)
IO	Interest Only (bond)
IRR	Internal Rate of Return
LC	Loss Coverage
LGD	Loss Given Default
LIBOR	London Inter-Bank Offered Rate
LTV	Loan-To-Value (Ratio)
MBS	Mortgage-Backed Security

MPR	Monthly Payment Rate (credit cards)
MPS	Mathematical Programming System
NAS	Non-Accelerating Senior (bonds)
NIM	Net Interest Margin
O/C	Over-collateralization (Test)
OTE	Owner's Trust Equity
PAC	Planned Amortization Class (bond)
PIK	Pay In Kind (bond)
PMF	Probability Mass Function
PO	Principal Only (bond)
PPR	Principal Payment Rate (credit cards)
PSA	Public Securities Association–Bond Market Association
REMIC	Real Estate Mortgage Investment Conduit
RICO	Racketeer-Influenced Corrupt Organization (act)
RMBS	Residential Mortgage-Backed Security
S&P	Standard & Poor's
SMM	Single Monthly Mortality
STCDO	Single-Tranche CDO
VBA	Visual Basic for Applications
WAC	Weighted-Average Coupon
WAL	Weighted-Average Life
WAM	Weighted-Average Maturity
WARF	Weighted-Average Rating Factor
ZPB	Zero Prepay Balance

Acknowledgments

I thank my colleagues at IXIS Capital Markets for their friendship over the years and for creating a great working environment. Rob Catarella, Joe Falcone, Bill Greenberg, John Hatzoglou, Rick Martino, Rene Mendez, Chris Nolle, Steve Pasko, Vaclav Polasek, Eric Raiten, and Andre Romain all shared their insights and expertise in developing this book. I am especially grateful to Andre, Eric, and Joe for reviewing early drafts, and William Dellal and Paul Monaghan for their support over the years. I also thank Young-Sup Lee at Morgan Stanley, Tim McLaughlin at Nomura Securities, Sylvain Jousseaume at Merrill Lynch and Ian Adelson for ongoing friendships and technical discussions. Special thanks go to Bill Falloon and his staff at Wiley.

About the Author

Evan Tick studied Electrical Engineering at MIT (MS, BS, 1982) and Stanford (PhD, 1987), before teaching at The University of Tokyo and The University of Oregon. He moved to New York in 1996 to work for Morgan Stanley and then Caisse des Dépôts CDC (now IXIS) soon after. He has been involved in fixed-income markets, focusing on portfolio optimization, risk management, asset-backed conduits, mortgage securitization, and credit derivatives. Perhaps his most crowning achievement was coaching the Douglass Panthers, who finished in sixth place in the 2005 First Lego League NYC-wide robotics tournament. Or it could have been cycling from Bolzano to the top of the Passo di Stelvio one horrible day in a freezing rainstorm in August 2000.

CHAPTER 1

Cash-Flow Structures

If I listened to my customers, I would have invented a very fast horse.

—Henry Ford

1.1 GETTING STARTED

A simplified "cash" structure, also known as a "true sale" structure, is illustrated in Figure 1.1. A seller sells assets into a trust from which bonds are issued to investors. The adjective "cash" is used to denote that real assets are purchased with cash collected from issued bonds. This is opposed to a synthetic structure where credit default swaps (CDSs) are entered into (discussed later in this chapter). The adjective "true sale" refers to the transfer of the assets into a trust or special-purpose vehicle (SPV) from the sellers. The transfer is a legal sale, isolating the assets from the seller.

The assets reside in the trust and generate interest and principal (I + P) cash flows. These collateral cash flows are routed to the various bonds that were issued as liabilities. The rationale behind this generic structure is to transform a group of assets with certain average credit risk into a set of bonds of *distinct* credit risks. These risks may be formalized by virtue of having a rating agency assign ratings (e.g., senior bonds are rated AAA).[1] The bonds are partitioned in an attempt to meet investor demand for different risks. The structure satisfies various counterparties in different ways. Senior investors may gain the ability to invest in asset types that were previously unavailable to them because of their raw risk. Equity investors may exploit

---

[1] Throughout this book, S&P ratings are given unless the distinction between the different agency ratings is relevant.

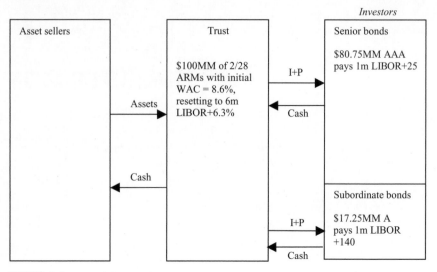

FIGURE 1.1   Simplified Cash Securitization Structure (Not Drawn to Scale)

the excess spread "arbitrage" between asset yields and issued bond costs. Seller/securitizers, underwriters, guarantors, and the like look to earn fees.

The AAA senior bonds, for example, achieve their low risk and high rating because they are supported (at a higher priority than other bonds) by asset cash flows and they have various forms of credit enhancement. One type of credit enhancement is the subordinate bonds shown in Figure 1.1. These bonds absorb any losses before the seniors do—*all* the subordinates need to be written down before the seniors realize *any* loss. The alchemy of transforming collateral of one rating into a security of another rating is subtle. Do the senior bonds have the same credit risk as other securities rated AAA (perhaps backed by different collateral) by the same rating agency? Where does the similarity end, making the rating nonequivalent (Davies 2006)?

Both the assets and the liabilities have various characteristics that are glossed over in this figure. Structural complications are hidden. How are interest and principal allocated to each bond over time? Are there triggers that cause cash flows to be rerouted or even terminate the deal? Are there auxiliary accounts, and how do they operate? Consider that a prospectus can be 150 to 250 pages long. The main difficulty in accurately modeling the structure (i.e., estimating the value of the bonds) *is not necessarily this complexity, although complexity does make such models intricate.* No, the *key difficulty is in making the right input assumptions*: Will the assets prepay and at what rate? How heavy will losses be, and what is their timing? Will forward interest rates be used or another view of rates taken?

Table 1.1 sketches a possible cash flow for this structure. Assets consist of $100MM worth of what is known as "2/28 hybrid ARM" loans. For simplicity, all the loans are considered to be the same: They remain fixed at 8.6% for two years until they float at six-month LIBOR + 6.3%. The collateral cash flows are shown on the left and the bond cash flows on the right. There are no losses assumed, although there *are* voluntary prepayments made on the collateral. Senior and subordinate floating-rate bonds are issued for a total of $98MM, thus implying that the deal is initially over-collateralized by 2%. Annualized one-month LIBOR rates are listed—the two bonds are floating on this rate: the senior bond at a 25 bps spread and the subordinate at a 140 bps spread. There is enough "excess spread" between the assets and liabilities that even after bond interest and principal is paid, there is a residual (rightmost column in Table 1.1). Note that the seniors get paid down entirely before the subordinates are paid any principal. In this structure, O/C is held constant at $2MM until the bonds pay down entirely, at which point the O/C slowly releases to the residual.

An overly simple example with actual numbers is introduced to help the reader visualize the core of all cash flow models. There are assets generating cash fed to liabilities absorbing cash. Both sides are driven by market rates, perhaps unevenly. The collateral can be driven by several factors, including losses and prepayments. The bonds are managed by potentially complex payment priorities. If one were to invest in the residual of this deal, for example, then an accurate present valuation of the residual cash flow would be necessary, under alternative scenarios. The sensitivity of the residual to various factors would be important to ascertain (e.g., how does its value change with a change in prepayment rate?).

The details of collateral cash flows are discussed in Chapter 3. The intricacies of bond cash flow generation are discussed in Chapter 4. How the over-collateralization amount, as well as the bond allocations, is optimally chosen is discussed in Chapter 5. The trade-offs between over-collateralization and excess spread are discussed in Chapter 6.

1.2 SECURITIZATION

Collateralized mortgage obligations (CMOs) and, in general, mortgage-backed securities (MBSs) are investment vehicles that support bond issuance with an underlying pool of mortgage assets. In general, interest cash flows from the assets support interest paid to the bonds, and principal cash flows from the assets support amortization of the bonds. In actuality, the transfer of cash flows can be a complex priority of payments as described in what is known as a waterfall. In general, the asset and liability balances match more

4

TABLE 1.1 Simplified Cash Securitization Structure: Cash Flows (x000). Monthly periods 1–12 and 45–60 shown. Rates are annualized (6m LIBOR not shown)

Period	Collateral Int	Collateral Prin	Prepay	Bal	Bonds 1m L	Senior Int	Sub Int	Prin Dist	Senior Prin	Sub Prin	Senior Bal	Sub Bal	Residual
0	—	—	—	100,000	—	—	—	—	—	—	80,750	17,250	—
1	717	59.3	1,344	98,596	3.15%	229	65	1,404	1,404	—	79,346	17,250	423
2	707	59.0	1,326	97,212	3.29%	234	67	1,384	1,384	—	77,962	17,250	405
3	697	58.6	1,307	95,846	3.44%	248	72	1,365	1,365	—	76,596	17,250	377
4	687	58.2	1,289	94,500	3.58%	253	74	1,347	1,347	—	75,250	17,250	360
5	677	57.8	1,270	93,171	3.73%	250	74	1,328	1,328	—	73,921	17,250	354
6	668	57.5	1,253	91,861	3.88%	263	78	1,310	1,310	—	72,611	17,250	327
7	658	57.1	1,235	90,569	4.02%	258	78	1,292	1,292	—	71,319	17,250	322
8	649	56.7	1,218	89,295	4.17%	271	83	1,274	1,274	—	70,045	17,250	295
9	640	56.4	1,200	88,038	4.31%	275	85	1,257	1,257	—	68,788	17,250	280
10	631	56.0	1,184	86,798	4.46%	252	79	1,240	1,240	—	67,548	17,250	300
11	622	55.7	1,167	85,576	4.60%	282	89	1,223	1,223	—	66,326	17,250	251
12	613	55.3	1,150	84,370	4.75%	276	88	1,206	1,206	—	65,120	17,250	249
45	255	8.6	826	22,597	6.75%	25	121	835	835	—	3,347	17,250	109
46	246	8.4	797	21,792	6.75%	18	109	805	805	—	2,542	17,250	118
47	237	8.2	768	21,016	6.75%	15	121	776	776	—	1,766	17,250	101
48	229	8.0	741	20,267	6.75%	10	117	749	749	—	1,017	17,250	101
49	220	7.8	714	19,545	6.75%	6	121	722	722	—	295	17,250	93
50	213	7.6	689	18,848	6.75%	2	117	697	295	402	—	16,848	94
51	205	7.4	664	18,176	6.75%	—	118	672	—	672	—	16,176	87
52	198	7.2	641	17,528	6.75%	—	114	648	—	648	—	15,528	84
53	191	7.1	618	16,904	6.75%	—	105	625	—	625	—	14,904	85
54	184	6.9	596	16,301	6.75%	—	105	603	—	603	—	14,301	79
55	177	6.7	575	15,720	6.75%	—	97	581	—	581	—	13,720	80
56	171	6.6	554	15,159	6.75%	—	96	561	—	561	—	13,159	75
57	165	6.4	534	14,618	6.75%	—	92	541	—	541	—	12,618	73
58	159	6.2	515	14,097	6.75%	—	80	521	—	521	—	12,097	79
59	153	6.1	497	13,594	6.75%	—	85	503	—	503	—	11,594	68
60	148	5.9	479	13,109	6.75%	—	79	485	—	485	—	11,109	69

or less. When the asset balance exceeds the liability balance, the structure is over-collateralized. This is beneficial to the bond holders because the excess can absorb defaulted mortgages. Most structures require a certain amount of over-collateralization (O/C) and when the OC is less than the target, the structure is undercollateralized. In such a case, payment priorities are shifted to pay down more senior bonds, hence increasing the OC.

Let's look in more detail at a typical deal, jumping into the deep water. The reader may wish to skim the remainder of this chapter and return to it after reading subsequent chapters. However, it is important to understand how the securitization business works before appreciating why models are built as they are. Subsequent chapters describe many of the points introduced here in greater detail.

The phases of a typical "cash" mortgage securitization are:

1. The Seller buys assets (it is called the Seller because it sells these assets into a Trust).
2. Underwriters bid to do the bond underwriting (potentially the Seller does its own bond issuance, in which case it is an underwriter).
3. The Seller picks a syndicate of underwriters with a lead.
4. The Seller works with the syndicate lead and the rating agencies to size and rate the structure.
5. The syndicate starts to sell the deal (i.e., solicit interest from Investors).
6. On Trade Date, the Seller and syndicate lead price the deal with live market spreads and interest rates. The syndicate finalizes sales to Investors at these prices for settlement on the Settle Date. Usually, all bonds are sold at this time.
7. The Seller books a sale of the assets on the Trade Date but retains certain risks until the Settle Date (around one month later). For example, should a loan entirely prepay, that loan must be replaced by the Seller. If the loan was purchased at a premium, since it prepays at par, there will be a loss to the Seller.
8. On settlement, the Seller sells the assets into the Trust.
9. The syndicate issues bonds supported by the Trust to Investors.
10. After settlement the Seller may be required to supply additional assets within some short period of time (called the prefunding period).
11. The Seller may also be allowed to trade assets during a period of time (called the reinvestment period).

Mortgage assets are sold in pools of loans by Originators who underwrite the individual loans. The pools are sold at auction. The first step above, buying assets, involves the following steps:

1. The Seller models the loan collateral to estimate a price.
2. The Seller wins its bid for the pool.

3. The Seller conducts due diligence on pool, potentially kicking out non-compliant loans.
4. The Trustee verifies that the collateral is compliant, issuing a Trust Receipt to the Seller.
5. The pool is now settled, that is, owned by the Seller.
6. The Seller monitors Servicer reports and reconciles invoices with cash receipts.
7. The Seller updates the loan balances and paid-through dates.
8. Within some short period of time after settling the pool, the Seller can put back noncompliant loans to the Originator.

Figure 1.2 summarizes a typical "cash" structure *just at the point of settlement*. Investors in the structure (also called Certificate Holders) pay cash to buy various bonds or tranches of the Trust (1). The Trustee is potentially paid up-front fees (2). The Trust buys the loans from the Seller (3). Previously, the loans were analyzed and bid, and due diligence was conducted by a third party (the Trustee). The final loan portfolio is passed into the Trust. Swap counterparties ("Basis Risk Cap Provider" and "NIM Cap Provider" in the diagram) may provide interest rate swaps and/or caps to the Trusts. Here, caps are assumed, requiring up-front fees (4,5). The caps reduce Trust exposure to any fixed-floating-rate mismatch. Servicing rights are sold to the Seller along with the loan portfolio. The Seller may sell these rights to a new Servicer, receiving cash (6).

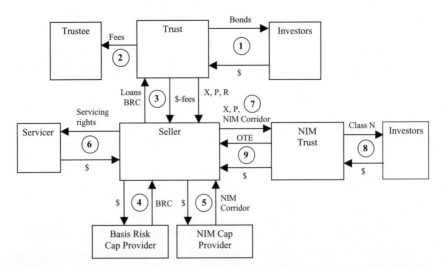

FIGURE 1.2 Typical Trust Structure with Corridors, Assumes the Seller Sells the NIM and Retains the OTE; Snapshot Taken at Deal Settlement

The Net Interest Margin (NIM) Trust is a monetized portion of the residual (equity) tranche of the structure. Potentially, three cash flows can be placed into the NIM Trust (7). Class X is residual interest, and class P is prepayment penalties. The NIM "corridor" is the flows from optional interest rate caps (the "NIM Cap Provider"). Class N is the NIM outflows, perhaps sold to Investors (8). The cash paid by NIM Investors flows through to the Seller (8,9) and into the original Trust in purchase of Classes X and P. This flow is implicitly netted against (3). A "post" NIM piece (OTE, or "Owner's Trust Equity") is the residual after Class N is paid. This may be retained by the Seller or sold to a counterparty (9). This example has one NIM, although a chain of NIMs is possible. Class R is constructed for tax purposes and related to real estate mortgage investment conduits (REMICs), a topic beyond the scope of this text. For one explanation of how this type of structure is taxed, see Morgan Stanley (2004a).

Figure 1.3 shows the structure in the *steady state*. The assets in the Trusts pay interest and principal to the Investors (1,6). These payments are supported by the Basis Risk Cap (BRC) paid by the Cap Provider should interest rates exceed the strike (2,3). These payments are also supported by the Servicer should any assets miss payments due to delinquency or default (4). Should recoveries be made on defaulted assets, the servicer is repaid any advances from recoveries (4). The Trustee distributes payments from the Cap Providers and Servicers to the Trusts (2,5). The assets also make payments to the Trustee: ongoing Trustee fees and Class X, P, and R cash flows (2). The Class X and P flows are paid to the NIM Trust (5). The post-NIM residual is paid back to the Trustee (7) and ultimately to its owner.

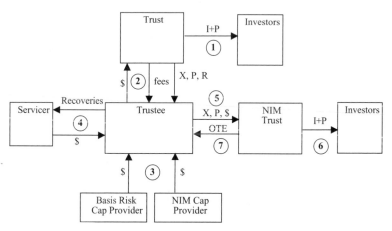

FIGURE 1.3 Typical Trust Structure: Steady State Cash Flows

The first phase of syndication (bidding on an asset pool) is illustrated in Figure 1.4. These actions occur within a few days and are repeated throughout the period when assets are warehoused, leading to a securitization takeout. Collateral data, arriving from an originator, are scrubbed and entered into a collateral management system. The system then produces stratification reports for traders to ascertain pricing assumptions for the pool, perhaps by comparing to similar pools. Loss distribution models are run (rating agencies may have their own proprietary models), producing loss severity and foreclosure frequency reports. A repline file (describing the collateral) is generated for structurers to lay out a tentative structure (what tranches at what ratings) that is then fleshed out (how large each tranche is) in the sizing model. The sizing model requires market inputs for curves and spreads, as well as rating agency constraints. The sizing model generates a final structure that can then be priced with the pricing model. Over time, if the model price drifts from other bids in the market, the model inputs should be reconsidered. For instance, one might ask: Are the assumed market spreads still correct?

To summarize, for each asset pool of interest, the models outlined take the best available input assumptions at the time and generate a bid price. This price is an estimate of pool value assuming eventual securitization takeout. The pool can be viewed on its own (as if the securitization were supported only by these assets) or in conjunction with what is already owned.

In reality, securitization is more complex than previously described. Figure 1.5 illustrates the purchase of assets over time. Starting on the left of the time line, an ongoing operation is to bid and purchase loan pools. These loans are added to the overall open position of the Desk. A securitization "closes" on the Settle Date. One month prior to this, the bonds are structured, priced, and sold vis-à-vis a Prosup (short for Prospectus Supplement) pool. This pool has the required collateral size and characteristics for closing. The rating agencies bless this pool and certain stressed performance results are published in the Prosup for sales purposes. One week prior to settlement, the initial settlement pool is selected. This pool must adhere to the Prosup pool characteristics within very tight bands. The rating agencies again need to bless this pool. Loans originally in the Prosup pool that have settled and pass all performance constraints can be removed from the initial settlement pool and substituted with other loans, as long as the overall profile is acceptable. After closing, the prefunding account is used to buy additional loans to complete the collateral. These loans are usually selected in three phases, one per month, each reviewed by the rating agencies.

Figure 1.4 also summarizes daily mark-to-market of the bonds. Every day, the current aggregated assets are run through the pricing model. The only inputs that should change are market curves and (less frequently) market

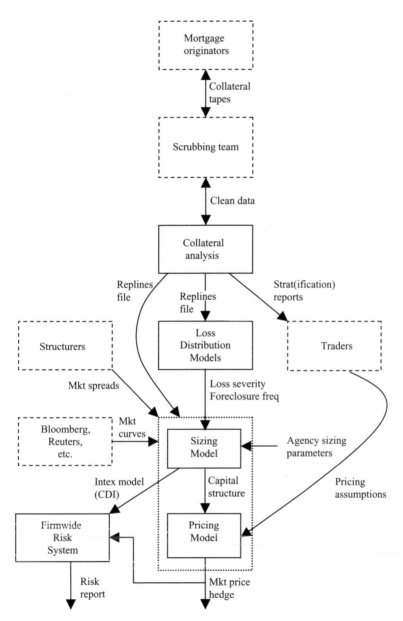

FIGURE 1.4 Modeling Procedure for Assets Not Yet Securitized

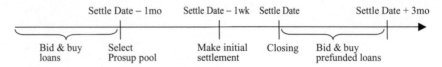

FIGURE 1.5   Typical Timeline Describing Loan Purchase for Securitization

spreads. The pricing model generates a price estimate for the loan portfolio. In the next chapters, the pricing and sizing models in this diagram are described.

Once a portfolio of loans gets securitized and the deal has settled, commercial models can be used, for example, Intex (www.intex.com). Industry standard has evolved to use the Intex CMO Description Information (CDI) meta-language for describing a deal and its waterfalls. The models outlined in this book are are not CDI interpreters, nor do they produce CDI to run on the Intex interpreter. The models described here take a different approach.

The securitizations described above involve "cash" structures involving actual or real collateral (loans or bonds). "Synthetic" deals are structured with swaps that mimic bond cash flows. Among securitizations over the past few years, synthetic and hybrid (synthetic and cash) deals outnumbered cash deals. Synthetics are introduced next and revisited in section 7.5.

1.3   SYNTHETIC STRUCTURES

A "synthetic" structure uses credit default swaps (CDSs) or, in the case of mortgages, asset-backed credit default swaps (ABCDSs) instead of real assets. In a CDS transaction one party pays a periodic fixed premium to buy protection on a given name or credit (a reference bond). The counterparty receives these premiums. Should the reference bond miss interest or principal payments, the counterparty pays some related compensation to the insurance buyer. Hence, the counterparty is selling protection. This is a gross overview of the swap—there are several other details concerning how the counterparty pays given certain events, and how the swap is terminated.

Even with this simple description, we can see how the swap can be used as a *hedge* for a cash deal. If the reference credit starts to deteriorate (e.g., its spread widens), then the protection buyer sees an increase in the swap value. A securitizer might enter into a swap to hedge the value of an underlying real asset warehoused prior to securitization settlement. It is painful if a separate swap is required for every name in the portfolio. To facilitate this, it is possible to swap on an *index* of names. For example, ABX is an index

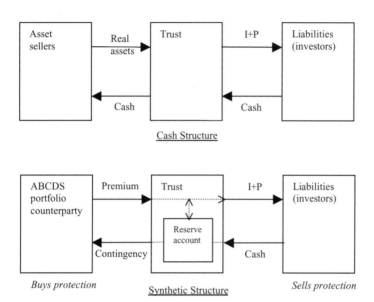

FIGURE 1.6   Cash vs. Synthetic Structures (Funded)

of 20 mortgage deals, each with various rated tranches (Lehman Brothers 2005, 2006; Credit Suisse 2006). If your asset portfolio has the same general characteristics as the ABX, it can be hedged by entering into an ABX swap as the protection buyer. For example, you can buy protection on the ABX BBB subindex, which means that you pay a premium and receive a contingency payment should the ABX BBB tranches miss a payment of some sort.

Furthermore, synthetic structures can be built entirely out of CDSs rather than real assets. Cash and synthetic deals are contrasted in Figure 1.6. In a typical cash deal, the investors pay cash that is used to buy real assets in the collateral portfolio. The assets throw off interest and principal payments (I + P). These are paid through a waterfall to the investors. The issued bonds amortize at the natural rate of the collateral amortization.

This description is simplified in many areas. No prior funding of assets is assumed—it is as if all the assets were purchased at settlement. In reality, most assets are purchased beforehand, and this requires funding. There is some counterparty off to the left that funds the deal at some funding rate, and is paid off on settlement date by the investor's cash. Also, on settlement, all assets are assumed to have been purchased—in reality, there may be a prefunding period. There may also be a reinvestment period, which is assumed here to be absent. Finally, termination conditions are ignored. These same simplifications are assumed when considering the synthetic deal next.

In a typical (funded) synthetic deal, the investors pay cash to buy bonds. This cash is invested in relatively risk-free securities (reserve account) that pays a floating rate (London Interbank Offered Rate [LIBOR]). A portfolio of (AB)CDS is entered into. These swaps pay fixed premiums. Supposing the issued bonds are floaters, the premium (from swaps) plus LIBOR (from the reserve account) combine to form the interest payment to the bonds. Any excess interest goes into the reserve account. During amortization, cash from the reserve account is paid out as principal to the bonds. The amortization rate tracks the amortization rate of the (AB)CDS reference bonds. Should losses be taken in the reference bonds, the reserve account makes a contingency payment to the swap counterparty. Finally, any cash remaining in the reserve upon termination is distributed to the residual.

This type of synthetic structure is called a "funded" deal because bonds are issued for *cash*. The trust has been created to ensure that the assets in the reserve account are bankruptcy remote. It is possible to issue an *unfunded* tranche if the investor is so highly rated that it can be trusted to make contingency payments. Such a tranche is usually (but not always) the senior-most, called the "super senior," that is, effectively rated even higher than AAA. The super senior is supported directly by entering into a CDS; that is, the investor pays no initial cash.

What are the advantages of a synthetic structure? Primarily, it should allow optimal asset selection without having to bid on newly issued asset portfolios or bonds. Assets on the secondary market can be evaluated, compared, and selected prior to execution. A cash portfolio organically grown over time is perhaps less optimal. Also, synthetics enable cheaper funding. CDSs can be cheaper than their corresponding cash assets. In addition, unfunded "super seniors" have lower spreads than funded seniors (hence are cheaper to the issuer). What is the main disadvantage? (AB)CDS counterparties to buy protection must be found, which may not be easy.

A *bespoke* tranche (also called a single-tranche CDO or STCDO) is a synthetic structure consisting of a single tranche. It is simpler than a traditional synthetic structure (above), and can be optimized to an investor's preferences. The investor can specify the collateral, the amount of credit enhancement, and the tranche width. If there is only one investor, then there can be no conflicts of interest with other investors, for example, the seller/structurer who often retains the equity. This can result in increased spread to the investor for equivalent risk. One investor also implies that the deal can be closed even faster than a traditional synthetic deal. Unlike a structure in which the seller has sold all tranches and hence holds no risk position, if the seller sells a bespoke to an investor, then the seller is short risk (i.e., it has bought protection). To hedge this, the seller may choose to sell protection in the right ratio (more about this in section 7.5.3). Either the entire index, a sector within the index, a subset of individual names in the index, or a combination of these can be sold as the hedge. A seller retaining the equity tranche of a cash structure has a similar hedging problem, as does any investor in any tranche.

Synthetic structures are a topic worthly of an entire book (e.g., Chaplin 2005). The reader interested in learning more about synthetics is also referred to Tavakoli (2003), Cifuentes and Lancaster (2004), Lucas (2006), Mahadevan (2006a, 2006b), Whetten and Adelson (2004a, 2004c, 2004d), and Bank of America (2004).

1.4 PUTTING IT ALL TOGETHER

In this chapter, cash and synthetic structures have been introduced. The taxonomy of securitizations goes beyond this one dimension. Other key dimensions include type of asset and type of analysis, as illustrated in Figure 1.7. Only a sample of links is shown here. Hybrid deals are structures where both the assets and liabilities are constructed with both cash and synthetic assets. In addition to the asset-backed securities (ABS) and residential mortgage-backed securities (RMBS) emphasized in this book, there are also commercial mortgage (CMBS), corporate (investment grade and high yield), and emerging market (EM) deals.

All these assets are valued primarily based on interest, default, and recovery rates. For assets such as corporate bonds, credit spreads are translated

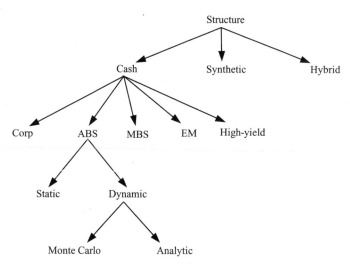

FIGURE 1.7 Taxonomy of Securitization Structures (Not All Links Shown)

into default probabilities (see Chapter 7). Mortgages and some ABS loans have the additional stochastic variable of prepayment rate. Each deal can be analyzed either statically or dynamically. Static analysis involves valuing a relatively small set of stressed economic scenarios as represented by interest, default, and prepayment curves. Dynamic analysis represents an unlimited number of scenarios by interest, default, and prepayment probability distributions. Finally, dynamic analysis can be implemented in various ways. Monte Carlo simulation evaluates thousands of scenarios sampled from the (marginal) probability distributions to construct empirical (joint) value distributions. In rare cases, the mathematics of the dynamic input distributions are sufficiently simple to allow semianalytical solutions to the output value distributions.

Not all of the combinations in this taxonomy are used in practice. Let's trace some of the popular combinations. This book concentrates on ABS/MBS cash deals with static analysis (Chapters 3 through 6). Static analysis has been used by rating agencies to rate deals (i.e., assign ratings to tranches). Dynamic analysis with Monte Carlo simulation is introduced in Chapter 7, in the context of both cash deals and synthetic deals. In general, dynamic analysis is used by sellers/securitizers to get a more detailed view of risk versus return, and has recently been adopted by rating agencies.

Mortgage taxonomy is quite rich. MBSs can be split between residential (RMBS) and commercial (CMBS). RMBSs can be split between government-guaranteed and nonguaranteed mortgages. The three agencies (Ginnie Mae, Fannie Mae, and Freddie Mac) issue "conforming" collateral, and nonagency originators issue "nonconforming" collateral.[2] RMBSs can also be split between pass-throughs and collateralized mortgage obligations (CMOs). The latter have tranched bonds in their liability structure. Nonagency CMOs are also called "whole loan" CMOs or CDOs because the collateral is raw mortgage loans. Other types of CDOs often have bonds for collateral, for example, pass-through mortgage bonds, corporates, and so on. Nonagency RMBSs, by virtue of not being guaranteed by the government, need other types of credit enhancement, as discussed in later chapters. Their collateral is split along a credit dimension: prime ("A" rated), midprime ("alt-A" rated), and subprime ("B" and "C" rated). "Home equity" is a term commonly used for subprime mortgages. However, technically it refers to second-lien mortgages of any quality. To avoid this ambiguity, the term will be avoided when possible.

Synthetic ABS deals with static analysis were touched upon in the previous section. Although the construction of synthetic deals is radically different

---

[2] Throughout the book, "agency" refers to rating agency, not government mortgage agency, unless otherwise noted.

than cash deals, the analysis for ABS/MBS/CMBS is similar. These asset types require detailed cash flow analysis for accurate valuation; that is, picking an optimal portfolio requires understanding cash flows. Thus, the techniques described in this book apply also to synthetic ABS deals. Synthetic deals based on corporate credits differ in that cash flow analysis is simpler because premiums are fixed and assets do not amortize. Synthetic deals based on indexes differ in that the portfolio is fixed. The waterfalls in such structures are usually quite simple. As a result, dynamic analysis is practical for this market, as discussed in section 7.5 in the context of Monte Carlo simulation. Semianalytical solution of such structures is used by the market as a de facto "street model" for pricing such indexes.

CHAPTER 2

Modeling

Irrationally held truths may be more harmful than reasoned errors.
—Thomas Huxley

Guildenstern: *We only know what we're told and that's little
enough. And for all we know it isn't even true.*

Player: *For all anyone knows, nothing is. Everything has to be
taken on trust; truth is only that which is taken to be true. It's the
currency of living. There may be nothing behind it, but it doesn't
make any difference so long as it is honoured. One acts on
assumptions. What do you assume?*
—Tom Stoppard, *Rosencrantz & Guildenstern Are Dead*

The purpose of this book is to introduce modeling cash flow–driven financial structures—specifically, modeling mortgage securitizations with spreadsheets (Excel) and object-oriented programming (Visual Basic). Why these specific choices? The abstract modeling concepts introduced are best learned in the context of rich and complex applications. Mortgages are notoriously complex deal structures because of the variability and detail of the assets and liabilities. Spreadsheets are chosen because for many businesses they are the quickest and most intuitive way to build financial models (Benninga 2000; Jackson and Staunton 2001). Object-oriented programming is chosen, as opposed to other programming paradigms, because it engenders modular organization required for complex applications.

Many textbooks cover financial modeling in Excel or C++. The main trouble with Excel is that models rapidly hit a complexity barrier. At some point, most serious models require increased data dimensionality, flexibility, expressivity, and speed that cannot be delivered by Excel. At this point the model is usually reimplemented in C++ (or Java, etc.). Having a spreadsheet as a prototype is handy for initially testing the new implementation.

It cannot be denied that this dual approach has an ecological niche in the business world because of its economy of effort. There is no need to pull out the big guns of C++ implementation unless the business proves its profitability and scalability. A spreadsheet may be sufficient for the initial phases of the business or for one-off trades.

The approach here is a hybridization of these two—implementing a model in a *simple* object-oriented language (VBA) *directly integrated* with a spreadsheet. The advantages of this approach are numerous. Models can be built quickly, even with spreadsheet formulae (eventually migrated to code). Models can be fast—perhaps not as fast as C++, but significantly faster than Excel. Models can exploit many of the advantages of class architecture: modularity, stability, flexibility, abstraction, elegance, expressivity, extensibility, and so on. User interfaces to models come "for free" with the spreadsheet; fancy interface toolboxes are available, but you don't have to use them. To be fair, because this is a hybrid approach, models aren't completed as quickly as in pure Excel, nor are they as powerful as in C++. As this book will hopefully illustrate, by taking a middle road we can get a majority of the best of both worlds.

This approach, and this text, is specifically meant for nonprogrammers. It is meant for those in the business world who are *not* quants or financial engineers. Anyone with Excel experience is a prime candidate for learning this material and exploiting this approach. There is a large population of financial analysts whose expertise and professional interest is business, not modeling or programming. Yet many of these analysts need to model. It is inevitable. Since most everyone has extensive spreadsheet skills, it is reasonable to *incrementally* extend those abilities with object-oriented programming—not a radical leap, such as would be required to exploit the esoteria of C++, but a minor jump into VBA. Granted, VBA lacks certain advanced features[1] but it is powerful enough to get many jobs accomplished.

2.1 DIPPING A TOE IN THE SHALLOW END

The purpose of this section is to get you programming in VBA as quickly as possible. Few language facilities will be introduced, only enough to start modeling. Before we begin, consider borrowing $100,000 over 30 years,

---

[1] Such as inheritance and templates. These are specifically mentioned, for those readers familiar with them, because they are key weaknesses of VBA. However, programming techniques are reviewed in this book for mimicking inheritance to some degree.

	A	B	C	D	E	F	G	H	I	J	K
1		period	Int	Prin	Bal						
2		0			100,000.00		bal	100,000			
3		1	625.00	74.21	99,925.79		npds	360			
4		2	624.54	74.68	99,851.11		freq	12			
5		3	624.07	75.15	99,775.96		coup	7.50%			
6		4	623.60	75.61	99,700.35		pymt	699.21			
7		5	623.13	76.09	99,624.26		WAL	20.2			
8		6	622.65	76.56	99,547.70						
9		7	622.17	77.04	99,470.66						
10		8	621.69	77.52	99,393.13						
11		9	621.21	78.01	99,315.13						
12		10	620.72	78.49	99,236.63						
13		11	620.23	78.99	99,157.64						
14		12	619.74	79.48	99,078.17						
351		349	50.37	648.84	7,410.58						
352		350	46.32	652.90	6,757.68						
353		351	42.24	656.98	6,100.70						
354		352	38.13	661.09	5,439.61						
355		353	34.00	665.22	4,774.40						
356		354	29.84	669.37	4,105.02						
357		355	25.66	673.56	3,431.47						
358		356	21.45	677.77	2,753.70						
359		357	17.21	682.00	2,071.69						
360		358	12.95	686.27	1,385.43						
361		359	8.66	690.56	694.87						
362		360	4.34	694.87	0.00						

Formula annotations:
- =-PMT(coup/freq, npds, bal)
- =E7-D8
- =pymt-C8
- =E7*coup/freq
- =SUMPRODUCT(D3:D362, B3:B362) / E2 / 12

FIGURE 2.1 Fixed Loan Cash Flows in Excel. Cells in Column H Have Range Names Listed Next to Them in Column G. Periods 0–12 and 349–360 Shown

paying a fixed monthly payment based on an annual rate of 7.5%. Figure 2.1 shows the amortization schedule of this loan as calculated in an Excel spreadsheet. PMT and SUMPRODUCT are Excel built-ins discussed in section B.1 of Appendix B and section 3.9. Throughout this book, key formulae are shown in boxes pointing to their cells (e.g., cells C8:E8 here). When shown in a vector or array, it is assumed that one can simply copy such formulae (up and down in this instance) to recreate the spreadsheet.

Even this simple task illustrates the power of spreadsheets. Spreadsheets allow one to build models while viewing their outputs, facilitating correcting errors and spotting patterns. For example, if the ending balance in period 360 were not zero, that would indicate an error. Errors can be tracked down by stressing inputs and with Excel's Tools→Formula Auditing. On the negative side, this simple task has used *both* of the two dimensions available in a single spreadsheet. There are other dimensions still available: (1) unused rows and columns of this sheet, (2) other sheets in the workbook, and (3) other workbooks. However, once the modeler starts to worry about efficiently mapping the problem onto this four-dimensional space, it detracts from thinking about building an accurate model.

The best way to manage spreadsheet real estate is by programming. For example, once the fixed loan sheet is built, a macro can be recorded or written that changes the inputs. The cash flows of thousands of similar loans could be generated with a simple loop. Data Tables and Pivot Tables are Excel tools that offer these features, with no programming necessary. Yet no matter how clever Excel is, at some point in realistic applications, some programming will be needed, and when it is needed, one should not shy away from doing it right. The power of simple spreadsheets can be immensely leveraged with a little programming (as explained in this book). The cynical reader will argue that spreadsheets are just fine and if it can't be done in a spreadsheet, let a C++ programmer in the back office take care of it. Cynics are asked to suspend their disbelief and imagine how they could be more productive with only a marginal investment. The machinery of object-oriented programs may look unwieldy, but one must realize that it is shoring up many of Excel's defects. It offers an effectively unlimited dimensional data space and flexible control (loops and recursive functions) in a modular way. As problems get more difficult, the machinery increasingly shows its merit.

Consider another simple problem. A portfolio of 1,000 fixed-rate loans has varying coupons, maturities, and balances. For loan j:

$$Coupon_j = 12\% - e^{j/600} \div 100$$
$$Maturity_j = 480 - \lfloor j/6 \rfloor$$
$$Balance_j = 100,000 + 20j$$

Find the weighted-average lives (WALs) of the individual loans as well as the WAL of the aggregate portfolio. Were we to attempt this in Excel, the previous spreadsheet would need to be extended to hold 1,000 loans! Let's consider a programming solution. To prevent "programming shock," certain simplifying assumptions will be made that we will readdress in the next section.

Figure 2.2 shows the entire VBA program. Each of these procedures will be described in detail below, but it helps to look at the whole structure of the program first. There are four modules in this program, each shown in their entirety in a separate window pane. The main macro (in the "main" module) is the top-level procedure. The other three "class" modules each define an object-oriented class. A class is a group of procedures that represent an abstraction. For example, FixedLoan is a class that models a fixed-rate loan. Portfolio models a group of loans and CFs models a series of cash flows. The key advantage of a class architecture is that one doesn't necessarily need to know *how* a class works, just *what* it does. In the main procedure here, loans are created, added to a portfolio, their cash flows are computed, and the WALs are calculated. All this can be done without knowing how any of the classes work!

Let's look at each of the classes in more detail. A FixedLoan class consists of four data items, or *members*, at the top of the pane and four procedures, or

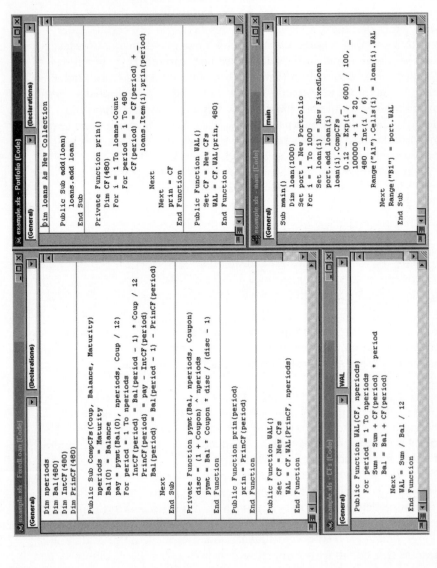

FIGURE 2.2 Visual Basic Editor in Excel. Clockwise from the Bottom Right: One Module (Main) and Three Class Modules (CFs, FixedLoan, and Portfolio)

methods. Three of the methods are public and one is private. A public method can be used by other classes, whereas a private method cannot. The code has been simplified by making certain assumptions, such as the periodicity is monthly and the maximum maturity is 40 years, by not specifying *types*, by including only those members and methods needed for this one example, and by cutting corners. These will be repaired in the next section.

The CompCFs method takes a coupon, balance, and maturity, and creates cash flows for interest paid, principal paid, and amortizing balance. To accomplish this it calls a private function pymt (similar to Excel's PMT built-in). The prin method returns the principal cash flow vector. Up to this point, the code is vanilla VBA, using iteration and simple arithmetic.

The WAL method returns the weighted-average life of the loan. This is where we begin to see how classes work. The New operator *instantiates* the CFs class into an *object* and assigns that object to CF. In the next statement, CF.WAL *invokes* the (CFs class) WAL method in the CF object.

```
Public Function WAL()
    Set CF = New CFs
    WAL = CF.WAL(PrinCF, nperiods)
End Function
```

Whereas a class is an abstraction, an object is an instance. So there can be more than one object of the same class. For example, in main there are 1,000 loan objects each instantiated from the FixedLoan class. WAL illustrates how one class is built from other classes. Both the FixedLoan and Portfolio classes need to compute WAL on cash flows. They both instantiate CFs objects for this purpose.

The Portfolio object has two public methods: add includes a loan in the portfolio, and WAL returns the portfolio's WAL. The private method prin is needed to sum the principal cash flows from all the loans in the portfolio. This illustrates the use of the VBA built-in Collection class. The data member loans is instantiated to be an (empty) Collection object. Three methods of the Collection class are used here: add includes another item to the object, Count returns the number of items in the object, and Item returns an indexed item from the object (see section A.2 in Appendix A for more details).

Finally, the main module puts all these components together to solve the problem. A portfolio object is instantiated (port):

```
Sub main()
    Dim loan(1000)
    Set port = New Portfolio
```

1,000 FixedLoan objects are instantiated:

```
    For i = 1 To 1000
        Set loan(i) = New FixedLoan
```

added to port:

```
        port.add loan(i)
```

and the cash flows of each loan are computed (given the coupons, balances, and maturities outlined previously):

```
        loan(i).CompCFs 0.12-Exp(i/600)/100, _
            100000 + i*20, 480-Int(i/6)
    ...
End Sub
```

The WAL of each loan is computed and written to the spreadsheet, as is the portfolio's WAL.[2] The answer, by the way, is 23.9 years for the portfolio WAL. Note that the portfolio WAL is *not* the average of the loan WALs. Although the problem is artificial, it manages to illustrate some important points. It would be difficult to extend the Excel solution to 1,000 loans, and even if that were accomplished, the spreadsheet would solve this one problem and no other. In comparison, the code can easily be extended in a number of directions. For example, to price the loans, all we need do is write a present valuation method in either the CFs or FixedLoan class. If we wanted floating-rate loans in the portfolio, then a new FloatLoan class is needed, and so on.

2.2 SWIMMING TOWARD THE DEEP END

Many things were simplified in the previous example in order to give an easy-to-digest introduction to object-oriented programming. Among these is the fact that variables and parameters used in the program have no *types*, making the program difficult to debug and maintain. Furthermore, objects are instantiated but never cleaned up afterward, potentially leading to memory usage problems and slower speed. The program makes certain assumptions, for example, 480 periods per loan. Let's revisit the FixedLoan class not only to repair these problems, but also to further examine programming syntax and semantics.

Consider the simple example of a fixed-coupon loan. A *class* is defined encapsulating what such a loan *is* and what it *does*. Each class is defined by

---

[2] Interestingly (or maybe not!), Range is a method of a "hidden" Application class object that is instantiated when executing a user-defined macro from Excel. Range returns a class object that has Cells as a method. The built-in Excel class architecture is quite intricate—a few key methods can go a long way.

VBA code in its own "class module." All the code discussed in this section is in the FixedLoan class module.

```
Option Explicit

Dim Coup As Double
Dim Freq As Integer
Dim nperiods As Integer
Dim IntCF() As Double
Dim PrinCF() As Double
Dim Bal() As Double

Public Sub Init( _
    Coup_ As Double, _
    Maturity As Integer, _
    Freq_ As Integer, _
    InitBal As Double)

    Coup = Coup_
    Freq = Freq_
    nperiods = Maturity * Freq

    Redim IntCF(nperiods) As Double
    Redim PrinCF(nperiods) As Double
    Redim Bal(nperiods) As Double

    Bal(0) = InitBal
End Sub
```

"Option Explicit" is a constraint stating that types in the module must be *explicitly declared*. It is strongly recommended that this be used (at the top of every module) and, with time, type declarations will become second nature. The benefits of types are discussed later in this section, but for now it can be appreciated that types help both the modeler and the language implementation (the interpreter or compiler) understand what is intended. The *data members* of the class are declared at the top of the module. The *scope* of these variables is over the entire class. In other words, these are essentially "global variables" within the class.

```
Dim Coup As Double
Dim Freq As Integer
Dim nperiods As Integer
Dim IntCF() As Double
Dim PrinCF() As Double
Dim Bal() As Double
```

In this case, a fixed loan is comprised of annual coupon (Coup), payment frequency (Freq), number of periods (nperiods), and three vectors: interest and principal cash flows (IntCF and PrinCF) and loan balance (Bal). Here two primitive types are used: Integer and Double (real number). An array of undisclosed size is indicated by "()" coupled with a type. These members are *private* to the class; that is, they cannot be directly accessed by other classes.[3] In this case, they represent the internal state of the fixed-loan abstraction. Because they are hidden from outsiders, they can be modified (various members removed, added, or their types changed) without affecting the rest of the program. Later in the book, programming methods are discussed that help ensure that this is actually the case.

Note that these are data member *declarations*, not *definitions*. Primitive types and abstract types can be used in declarations (section 2.3 discusses types at length). Abstract types include user-defined types and types defined as classes. As an example of the latter, if a FixedLoan required a fixed loan as a member, the member could be declared as:

```
Dim InternalLoan As FixedLoan
```

Don't worry about the recursion here—it is perfectly acceptable as a declaration. In the case of primitive types, the data members are allocated upon instantiation of the class (shown in a moment). However, certain data members are *not* allocated. For example, the arrays above have no size specified, so they cannot yet be allocated. The InternalLoan member is not allocated here either. These require allocation in a class procedure or method, as discussed next.

Procedural members of the class are now defined. There are two types of procedures in VBA: Sub and Function. These are also called *methods* of the class. A Function returns a value, whereas a Sub does not. The first method in this class is named Init. The procedure header is:

```
Public Sub Init( _
    Coup_ As Double, _
    Maturity As Integer, _
    Freq_ As Integer, _
    InitBal As Double)
```

There are four input parameters to this subroutine. Recall "_" (i.e., space-underscore) indicates line continuation. Each parameter is given a

---

[3] One can declare a data member to be public, e.g., Public Coup as Double instead of Dim Coup as Double. This practice is discouraged—the ramifications of this restriction are discussed in a later section.

name and type. The names ending in "_" are treated as are any other name. All invocations of this method must pass four arguments whose types match these formal parameter types.[4] The discussion of what constitutes a match is delayed until the next section, but for now one can assume an *exact* match. For example, you had better pass a Double for the coupon to Init or else you will get an error. The procedure body extends until the "End Sub" statement.

```
    Coup = Coup_
    Freq = Freq_
    nperiods = Maturity * Freq

    Redim IntCF(nperiods) As Double
    Redim PrinCF(nperiods) As Double
    Redim Bal(nperiods) As Double

    Bal(0) = InitBal
End Sub
```

Because this method is intended to *initialize* the class object, it *defines* the data members for later use. The first three statements copy the input arguments into members. The next three statements allocate memory for the vectors. This memory will be automatically deallocated when the object is "destroyed"—more about that later. Finally, the initial loan balance is saved as the zero element of the Bal array. As previously mentioned, the scope of the data members is the entire class. Thus, in the first assignment above, Coup is the data member. The scope of procedure parameter names is local to the procedure. Thus, in the same assignment above, Coup_ is a local variable. If the parameter name were declared as Coup in Init, there would be no way to reference the data member within Init (the innermost scoping context takes precedence). Naming the variables Coup_ and Coup is a convention to make their relationship explicit—this convention is not required, only recommended.

Although this class doesn't do anything yet (other than initialize itself), let's see how to create or "instantiate" an object of this class:

```
...
Dim Loan As FixedLoan

Set Loan = New FixedLoan
Loan.Init 0.010, 30, 12, 150000
...
```

---

[4] One can specify optional parameters, e.g., `Optional InitBal as Double` as the last parameter above. Note that optional arguments must be the *last* arguments listed for the procedure.

This code segment[5] declares a Loan to be an object of the FixedLoan class type. This is subtle: A class defines an abstract type analogous to an Integer or array of Doubles. The class name identifies the type, and variables can be declared to be of that type. The declaration *must precede* any definition of or reference to that variable. The second statement *instantiates* Loan. Instantiation means that a new object (of that class) is created and the data members are allocated.[6]

Next the Init method is invoked with the "object.method" notation. However, unlike a call in a typical procedural programming language, a method invocation can leave side effects in the object. In this case, by initializing Loan, the first element of the Bal vector gets the value 150,000. If one accesses that element later in the code, it will have retained that value. The object is said to have *persistence* or *state*. VBA has alternative syntax for procedure/method calls. The following four calls are equivalent:

```
. . .
Loan.Init 0.010, 30, 12, 150000
Call Loan.Init(0.010, 30, 12, 150000)
Loan.Init Maturity:=30, Freq_:=12, Coup_:=0.01, _
  initbal:=150000
Call Loan.Init(Freq_:=12, Coup_:=0.01, Maturity:=30, _
  initbal:=150000)
. . .
```

Declaring and instantiating a class type variable are different and are not necessarily used in tandem. Declaration defines the variable but does not give it substance. Such a variable will start its life (after the declaration) as "Nothing," a special nil value. Such a variable can be assigned to another variable of the same type. The "New" operator effectively returns an entirely fresh object of the specified type. As a shortcut, an object declaration and instantiation can be combined. These issues are illustrated below:

```
. . .
Dim flag(1 To 2) As Boolean
Dim Loan1 As FixedLoan
Dim Loan2 As FixedLoan
Dim Loan3 As New FixedLoan
```

---

[5] This code snippet can be in another class or it can be unaffiliated with any class. In the latter case, it would be placed in a VBA "code module" rather than a "class module."

[6] Instantiation in C++ means more than this. C++ not only allocates the data members, but *implicitly* executes a "constructor" method if one is defined. In VBA it is the programmer's responsibility to *explicitly* execute a constructor if so desired. That is the purpose of the Init method.

```
flag(1) = Loan1 Is Nothing
Set Loan1 = New FixedLoan
flag(2) = Loan1 Is Nothing
Set Loan2 = Loan1
Loan1.Init 0.01, 30, 12, 150000
...
```

Loan3 uses a combined declaration and instantiation. Loan1 is also instantiated and Loan2 is not. Loan2 is simply assigned to reference Loan1. Changes to Loan1 will appear to Loan2 and vice versa. They are identical. (One might say that Loan2 is a "pointer" to or "alias" of Loan1.) After execution of this code snippet, flag(1) is True and flag(2) is False.

Let's add some other methods so that the class does something, as in Figure 2.2. Suppose we want to compute the cash flow vectors with a CompCFs method. This procedure uses a (private) function to help.

```
Public Sub CompCFs()
    Dim period As Integer
    Dim pmt_ As Double

    pmt = pymt(Bal(0), nperiods, Coup/Freq)
    For period = 1 To nperiods
        IntCF(period) = Bal(period-1) * Coup / Freq
        PrinCF(period) = pmt - IntCF(period)
        Bal(period) = Bal(period-1) - PrinCF(period)
    Next
End Sub

Private Function pymt( _
    Bal As Double, _
    nperiods As Integer, _
    coupon As Double) As Double

    Dim disc As Double

    disc = (1 + coupon) ^ nperiods
    pymt = Bal * coupon * disc / (disc - 1)
End Function
```

CompCFs has no arguments and returns no value. That is not exceptional because a method is within the scope of the class data members. These data members can be used as the inputs and outputs of the method. That is exactly what it does as it loops through the amortization schedule computing the interest and principal payments.

```
pmt = pymt(Bal(0), nperiods, Coup/Freq)
For period = 1 To nperiods
    IntCF(period) = Bal(period-1) * Coup / Freq
    PrinCF(period) = pmt - IntCF(period)
    Bal(period) = Bal(period-1) - PrinCF(period)
Next
```

The pymt function computes a constant mortgage payment for a fixed-rate loan. It needs to be computed only once so it is invoked outside of the loop. The loop iterates from 1 to nperiods (with an implicit step size of one). In the loop body, the interest paid is computed first and then subtracted from the aggregate payment to derive the principal paid. The balance is then updated so that the next iteration works properly.

The pymt function has a few quirks. First, it is defined to be Private rather than Public. This means that an instantiated FixedLoan object cannot invoke the pymt function. It is advantageous to "hide" this definition so that no outside code will use it and start to depend on its interface (i.e., how its arguments are declared) and its particular properties. Also, we see an example of a local variable name (nperiods) overriding access to the global data member name. In this case, the function requires that the number of periods remaining to loan maturity be passed as an argument. The scope of nperiods in

```
disc = (1 + coupon) ^  nperiods
```

is local. We can extend our previous instantiation example to include an invocation of this CompCFs method:

```
...
Dim Loan As FixedLoan

Set Loan = New FixedLoan
Loan.Init 0.010, 30, 12, 150000
Loan.CompCFs
...
```

It would be erroneous to invoke Loan.pymt because it is private. This would display the error: "Method or data member not found."

Still, the class is incomplete because we don't have ways to observe the results. The WAL function in Figure 2.2 is one such method. Another idea is a method that dumps the cash flows to a spreadsheet or a method that returns individual elements of the cash flows upon demand, and so on. Let's break here to discuss why typing is important.

2.3 TYPES

Although types are critical to good programming practice, readers may wish to skip this section and return later after they have more modeling experience from later chapters. Using types is voluntary in VBA, so the beginner can start without the additional complexity introduced here and then gradually fill in this knowledge.

With "Option Explicit" the type matching rule within a module is:

All invocations of a method must pass the correct number and types of its arguments.

Without "Option Explicit," certain type coercions may be implicitly performed if argument types do not match exactly. In the former case, or in the latter case when coercions are impossible, a type error will occur in violation of this rule. With "Option Explicit," type checking is done *prior* to program execution. Without "Option Explicit," type checking is done *during* program execution. That is a critical difference for reasons outlined later in this section. First, let's consider some examples (assume "Option Explicit" is specified).

An example of a type error follows:

```
. . .
Dim Loan As New FixedLoan
Dim Freq As Double
Dim InitBal As Long

Freq = 12
InitBal = 150000
Loan.Init 0.010, 30, Freq, InitBal
. . .
```

This displays the error "ByRef argument type mismatch" for the Init call's last two arguments (more about ByRef in the next section). Type coercion is achieved (for such primitive types) as follows:

```
. . .
Dim Loan As New FixedLoan
Dim Freq As Double
```

```
Dim InitBal As Long
Freq = 12
InitBal = 150000
Loan.Init 0.010, 30, (Freq), (InitBal)
...
```

The "()" wrappers will do the "obvious" conversions of Double → Integer and Long → Double. Thus no errors will be generated. Complex types, such as the class type FixedLoan, cannot be coerced in such a manner. However, there is a wild card type, Variant, that matches *any* other type. For example,

```
...
Dim Loan As New FixedLoan
Dim x As Variant

x = 12
Loan.Init 0.010, 30, x, 150000
Set x = Loan
...
```

The variable "x" is declared to be Variant. Initially, it holds the Integer payment frequency. Next, it holds a reference to the Loan. Neither assignment causes an error. Declaring a variable with *no type* is equivalent to declaring it as Variant:

```
Dim x
```

"Variant" types can be useful, but use sparingly—they can be notoriously slow! The more Variants, the fewer the advantages of type checking previously outlined. However, in certain situations—for example, a function that genuinely takes an argument that can be one of two or more distinct types—it is useful.

A user type is an anemic class with no methods. Historically, programming languages had user types before they evolved into classes. Consider the following user type (must be declared at the top of a module prior to procedures or methods):

```
Private Type LoanType
    Coup As Double
    freq As Integer
    nperiods As Integer
    margin As Double
    init_pdc As Double
```

```
      init_reset As Integer
      life_cap As Double
      life_floor As Double
      pdc As Double
      reset_freq As Integer
End Type
```

This type is private, so its scope extends only within its module. This is a type declaration, so its component types must all be declared. Component types can be practially anything, but recursion or a circular chain among user types is erroneous. A user type is used in a variable declaration within the scope of that type. For example,

```
. . .
Dim Loan1 As LoanType

Loan1.margin = 0.05
. . .
```

The first statement both declares and defines (i.e., instantiates) Loan1. This is similar to a variable with a primitive type declaration. The second statement above shows how the components of the variable are referenced. Advantages of user types are extensibility (the ability to add fields to the type without rewriting preexisting code) and random access (the ability to directly reference a field). Note that LoanType could be defined as a class with 10 data members, giving a similar capability.

```
Public Coup As Double
Public freq As Integer
. . .
Public reset_freq As Integer
```

It is interesting to review why class types are allowed to have recursive or circular declarations when user types are not. First, consider the user type defining a TreeType:

```
Private Type TreeType
    left As TreeType
    right As TreeType
    node As Integer
End Type
```

Compilation displays the error: "Circular dependencies between modules" because the compiler cannot complete type checking over this infinitely

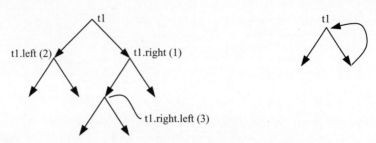

FIGURE 2.3 Two Examples of Tree Objects: Standard Tree (Left) and Circular Graph (Right)

recursive definition. Now consider the following Tree class (with no methods):

```
Public left As Tree
Public right As Tree
Public node As Integer
```

A circular data member declaration in a class is instantiated to Nothing when the class object is instantiated. Thus no infinite reference loop is triggered. The circular (and potentially infinite) expansion of such an object is under program control – an object can be instantiated only with the New operator. For example the following is a valid finite structure built from Tree objects (illustrated in Figure 2.3):

```
Dim t1 As Tree

Set t1 = New Tree
Set t1.right = New Tree
Set t1.left = New Tree
Set t1.right.left = New Tree
t1.right.node = 1
t1.left.node = 2
t1.right.left.node = 3
```

Although classes allow circular declarations, one must still be careful when building infinite structures from such classes. The following is an infinite structure built from Tree objects (it is effectively a graph rather than a tree):

```
Dim t1 As Tree

Set t1 = New Tree
Set t1.right = t1
...
```

This structure can be created but one can potentially have trouble traversing it. From a typing perspective, it is perfectly valid.

Type checking prior to execution (with "Option Explicit") is recommended for several reasons. First, catching a type mismatch with type checking finds a problem at its source. Without type checking, an error may occur later downstream where it is difficult to reconstruct what precipitated it. Second, with types declared, the error will occur where and when the procedure is called and the passed arguments are matched against their formal declarations. Thus the procedure body will not be executed (which in general can be time consuming) and the error will be found relatively quickly. Third, one can "compile" the program in its entirety prior to running it. (In the VBA Editor this is the Debug→Compile VBAProject menu option.) The error will be quickly caught, at its source, during compilation before *any* code is executed. Fourth, even without errors, typing is good practice because it indicates to others what is the intended use of the code. Fifth, if coercions are needed, they must be made explicit, so mysterious behavior is less likely.

2.4 CLASS ARCHITECTURE

A class architecture is a group of classes that in aggregate describe an abstract model or system. For example, previously a FixedLoan class was defined that describes a fixed-rate mortgage loan. Consider an asset portfolio that consists of both floating and fixed loans. The goal is to abstract FixedLoan into a more general loan class type.

Let's start by defining a floating-rate mortgage loan (known as a hybrid adjustable-rate mortgage) as a FloatLoan class. There are seven new data members in this class (in bold below) that don't appear in FixedLoan.

```
Dim Coup As Double
Dim freq As Integer
Dim nperiods As Integer
Dim IntCF() As Double
Dim PrinCF() As Double
Dim Bal() As Double

Dim margin As Double
Dim init_pdc As Double
Dim init_reset As Integer
Dim life_cap As Double
Dim life_floor As Double
Dim pdc As Double
Dim reset_freq As Integer
```

The initialization method assigns values to the scalar members and re-allocates the vectors. All of the scalar data members are static (they do not change value) *except for Coup because the loan floats*. In the following code, Coup is overwritten whenever the loan resets. In the simplest of all floaters, one would need only the margin to add to some changing market rate. The loan described here is a hybrid adjustable-rate mortgage (ARM), so it is more complex.

The additional six members are: init_pdc (initial periodic cap: caps the rate on the loan's first reset date), init_reset (initial reset period: the coupon is initially reset and the aggregate interest plus principal payment changes in this period), life_cap (lifetime cap: caps the rate for all reset dates), life_floor (lifetime floor: guarantees a minimum rate for every reset date), pdc (periodic cap: caps the rate on the loan's subsequent reset dates), and reset_freq (reset frequency: how many periods between each reset date from the initial reset period).

```
Public Sub Init( _
    Coup_ As Double, _
    Maturity As Integer, _
    Freq_ As Integer, _
    initbal As Double, _
    Margin_ As Double, _
    pdc_ As Double, _
    init_pdc_ As Double, _
    init_reset_ As Integer, _
    life_cap_ As Double, _
    life_floor_ As Double, _
    reset_freq_ As Integer)

    Coup = Coup_
    margin = Margin_
    freq = Freq_
    nperiods = Maturity * freq
    init_pdc = init_pdc_
    init_reset = init_reset_
    life_cap = life_cap_
    life_floor = life_floor_
    reset_freq = reset_freq_
    pdc = pdc_

    ReDim IntCF(nperiods) As Double
    ReDim PrinCF(nperiods) As Double
    ReDim Bal(nperiods) As Double

    Bal(0) = initbal
End Sub
```

We define a method for computing cash flows as follows. This method differs from a fixed loan because the floater requires a vector of market interest rates. The method requires a subordinate procedure, CalcCoup, for recalculating the coupon and aggregate payment on reset dates.

```
Public Sub CompCFs( _
    Rates() As Double)

    Dim period As Integer
    Dim pmt As Double

    pmt = pymt(Bal(0), nperiods, Coup/Freq)

    For period = 1 To nperiods
        CalcCoup period, Rates(period), pmt
        IntCF(period) = Bal(period - 1) * Coup / freq
        PrinCF(period) = pmt - IntCF(period)
        Bal(period) = Bal(period - 1) - PrinCF(period)
    Next
End Sub
```

CalcCoup is defined as follows.[7] It has two input arguments (period and market interest rate) and one output (Pmt–aggregate payment). The payment is returned only on reset periods; otherwise, we continue to use the previously computed payment. Reset periods happen at the initial reset period and a fixed number of periods after that, as defined by the reset frequency.

```
Private Sub CalcCoup( _
    period As Integer, _
    MktRate As Double, _
    Pmt As Double)

    Dim InitReset As Boolean
    Dim lim As Double
    Dim rate As Double

    InitReset = True

    If (Bal(period - 1) > 0) And (period >= init_reset) Then
        If (period - init_reset) Mod reset_freq = 0 Then
```

---

[7] The functions Min and Max are not defined as primitive operators in the VBA language. Instead, they can be invoked as methods of the Application.Worksheet Function object, for example, Application.WorksheetFunction.Max(x,y). *Caution:* The implementation of the Application.WorksheetFunction is slow! When speed is important, min and max should be explicitly rewritten.

```
      If InitReset Then
          lim = init_pdc
          InitReset = False
      Else
          lim = pdc
      End If

      rate = MktRate + margin
      rate = Max(rate, Coup - lim, life_floor)
      rate = Min(rate, Coup + lim, life_cap)
      Coup = rate

      Pmt = pymt(Bal(period - 1), nperiods - period,_
      Coup/Freq)
    End If
  End If
End Sub
```

CalcCoup introduces a few quirks we have not yet seen. It produces two results: the new coupon and new aggregate payment. The former is assigned to a data member; the latter is passed back through a procedure argument. The latter is known as "call by reference." Although most procedure arguments do not require this capability, it happens to be the default setting in VBA. Call by reference is implemented with a pointer to the variable residing back at the caller. An alternative methodology is "call by value," wherein the procedure argument is copied into a local variable at procedure call. Thus any value that variable finally gets within the method is not transmitted back to the caller. To force VBA to treat a procedure argument in this manner, use the ByVal keyword. For example,

```
Private Sub CalcCoup( _
    ByVal period As Integer, _
    ByVal MktRate As Double, _
    ByRef Pmt As Double)
```

Explicitly declaring these parameters as above is safer. For example, if MktRate is updated within CalcCoup, its modified value is not transmitted back to the caller. A caller should never be surprised that seemingly invariant data is inadvertently modified by a benign method. This is especially important for public methods written by different people. Although ByVal/ByRef declarations are omitted in this book, they are strongly recommended.

The pymt method is the same as in FixedLoan—the code is copied from the FixedLoan module to the FloatLoan module. An example of declaring, instantiating, initializing, and evaluating a floating-rate loan follows:

```
. . .
Dim Loan As FloatLoan
Dim Rates(360) As Double
. . .
Set Loan = New FloatLoan
Loan.Init 0.0625, 30, 12, 150000, 0.0525, 0.01, 0.02, 35,_
  0.125, 0.0625, 6
Loan.CompCFs Rates
. . .
```

The reader should be dissatisfied at this stage. Fixed and floating loans are quite similar, and yet the two classes share no code. The Init and CalcCFs methods are almost identical, but the slight changes required that we write different code for each class. In developing a model, it is not unusual to first implement classes from the "bottom up" as was done here, because one may not recognize the similarities between the classes. As the model develops, one of two trends occurs. Either the two (or more) related classes retain their similarity and thus are candidates to coalesce, or they become more and more dissimilar. In the latter case, it's best to keep them separate.

Thinking about it more deeply, mortgages can be split into more categories than simply fixed and floating. There are categories within floating loans, such as ARMs and option ARMs. Loans can also be split by modeling assumptions. For example, in FixedLoan we assumed no losses and no prepayments (voluntary principal paydowns). Once loss and prepays are introduced, subcategories can be created corresponding to which rating agency assumptions are used to evaluate loss and prepay.

These perplexing issues are mentioned early (the details of which are discussed at length in later chapters), to raise the reader's consciousness that *class architectures are difficult to design perfectly.* They are difficult to design initially and they will change over time. Any nontrivial problem will have alternative abstractions. The best one can do is to *design an architecture with the expectation that it will need to be changed.*

2.4.1 Weak Inheritance

Coalescing two or more similar classes is done differently in various programming languages. The concept of *inheritance*, although not fully supported in VBA, is important in this regard. FixedLoan and FloatLoan can be thought of as *inheriting* their methods from a *generic* or *parent* Loan class. Each of these *child* or *specialized* classes would then be permitted to redefine any methods that they do differently than does the parent. In weak inheritance:

All of the parent's methods must be defined in each child class.

In this case the parent specifies an *interface* and the children deliver on this specification. How each child accomplishes this is its own business. The outside world (i.e., other classes) care only about the interface. This limited type of inheritance *is* supported by VBA. We can define a parent and child classes and state that each child "Implements" the parent.

Here is the parent Loan class in our architecture:

```
Public Sub Init( _
    Coup_ As Double, _
    Maturity As Integer, _
    Freq_ As Integer, _
    initbal As Double, _
    Margin_ As Double, _
    pdc_ As Double, _
    init_pdc_ As Double, _
    init_reset_ As Integer, _
    life_cap_ As Double, _
    life_floor_ As Double, _
    reset_freq_ As Integer)
End Sub

Public Sub CompCFs(Rates() As Double)
End Sub
```

This is it—it is simply a list of public method declarations or specifications. Any Loan is required to deliver definitions for these methods.

The following is the Loan_Fixed child class in our architecture. The name of each shared public member must be prepended with the name of the parent class followed by "_". Thus Init becomes Loan_Init.[8] Code that was listed previously is not repeated below. The "Implements Loan" constraint is critical. The number of parameters for Init and CompCFs has been expanded

---

[8] Public methods in inherited classes cannot contain other "_" characters in their names; for example, Comp_CFs is an illegal method name in the example above. In this book, child classes are always named with their parent class as a prefix, for example, Loan_Fixed. This is only a convention to clarify the relationships among the classes.

but these new arguments are *not used* in the procedure bodies. They are included in order to satisfy the parent's specification.

Implements Loan

```
Dim Coup As Double
Dim Freq As Integer
Dim nperiods As Integer
Dim IntCF() As Double
Dim PrinCF() As Double
Dim Bal() As Double

Public Sub Loan_Init( _
    Coup_ As Double, _
    Maturity As Integer, _
    Freq_ As Integer, _
    initbal As Double, _
    Margin_ As Double, _
    pdc_ As Double, _
    init_pdc_ As Double, _
    init_reset_ As Integer, _
    life_cap_ As Double, _
    life_floor_ As Double, _
    reset_freq_ As Integer)
    <definition given previously for FixedLoan.Init>
End Sub

Public Sub Loan_CompCFs(Rates() As Double)
    <definition given previously for FixedLoan.CompCFs>
End Sub

Private Function pymt(Bal As Double) As Double
    <definition given previously in FixedLoan>
End Function
```

The following is the Loan_Float child class in our architecture.

Implements Loan

```
Dim Coup As Double
Dim freq As Integer
Dim nperiods As Integer
Dim IntCF() As Double
Dim PrinCF() As Double
Dim Bal() As Double
```

```
Dim margin As Double
Dim init_pdc As Double
Dim init_reset As Integer
Dim life_cap As Double
Dim life_floor As Double
Dim pdc As Double
Dim reset_freq As Integer

Public Sub Loan_Init( _
    Coup_ As Double, _
    . . .
    reset_freq_ As Integer)
    <definition given previously for FloatLoan.Init>
End Sub

Public Sub Loan_CompCFs(Rates() As Double)
    <definition given previously for FloatLoan.CompCFs>
End Sub

Private Sub CalcCoup(. . .)
    <definition given previously in FloatLoan>
End Sub

Private Function pymt(. . .) As Double
    <definition given previously in FloatLoan>
End Function
```

Note that children can have their own individual private members; for example, Loan_Float defines CalcCoup whereas Loan_Fixed does not. These class objects are instantiated as illustrated in the following example. The GetLoan function would be used to create a loan of some type (indicated by the string "fixed" or "float"). The function returns type Loan, the parent class, even though child objects are instantiated. Type checking accepts this because Loan_Fixed and Loan_Float inherit from Loan.

```
Private Function GetLoan(LoanType As String) As Loan
    Select Case LoanType
        Case "fixed"
            Set GetLoan = New Loan_Fixed
        Case "float"
            Set GetLoan = New Loan_Float
        Case Else
            Stop
    End Select
End Function
```

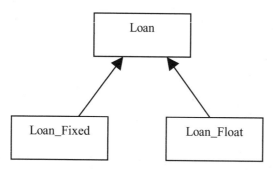

FIGURE 2.4 Weak Inheritance Schema: Children Point Up to Parent Class

For most client classes (i.e., classes that use loans) only the type Loan is needed. From the caller's perspective, all loans have a uniform interface. Figure 2.4 diagrams the relationships so far, where upward arrows represent weak inheritance.

The advantages of even this simplest form of inherence are numerous. First, it forces the modeler to think in terms of consistent and clear class interfaces. If Loan_Fixed and Loan_Float are almost the same, they should appear the same to the outside world. In other words, requesting that a cash flow be computed should require the same method call. Second, it allows the child objects to be declared as the parent class type. This increases the flexibility of the model. For example, one could now declare an array of Loan type and assign either Loan_Fixed or Loan_Float objects to it (but no other types, as would be enabled by using Variant). Third, it abstractly defines a class architecture so that other modelers do not necessarily need to know or understand the children, only the parent.

This simple form of inherence has its drawbacks also. The pymt method is identical for both children, yet each child has its own copy of the code. If we decide to later change the implementation of this method, then we must remember to change it in *each* class and propagate the changes in each. This is both error prone and extra work. This disadvantage is addressed in section 2.4.3.

Full inheritance allows the parent to contain method definitions that by default will be inherited by the children. If a child redefines a method, then the local, more specific, definition is used. Otherwise, the default (from the parent) will be used. This allows both code sharing and specialization as needed. Methods are seamlessly passed down from parents to children, and from those children to their children and so on, with no explicit control by the modeler. Thus languages that support full inheritance (e.g., C++) facilitate richer class architectures.

2.4.2 Parameterized Class

Another approach to coalescing two or more similar classes is to combine them into one *parameterized* class. For example, we can add a new LoanType member to a Loan class and use this parameter to select what to do in each method. Let's call this the ParamLoan class.

```
Dim Coup As Double
Dim Freq As Integer
Dim nperiods As Integer
Dim IntCF() As Double
Dim PrinCF() As Double
Dim Bal() As Double

Dim margin As Double
Dim init_pdc As Double
Dim init_reset As Integer
Dim life_cap As Double
Dim life_floor As Double
Dim pdc As Double
Dim reset_freq As Integer
Dim LoanType As String

Public Sub Loan_Init( _
    LoanType_ As String, _
    Coup_ As Double, _
    . . .
    life_floor_ As Double, _
    reset_freq_ As Integer)

    LoanType = LoanType_
    <definition given previously for FloatLoan.Init>
End Sub

Public Sub CompCFs( _
    Rates() As Double)

    Dim period As Integer
    Dim pmt As Double

    pmt = pymt(Bal(0), nperiods)

    For period = 1 To nperiods
        If LoanType = "float" Then
            CalcCoup period, Rates(period), Pmt
        End If
```

```
        IntCF(period) = Bal(period - 1) * Coup / freq
        PrinCF(period) = pmt - IntCF(period)
        Bal(period) = Bal(period - 1) - PrinCF(period)
    Next
End Sub

Private Sub CalcCoup(...)
    <definition given previously>
End Sub

Private Function pymt(...) As Double
    <definition given previously>
End Function
```

This technique has the main advantage of sharing code. Thus if we need to modify the definition of pymt, it is done just once.

However, the technique has a disadvantage of requiring all specializations of the similar classes to be encoded together. In the small example here, the parameterization with LoanType is manageable—it affects only one method. In a more complex class, the parameterization will be more invasive and can be confusing. The declarativity paradigm is fundamentally broken by coalescing in this manner. Suppose we debug this simple Loan class and are happy with the results. Then in the future changes are needed for floating loans. We must install these modifications in the shared class, so potentially an error may be introduced that causes fixed loans to malfunction. In the inheritance technique, we would need only to modify Loan_Float. It would be impossible to introduce an error into Loan_Fixed.

2.4.3 Which Is Better?

Which technique is better depends on the complexity and stability of the class. If the class is sufficiently simple and/or stable, then a parameterized class can be better than simple inheritance. If the class is sufficiently complex or unstable, then inheritance can be better. Stability refers to the necessity of extending and/or modifying the class in the future. The key disadvantage of simple inheritance is the need to copy code. This can be assuaged by introducing new auxiliary classes that supply these shared methods. Consider the previous loan example. Suppose a BondMath class is introduced that is nothing more than a library of methods for computing various bond characteristics. The MtgPymt method is what was previously called pymt in the Loan classes. It now requires additional arguments.

```
Public Function MtgPymt( _
    Bal As Double, _
    nperiods As Integer, _
    Coup As Double, _
    freq As Integer) As Double

    Dim disc As Double

    disc = (1 + Coup / freq) ^ nperiods
    MtgPymt = Bal * (Coup / freq) * disc / (disc - 1)
End Function
```

Now the Loan_Fixed child class is modified to use the BondMath class. A local variable, calc, is instantiated to be a BondMath object. The aggregate payment is computed via the method supplied by this object. When CompCFs has completed its computation of the cash flows, the calc object is *destroyed*. By setting the object to Nothing, its internal representation, including the memory allocated for its data members, is recycled.

```
Public Sub CompCFs( _
    Rates() As Double)

    Dim period As Integer
    Dim pmt As Double
    Dim calc as New BondMath

    pmt = calc.MtgPymt(Bal(0), nperiods, Coup, freq)

    For period = 1 To nperiods
        IntCF(period) = Bal(period - 1) * Coup / freq
        PrinCF(period) = pmt - IntCF(period)
        Bal(period) = Bal(period - 1) - PrinCF(period)
    Next

    Set calc = Nothing
End Sub
```

Note, however, that an object B instantiated *within* an object A is *not* implicitly destroyed by destroying A. In other words, cleanup is not recursive, nor should it be. For example, suppose object A instantiates objects B and C. Object B is a temporary result that is only needed to produce C, a long-living result. Thus when we recycle A, we want to also recycle B but keep C. One can see that recursive cleanup would erroneously recycle *all three* objects. In general, classes that instantiate class objects should supply method(s) for disallocating these objects. In our example, A should define a Destroy method that cleans up B but not C. Thus after A has been used to create the result C, we would call A.Destroy *prior* to destroying A itself.

Modification of Loan_Float is similar, but has the added complication that the private CalcCoup method also performs a payment calculation in some instances. In Loan_Float, we could pass the calc object *into* CalcCoup to enable this calculation. Thus we have accomplished sharing code, yet kept the two loans distinct and conforming to a generic parent class.

Stability or extensibility is another issue. If we need to expand our loan definitions in the future (which is most likely), then which class architecture is best? As a *Gedankenexperiment*, consider the simple loan classes previously defined. We know (in hindsight) that the following extensions were eventually required:

- an interest-only period when no principal is paid down.
- a balloon payment period when all remaining principal is paid down.
- aging, wherein the loan has already aged a certain number of periods.
- optionality, wherein a floating-rate borrower can make various payment decisions, potentially leading to negative amortization (more about this in section 3.7).
- accounting for losses and prepayments.

How well would simple inheritance and parameterized classes handle these extensions? The first three affect both fixed and floating loans. CompCFs would need modification. In the parameterized class this modification occurs once. In the inheritance scheme both child class methods would need to be modified, a duplication of effort. Can we pull off the same trick of lifting CompCFs into an auxiliary class? In the case of lifting pymt into MtgPymt, the two child classes shared the exact same code. In the case of CompCFs, the two methods differ, as parameterized by loan type. This auxiliary class, call it LoanAux for instance, is directly linked to the parent class. In fact, the MtgPymt method can be thought of as a member of LoanAux rather than BondMath, depending on how the architecture is abstracted. Notice that because the loan example is so simple, lifting up both pymt and CompCFs essentially *hollows* out the children.

Introducing optionality (these loans are known as "option ARMs") requires major renovation within the rules governing floating-rate loans. It would be foolhardy to attempt this in a parameterized class. The number of if-then-else contortions would lessen the declarativity and potentially introduce errors into fixed-rate loans.

The loan example was chosen to be simple enough to illustrate certain trade-offs. The key simplification is the assumption that no losses or prepayments occur. Eventually, any mortgage model will need to deal with these and other stresses. Furthermore, different counterparties may require different approaches to these stresses. For example, the trading desk, rating agencies, and auditors may have different views. The views may differ not only in the level of losses and prepayments, but also the timing.

In the simple inheritance Loan class, the main axis of the architecture is loan type. If the modeling complexity of loss and prepayment is much greater than fixed versus floating loans, then perhaps this architecture is not optimal. Consider an alternative wherein the main axis is counterparty. A Loan parent class would be specialized by children corresponding to different counterparties, e.g., Loan_Desk, Loan_Moodys, Loan_SP, and so on. Each of these children could use a SimpleLoan object (formerly called a Loan) for modeling cash flows without stresses, and then use these cash flows with stress assumptions to produce final cash flows. From the view of client classes, a Loan object would still have initialization and cash flow calculation methods.

2.5 EXERCISES

2.1. Build a spreadsheet model for the interest and principal cash flows of a mortgage and then reimplement in VBA. Extend these models to include prepayments, based on a prepayment rate, say as percentage of remaining balance. A prepayment rate curve (because rates can change every period) is given as an input to the model. Convert this into a Mortgage class, similar to that described in this chapter. Note that class methods cannot be directly invoked from spreadsheet cells. Instead, a macro must be written in a "code" module that instantiates the class object and invokes the method.

2.2. Review the algorithm presented in section B.2 of Appendix B for computing price from yield. Implement this in VBA as a method in a BondMath class. Test the method in either a spreadsheet or VBA code. Evaluate a Mortgage (Exercise 2.1) to return cash flows. These cash flows are passed as arguments to the yield-to-price method, resulting in a price.

2.3. Extend your program in Exercise 2.2 to operate on a portfolio of Mortgages. In either a spreadsheet or a VBA program, evaluate a set of loans, invoking the yield-to-price function for each.

2.4. Review the algorithm presented in section B.3 of Appendix B for computing yield from price. Implement this in VBA as a method in a BondMath class. Test the method in either a spreadsheet or VBA code as for Exercise 2.2.

2.5. Review the algorithms presented in section B.4 of Appendix B for computing interest rate (index), spread, and discount margin durations. Implement these in VBA as three methods in a BondMath class. Test the methods in either a spreadsheet or VBA code as for Mortgages. To better test index duration, you may want to replace the static prepayment curve (assumed in Exercise 2.1) in the Mortgage class with an alternative prepayment function based on interest rates. In general, as interest rates increase, prepayment rates decrease and vice versa.

2.6. Write a Portfolio class that manages a set of Assets. This class should have methods such as yield-to-price that are invoked on each item in the Portfolio. A possible way to implement the set of Mortgages is with the built-in Collection class.

2.7. Implement the credit card model presented in section B.6 of Appendix B as a CreditCard class.

2.8. Redesign and implement an object-oriented architecture that supports the Mortgage, BondMath, CreditCard, and Portfolio classes. Can you use weak inheritance to some advantage in the architecture? Feel free to rearrange the architecture, removing or adding classes.

CHAPTER 3

Assets

*Life is constantly providing us with new funds, new resources,
even when we are reduced to immobility. In life's ledger there is no
such thing as frozen assets.*

—Henry Miller

Many asset types are securitized: corporate bonds, credit card debt, auto loans, student loans, residential and commercial mortgages, and so on. The purpose of this chapter is to introduce residential mortgages. Although mortgages are in general more complex than the "average" securitized asset, they still demonstrate how assets are placed into a securitization and how the asset characteristics affect the structure. Once the reader has learned about residential mortgages, it is a relatively small step in complexity to analyze other asset-backed securities (ABSs).

Consider credit card debt, for example. Credit card securitization operates on the same principles as mortgage securitization in that excess spread and over-collateralization give the credit enhancement needed to protect the structure. Debt holders have the option to prepay their loans, just as in mortgages. Like mortgages, credit cards usually charge floating rates. The trust into which the debt is placed may have caps or swaps to protect it against basis risk. Unlike a generic mortgage, credit card debt revolves; that is, it can grow and shrink. There are mortgages that exhibit similar behavior, for example, a home-equity line of credit ("second mortgage") and an option ARM (an adjustable-rate mortgage that can grow in balance). A simple credit card model is given in section B.6 of Appendix B.

In this chapter, first mortgage assets are introduced, then a basic collateral cash flow model, followed by a discussion of how rating agencies differ in their modeling approaches.

3.1 REPLINES

Simple loans were introduced in the previous chapter as an example of object-oriented modeling. In this chapter, the loan definition is expanded to be more realistic. These loans are still abstractions—actual loans as underwritten contain much more information than listed here (see, for example, Pratt 2006). For example all of the credit quality information of the borrower is absent here. This information is certainly needed to determine the expected losses. The abstraction here is sufficient to flesh out the mortgage collateral model, given loan loss characteristics from another model.

A repline ("representative line") is the loan abstraction we will use. A repline can represent a single mortgage or a group of mortgages. Both cases refer to the weighted-average coupon (WAC), the weighted-average maturity (WAM), and so on. A fixed-rate repline is comprised of all fixed-rate loans. Typically, fixed and floating loans are not aggregated into the same repline. However, different types of floating-rate loans (e.g., loans with different initial reset periods) can be aggregated into a single repline. Historically, replines were introduced because it was computationally burdensome to model individual loans. These days, it is not a hardship to model upward of thousands of loans, but this abstraction is retained nonetheless.[1]

Table 3.1 summarizes the fields in a simplified repline. Each of these fields is expounded in the following notes:

1. *Type*: string specifying fixed-rate (*FRM*), floating-rate (*ARM*), or option ARM (*OPTARM*). Option ARMs are addressed in section 3.7—they require additional loan parameters that are not listed in Table 3.1.
2. *Balance*: initial balance in dollars.
3. *WAC*: initial balance weighted average (gross) coupon of constitutent loans comprising the repline. For a fixed-rate repline, the WAC is static over the life of the repline. For a floating-rate repline, this coupon changes every reset period.
4. *ExpRate*: these fees (stated as annualized rates on the loan balance) must be paid out from the repline before interest flows are paid.
5. *WAM*: initial balance weighted average maturity of constituent loans comprising the repline, in months. This is the remaining amortization term as opposed to the remaining term to maturity. The remaining term to maturity plus age must equal the original term.

---

[1] Some deals in the market have on the order of 100,000 individual loans, making aggregation into fewer replines still useful for modeling efficiency.

TABLE 3.1 Mortgage Repline Definition (All Rates are Annualized; Times are in Months.)

	Field	Typical Value	Comment
1	*Type*	ARM	FRM, ARM, or OPTARM
2	*Balance*	125,000	Initial loan balance in dollars
3	WAC	7.57	Weighted-average coupon (%)
4	*ExpRate*	0.52	Servicing + trustee rates (%)
5	WAM	355	Weighted-average maturity in months
6	*Age*	5	Months since settlement
7	*PrepayPenaltyPeriod*	20	Months
8	*PrepayPenalty*	60 IP 4.8	String describing prepay penalty
9	*BalloonPeriod*	180	Month of balloon payment
10	*IOPeriod*	0	Interest-only period in months
11	*PrefundPeriod*	2	Months of prefunding
12	*PrefundRate*	1.00	Int. rate earned during prefunding (%)
13	*Margin*	5.94	ARM margin (%)
14	*Index*	1yCMT	ARM basis (interest rate curve) Id.
15	*InitResetPeriod*	19	Coupon first reset in next month
16	*ResetFreq*	6	Subsequent coupons reset at this freq.
17	*InitPdcCap*	2.12	Rel. diff. allowed in initial reset WAC (%)
18	*PdcCap*	1.32	Rel. diff. allowed in subs. reset WACs (%)
19	*LifeCap*	14.18	Absolute WAC max (%)
20	*LifeFloor*	7.54	Absolute WAC min (%)
21	bond prepay curve	. . .	Prepay curve used for bonds
22	NIM prepay curve	. . .	Prepay curve used for NIMs
23	OTE prepay curve	. . .	Prepay curve used for OTE
24	*Speed*	150	Multiplier for prepay curve (%)
25	*Lien*	1	1 or 2
26	*Group*	1	Collateral group identifier

6. *Age*: months since settlement.

7. *PrepayPenaltyPeriod*: the number of months following settlement during which the borrower is penalized should the loan be prepaid.

8. *PrepayPenalty*: this string encodes the prepayment penalty conditions. For example, "36 C 105" means that prior to month 36, the penalty is 5% of the current loan balance. "24 IP 4.8" means that prior to month 24, the penalty is 4.8 times the current monthly periodic WAC times the current loan balance. The 4.8 is essentially 80% of six months. The penalty can be more complex, for instance "12 C 105 12 C 104" indicates a 5% penalty for the first year and a 4% penalty for the second year.

9. *BalloonPeriod*: if this is positive, the loan pays off its remaining balance as a principal paydown on this month.

10. *IOPeriod*: up to and including this month, the loan pays "gross" interest only, that is, WAC × Balance. After the interest-only period, the loan pays a standard mortgage payment, that is, the constant periodic payment needed to pay off the balance in the remaining life of the loan at the current coupon.

11. *PrefundPeriod*: if positive, the loan balance represents cash that has not yet been converted into assets as of the settlement date. Up to *Prefund-Period*, the cash earns interest at *PrefundRate*. At *PrefundPeriod*, loans are purchased with the characteristics specified in the repline. These loans begin to pay interest, principal, prepayments, and so on, after the *PrefundPeriod*.

12. *PrefundRate*: up to and including the prefunding period, the repline pays interest only at this rate.

ARMs:

13. *Margin*: the additional interest earned by a floating-rate repline over its index rate.

14. *Index*: string descriptor of interest rate curve—*1mL, 6mL, 1yCMT, PRIME*, and so on. Floating-rate repline WAC is reset to the index plus margin, constrained by the following caps and floors.

15. *InitResetPeriod*: the month in which an ARM WAC is first reset.

16. *ResetFreq*: after the initial reset period, an ARM WAC is reset at the reset frequency (in months). For example, if the initial reset period is 24 months and the reset frequency is 6 months, the model resets the coupon on month 25, 31, 37, and so on.

17. *InitPdcCap*: no jump in ARM WAC (compared to the previous reset) can exceed this rate. Applies to the first reset only.

18. *PdcCap*: no jump in ARM WAC (compared to the previous reset) can exceed this rate. Applies to resets subsequent to the first reset.

19. *LifeCap*: no ARM WAC can exceed this rate.

20. *FloorCap*: no ARM WAC can be less than this rate.

21. *Bond prepay curve*: prepayment speeds for modeling bonds for this repline for each month. In other words, every repline can specify its own prepay curve for use in the evaluation of issued bonds. In practice this generality is not fully used.

22. *NIM prepay curve*: prepayment speeds for modeling NIMs for this repline for each month.

23. *OTE prepay curve*: prepayment speeds for modeling the post-NIM for this repline for each month.
24. *Speed*: multiplier for all prepay curves used in this repline (above).
25. *Lien*: specifies either first or second lien. A first lienholder gets priority over a second lienholder for the collateral that they share. Second liens can be attached to mortgages—they can be used to effectively buy a property with no cash. For example, a mortgage with an attached first lien is taken on 80% of a property value. A second mortgage with attached second lien is taken on the remainder (called an "80–20"). Second-lien loans are riskier and thus have higher coupons. They are penalized by rating agencies with greater loss coverages (e.g., Standard & Poor's 2006).
26. *Group*: string identifier of collateral group. Each repline must be a member of one and only one collateral group. In the simplest case, all replines belong to a single group. In more complex deals the collateral is split up, with different groups attached to different bonds.

This template covers several types of loans. First-lien mortgages when purchasing a house are most obvious. Second-lien mortgages are loans against the equity of an owned property. They can be a lump sum (called home-equity loans) or a line of credit, and can pay either a fixed or floating rate. Cash-out refinancing is the transaction of taking cash out of ownership equity, either in terms of a bigger first-lien mortgage or a new second-lien. Historically low interest rates of the 10 years (1996–2005) coupled with asset appreciation led to growth in second liens (especially in the subprime sector). This has subsequently declined.

As interest rates rise, slowly deflating the real estate appreciation, consumers decrease borrowing and increase refinancing floating debt into fixed. This leads to interesting new options offered on loans. One such instrument is an option ARM, which acts like a loan and a line of credit, as discussed in section 3.7. Another is a fixed-rate option on a floating-rate loan (Simon 2006b): the borrower has the option to lock and unlock the rate (for a fee).

3.2 PORTFOLIO OPTIMIZATION

Selecting an optimal loan portfolio for securitization can be difficult. Negotiations between the securitizer and the rating agencies arrive at a set of constraints that characterizes an acceptable portfolio. For example, the securitization must deliver a set of loans with a certain average WAC and FICO score and the like. At settlement the entire balance may not yet be funded—the "prefunded" cash amount is used over a certain number of periods to buy more assets that meet the required constraints.

Choosing the loans to be delivered at settlement from a universe of assets on hand can be difficult if constraints are "tight," the delivery amount is a large percentage of the universe, and the universe is large. The selection problem is combinatorial; that is, doubling the size of the universe increases the number of possible delivery portfolios much more than twice. The constraints are linear; for example, they ensure that average FICO is greater than a constant value. The unknowns in the problem are a set of binary variables, each indicating if a given loan is selected.

In this section two methods for solving such combinatorial problems are reviewed: linear (zero-one) programming and simulated annealing.

3.2.1 Zero-One Program

A zero-one (or binary) program is a linear program with binary variables (e.g., Papadimitriou and Steiglitz 1998). Let x_i indicate if loan i is selected, for $i \in [1..n]$ where there are n loans in the universe. Consider the following constraints (a subset of those required in an actual securitization):

$$\sum_{i=1}^{n} Bal_i x_i \leq Bal_+$$

$$\sum_{i=1}^{n} Bal_i x_i \geq Bal_-$$

$$\sum_{i=1}^{n} Bal_i FICO_i x_i \div \sum_{i=1}^{n} Bal_i x_i \geq FICO_-$$

$$\sum_{i=1}^{n} Bal_i WAC_i x_i \div \sum_{i=1}^{n} Bal_i x_i \geq WAC_+$$

$$\sum_{i=1}^{n} Bal_i CLTV_i x_i \div \sum_{i=1}^{n} Bal_i x_i \leq CLTV_+$$

Loan i has an initial balance Bal_i, and characterizing metrics, for example, $FICO_i$ (credit quality) and WAC_i (weighted-average coupon). Two constraints bound the total balance, whereas the rest bound the balance-weighted average metrics. Bal_+, Bal_-, $FICO_-$, WAC_+, and $CLTV_+$ are constant bounds on the constraints. For example, the last constraint above indicates that the balance-weighted average combined loan-to-value ratio

(CLTV) of the loan portfolio must be less than or equal to $CLTV_+$. An actual deal has several additional constraints. The constraints above are normalized as follows:

$$\sum_{i=1}^{n} Bal_i x_i \leq Bal_+$$

$$\sum_{i=1}^{n} Bal_i x_i \geq Bal_-$$

$$\sum_{i=1}^{n} Bal_i (FICO_i - FICO_-) x_i \geq 0$$

$$\sum_{i=1}^{n} Bal_i (WAC_i - WAC_+) x_i \geq 0$$

$$\sum_{i=1}^{n} Bal_i (CLTV_i - CLTV_+) x_i \geq 0$$

In addition to the constraints, an objective function can be specified. The goal of solving the problem is to minimize (or maximize) the objective subject to the constraints. One could minimize cost, maximize price, and so on. A portfolio x is *feasible* if it satisfies the constraints. A portfolio x is *optimal* if its objective function valuation is less than or equal to that of all other feasible portfolios (for a minimization problem).

In the case of a loan securitization, it may be sufficient to omit the objective—finding a feasible solution may be difficult enough! Figure 3.1 illustrates a constraint space in n-dimensions (flattened here using artistic license). The constraints partition the space, forming a feasible region (probably very small compared to the infeasible area outside this region). In general, a search moves from one candidate portfolio to another attempting to get into the feasible space and ultimately onto the border of the space where the optimal solution resides. The Simplex method is a classic search algorithm that works well for variables over the real numbers (e.g., MCS 2006). Unfortunately, the variables in our problem are binary—much harder!

Several companies sell software packages for solving mathematical programs, for example, ILOG and Frontline Systems Inc. CPLEX by ILOG (www.ilog.com, ILOG 2002) is notoriously fast, and Solver by Frontline (www.solver.com) is known for its Excel origins. Both these systems and others use the Generalized Reduced Gradient (GRG) algorithm, which is sufficiently efficient to solve large problems like ours. There are a variety

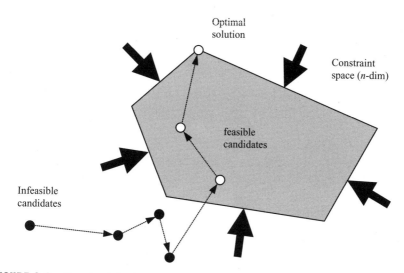

FIGURE 3.1   Sketch of Optimization Space; Path Shows General Search

of ways to specify the problem, not all of which may be available in each commercial system:

- Problems with few variables can be symbolically described in systems such as LINDO (www.lindo.com).
- For arbitrarily large problems, some systems allow one to generate the problem specification on the fly via a C++ (or VBA, etc.) Application Program Interface (API).
- Most systems accept an MPS file, the industry standard for describing such problems. Essentially, MPS is a flat text file with approximately one line for each nonzero constant coefficient in the constraints and objective (e.g., MPS 2006).
- Finally, problems can be specified directly in Excel in systems such as Solver. Excel also has a tool called the "Solver Add-In" that allows the solution of small linear and nonlinear programs under linear constraints. Unfortunately, it does not solve large problems—its big brother is the Frontline System's product. See section 5.7 for an example of optimization with Excel's Solver.

As an example, consider a universe of 6,819 loans under 14 constraints similar to those given above and a certain objective function. The MPS file has 116,000 lines but is quite easy to generate. A commercial optimizer was used to find an optimal portfolio in a few seconds. In comparison, simulated annealing, as described next, took a few minutes to solve the problem, producing a feasible but nonoptimal portfolio.

3.2.2 Simulated Annealing

Another approach is randomized search. Here, a candidate portfolio is randomly selected (i.e., the x_i variables are randomly assigned). Once the variables are assigned, the average FICO, average WAC, and the like can be computed. A penalty or error can be computed measuring the "distance" of a candidate from a theoretical optimum. The search proceeds by choosing successive candidates in an attempt to minimize the penalty.

There are three critical issues in fashioning such a search algorithm: how to generate a new candidate, how to compute a candidate's penalty, and when to "accept" a candidate. Simulated annealing (e.g., Press 1992 and Weisstein 2006) and genetic algorithms belong to this class of randomized combinatorial search methods. These algorithms can handle any type of constraints—linear or nonlinear—which makes them powerful tools.

The remainder of this section considers a simple simulated annealer. The search starts with an initial random candidate portfolio. A new candidate portfolio is derived by perturbing the previous candidate. If the new candidate's penalty is smaller than the previous, then the new candidate is "accepted"; that is, the next candidate is derived from it. A candidate is not necessarily rejected if its penalty is larger than the previous—this subtle point is discussed below. A series of candidates is generated in the course of the search. The one with the lowest penalty is the "solution" to the search, although it may not be optimal or even feasible.

How is a new candidate generated? Randomization is useful because it allows the search to avoid getting "sucked" into a local optimum. However, pure randomization makes it impossible to follow a gradient—a promising perturbation of the previous candidate. A reasonable compromise is to base candidate generation on a random walk defined by the transition matrix:

$$P = \begin{bmatrix} 1-p & p \\ q & 1-q \end{bmatrix}$$

where $P_{i,j}$ is probability of a given loan changing from state i to state j. There are only two states: The loan is selected or not. p is the conditional probability of selecting a loan given that it was previously not selected. Similarly, q is the conditional probability of rejecting a loan given that it was previously selected. This represents a Markov process, allowing us to relate p and q (e.g., Mansour 1999; Drake 1967):

$$p = q \times \frac{m}{n-m}$$

where m is the sample size (i.e., estimated number of loans that will be selected) and n is the total number of loans in the universe. A simplifying assumption is that every loan uses the same transition matrix. To transition the state of a loan, generate a uniform random variable $Rnd(0,1)$. Let $x(k)$ be the k-th candidate.

$$x_i(k) = \begin{cases} 1 & [x_i(k-1) = 1] \wedge [Rnd(0,1) < q] \\ 1 & [x_i(k-1) = 0] \wedge [Rnd(0,1) > p] \\ 0 & \text{otherwise} \end{cases}$$

How is the penalty defined? For example, the following are possible FICO penalties:

$$abs(FICO - FICO_-)$$
$$(FICO - FICO_-)^2$$
$$\frac{FICO - FICO_-}{FICO_-}$$

A total penalty is the sum of individual penalties. Mansour (1999) defines a set of penalty functions for equality, inequality, and other constraints. The basic structure of all his penalty functions, in the context of the FICO constraint, is:

$$Penalty = \max\left[0, \left(\frac{FICO - FICO_-}{d}\right)^g\right]$$

for some tolerance d and stress g. Define the achieved FICO score as follows:

$$FICO \equiv \sum_{i=1}^{n} Bal_i FICO_i x_i \div \sum_{i=1}^{n} Bal_i x_i$$

Consider two alternative FICO constraints:

$$FICO \geq FICO_-$$
$$FICO = FICO_-$$

For the inequality, d is some very small number and $g = 1$, resulting in a large penalty should the actual FICO score exceed its bound. For the equality, d is a positive tolerance and $g = 2$. As the tolerance decreases, the penalty increases. For example, if $FICO_- = 650$, $FICO = 648$, and the tolerance $d = 0.5$, then the penalty is 16.

When to accept a new candidate? Metropolis invented an acceptance method based on the concept of a "temperature" that starts hot and cools down over the search (e.g., Press 1992). When the temperature is hot, there is a greater probability of accepting a new candidate that is no better than the previous. These acceptances "pop" the search out of local optima. When the temperature cools down, so does the probability of accepting an inferior candidate. The famous analogy is with annealing steel: When the metal is very hot, the atoms jump around, settling into gaps and creating a smooth surface. The temperature must be cooled slowly to facilitate this.

In simulated annealing, current temperature is defined as:

$$T = T_0 R^{\lfloor k/s \rfloor}$$

where T_0 is the initial temperature, R is the rate of cooling, k is the iteration, and s is the step size. The acceptance criterion is defined as:

$$\Delta = Penalty_{new} - Penalty_{prev}$$

$$Accept = \begin{cases} Rnd(0, 1) < e^{-\Delta/T} & \Delta > 0 \\ True & \text{otherwise} \end{cases}$$

Consider an example: The universe has $n = 6{,}259$ loans with an average loan size of \$171,000. The estimated sample size $m = \$500MM/\$171{,}000 \approx 3{,}000$. For a probability of rejection $q = 5\%$, $p = 5\% \times [4000/(6259 - 4000)] = 8.85\%$. The search is run for 25,000 iterations with a step size of $s = 100$. The initial temperature is $T_0 = 10$ and $R = 0.9$. The five constraints listed in the previous section were modeled, where:

$$Bal_+ = 500MM + 0.5MM$$
$$Bal_- = 500MM - 0.5MM$$
$$FICO_- = 636$$
$$WAC_+ = 7.65$$
$$CLTV_+ = 80.8$$

The first two constraints are inequalities and the last three are now *equalities with tolerances*: 1, 0.02, and 0.02. Annealing resulted in a portfolio of 2,965 loans with balance of \$500,026,195, average FICO of 635.8, average WAC of 7.65, and average CLTV of 80.8. The total penalty of this

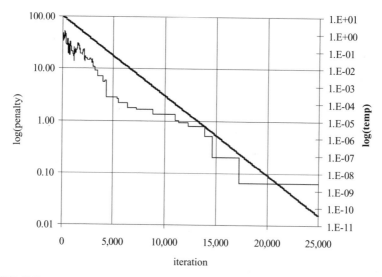

FIGURE 3.2 Example of Simulated Annealing: Log(penalty) and Log(temp) vs. Iteration

portfolio is 0.06—not quite feasible, but acceptable. Figure 3.2 shows the penalty and temperature evolving over the annealing schedule. The points where the penalty jumps *up* (near the beginning of the schedule) are when inferior candidates are accepted according to the Metropolis criterion. Inferior candidates were accepted 72 times out of 25,000 iterations. It is quite easy to implement this algorithm in Excel and VBA (these results were generated with three pages of VBA code).

If the constraints were not met, one might try splitting the optimization into two equal-sized problems in an effort to achieve a feasible solution. The first partition is selected from the total universe, and the second partition is selected from those loans not yet selected. Thus finding a feasible first partition is easier, but finding a feasible second partition may not be. Alternatively the universe can be split in two. Either way, an *optimal* solution cannot be found this way, other than by *luck*.

An objective function can be implemented by adding a new component to the total penalty. This component measures the distance of the candidate's objective value from a theoretical minimum (the case of maximization is problematic). For example, say you want to minimize some attribute of the portfolio. Add the sum of this attribute of the selected loans in the candidate (or some function thereof) to the penalty—the "theoretical" minimum being zero. It is difficult to correctly weigh the penalty components related to feasibility and optimality.

3.3 LOSSES, PREPAYMENTS, AND INTEREST RATES

The replines, representative of mortgage loans, are critically influenced by their loss and prepayment characteristics, as well as market interest rates. The usefulness of the overall analysis and pricing of a securitization structure will depend on the accuracy of modeling losses, prepayments, and interest rates. Unfortunately this is difficult.

The model introduced here is static in the sense that a static view of the world, called a scenario, is assumed. A scenario indicates what loss, prepayment, and interest rate assumptions should be made for the collateral. Each such attribute can be arbitrarily complex. For example, losses might be characterized by a single loss "coverage" value, the product of default frequency and severity. This value represents the cumulative losses incurred by the collateral. Alternatively, each repline within the collateral might be assigned its own loss coverage value. An even more sophisticated model (as discussed in section 7.2) might assign a probability distribution of loss to the collateral or to each repline within the collateral. Similarly, recovery, prepayment, and interest rate models range from simple to complex.

The rating agencies have proprietary models for these attributes and periodically publish empirical results that structurers use as inputs to their models. For example, although there is an interest rate forward curve in the market each day, the agencies may prefer their own stylized forward curve, anchored by the market spot rate, in order to stress the structure.

Prepayment rates are more problematic. The rate at which borrowers prepay their loans is a function of forward interest rates, if the loan is fixed or floating, and if floating, its first reset date. Models have been built to predict prepayment rates. Alternatively, one can use the enormous amounts of empirical data from the servicing of issued deals to build predictive prepayment curves. Periodically, as interest rates undergo significant shifts, new curves are derived. For such a regime change, old deals are kicked out, and newer deals are more heavily weighted to capture the latest market effects. Note that a prepayment curve can be customized both for loans and bonds. For example, prepayment speed will generally increase going into the first reset date of an ARM. Thus ARMs with different reset dates are best modeled by different prepayment curves. Furthermore, one might wish to apply different stresses to different bonds in the liability structure. One way to do this is to construct prepayment curves of varying stresses.

Rating agency loss models are essentially "black boxes" to structurers. Their input is the collateral replines and their output is the loss coverage (or its components: foreclosure frequency and loss severity) at a given rating. Standard & Poor's (S&P) makes their model available to the public: LEVELS is a software application with which the structurer can model losses

(Standard & Poors 2003a,b). Moody's and Fitch do not currently make their models available, and supply loss coverages to a structurer only at the final stages of a deal. Although the rating agency models are hidden, there are some things that can be deduced about them.

In broad strokes, these models break down mortgage collateral into *factors*, for example, fixed versus floating, size, LTV (loan-to-value ratio), FICO score (credit quality), lien, loan purpose (home purchase vs. cash out/refinance), loan type (single family vs. two to four families), occupancy (owner vs. investor), and so on. Each of these factors has a loss function, that is, how loss varies when that factor is varied. Overall loss is estimated as the loan-balance-weighted average of the factor values for any given collateral.

3.4 CASH-FLOW MODEL

In this section, a collateral cash-flow model is described. This model is based on that given by the Public Securities Association PSA (1993), considered to be the industry standard. Throughout the book, this collateral model is refered to as the PSA model. Unfortunately, the term "PSA model" has commonly come to mean a specific ramped prepayment curve. This is *not* my intention—PSA model refers here to the cash-flow model formalized in PSA (1993). Later sections summarize rating agency collateral models as modifications of this PSA model.

For the most part, agencies differ in their assumptions of data inputs (such as loss and prepay) rather than the cash-flow mechanics. The models described do *not* estimate the behavior of prepayments, delinquencies, or recoveries (although a default model is discussed in Chapter 7). There are a host of econometric, option-based, socioeconomic, and other models to estimate these characteristics. The framework presented here is built on some view of these key factors, whether it be that of the seller/securitizer, rating agencies, or some other party. Although published rating agency views are given in sections 3.5 and 3.6, it would be presumptuous to give a "typical" seller's view.

Figure 3.3 illustrates three uses of the collateral model. The PSA model is used to generate collateral cash flows for a variety of purposes. The main use is in conjunction with the liability cash-flow model (the "waterfall"), once the structure allocation is *known*. This is sketched on the top of Figure 3.3. In other words, given a bond allocation, the bond ratings, and collateral cash flows (from the PSA model), the waterfall produces the price of the structure.

The middle and last illustrations in Figure 3.3 summarize uses of the rating agency collateral models. The agency models are used in "sizing" the

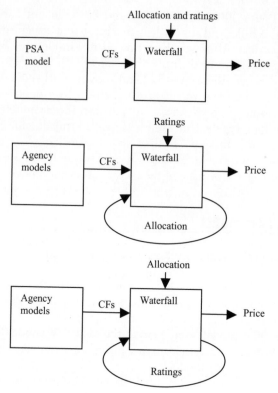

FIGURE 3.3   Using the Collateral Cash-Flow Models

structure, that is, determining the bond allocation from given ratings (see Chapter 5). Sizing is a search procedure that iterates over the allocation until it converges on an optimal solution. Alternatively one can fix the allocations and derive the maximum ratings consistent with those allocations.

There are two sources of inputs to the model. First, the loan portfolio is described by a set of replines. Recall that, among other things, the repline specifies prepay curves and for floating-rate loans, a (benchmark) rate curve, and the like. Second, the loss and prepay characteristics shared by all replines are given in Table 3.2. Loss is described for all replines by a single loss distribution $LossDistr(t)$, cumulative loss, loss delay, loss severity, and servicer advance. There are exceptions to this; for instance, S&P does not share the loss rate and severity among all replines. For different applications, these parameters may vary; we shall see how rating agencies construct them later in this chapter. Yet fundamentally they are the loss-related input parameters

TABLE 3.2 Collateral Model Input Parameters (Shared Across Replines)

Parameter	Meaning
LossDelay	# months delay between any default and its realized loss
LossSeverity	One minus recovery rate (used to compute loss from default)
CumLoss	Scale down defaults by constant factor
LossDistr(t)	Loss distribution curve—must sum to one
Advance	TRUE = servicer advances principal and interest for defaulted loans
Speed	CPR multiplier (prepay curve is scaled by this speed)
WACReductPeriod	WAC is reduced for periods ≥ *WACReductPeriod*
WACReduction	WAC is reduced by this factor

of the collateral cash-flow model.[2] Similarly, prepayment is described for all replines by speed—used as a scalar multiplier of the prepayment curve specified in the individual replines. Note that parameters controlling delinquencies are conspicuously absent. The model introduced simplifies delinquencies by coupling them with defaults (see section 3.4.2). The same loan loss characteristics are applied to each repline (not so for rating agencies), whereas each repline has the flexibility to specify different prepayment characteristics.

The overall algorithm is sketched in Figure 3.4. For each repline in the asset portfolio, first "zero-prepay" cash flows are generated. These assume no losses or prepayments. Second, the zero-prepay balances are used to derive cash flows with loss and prepayment assumptions. These two phases are described in detail next. Table 3.3 summarizes some of the notation used throughout the book.

3.4.1 Zero-Prepay Cash Flows

This cash-flow algorithm takes a repline (Table 3.1) and an interest rate curve as inputs, and produces the amortizing loan balance as output, assuming no losses or prepays. This is known as the zero-prepay balance $ZPB(t)$. The following recurrence equations are iterated over for successive periods t until $ZPB(t)$ amortizes to zero. $ZPB(t)$ will then be used to produce amortization and survival rates, which will be useful when we apply defaults and prepayments in the next section.

---

[2] Note that the term structure of default rates is artificially created by multiplying a mean default rate by a set distribution over time, in contrast to using market spreads to derive these default rates as in CDO and synthetic index models (see Chapter 7). There are no market spreads for these raw loans because they are not traded, hence this approximation.

for each repline
for each period
compute zero-prepay cash flows
for each period
compute actual cash flows

FIGURE 3.4 Collateral Model Overview

Repline components are preceded with "*Loan.*" (e.g., *Loan.Balloon-Period*) to differentiate them from other parameters. Some initial conditions are required:

$$WAC(0) = Loan.WAC$$

$$ZPB(0) = Loan.Balance$$

$$Pmt(1) = MtgPmt(ZPB(0), Loan.WAM, WAC(0), Freq)$$

where WAC is annualized. Most of the algorithm has already been implemented in Chapter 2 as the Loan class. In reading the full formal specification below, think back to the Loan class with data members extended by the repline definition in Table 3.1. The FixedLoan class needs to be modified to implement an interest-only period. A new method GetZPB is needed to return the balance after executing CompCFs.

$$ZPI(t) = ZPB(t - 1) \times WAC(t - 1) \div Freq \tag{3.1}$$

$$ZPP(t) = \begin{cases} 0 & t \leq Loan.IOMonths \\ Pmt(t) - ZPI(t) & \text{otherwise} \end{cases} \tag{3.2}$$

$$ZPB(t) = \begin{cases} 0 & t \geq Loan.BalloonPeriod \\ ZPB(t - 1) - ZPP(t) & \text{otherwise} \end{cases} \tag{3.3}$$

TABLE 3.3 Some Notation Used to Specify Algorithms

$x \wedge y$	x AND y
$x \vee y$	x OR y
$\neg x$	NOT(x)
$x = \begin{cases} a & condition1 \\ b & condition2 \\ \vdots & \vdots \\ z & \text{otherwise} \end{cases}$	conditional definition
$x > y$	For tranches x and y, x is senior to y, e.g., A1 > A2
$v(t)$	Time series v at discrete period t, initial value always at $t = 0$

The *Recalc* flag indicates that the aggregate payment $Pmt(t)$ needs to be updated. If a fixed-rate loan has an interest-only period then $Pmt(t)$ needs to be updated at the end of the interest-only period. An ARM will reset on its initial reset date and at regular intervals after that, as specified by the reset frequency.

$$Reset_{FRM}(t) = [Loan.Type = FRM] \wedge [t = Loan.IOMonths] \tag{3.4}$$

$$NextReset(t) = (t - Loan.InitReset) \bmod Loan.ResetFreq \tag{3.5}$$

$$Next_{ARM}Reset(t) = [Loan.Type = ARM] \wedge [NextReset(t) = 0]$$

$$Reset_{ARM}(t) = \begin{cases} Next_{ARM}Reset(t) & t \geq Loan.InitResetFreq \\ False & \text{otherwise} \end{cases} \tag{3.6}$$

$$Reset_{ARM1}(t) = Reset_{ARM}(t) \wedge toggle(t-1) \tag{3.7}$$

$$Recalc(t) = Reset_{FRM}(t) \vee Reset_{ARM}(t) \tag{3.8}$$

The $Reset_{ARM1}(t)$ flag represents the *first* ARM reset. A toggle enables this definition.

$$toggle(t) = \begin{cases} True & t = 0 \\ False & Reset_{ARM1}(t) \\ toggle(t-1) & \text{otherwise} \end{cases} \tag{3.9}$$

The WAC is reset when floating-rate loans reset. When the ARM first resets, its rate cannot increase or decrease more than a fixed percentage, called the initial cap (*Loan.InitPdcCap*). For the subsequent reset dates, a periodic cap applies (*Loan.PdcCap*). Moreover, the rate of the ARM can never exceed *Loan.LifeCap* or be lower than *Loan.LifeFloor*. The curve $Rates(t)$ is chosen according to *Loan.Index* (usually six-month LIBOR) among various market data. Rates are shifted by the prefunding period because these cash flows are all computed with respect to $t = 1$ being the end of the prefunding period. See Figure 3.5 for an illustration of how this shift works. Note that a 30/360 day count is assumed below—if the loan uses act/360, then an adjustment is needed.

$$cushion(t) = \begin{cases} Loan.InitPdcCap & Reset_{ARM1}(t) \\ Loan.PdcCap & \text{otherwise} \end{cases} \tag{3.10}$$

$$RawRate(t) = Rates(t + Loan.PrefundPeriod) + Loan.Margin \tag{3.11}$$

$$WAC_{ARM}(t) = \min[Loan.LifeCap, \; WAC(t-1) + cushion(t), \tag{3.12}$$
$$\max[Loan.LifeFloor, \; WAC(t-1) - cushion(t), \; RawRate(t)]]$$

$$WAC(t) = \begin{cases} WAC_{ARM}(t) & Reset_{ARM}(t) \\ WAC(t-1) & \text{otherwise} \end{cases} \tag{3.13}$$

When the *Recalc* flag is true the aggregate mortgage payment is recomputed. The new required payment will pay down the entire remaining zero-prepay balance (ZPB) at the maturity of the loan assuming the current WAC. The *MtgPmt* function is listed in section 2.4.3.

$$Pmt(t+1) = \begin{cases} MtgPmt(ZPB(t), Loan.WAM - t, WAC(t), Freq) & Recalc(t) \\ Pmt(t) & \text{otherwise} \end{cases}$$

$$(3.14)$$

The ZPB traces an amortization schedule through time. Amortization and survival percentages are defined for $t_1 < t_2$:

$$amort(t_1, t_2) = \frac{ZPB(t_1) - ZPB(t_2)}{ZPB(t_1)} = 1 - survival(t_1, t_2) \qquad (3.15)$$

$$survival(t_1, t_2) = \frac{ZPB(t_2)}{ZPB(t_1)} = 1 - amort(t_1, t_2) \qquad (3.16)$$

3.4.2 Actual Cash Flows

The actual cash-flow generation algorithm iterates for successive periods t until the ZPB amortizes to zero. The algorithm is described here for a single repline. The algorithm produces period-by-period cash flows for interest paid, principal paid, prepayments, and so on. The key outputs produced by this algorithm for use in the liability model are:

- $Int_{net}(t)$: interest
- $Prin(t)$: scheduled principal
- $PrepayAndRecovery(t)$: voluntary and involuntary prepayments[3]
- $Bal_{act}(t)$: actual balance
- $Loss(t)$: principal loss
- $PrepayPenalty(t)$: prepayment penalty

For a portfolio of replines, the algorithm must be repeated once per repline. The aggregate cash flows are the sum of the cash flows from each repline.

Defaults and Losses Each period, new defaults are generated from loss characteristics, but losses are realized after some delay. It is this delay and

---

[3] Cash recovered or salvaged from a defaulted loan is used to pay down the liabilities, hence is considered to be an *involuntary* prepayment.

its proper treatment that transforms an otherwise straightforward algorithm into the convoluted specification you see here. Let's first see how new defaults are calculated.

Foreclosure frequency $FF(t)$ is the product of $CumLoss$ and $LossDistr(t)$. $CumLoss$ is the Cumulative Default Rate (CDR), and $LossDistr(t)$ describes the loss distribution over time. The loss distribution spreads the total foreclosures over the loan horizon.

$$FF(t) = CumLoss \times LossDistr(t) \tag{3.17}$$

$$\sum_t LossDistr(t) = 1$$

New defaults $Def_{new}(t)$ are the product of foreclosure frequency $FF(t)$ and loan balance $base(t)$. New defaults cannot exceed the performing balance $Bal_{pref}(t)$. There are alternative definitions of $base(t)$ that can be justified, for example, the initial balance, the performing balance last period, and the ZPB last period. These options are given in Equation (3.18). Throughout this section, an equation in annotated as "non-PSA" if it does *not* conform to the PSA standard (PSA 1993). All other equations conform.

$$base(t) = \begin{cases} ZPB(0) & \text{initial balance (non-PSA: S\&P)} \\ ZPB(t-1) & \text{zero-prepay balance (non-PSA)} \\ Bal_{pref}(t-1) & \text{performing balance} \end{cases} \tag{3.18}$$

$$Def_{new}(t) = \min[Bal_{perf}(t-1), \quad FF(t) \times base(t)] \tag{3.19}$$

A new default is delayed for a fixed number of periods $LossDelay$ and then the loss is realized. This delay models the foreclosure process.

$$\overline{Def_{new}}(t) = \begin{cases} Def_{new}(t - LossDelay) & t > LossDelay \\ 0 & \text{otherwise} \end{cases} \tag{3.20}$$

We assume that defaults occur at the *beginning* of the period. Hence, $BalLessDef(t)$ is defined as the performing balance in period $t-1$ less new defaults in period t. Note that defaults are immediately netted from performing balance—these assets are no longer performing even if their loss has not been realized yet.

$$BalLessDef(t) = Bal_{perf}(t-1) - Def_{new}(t) \tag{3.21}$$

This definition of defaults implies that a *default occurs as soon as a payment is missed,* and that each loan that defaults ends up in foreclosure. Thus delinquencies are not modeled independently of defaults. One can think of modeling delinquencies by adjusting *LossDelay* and *CumLoss*. For example, to model an increase in delinquent loans (and/or an increase in their average delinquency) *LossDelay* is increased. To model an increase in delinquent loans that become current, *CumLoss* is decreased.

Cumulative defaults $Def_{new}(t)$ less realized losses and salvage (also known as recovery) occurring in all periods prior to t is $Def_{roll}(t-1)$ (known also as $FCL(t)$—"foreclosures"—in PSA methodology). Def_{roll} is defined later in Equation (3.42). Loss and salvage are assumed to be realized at the *end* of the period.

Loss is the delayed application of default multiplied by *loss severity*. Note that severity, by convention, is with respect to the original defaulted balance (i.e., $Def_{new}(t)$ delayed *LossDelay* periods)—not with respect to the *amortized defaulted balance* (ADB) surviving to t. The *survival* function is defined in Equation (3.16). Loss cannot exceed the ADB, a tighter bound than the performing balance. Loss severity (sometimes called Loss Given Default or LGD) can also be expressed as 1 – recovery rate.

$$ADB(t) = \begin{cases} \overline{Def_{new}}(t) \times survival(t - LossDelay - 1, t - 1) & Advance \\ 0 & otherwise \end{cases}$$

$$(3.22)$$

$$Loss(t) = \min[ADB(t), \ \overline{Def_{new}}(t) \times LossSeverity] \qquad (3.23)$$

ADB is used in later computations, so it is worth groking now. The servicer can advance interest and principal payments for defaulted loans over the period of time between when the default occurs and when a loss is realized. (This modeling option is controlled by the *Advance* flag, Table 3.2.) When the loss is realized the servicer is repaid from any recoveries. The servicer is effectively making the trust (where the assets reside) whole during the foreclosure process.

Suppose a loan defaults in the first period, $Def_{new}(1) = 100,000$, *LossDelay* = 6 and *LossSeverity* = 30%. The default experienced in period 1 is delayed six periods until period 7 when a loss is realized (i.e., $\overline{Def_{new}}(7) = 100,000$). The servicer advanced both interest and principal payments related to the defaulted amount of 100,000 over six periods. Suppose the survival rate (based on the ZPB) over these six months is 98%. Thus the servicer advanced 2,000 in principal payments to be applied against this default. The defaulted amount amortizes down to $ADB(7) = 98,000$ by period 7. The realized loss in period 7 is $Loss(7) = \min[98,000, 30\% \times 100,000] = 30,000$. The recovered amount of $100,000 - 30,000 = 70,000$ is used to help pay back the servicer for advancing payments on the defaulted loans (see "Recovery" below).

Interest Calculation The interest computation is now described. This is the PSA methodology and differs slightly from those required by the rating agencies (more about that later). Weighted-average coupon (WAC) is initially computed as described previously. Starting on the WAC reduction period, net WAC is WAC less a reduction. *WACReduction* can depend on WAC itself (e.g., see Table 3.6). For the PSA model, the reduction rate is zero, although the agencies generally require it. Effective WAC is net WAC less expenses *ExpRate* (servicing, trustee, and custodial fees).

$$WAC_{net}(t) = \begin{cases} WAC(t) & t < WACReductPeriod \\ WAC(t) - WACReduction & otherwise \end{cases} \tag{3.24}$$

$$WAC_{eff}(t) = WAC_{net}(t) - Loan.ExpRate \tag{3.25}$$

Net interest $Int_{net}(t)$ is the interest paid through to securitization bond holders. Net interest is comprised of performing interest $Int_{perf}(t)$ plus advanced interest $Int_{adv}(t)$ (assuming the servicer is advancing). Performing interest is the effective WAC times the performing balance less new defaults. Defaulted loans are immediately subtracted from the balance to account for their inability to pay interest. Advanced interest (by the servicer) is the effective WAC times previously rolling defaults plus new defaults. The servicer pays the interest missing from both new and old defaulted loans. Note that a 30/360 day count is assumed in the formulae below—if the loan uses an actual/360 convention then an adjustment is needed.

$$Int_{perf}(t) = BalLessDef(t) \times WAC_{eff}(t) \div Freq \tag{3.26}$$

$$Int_{adv}(t) = [Def_{roll}(t-1) + Def_{new}(t)] \times WAC_{eff}(t) \div Freq \tag{3.27}$$

$$Int_{net}(t) = \begin{cases} Int_{perf}(t) + Int_{adv}(t) & Advance \\ Int_{perf}(t) & otherwise \end{cases} \tag{3.28}$$

By using effective WAC, higher priority payments to the servicer and stress ("WAC reduction") are implicitly accounted for. Note that servicer fees are not explicitly computed in the algorithm—there is simply that much less cash available to net interest. Also note that servicer fees do not pay for servicer advances.

Principal Calculation   Scheduled principal payments are composed of performing and advanced principal payments. Performing principal payments are the performing loan balance minus new defaults times the amortization percentage. Advanced principal payment (by the servicer) is amortization percentage times a default balance. The default balance is the previous period's rolling defaults plus new defaults less ADB. ADB is subtracted because it becomes realized loss and salvage in this period.

$$Prin_{perf}(t) = BalLessDef(t) \times amort(t - 1, t) \tag{3.29}$$

$$Prin_{adv}(t) = [Def_{roll}(t - 1) + Def_{new}(t) - ADB(t)] \times amort(t - 1, t) \tag{3.30}$$

$$Prin(t) = Prin_{perf}(t) + Prin_{adv}(t) \tag{3.31}$$

Note that advanced principal is characterized as an amortized default because it is the amortized portion of the defaulted loan amount. Also note that the advanced interest calculation (Equation (3.27)) does *not* subtract ADB as here. At first blush this seems strange: why compute interest and principal payments from different balances? The rationale is that the interest is still owed on the amortized default balance for the current period (it does not amortize until the end of the period).

Recovery   Raw salvage (i.e., recovery) is defined against amortized default balance, ADB. Thus loss and recovery are defined against different notionals. An alternative is to define raw salvage as the delayed default minus loss.

$$RawSalvage(t) = \begin{cases} ADB(t) - Loss(t) & PSA \\ \overline{Def_{new}(t) - Loss(t)} & \text{non-PSA} \end{cases} \tag{3.32}$$

Raw salvage is used to pay the interest and principal owed to the servicer for its advanced payments on the behalf of defaulted loans. Initially, $AdvOwed(0) = 0$. Advanced interest and principal accumulates until it is paid by salvage.

$$AdvOwed'(t) = AdvOwed(t - 1) + Int_{adv}(t) + Prin_{adv}(t) \tag{3.33}$$

$$AdvOwed(t) = \max[0, AdvOwed'(t) - RawSalvage(t)] \tag{3.34}$$

$$Salvage'(t) = \max[0, RawSalvage(t) - AdvOwed'(t)] \tag{3.35}$$

Accounting for repaying servicer advances is not part of the PSA model.

$$Salvage(t) = \begin{cases} RawSalvage(t) & \text{PSA} \\ Salvage'(t) & \text{non-PSA} \end{cases} \tag{3.36}$$

Prepayments   Constant prepayment rate (CPR) is computed as a prepayment curve $PP(t)$ specified for each repline multiplied by a scalar multiplier *Speed*. Prepayments are taken on the amortized performing balance. The two alternative definitions below are not equivalent, although they might appear so at first glance. The performing principal payment is calculated from the performing balance *less new defaults* (Equation (3.29)). Yet the PSA definition assumes that prepayments are from the entire performing balance (Equation (3.39)). This seems to contradict the assumption that new defaults occur at the beginning of the period.

$$CPR(t) = PP(t + Loan.Age) \times Speed \tag{3.37}$$

$$SMM(t) = 1 - [1 - CPR(t)]^{1/Freq} \tag{3.38}$$

$$Prepay(t) = \begin{cases} \max[0, SMM(t) \times Bal_{perf}(t-1) \times survival(t-1,t)] & \text{PSA} \\ \max[0, SMM(t) \times (Bal_{perf}(t-1) - Prin_{perf}(t))] & \text{non-PSA} \end{cases} \tag{3.39}$$

Prepay and recovery are added together because they represent cash flow other than scheduled principal and interest.

$$PrepayAndRecovery(t) = Prepay(t) + Salvage(t) \tag{3.40}$$

Prepayment penalty is computed based on each loan's prepayment penalty descriptor, *PrepayPenalty*. The *PPP* function is not presented here. See Table 3.1 for examples.

$$PrepayPenalty(t) = PPP(Loan.PrepayPenalty, Loan.Age, t,$$

$$Prepay(t), WAC(t)) \tag{3.41}$$

Advancing Balances   Defaulted loans accumulate in rolling defaults.

$$Def_{roll}(t) = \max[0, Def_{roll}(t-1) + Def_{new}(t)$$

$$- Prin_{adv}(t) - Loss(t) - Salvage(t)] \tag{3.42}$$

Performing balance is the previous period's performing balance less new defaults less (performing) scheduled and prepaid principal.

$$Bal_{perf}(t) = \max[0, BalLessDef(t) - Prin_{perf}(t) - Prepay(t)] \tag{3.43}$$

Actual balance is the previous period's actual balance less performing and advanced principal less prepaid principal less loss and salvage. If *LossDelay* is zero, then the actual balance equals the performing balance.

$$Bal_{act}(t) = \max[0, Bal_{act}(t-1) - Prin(t) - Prepay(t) - Loss(t) - Salvage(t)]$$
$$\tag{3.44}$$

See Exercise 3.2 concerning the relationship between these key variables.

Prefunding   If the repline is prefunded, its balance represents cash in a prefunding account until the *PrefundPeriod* when loans are purchased. During prefunding, the cash is invested and earns the *PrefundRate*. Thus collateral cash flows generated for this repline during this period have zero principal payments, prepayments, etc. The cash balance remains fixed at the initial loan balance. After the *PrefundPeriod*, collateral cash flows are generated with the repline's characteristics. The recurrence equations below specify this by shifting the previously defined cash flows by *PrefundPeriod*.

$$\Delta = Loan.PrefundPeriod$$

$$\overline{Bal}_{act}(t) = \begin{cases} ZPB(0) & t \leq \Delta \\ Bal_{act}(t - \Delta) & \text{otherwise} \end{cases}$$

$$\overline{Int}_{net}(t) = \begin{cases} ZPB(0) \times Loan.PrefundRate/Freq & t \leq \Delta \\ Int_{net}(t - \Delta) & \text{otherwise} \end{cases}$$

$$\overline{Prin}(t) = \begin{cases} 0 & t \leq \Delta \\ Prin(t - \Delta) & \text{otherwise} \end{cases}$$

$$\overline{PrepayAndRecovery}(t) = \begin{cases} 0 & t \leq \Delta \\ PrepayAndRecovery(t - \Delta) & \text{otherwise} \end{cases}$$

$$\overline{PrepayPenalty}(t) = \begin{cases} 0 & t \leq \Delta \\ PrepayPenalty(t - \Delta) & \text{otherwise} \end{cases}$$

$$\overline{Loss}(t) = \begin{cases} 0 & t \leq \Delta \\ Loss(t - \Delta) & \text{otherwise} \end{cases}$$

A sketch of how prefunding is modeled is given in Figure 3.5. Interest rates are shifted when computing the *ZPB*. The *ZPB* is translated into the

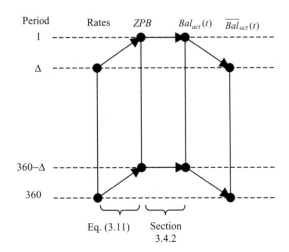

FIGURE 3.5 Illustration of How Rates and Balances are Manipulated to Model Prefunding

actual balance by the previous algorithm. The final step is to shift the actual balance in time. This shift is the prefunding period.

Discussion This section reviews the alternatives to the PSA model introduced above, as summarized in Table 3.4.

1. PSA defines new defaults from performing balance, not ZPB. Alternatively, S&P models the latter.
2. PSA defines raw salvage (prior to reimbursing the servicer for any advances) from ADB, yet losses are defined from delayed defaults (nonamortized). An alternative is to define both raw salvage and losses from the same base: delayed defaults. The PSA definition is more logical.
3. For PSA, ultimate salvage and raw salvage are equivalent. Alternatively recovered cash is used for reimbursing the servicer for any advances.
4. PSA defines prepayments on last period's performing balance surviving to the current period. Since survival rates are defined from ZPB, the surviving performing balance contains loans about to default this period. Alternatively, prepayments can be defined on last period's performing balance less this period's performing principal payment. In this formulation, this period's defaults are not included. In other words, within a given period, PSA treats prepayments occurring before defaults, whereas the alternative treats defaults occurring before prepayments.

TABLE 3.4 Comparison between PSA and Alternatives

	PSA	Alternative	Equation
1 $Def_{new}(t)$	$\min[Bal_{perf}(t-1),$ $FF(t) \times ZPB(t-1)]$	$\min[Bal_{perf}(t-1),$ $FF(t) \times ZPB(t-1)]$	(3.18)
2 $RawSalvage(t)$	$ADB(t) - Loss(t)$	$\overline{Def_{new}} - Loss(t)$	(3.32)
3 $Salvage(t)$	$RawSalvage(t)$	$Salvage'(t)$	(3.36)
4 $Prepay(t)$	$SMM \times Bal_{perf}(t-1) \times$ $survival(t-1,t)$	$SMM \times [Bal_{perf}(t-1) -$ $Prin_{perf}(t)]$	(3.39)

3.4.3 Examples

Aggregate output cash flows from the PSA collateral model for 2004-HE2 (Morgan Stanley 2004a) are shown in Figure 3.6. This deal and others in the series are used as examples in this book. This assumes a 1% CDR (constant default rate) at 50% loss severity. Figure 3.7 compares this scenario for various losses, showing balances in log scale. The losses cause faster amortization of the collateral balance.

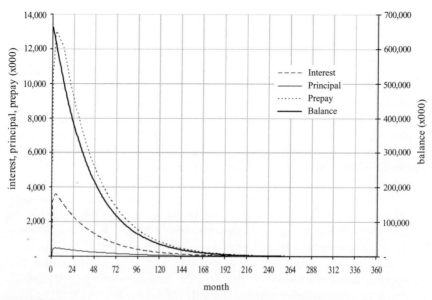

FIGURE 3.6 Major Collateral Cash Flows ($\times$000) for 2004-HE2

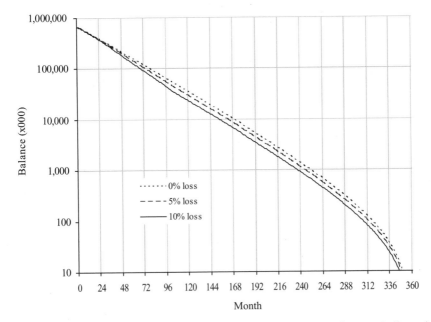

FIGURE 3.7 Collateral Balance (×000) for Various Losses with PSA Collateral Model, 2004-HE2

3.5 S&P CASH-FLOW MODEL

This section describes the static cash-flow model recommended by Standard and Poor's (S&P) for residential mortgages (Standard & Poor's 2005a). S&P outlines input stresses but does not detail the cash-flow algorithm per se—that is the responsibility of the securitizer. S&P uses the PSA standard model (as described in the last section) with a few modifications. Their modifications to the algorithm do not materially affect the model's results—much more significant are the S&P assumptions concerning loss, prepayment, and interest rate characteristics.

Note that in this section the S&P collateral cash-flow model only is summarized. In fact, S&P requires some deviations from a "standard" liability cash-flow model; these are explained in the next chapter. Also note that S&P updates their assumptions in periodic publications (Standard & Poor's 2005a, 2006). The indicative S&P values given in this section are for illustrative purposes only and are subject to change due to market movements and changes in analysts' views.

TABLE 3.5 Sample Foreclosure Frequencies and Loss Severities (from S&P LEVELS)

	ARM FF	Sev	FRM FF	Sev
AAA	37.37%	60.21%	41.88%	59.70%
AA+	33.49%	55.99%	38.46%	53.95%
AA	28.27%	53.94%	32.30%	51.09%
AA−	26.48%	52.87%	30.27%	49.56%
A+	24.51%	51.00%	28.78%	46.90%
A	22.52%	49.95%	26.44%	45.39%
A−	20.95%	48.92%	25.07%	43.88%
BBB+	19.16%	48.29%	22.71%	42.93%
BBB	17.83%	47.66%	21.43%	41.99%
BBB−	15.88%	47.24%	18.80%	41.22%
BB+	14.10%	46.82%	14.83%	40.46%
BB	12.02%	46.60%	13.72%	40.08%
B	7.40%	45.94%	7.19%	38.93%

Foreclosure frequency and loss severity values are supplied by the S&P LEVELS (Standard & Poor's 2003a,b) model for each rating, for each repline. Table 3.5 shows S&P LEVELS output for two typical (floating and fixed) loans. Foreclosure frequency (FF) corresponds to *CumLoss* in Equation (3.17) and loss severity (Sev) corresponds to *LossSeverity* in Equation (3.23). These mean loss characteristics are used to model the replines. Given two different replines, the one with better credit characteristics will be granted lower loss characteristics for a given rating. The ratings here correspond to bond ratings. Thus the higher the rating, the more severe the loss characteristics.

The previous explanation of S&P LEVELS is simplified. For example, the tool can be run in two modes: aggregate and loan-level losses. In aggregate, *three* sets of loss characteristics are computed for the entire asset portfolio: the average floating, fixed first-lien, and fixed second-lien loan loss characteristics. The floating (fixed) loan loss characteristics will be used for all floating (fixed) loans, from the most to the least creditworthy. When loan-level losses are computed, loss characteristics are computed for each individual repline.

Before getting into the details of the S&P collateral model, it is important to preview how these loss characteristics are used in the general asset/liability model. For a given structure, to achieve a given bond rating, the loss characteristics corresponding to that rating need to be *achieved*. Let's make this statement more formal. Define the breakeven loss as the *maximum* foreclosure frequency applied to the model (all other assumptions left unchanged) that achieves *zero* losses in the reference bond and all bonds senior to the reference bond. If (and only if) the breakeven loss is greater or equal to the rating agency foreclosure frequency, then the corresponding bond rating has been achieved.

For example, consider the loss characteristics given in Table 3.5. Suppose these are aggregate characteristics and our asset portfolio consists only of ARMs. Suppose our structure is already allocated; that is, the notional amounts to be issued for each bond have been decided. Assume we want to issue one of these bonds as AA rated. If we evaluate the model assuming 26% loss rate (over some distribution in time, discussed later in this section), the reference bond and all senior bonds experience no loss. However, if we assume a 27% loss rate, bond losses appear. Thus the bond cannot be rated AA, although it can be rated AA−.

Viewed another way, suppose we already decided on bond ratings, but not bond allocations. We can use this degree of freedom to achieve the rating we have already selected. Define the breakeven subordination as the *minimum* subordination applied to the tranche that achieves *zero* losses in the reference bond and all bonds senior to the reference bond. If (and only if) the breakeven subordination is less than or equal to the actual subordination of the reference bond, then the corresponding bond rating has been achieved.

Returning to the previous example, recall we want to issue an AA rated bond at some priority in the structure. If we evaluate the model assuming 28.27% loss rate, we find that at least 10% subordination is required below the AA bond to achieve zero loss in the AA bond and above. Thus, for instance, we can allocate a structure with 10% subordination to the AA bond. Two clarifications are necessary: First, there is usually no benefit to allocating more subordination than is minimally required by the agencies. However, one rating agency will likely trump the others, that is, require more stringent requirements. Thus, for example, although S&P may require 10%, Moody's may require 11%. Second, when minimum subordination amounts are stipulated, the tranches must be allocated one after the other in priority order. A methodology for performing this "sizing" is given in Chapter 5.

3.5.1 Model Parameters

The model is parameterized as follows (in addition to the PSA parameters previously introduced in Table 3.2):

- *Interest rates.* S&P periodically issues interest rate curves for use in evaluating securitization models. The curves reflect their view on future rates. The set of curves is referenced by vintage, rating, and loan index.

Vintage is the date of the curve (new deals are run with the latest curves, but old deals may be run on their original curves for benchmarking purposes).

Different curves are supplied for different ratings. In general, higher ratings correspond to higher interest rate curves. Greater stress is required to achieve the higher rating. Because some of the collateral may have fixed rates for certain periods, and the bonds are generally floaters, the basis risk is stressed by increasing rates. The loan index indicates the interest rate basis, for example, one-month LIBOR (see *Index* in Table 3.1).

Figure 3.8 shows the S&P, Moody's, and market forward curves for one-month LIBOR on May 23, 2006. This corresponds to *Rates* in Equation (3.11). The forward curve is flat, greatly exaggerating the stresses of the rating agency models. By steepening interest rates, the agencies are highly stressing excess spread. Unlike stressing loss, which affects the subordinate tranches first, stressing interest rates affects all the tranches at once. Loss rarely burns through to highly rated mezzanine tranches, but very high interest rates can cause their interest payments to be deferred as described in section 4.4. This means that the senior credit enhancement levels required by S&P (and Moody's) will increase (Agarwal 2005).

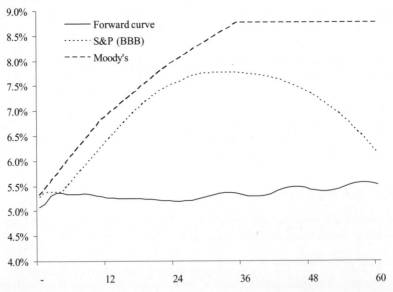

FIGURE 3.8 Interest Rate Curves on May 23, 2006 (One-Month LIBOR Models)

TABLE 3.6   WAC Reduction Rate for S&P Model

Rating	WAC < 10%	10 ≤ WAC < 12%	WAC ≥ 12%
AAA	0.14%	0.45%	0.60%
AA+	0.13%	0.40%	0.55%
AA	0.12%	0.37%	0.50%
AA−	0.11%	0.35%	0.47%
A+	0.09%	0.30%	0.44%
A	0.08%	0.25%	0.40%
A−	0.07%	0.22%	0.35%
BBB+	0.06%	0.18%	0.30%
BBB	0.06%	0.18%	0.30%
≤BBB−	0.06%	0.18%	0.28%

- *WAC reduction.* From the WAC reduction period onwards, S&P requires that a penalty is assessed to interest cash flow. The idea behind the penalty is that effectively the WAC has been decreased. S&P specifies the penalty in Table 3.6. This corresponds to *WACReduction* in Equation (3.24). The reduction to monthly interest cash flow is effectively actual balance × adjustment ÷ 12. For the purpose of indexing this table, the reference WAC is equal to the loan's WAC for floating loans. For fixed loans, the reference WAC is equal to the BB− spot rate plus the loan's margin.
- *Prepayments.* S&P requires the use of certain static prepayment curves, always ramps. The general ramp is specified by an initial and terminal constant prepayment rate (CPR) and a ramp-up period. This model is stressed below. *PP*(*t*) is used in Equation (3.37).

$$PP'(t) = Initial + (t + Loan.Age - 1) \times \frac{Terminal - Initial}{Ramp - 1}$$

$$PP(t) = \min[Terminal, PP'(t)] \tag{3.45}$$

Different curves are used for ARM and FRM loans, as well as among ARMs with different initial reset periods. Intuitively, prepayments increase as an ARM gets closer to resetting. The detailed features of the peak can be derived from empirical data—a ramp is a gross approximation.

For a given target rating, S&P requires that the prepayment curve be stressed by the adjustments in Table 3.7. A *reduction* in CPR is applied throughout the prepayment curve as follows. Prepayments are

TABLE 3.7   CPR Stress in S&P Model

Rating	Adjustment
AAA	−6.00%
AA+	−5.00%
AA	−4.00%
AA−	−3.00%
A+	−1.50%
A	−1.50%
A−	−1.00%
BBB+	−0.50%
≤BBB	0.00%

stressed downward in order to further exacerbate the other stresses, namely losses and basis risk.

$$CPRMultiple = \frac{Terminal + CPRStress}{Terminal}$$

$$Initial' = Initial \times CPRMultiple$$

$$Terminal' = Terminal \times CPRMultiple$$

$$PP'(t) = Initial' + (t + Loan.Age - 1) \times \frac{Terminal' - Initial'}{Ramp - 1}$$

$$PP(t) = \min[Terminal', PP'(t)] \tag{3.46}$$

- *Loss distribution.* As specified in Equation (3.17), foreclosure frequency for a given period t, $FF(t)$, is the product of the cumulative loss (*CumLoss*) and a loss distribution, $LossDistr(t)$, supplied by S&P as shown in Table 3.8.
- *Loss delay.* S&P requires a 12-month delay between default and realized loss. This parameter (*LossDelay*) is used in Equation (3.20).

3.6   MOODY'S CASH-FLOW MODEL

This section describes Moody's collateral model. The discussion presupposes familiarity with the previous models. Moody's, like the other agencies, periodically publishes new guidelines for analytical assumptions in modeling mortgages (e.g., Agarwal 2005). In such reports, the latest interest rate, loss,

TABLE 3.8 Loss Distributions for S&P Model: First and Second Liens Differ

Months	First Liens	Second Liens
1	4.00%	2.50%
6	5.75%	7.75%
12	6.25%	12.75%
18	13.00%	13.00%
24	10.25%	12.00%
30	10.00%	10.25%
36	9.50%	10.25%
42	9.00%	9.50%
48	9.00%	7.75%
54	7.75%	5.75%
60	5.75%	5.00%
66	5.50%	3.50%
72	4.25%	2.50%

and prepayment characteristics are specified. Unlike S&P, all loans utilize the same loss characteristics.

The indicative Moody's values given in this section are for illustrative purposes only and are subject to change due to market movements and changes in analysts' views.

Loss coverages for a typical pool of collateral, as generated by the proprietary Moody's loss model, are shown in Table 3.9. Like S&P, models are stressed by target rating. For instance, for a tranche to achieve an Aaa rating it must perform with highly stressed losses, in this case 26.45% ÷ 60% = 44% foreclosure frequency (see Table 3.10).

TABLE 3.9 Loss Coverage for Moody's Model (Typical Deal)

Rating	Loss Coverage	Rating	Loss Coverage
Aaa	26.45%	Baa2	9.35%
Aa1	22.70%	Baa3	8.35%
Aa2	19.30%	Ba1	7.50%
Aa3	17.25%	Ba2	6.80%
A1	15.35%	Ba3	6.15%
A2	13.60%	B1	5.55%
A3	12.00%	B2	5.05%
Baa1	10.00%	B3	4.35%

TABLE 3.10   Loss Distributions for Moody's Model

Month		First Liens		Second Liens	
Start	End	FRM	ARM	FRM	ARM
1	6	0%	0%	0%	0%
7	12	3%	3%	3%	3%
13	24	12%	17%	17%	17%
25	36	20%	25%	25%	25%
37	48	25%	25%	25%	25%
49	60	20%	20%	20%	20%
61	72	15%	10%	10%	10%
73	84	5%	0%	0%	0%
85		0%	0%	0%	0%

3.6.1   Model Parameters

The model is parameterized as follows (in addition to the PSA parameters previously introduced in Table 3.2).

- *Interest rates.* A few interest rate curves are used in the Moody's models. Piecewise linear models are used based on the current one-month and six-month LIBOR spot rates. If there are no derivatives in the trust, the linear model has a rise of 1.5% over the first year, 1% over the second year, and 0.75% over the third year. If there are derivatives, then the linear model has a rise of 1.65% over the first year, 1.1% over the second year, and 0.825% over the third year. Floating loans are indexed from these curves, as indicated by the repline *Loan.index*. Figure 3.8 shows a (nonderivative) curve on May 23, 2006. This corresponds to *Rates* in Equation (3.11). Moody's curves may be shocked in parallel by 10 bps for extra stress.
- *WAC reduction.* Similar to S&P, to stress the WAC, a penalty is assessed based on the stress curve given below. Unlike S&P this stress is not based on rating, but rather on time. Stress linearly increases with period until it reaches 0.36% (this is an annualized rate). This corresponds to *WACReduction* in Equation (3.24).

$$WACReduction(t) = \begin{cases} -0.01\ \% \times t & t < 36 \\ -0.36\ \% & \text{otherwise} \end{cases}$$

- *Prepayments.* FRM and ARM loans are assigned different CPR curves, as shown in Figure 3.9. This corresponds to *PP(t)* in Equation (3.37).

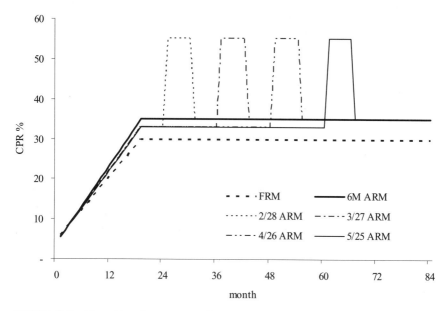

FIGURE 3.9 First-Lien CPR Curves for Moody's Model (Prior to Stress by CPR Multiplier). Each ARM Peaks at 55% for Six Months, Starting at Reset, Simulating Refinances.

There are multiple ARM curves, depending on reset period. All ARM curves plateau at 35% and have a six-month 55% spike starting at reset, except for six-month ARMs which have no spike. These CPR curves have an origin at loan inception. The spikes model refinancing after the initial "teaser" rates are replaced by a floating rate. Fixed loans plateau at 33% CPR.

- *Loss severity and prepayment stress.* These parameters are fixed across all deals (subject to change by Moody's). Foreclosure frequency (*CumLoss* in Equation (3.17)) can be derived as loss coverage ÷ severity (*LossSeverity* in Equation (3.23)). CPR multiple is a stress factor multiplied by the CPR curve selected for a specific loan type. The rationale behind further increasing prepayment speeds for higher ratings is that this stresses excess spread downward. Note, however, that this approach is the opposite to that of S&P, where prepayment speeds are stressed downward, in order to exacerbate losses.
- *Loss distribution.* ARMs and FRMs each have its own loss distribution, *LossDistr(t)*, shown in Table 3.10. First and second liens are potentially different. Loss distribution is used in Equation (3.17).

- *Loss delay*. Unlike the S&P model, here defaults cause instant realized losses. This parameter (*LossDelay*) is used in Equation (3.20).
- *Default cap*. The cap is the current prepay amount scaled by a constant shown as column "default to prepay ratio" in Table 3.11. New defaults generated for a given period are capped by this amount. This is not implemented in the PSA model as described in Equation (3.20).

3.6.2 Algorithm

The Moody's procedure differs from PSA and S&P. These minor differences are beyond the scope of this book; however, one important point should be emphasized.

Defaults are computed in a different manner than PSA. Rather than multiply the foreclosure frequency by *last period's* ZPB, it is multiplied by the *initial* balance. Since default will grow independent of the amortized principal using this method, it must be capped. The cap is the current prepay amount scaled by a constant, *MaxDefPrepayRatio*, shown in the rightmost column of Table 3.11.

One input to the core algorithm is *CumLoss*, the base foreclosure frequency, computed as the loss coverage divided by the severity. Moody's defines realized loss coverage as the total *undiscounted* losses over the horizon divided by the initial balance. Realized loss coverage does not necessarily equal input loss coverage because of the aforementioned default cap. Another way that this can happen is if prepayment speeds are high, shortening the life of the structure and thereby cutting off some scheduled losses.

Moody's requires that all input losses be realized in the model (Agarwal 2005). This is implemented by *adjusting* the input loss coverage until the *realized* loss coverage achieves a *target* value. Table 3.9 gives the target loss coverages for each rating. For example, for Aaa stress Moody's specifies a target loss coverage of 23%. For a given structure, applying 23% loss coverage to the model generates cash flows with only 19% realized loss coverage (*actual* losses divided by initial collateral balance). To reiterate, this happened because the collateral paid down before all the losses were scheduled to appear. We have to increase the input loss coverage to 38% to achieve the 23% target.

Because the collateral model is fairly linear with respect to loss coverage, a simple search method suffices to achieve the target loss coverage. An extrapolating/interpolating search is shown in Figure 3.10. Let the *target* value be φ, the *realized* value (in period t) be χ_t, and the *estimated* value be $\hat{\chi}_t$. Linear extrapolation is used in the first iteration to get started. After that, interpolation is used (which is equivalent to extrapolation if the two

TABLE 3.11 Loss Severity and Other Parameters for Moody's Model

Rating	First Liens				Second Liens			
	Severity	CPR Mult FRM	CPR Mult ARM	Default-to-Prepay Ratio	Severity	CPR Mult FRM	CPR Mult ARM	Default-to-Prepay Ratio
Aaa	60.00%	133.0%	115.0%	75.0%	100.00%	115.0%	115.0%	80.0%
Aa1	57.50%	126.0%	112.5%	70.0%	98.93%	112.5%	112.5%	75.0%
Aa2	55.00%	120.0%	110.0%	65.0%	97.86%	110.0%	110.0%	70.0%
Aa3	53.33%	117.0%	108.5%	62.5%	96.79%	108.5%	108.5%	67.5%
A1	51.67%	113.0%	106.5%	60.0%	95.71%	106.5%	106.5%	65.0%
A2	50.00%	110.0%	105.0%	57.5%	94.64%	105.0%	105.0%	62.5%
A3	48.33%	107.0%	103.5%	55.0%	93.57%	103.5%	103.5%	60.0%
Baa1	46.67%	103.0%	101.5%	52.5%	92.50%	101.5%	101.5%	57.5%
Baa2	45.00%	100.0%	100.0%	50.0%	91.43%	100.0%	100.0%	55.0%
Baa3	44.17%	97.0%	98.5%	47.5%	90.36%	98.5%	98.5%	52.5%
Ba1	43.33%	93.0%	96.5%	45.0%	89.29%	96.5%	96.5%	50.0%
Ba2	42.50%	90.0%	95.0%	42.5%	88.21%	95.0%	95.0%	47.5%
Ba3	41.67%	87.0%	93.5%	40.0%	87.14%	93.5%	93.5%	45.0%
B1	40.83%	83.0%	91.5%	37.5%	86.07%	91.5%	91.5%	42.5%
B2	40.00%	80.0%	90.0%	35.0%	85.00%	90.0%	90.0%	40.0%
B3	40.00%	77.0%	88.5%	35.0%	85.00%	88.5%	88.5%	40.0%

$$
\begin{array}{ll}
1 & t = 0 \\
2 & \hat{\chi}_t = \varphi \\
3 & \varepsilon = 0.1\% \times \varphi \\
4 & iterate = \text{True} \\
5 & while\ iterate \\
6 & \quad \chi_t = GenCashFlows(\dots \hat{\chi}_t \dots) \\
7 & \quad iterate = \left| \chi_t - \varphi \right| > \varepsilon \\
8 & \quad if\ iterate \\
9 & \quad\quad if\ t = 0 \\
10 & \quad\quad\quad \hat{\chi}_{t+1} = \varphi \times \hat{\chi}_t \div \chi_t \\
11 & \quad\quad else \\
12 & \quad\quad\quad \hat{\chi}_{t+1} = \hat{\chi}_t - (\chi_t - \varphi) \times (\hat{\chi}_t - \hat{\chi}_{t-1}) \div (\chi_t - \chi_{t-1}) \\
13 & \quad\quad t = t + 1
\end{array}
$$

FIGURE 3.10 Search Algorithm for Finding Loss Coverage Estimate $\hat{\chi}$ that Produces Realized Loss Coverage χ Equal to Target φ

previous estimates, $\hat{\chi}_{t-1}$ and $\hat{\chi}_t$, don't bracket the target φ). The required accuracy ε of the search is 0.1% of the target. Thus for poor ratings, such as Ba1, the loss coverage is low and hence the required accuracy is relatively high (compared to Aaa).

3.7 OPTION ARMS

Optional adjustable rate mortgages ("option ARMs") are based on the vanilla ARMs described in the previous sections. Vanilla ARMs allow the borrower to prepay the loan, but no other payment options. Option ARMs also allow prepayment, in addition to other payment choices most periods over the horizon of the loan. The fundamental idea behind option ARMs is to allow the borrower to make partial payments that may leave the unpaid principal balance unchanged or even cause the balance to *increase* (i.e., cause the loan to *negatively amortize*). This is similar to giving the borrower a revolving line of credit on top of his mortgage. In addition to these options, the borrower is allowed to make full payments, causing the loan to positively amortize.

In practice option ARMs have many nuances. In this section, a generic loan is described that fits many of the characteristics seen in actual option ARMs. The borrower makes a selection every payment period to pay either in full (normal amortizing payment), interest only (keeping the outstanding loan balance constant), or a "minimum payment" (causing negative amortization). In certain circumstances, as outlined below, the borrower's selection is *overruled* by the constraints of the loan. For example, every fifth year, for all periods in that year, only full payments can be made. In practice, before a payment period, the servicer determines what options are permitted. The servicer then mails the borrower an invoice listing only permissible choices.

The borrower is never allowed to pay *less* than the "minimum payment" (hence its name). If the borrower consistently makes full payments, then amortization proceeds as in a vanilla ARM. In this and all cases, the floating interest rate is taken from one-month LIBOR plus the loan margin. Usually an option ARM has a teaser rate as its initial WAC during an initial fixed-rate period of one month. This teaser rate is critically important, as we will see shortly.

The minimum payment definition is vital to understanding an option ARM. Figure 3.11 illustrates the relationships between the payment options over time for a given loan and LIBOR curve. In this model, the borrower attempts to make minimum payments in *every* period. The only time a minimum payment is not made is when the full payment is required. The bottom of the figure shows the switching between these two modes of payment. The

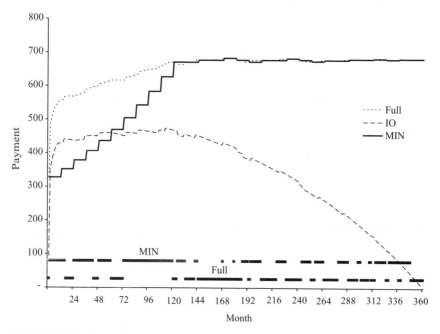

FIGURE 3.11 General Amortization Schedules of Option ARM (Payments Are Dollars)

upper three curves show the payment amount for each payment type (only one of which is the *actual* payment each month). The minimum payment (MIN) starts out less than the full payment and ratchets up every year until it reaches the full payment. Due to timing subtleties, the minimum payment sometimes slightly *exceeds* the full payment. Initially, the minimal payment may lie below the interest-only payment (IO) if the teaser rate is very low. Because the minimum rate ratchets up each year, it will cross above the interest-only rate within the first few years.

Most borrowers are expected to select the minimum payment whenever they are permitted, or at least this conservative assumption makes sense given lack of better data. First, define a "raw" minimum payment. For the first period of *every* year in the payment schedule, the raw minimum payment is equal to the full payment. The raw minimum payment does not change from its previous value for intermediate periods. Thus the raw minimum payment is a step function derived from the full payment. From this, the minimum payment is computed. The minimum payment is the lesser of the raw minimum payment and the minimum payment one year prior times 107.5%. The second term effectively caps the payment so that it cannot grow more than 7.5% per year (this cap is loan specific and changes with market conditions). Thus the minimum payment ratchets up each year as illustrated in Figure 3.11.

Each period two steps are used to compute the loan balance. The first step determines if the borrower's selection needs to be overruled with a full payment. The second step computes the final payment selection and applies it to the previous balance. A minimum payment or interest-only payment is disallowed in two cases:

- Pay full during each period of every fifth year of the loan (including the last year of the loan).
- Pay full for a period in which the borrower selects a minimum payment and the balance that would result from allowing such a payment exceeds 110% of the initial loan balance. Should this occur, for every subsequent period in that year, also pay full.

The *actual* payment is that made by the borrower for a given period. The actual payment is computed from the various components previously discussed. A final selection is used to choose a payment amount. If the actual payment is less than the minimum payment, then the minimum payment must be made. The payment can then be decomposed into interest and principal payments. The balance is adjusted by the principal payment (that can be *negative*, the whole point of the option ARM).

3.8 CLASS ARCHITECTURE: MULTIPLE INHERITANCE

A loss-free model was first introduced in Chapter 2 and extended to the zero-prepay model in section 3.4.1. The zero-prepay model is used to generate a zero-prepay balance (ZPB) that is required for the full collateral model with losses (section 3.4.2). As discussed in Section 2.4.3, there are subtle issues in the incorporation of losses within the simple Loan class architecture. These issues revolve around the trade-off between code sharing and code independence. To fully share the code specified above, a parameterized Loan class is required. But this means that fixed and floating loans coexist in one class, hence are not fully modular. On the other hand, to fully modularize fixed and floating loans, weak inheritance should be used. But this means that the complex code implementing the full collateral model needs to be replicated.

On top of these concerns, rating agency models were introduced in sections 3.5 and 3.6. The agencies make subtle changes to the core PSA model, in addition to requiring vastly different input assumptions. Furthermore, whereas the PSA model is set in stone, the agency models can change over time. Certainly the data assumptions shift, but the algorithm mechanics might also change. The agency dimension of the problem is at least as complex as the loan type dimension. This book focuses on mortgage assets. Different asset types add another dimension to the problem that is at least as complex as the agency issues.

Figure 3.12 illustrates one possible architecture with agencies as the main axis. Because this is nothing more than an interface, there is no code sharing among the children. For example, although S&P makes only a few changes to the core PSA algorithm, the entire code is replicated. The advantage of this, however, is that should S&P change their requirements in the future, the changes will be isolated—there will be no way to accidentally introduce bugs in the Moody's model for instance.

The CollatModel parent class is defined as follows. Each child needs to implement both Init, for initializing the object, and GenCashFlows, which runs the collateral cash flow algorithm and produces a set of cash flows in a

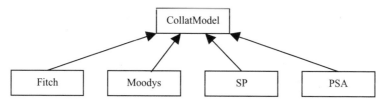

FIGURE 3.12   Sketch of (Weak) Inheritance in CollatModel Class

CashFlow object. The implementations of these methods are not presented, so the parameters are not important.

```
Public Sub Init(...)
End Sub

Public Function GenCashFlows() As CashFlow
End Function
```

The Moodys child class,[4] for example, indicates it is related to the parent as follows:

```
Implements CollatModel

Dim Cashflows as CashFlow
Dim LossCoverage as Double
. . .
```

and contains definitions for each procedural method. In actuality, Moodys has more than just the two data members shown above. These two, however, are important for the discussion below. Cashflows holds the result of running the collateral model. LossCoverage is the target loss associated with the rating being modeled (Table 3.10).

In a programming language with full inheritance, CollatModel would have the core PSA cash flow model within it, and the rating agency children would redefine certain methods to drive different behavior. The Moody's search raises an interesting issue. It would be nice to implement this search algorithm, along with other search/optimization techniques, in a class of their own, rather than distributed in the Moodys and other classes. This would allow code sharing and would keep the details of the algorithms hidden, away from the clients.

Each of these search/optimization algorithms involves, at its core, evaluation of an objective function. For example, to find the yield from bond price, the cash flows are discounted with a "guess" of the yield, and the search attempts to converge on the target price. In this case, the core function is present valuing some cash flows. Usually the core function is much *heavier* than this.

To collect the search algorithms into their own class and make them truly shareable among alternative clients requires that the core objective function

---

[4] In VBA, class and method names cannot contain certain symbols (e.g., apostrophe). So the "Moodys" class name is not a typo.

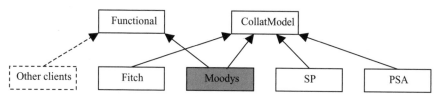

FIGURE 3.13 Sketch of Multiple (Weak) Inheritance for Moodys Class

be abstracted. Each client may have *different* core functions to search over, yet all must use the *same* search class. This is accomplished by extending the notion of inheritance to that of *multiple* inheritance, as illustrated in Figure 3.13.

Moodys (with the other children) weakly inherits from CollatModel. Moodys also inherits from another class, Functional, defined very simply:

```
Public Function Eval(param As Double) As Double
End Function
```

The Moodys class is modified slightly:

```
Implements CollatModel
Implements Functional

Public Function Functional_Eval ( _
    LossCoverage_ As Double) As Double
    LossCoverage = LossCoverage_
    Functional_Eval = GenCashFlows_()
End Function

Private Function GenCashFlows_() as Double
    . . .
    Dim RealizedLossCoverage As Double
    . . .
    <perform collateral cash flow model here>
    . . .
    GenCashFlows_ = RealizedLossCoverage
End Function
```

In addition to inheriting from CollatModel, Moodys now also inherits from Functional. Moodys then dutifully defines Functional_Eval as required in the Functional interface. Functional_Eval calls the cash-flow generation function, GenCashFlows_. This function returns the realized loss coverage (the cash flows themselves are saved in the data member, Cashflows). The public method GenCashFlows in Moodys is defined as follows:

```
Public Function CollatModel_GenCashFlows() As CashFlow

    Dim RealizedLossCoverage As Double
    Dim Search As New Search
    Dim Tolerance As Double

    Tolerance = 0.0005

    Search.InterpolationSearch Me, Tolerance, _
        LossCoverage, LossCoverage, RealizedLossCoverage

    Set Search = Nothing
    Set CollatModel_GenCashFlows = Cashflows
End Function
```

Instead of invoking the cash-flow generation algorithm directly by calling GenCashFlow_, a Search object is instantiated. The cash flow is indirectly generated by invoking the InterpolationSearch method of the Search object, *passing as its first argument Me*, that is, the Moodys object itself! This will make sense in a moment.

The interpolation search algorithm specified in Figure 3.10 can be implemented as the following method (in the Search class). This method requires as inputs: CoreFunction: a Functional object representing the core function to search over, Tolerance: the precision required, Target_: the value we aim to achieve, In_: the effective value needed to achieve the target, Out_: the realized output value (will be within Tolerance of Target_).

```
Public Sub InterpolationSearch( _
    CoreFunction As Functional, _
    Tolerance As Double, _
    Target_ As Double, _
    In_ As Double, _
    Out_ As Double)

    Dim Err As Double
    Dim PrevIn As Double
    Dim PrevOut As Double
    Dim iterate As Boolean
    Dim step As Integer
    Dim target As Double
```

```
      target = Target_
      Err = target * Tolerance
      iterate = True
      step = 0
      In_ = target

      While iterate
          PrevOut = Out_
          Out_ = CoreFunction.Eval(In_)
          PrevIn = In_
          step = step + 1
          iterate = (Abs(Out_ - target) > Err)

          If iterate Then
              If step = 1 Then
                  In_ = target * In_ / Out_
              Else
                  In_ = In_ - (Out_ - target) * _
                      (In_ - PrevIn) / (Out_ - PrevOut)
              End If
          End If
      Wend
End Sub
```

The "crux of the biscuit" is:

```
Out_ = CoreFunction.Eval(In_)
```

Here, everything comes together. CoreFunction is declared as a Functional object—it is the Moodys object, which is in fact Functional, as well as being CollatModel. Its Eval method, required to evaluate the core search function, is invoked with In_, the input argument. Both In_ and the output Out_ drive the interpolation. The search continues until Out_ is within Tolerance of the target. The methods can be generalized to allow more input arguments and the like.

The reader might ask: Is it really worth all this complication to do such a simple task? Consider that any client that needs to do an interpolation search can take advantage of this one. We will see in later chapters additional types of searches that can be added as methods to the Search class and thereby shared. Furthermore, the concept can be exploited for other kinds of algorithms (e.g., sort) that are orthogonal to the general application architecture.

3.9 *DOING IT IN EXCEL*: SUMPRODUCT

All sections in the book entitled *Doing It in Excel* give practical tips for modeling in Excel. The tips are generally related to the topics discussed in the chapter. In addition, Appendix A discusses Excel style and compilation tips. Although this book emphasizes object-oriented programming in VBA, Excel still plays a huge role in modeling.

SumProduct is a versatile function that can be exploited for many tasks. Consider the replines in Figure 3.14 and their weighted averages computed in Figure 3.15. SumProduct takes a variable number of vector arguments, each multiplied piecewise with the others, then added. For example, consider three named ranges in Figure 3.14: Type, Bal, and WAC. The following formulae (computing the balance-weighted average WAC of ARM loans) are equivalent:

```
=SUMPRODUCT(if(Type="ARM",1,0),Bal,WAC)/
    SUMPRODUCT(if(Type="ARM",1,0),Bal)

=SUMPRODUCT(--(Type="ARM"),Bal,WAC)/
    SUMPRODUCT(--(Type="ARM"),Bal)

=SUMPRODUCT(--(Type="ARM"),Bal,WAC)/SUMIF(Type,"=ARM",Bal)
```

The expression `--(Type="ARM")` converts a vector (TRUE, FALSE, FALSE, ...) into a vector (1, 0, 0, ...) by double negation. SumProduct subsumes SumIf so there is no need to remember SumIf.

3.10 EXERCISES

3.1. Implement a cash flow generation method for the PSA algorithm within a loan class.

3.2. By induction prove that $Bal_{act}(t) = Bal_{perf}(t) + Def_{roll}(t)$ with the PSA definitions in section 3.4. Thus, the actual collateral balance (as delivered to the liability cash flow model) is equal to the performing collateral balance plus the rolling cumulative defaults.

3.3. Equations 3.26 through 3.28 are sometimes written differently:

$$Int_{exp}(t) = [Bal_{perf}(t-1) + FCL(t)] \times WAC_{eff}(t) \div Freq$$

$$Int_{adv}(t) = [Def_{new}(t) + FCL(t)] \times WAC_{eff}(t) \div Freq$$

$$Int_{perf}(t) = Int_{exp}(t) - Int_{adv}(t)$$

$$Int_{net}(t) = \begin{cases} Int_{exp}(t) & Advance \\ Int_{perf}(t) & \text{otherwise} \end{cases}$$

where $FCL(t) = Def_{roll}(t-1)$. Prove this equivalence.

	A	B	C	D	E	F	G	H	I	J	K	L	M	N	O	P	Q
1	Type	Group	Bal	WAC	Serv	WAM	Age	PP Pen	Balloon	IO Months	Margin	Init Reset	Reset Freq	Init Pdc Cap	Pdc Cap	Life Cap	Life Floor
2	ARM	G1	408,546	7.765	0.52	478	2	34	360	0	6.322	34	6	2.406	1.400	14.625	7.702
3	ARM	G1	5,789,967	8.050	0.52	478	2	22	360	0	6.160	22	6	2.277	1.280	14.904	7.905
4	ARM	G1	38,411	7.540	0.52	476	4	8	360	0	5.468	20	6	2.355	1.215	13.970	7.540
5	ARM	G1	668,228	8.376	0.52	477	3	9	360	0	6.091	21	6	2.213	1.296	15.210	8.340
6	ARM	G1	27,877	8.210	0.52	477	3	9	360	0	7.589	33	6	3.000	1.500	15.210	8.210
7	ARM	G1	215,247	8.614	0.52	476	4	20	360	0	6.918	20	6	1.854	1.500	15.498	8.614
8	ARM	G1	296,659	8.422	0.52	478	2	34	360	0	6.772	34	6	2.330	1.500	15.422	8.399
9	ARM	G1	3,863,182	8.545	0.52	478	2	0	360	0	6.055	22	6	1.703	1.467	15.498	8.405
10	ARM	G1	239,461	7.839	0.52	478	2	34	360	0	5.333	22	6	2.316	1.228	14.839	7.364
11	ARM	G1	115,798	8.590	0.52	477	3	21	360	0	6.055	21	6	2.144	1.343	15.474	7.883
12	ARM	G1	22,490	8.965	0.52	477	3	9	360	0	6.875	21	6	3.000	1.292	15.965	8.965
13	ARM	G1	131,035	8.208	0.52	477	3	33	360	0	6.394	21	6	1.573	1.476	15.208	8.208
14	ARM	G1	500,142	7.898	0.52	477	3	9	360	0	5.615	21	6	1.500	1.500	14.898	7.898
15	ARM	G1	453,790	8.059	0.52	476	4	20	360	0	6.045	20	6	1.500	1.500	15.059	8.059
16	ARM	G1	330,861	8.055	0.52	478	2	10	360	0	5.538	22	6	1.555	1.482	15.055	8.055
17	ARM	G1	112,805	8.065	0.52	476	4	8	360	0	6.502	20	6	1.500	1.500	15.065	8.065
18	ARM	G1	52,913	9.070	0.52	477	3	33	360	0	6.963	21	6	1.500	1.500	16.070	9.070
19	ARM	G1	21,826	9.330	0.52	477	3	57	360	0	6.766	21	6	1.500	1.500	16.330	9.330
20	ARM	G1	46,520	7.253	0.52	475	5	13	360	0	3.315	19	6	1.500	1.500	14.253	7.253

FIGURE 3.14 Simplified Mortgage Repline Portfolio ("Loans" Sheet); Named Ranges Outlined

	A	B	C	D	E	F	G
1	G1	ARM	FRM	total			
2	Principal Balance	924,092,932	75,907,068	1,000,000,000	=SUMPRODUCT(		
3	Gross Coupon	8.1331	9.4134	8.2303	--(loans!$B$2:$B$1000=$A$1),		
4	Servicing	0.52	0.52	0.52	loans!$C$2:$C$1000)		
5	WAM	390.9	359.1	388.5			
6	Age	3.2	3.4	3.2	=SUMPRODUCT(		
7	Prepayment Penalty	15.9	20.3	16.3	--(loans!$B$2:$B$1000=$A$1),		
8	Balloon	102.4	92.9	101.7	--(loans!$A$2:$A$1000=B$1),		
9	IO Months	14.9	1.9	13.9	loans!$C$2:$C$1000)		
10	Margin	6.2			=IF(B$2=0,0,SUMPRODUCT(		
11	Initial Reset	22.1			--(loans!$B$2:$B$1000=$A$1),		
12	Reset Frequency	6.0			--(loans!$A$2:$A$1000=B$1),		
13	Initial Periodic Cap	2.4			loans!$C$2:$C$1000,		
14	Subsequent Periodic Cap	1.3			loans!$D$2:$D$1000)/B$2)		
15	Life Cap	14.9					
16	Life Floor	8.0					
17							

FIGURE 3.15 Computing Weighted Averages with Sumproduct

3.4. Implement a class for loss and prepay curves. A loss vector is created containing the monthly loss rates for each period. There are four methods for creating this vector. If the default type is "CMD," then each period is a constant, *simple* monthly default rate (somewhat unconventional). If the default type is "CDR" then each period is a constant, *compounded* monthly default rate, similar in construction to a bond equivalent yield.

If the default type is "VECT," then the loss vector varies from month to month. The variance comes from a loss curve given as input. There are two methods for creating a variable vector. If the vector type is "CMD," then each period is the product of the loss curve times a constant, *simple* monthly default rate. If the vector type is "CDR" or "SNP," then each period is the product of the loss curve times a constant, *compounded* monthly default rate.

3.5. Implement a cash flow generation method for the S&P algorithm within a loan class.

3.6. Implement a cash flow generation method for the Moody's algorithm within a loan class.

3.7. Combine above Exercises 3.1, 3.5, and 3.6 into a single implementation. What type of class architecture works best?

3.8. Implement option ARMs within your solution to Exercise 3.1. Does the introduction of a new loan type require you to rethink your architecture?

3.9. Implement the prepayment penalty function *PPP* discussed in section 3.1 and used in Equation (3.41).

3.10. Consider a *slow amortizing mortgage*. There is a "slow" WAM in addition to a standard WAM. For an initial number of periods, the loan amortizes as if its maturity is set to the slow WAM. After that initial period, the loan reverts back to amortizing with a maturity set to its standard WAM. Because the slow WAM is greater than the standard WAM, the loan amortizes slower during its initial phase. Implement this product within your framework.

3.11. Implement a fixed-rate interest-only (IO) mortgage within your collateral model (Simon 2006a). This type of loan typically has a 10-year initial period during which the rate is fixed. After that, the rate floats. This loan is made primarily to prime borrowers, that is, those with good credit. When people think that future rates will rise, they may be interested in locking in a fixed rate, assuming they will pay down the loan prior to the reset date. If rates get too high, however, the popularity of this loan drops off because of the high interest expense. There is a sweet spot in short rates where this rare loan type is most frequent.

3.12. Research an asset-backed security type (e.g., credit card debt, student loans, auto loans). The residential mortgage collateral cash flow architecture (as described in this chapter) is already stretched in two dimensions: agencies and asset subtypes. What is the most effective way to extend the architecture in a third dimension (new asset types)? Propose a new architecture in broad strokes.

3.13. For a small example, use Excel Solver to find the optimal portfolio of loans given constraints similar to those in section 3.2.1. Try to implement a universe of 10 loans, and constrain the problem so that about half of them are selected. Discuss alternative objective functions.

3.14. Implement a simulated annealer class. Test your code with the same problem as in Exercise 3.13.

3.15. Implement a Search class that works by multiple inheritance as discussed in section 3.8. Implement interpolation search and binary search. Create clients to illustrate the flexibility of the architecture.

CHAPTER **4**

Liabilities

Froth at the top, dregs at bottom, but the middle excellent.
—Voltaire

4.1 GETTING STARTED

The liabilities in a "cash" securitization are the bonds issued to investors (the debt holders) to raise cash to buy the asset portfolio. Review Figure 1.2 sketching a mortgage securitization. This chapter describes how to model the liability cash flows, that is, payments of interest and principal to debt holders. These cash flows are crucial to valuing or pricing the bonds.

The model described accommodates alternative liability structures and their controls, known as *priorities of payment* or *waterfalls*. A general liability structure is comprised of tranches or classes. Some tranches may be kept on the books of the seller/securitizer. However, most tranches correspond to bonds or notes that are sold to investors. Generally, bonds promise (fixed or floating) interest and principal payments each period. However, the aggregate periodic payment is not fixed as in mortgage loans. In addition, a bond might be guaranteed by a third-party insurer. In this case, payments cannot be late or lost, unless the guarantor defaults. If a bond is not guaranteed, then there is the chance that a bond payment is late or lost because an asset defers interest or defaults. Still, the servicer may agree to advance missing payments to the extent deemed recoverable, to be potentially reimbursed by later, excess cash flows.

Tranches are broadly categorized as *senior* or *subordinate*, corresponding to their rating quality and credit enhancement. Seniors have higher ratings due to more credit enhancement. Subordinates have lower ratings due to less credit enhancement. In general, the asset and liability balances are equal. The situation when the assets exceed the liabilities is known as over-collateralization (O/C). Tranches are enhanced by O/C. There are more assets than liabilities, so the excess assets can absorb loan defaults before interest and principal payments to the tranches get lost. Tranches can also enhance other tranches: They are prioritized in some order of payment. Thus missing payments (due to asset losses) are absorbed by the lowest-priority tranche first. Seniors are enhanced by both O/C *and* subordinate tranches. In broad strokes, seniors get paid in higher priority than subordinates, so the only way a senior would experience a missing payment is if all the subordinates failed to get paid. Hence seniors achieve higher ratings than subordinate tranches as judged by the rating agencies.

These concepts are also known as credit tranching (having lower-rated tranches absorb losses prior to higher-rated tranches) and sequential tranching (having a lower-priority tranche absorb losses prior to a higher-priority tranche). Both ideas help make bond cash flows more stable and predictable than a given mortgage loan cash flow, the key advantage of securitization.

The senior/subordinate categorization is clumsy—in fact, tranches rated AAA down to B− can be carved out of the structure, as we shall see in this chapter. Usually, seniors are rated AAA only. Highly rated (around AA+ to A−) subordinates are called *mezzanine* tranches. In this book, low-rated (around BBB+ and below) subordinates are called *junior* tranches. In addition to standard bonds that pay both interest and principal, there are alternative bonds, for example, IO, PO, Z, PAC, and NAS bonds (e.g., Fabozzi and Modigliani 1992). The framework described can support these bonds, although they are not emphasized.

An "I" structure represents the sequential ordering of the tranches, from most senior to most subordinate. Figure 4.1 shows an example of an "I" structure. There is one collateral group supporting eight issued bonds, followed by a NIM (Net Interest Margin) and OTE (Owner's Trust Equity)

Class		Rating	Alloc	Coupon
A1	Senior	AAA	82.1%	1mL+37bp
M1	Mezz	AA	6.8%	1mL+63bp
M2	Mezz	A	4.9%	1mL+115bp
M3	Mezz	A-	1.3%	1mL+125bp
B1	Sub	BBB+	1.1%	1mL+175bp
B2	Sub	BBB	0.8%	1mL+185bp
B3	Sub	BBB−	0.6%	1mL+311bp
B4	Sub	BB+	1.0%	1mL+375bp
N1	NIM	N/A	6.3%	544 bp
OTE	OTE	N/A	N/A	2600 bp

FIGURE 4.1 Illustration of "I" Structure: 2004-HE4 (Tranches Not Drawn to Scale)

(these latter notes are discussed in sections 4.10 and 5.5). All the issued bonds are floaters. By "sequential" it is meant that A1 is paid interest before M1 and so on. If there is sufficient collateral interest for all bonds, then one would observe interest cash flows to all outstanding bonds "simultaneously." If there were insufficient collateral interest, then some more senior bond would be paid interest at the expense of some more junior bond missing interest.

For principal, a purely sequential ordering would require A1 to completely pay down before any principal is paid to M1, and so on. In practice, structures may pay principal sequentially for a number of periods, but then pro rata distributions occur. The period of pure sequentiality is to protect the senior bond holders. There are additional waterfalls related to structure, for example, how cash possibly generated from options is paid. In general, the 2004-HE4 (Morgan Stanley 2004c) structure shown in Figure 4.1 is considered to be "sequential" because of its interest waterfall.

In certain cases, two tranches are considered to have no precedence. For example, two senior tranches may be paid interest *pro rata* (*pari passu* is a special case of a 50%–50% pro rata distribution). In related structures, collateral can be partitioned into groups supporting different tranches.

Consider a deal with nonsequential tranches visualized as a "Y" structure. Figure 4.2 shows the issued bonds of the 2004-HE2 structure (Morgan Stanley 2004a). For now, it suffices to squint one's eyes and see the "Y."

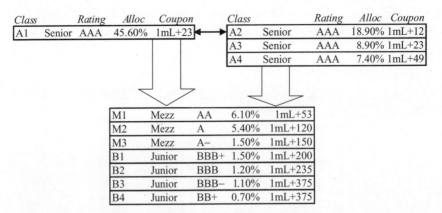

Class		Rating	Alloc	Coupon	Class		Rating	Alloc	Coupon
A1	Senior	AAA	45.60%	1mL+23	A2	Senior	AAA	18.90%	1mL+12
					A3	Senior	AAA	8.90%	1mL+23
					A4	Senior	AAA	7.40%	1mL+49

M1	Mezz	AA	6.10%	1mL+53
M2	Mezz	A	5.40%	1mL+120
M3	Mezz	A−	1.50%	1mL+150
B1	Junior	BBB+	1.50%	1mL+200
B2	Junior	BBB	1.20%	1mL+235
B3	Junior	BBB−	1.10%	1mL+375
B4	Junior	BB+	0.70%	1mL+375

FIGURE 4.2   Illustration of "Y" Structure: 2004-HE2 Interest Waterfall (Tranches Not Drawn to Scale)

This particular structure has two collateral groups supporting (A1) and (A2,A3,A4). With respect to interest payments there is no precedence among the senior tranches. Furthermore, among (A2,A3,A4), interest is paid in a pro-rata distribution. To top it all off, (A1) and (A2,A3,A4) are *cross-collateralized*, informally meaning that any extra collateral interest cash flow is shared between (A1) and (A2,A3,A4). This is illustrated with the small arrow. Cross-collateralized deals can also be viewed as "H" structures. Note that the 2004-HE2 principal waterfall is an entirely different beast that we will visit in section 4.11.

As a final example, consider the 2005-3 CWABS deal (Countrywide Home Loans 2004) illustrated in Figure 4.3. There are two large "legs:" Leg1 contains floating-rate bonds, and Leg2 contains primarily fixed-rate bonds. Each of these is supported by its own collateral groups. The senior bonds in each leg have complex pro-rata interest distributions, so each leg is really a "Y" structure. The legs "combine" in the sense that residual cash flows from each leg join together to support a NIM. Thus the deal is a kind of multiple "Y" or tree structure.

In summary, "I," "Y," and "H" mnemonics help visualize a structure but are not flexible enough. Actual structures can be quite complex and a model must be equally flexible.

Class		*Leg1* Rating	*Alloc*	*Coupon*	Class		*Leg2* Rating	*Alloc*	*Coupon*
2-AV-1	Senior	AAA	30.55%	1mL+19	AF-1A	Senior	AAA	27.94%	1mL+12
2-AV-2	Senior	AAA	7.64%	1mL+24	AF-1B	Senior	AAA	4.26%	1ySWAP+17
3-AV-1	Senior	AAA	21.43%	1mL+10	AF-2	Senior	AAA	4.29%	2ySWAP+20
3-AV-2	Senior	AAA	0 bp	1mL+15	AF-3	Senior	AAA	21.55%	3ySWAP+25
3-AV-3	Senior	AAA	8.13%	1mL+20	AF-4	Senior	AAA	6.19%	5ySWAP+52
3-AV-4	Senior	AAA	2.77%	1mL+30	AF-5A	Senior	AAA	5.78%	7ySWAP+78
MV-1	Mezz	AA+	5.45%	1mL+42	AF-5B	Senior	AAA	5.74%	7ySWAP+70
MV-2	Mezz	AA	4.10%	1mL+45	AF-6	Senior	AAA	10.00%	7ySWAP+36
MV-3	Mezz	AA−	2.20%	1mL+49	MF-1	Mezz	AA+	2.85%	5ySWAP+75
MV-4	Mezz	A+	1.90%	1mL+62	MF-2	Mezz	AA	2.50%	5ySWAP+80
MV-5	Mezz	A	1.80%	1mL+67	MF-3	Mezz	AA−	1.55%	5ySWAP+85
MV-6	Mezz	A−	1.70%	1mL+74	MF-4	Mezz	A+	1.35%	5ySWAP+95
MV-7	Mezz	BBB+	1.50%	1mL+130	MF-5	Mezz	A	1.25%	5ySWAP+100
MV-8	Mezz	BBB	1.30%	1mL+140	MF-6	Mezz	A−	1.25%	5ySWAP+120
BV	Junior	BBB−	1.35%	1mL+190	MF-7	Mezz	BBB+	1.00%	5ySWAP+135
					MF-8	Mezz	BBB	1.00%	5ySWAP+145
					BF	Junior	BBB−	1.00%	5ySWAP+185

N	NIM	N/A	N/A	500 bp
OET	Post-NIM	N/A	N/A	2500 bp

FIGURE 4.3 Illustration of Tree Structure with Two Legs (Tranches Not Drawn to Scale)

4.2   NOTATION

The notation used in this chapter is now introduced. In the context of a single collateral group, the liability model defines the following cash flows:

$$CollInt(t) = \overline{Int_{net}}(t)$$

$$CollPrin(t) = \overline{Prin}(t) + \overline{PrepayAndRecovery}(t)$$

$$CollPPP(t) = \overline{PrepayPenalty}(t)$$

$$CollBal(t) = \overline{Bal_{act}}(t)$$

$$CollLoss(t) = \overline{Loss}(t)$$

The right-hand sides of these equations are defined in section 3.4.2. Note that principal and prepayment cash flows are aggregated in the liability model. *CollPrin* is sometimes known as the Basic Principal Distribution Amount.[1]

As for the liabilities, the previous figures hint at the intricacies that the notation needs to express. A structure is supported by one or more *collateral groups*, each dedicated to subsets of tranches within the structure. Each tranche has a *primary* collateral group—the collateral it depends on before any others. Other associations, by cross-collateralization, are specified in a waterfall (section 4.11). Tranches can be combined into blocks and legs. A *block* is an *ordered* set of similar-type tranches that have the same primary collateral group. Blocks are needed when describing pro rata distributions. A *leg* is a set of dissimilar tranches that may be supported by different collateral groups, but share an O/C requirement or target. Among the deals previously introduced, 2004-HE4 and HE2 are each composed of a single leg, whereas CWABS is composed of two legs.

For an entire structure the following (nonempty) sets are defined:

$$Collat = \{G1, G2, \ldots\}$$

$$Tranches = \{A1, A2, \ldots, M1, M2, \ldots, B1, B2, \ldots\}$$

$$Blocks = \{Blk1, Blk2, \ldots\}$$

$$Legs = \{Leg1, Leg2, \ldots\}$$

---

[1] Term sheets, prospectuses, and other documents defining a structure often have "defined terms." These are the key variables in the deal. Defined terms are often capitalized. Various names for a variable, as encountered as defined terms in actual deals, are sometimes listed in the book. Shorter names are used here for manipulation in equations.

Class[2] names vary from deal to deal, but are generally labeled A, M, and B here. A tranche belongs to one and only one leg. A block belongs to one and only one leg. A tranche may belong to more than one block. Each leg has a few predefined blocks (possibly empty):

$$Senior = (A1, A2, \dots)$$

$$Mezz = (M1, M2, \dots)$$

$$Junior = (B1, B2, \dots)$$

$$Sub = Mezz \,\|\, Junior$$

$$Bond = Senior \,\|\, Sub$$

$$NIM = (NIM_1, NIM_2, \dots)$$

$$OTE = (OTE_1)$$

The "$\|$" operator concatenates two *ordered* sets. In this notion, A1 *precedes* A2 in *Senior*, represented as A1 > A2. The algorithms later described also use *reverse* sets. For example in *rev(Sub)*, M2 *precedes* M1. The NIM and OTE bonds are built from residuals after all the other bond payments have been satisfied (see Figure 1.2 for an example of a NIM). Other blocks can also be specified, such as (A2,A3,A4) in 2004-HE2.

The model has several internal variables. For example, $Bal(t)$ are the bond balances and $IntOwed(t)$ are the interest payments due the bond holders. The above sets are used to *index* all the model variables. Table 4.1 gives some examples of the notation.

Most of the liability model is described with recurrence equations. This is essentially an exercise of converting legal into symbolic specifications (see Figure 4.4). In fact, the prospectus is a perfectly valid model, albeit a bit wordy! The conversion here into cash flow equations is to expose the logic behind the structure. To achieve this, the mathematical symbolism must be simpler than English; otherwise, little has been accomplished. The specification is then implemented in an object-oriented programming language as a class architecture. Finally, the program is compiled into an executable model.

In this chapter both the mathematical specification and the class architecture are discussed. It is guaranteed that *this* model will fail to capture *some* aspect of *some* deal. Deals add new features or combine old features in ways

---

[2] "Class" is used interchangeably with bond and tranche. This should not be confused with a class in an object-oriented programming language, as can be determined from context.

TABLE 4.1 Examples of Notation Used in Model Specification

Notation	Meaning
$\forall k \in Tranches$	All tranches in structure
$\forall k \in Legs$	All legs in structure
$\forall k \in Leg$	All tranches in Leg
$\forall g \in Leg$	All collateral groups in Leg — from context
$CollInt_g(t)$	Interest from collateral group g
$CollInt_{Leg}(t)$	Interest from all collateral groups supporting Leg
$CollInt_G(t)$	Interest from all collateral groups in set G
$CollInt(t)$	Interest from all collateral groups in structure
$CollBal_\ell(t)$	Collateral balance contributed by loan ℓ
$Bal(t)$	Total balance from all tranches in structure
$Bal_k(t)$	Balance of tranche k
$Bal_{Leg}(t)$	Balance of all tranches in Leg
$Bal_{Blk}(t)$	Balance of all tranches in block Blk
$Bal_{Senior}(t)$	Balance of all Senior tranches in context of some Leg

that could not have been anticipated. This is the problem of brittleness—the model works fine until it suddenly fails to handle a new situation. The recommended approach to anticipating the unexpected is to define a waterfall class in the architecture. This class handles the complexity that the mathematics does not represent. For example, a deal may specify a priority of payments that does not fit the formalism presented in this chapter. This can be modeled in the waterfall class, which being part of a general programming language, can handle anything.

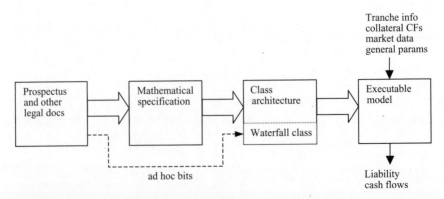

FIGURE 4.4 Building the Liability Model

Key inputs to the liability model are split between those describing individual tranches and those shared by all the tranches. It is best to introduce these many inputs with an example. Table 4.2 gives the parameters describing the 2004-HE2 issued bonds. The following notes give more detail.

- <u>Name</u>: a string representing the tranche.
- <u>Desc</u>: a string that defines the implicit blocks in each leg (e.g., Senior, Mezz, Junior, NIM, and OTE). Other blocks are defined explicitly in the waterfall.
- <u>Type</u>: Fixed or Float(ing) interest rate paid to bond holder.
- <u>SettleFlat</u>: if TRUE, then the bond settles without accrued. The usual convention is that floating-rate tranches do not settle flat.
- <u>DayCount</u>: day-count convention: either 30/360 or act/360. Usually floaters are act/360 and fixed tranches are 30/360, but not necessarily.
- <u>AccrualDate</u>: date when interest starts to accrue for this tranche.
- <u>CapKey</u>: string that references an interest rate corridor (also known as caps). If this field is empty, then no caps apply to that tranche. Caps can be globally turned on/off by a flag in the scenario (Table 4.3). *Caution*: These are not swaps that support all tranches. See section 4.8.1.
- <u>SPRating</u>: S&P rating.
- <u>MoodysRating</u>: Moodys rating.
- <u>Size</u>: tranche size is given as a percentage of the initial collateral balance. If the sum of these entries is less than 100% then the structure is initially over-collateralized.
- <u>Coupon</u>: specified for fixed-rate tranches only. This is the base rate to pay bond holders (prior to any caps that may be imposed on it).
- <u>Margin</u>: offered coupon specified for floating-rate tranches only. The margin plus the rate specified by the Benchmark index gives the base rate to pay bond holders (prior to any caps that may be imposed on it). For subordinate bonds, the margin can be capped by the available WAC supplied by the collateral.
- <u>Spread</u>: market spread used for computing yield. For most floaters market spread is equal to margin. For sufficiently subordinate bonds, since the spread is higher than the margin, the price falls below par. *Remember*: Margin (or coupon) is fixed once the bond is issued, whereas spread can change every day with the market. See section B.4 of Appendix B for a discussion about spread duration.
- <u>Benchmark</u>: for floating tranches this string represents the interest rate index: 1mL (one-month LIBOR), 6mL, 1yrCMT, Prime, etc.
- <u>WALTarget</u>: specified for senior bonds only—the senior sizing algorithm attempts to achieve the weighted-average life (WAL) target specified

TABLE 4.2 2004-HE2 Input Parameters Describing Pre-NIM Classes (T = TRUE, F = FALSE)

Name	A1	A2	A3	A4	M1	M2	M3	B1	B2	B3	B4
Desc	Senior	Senior	Senior	Senior	Mezz	Mezz	Mezz	Junior	Junior	Junior	Junior
Type	Float	Float	Float	Float	Float	Float	Float	Float	Float	Float	Float
SettleFlat	F	F	F	F	F	F	F	F	F	F	F
DayCount	act/360	act/360	act/360	act/360	act/360	act/360	act/360	act/360	act/360	act/360	act/360
AccrualDate	5-1-04	5-1-04	5-1-04	5-1-04	5-1-04	5-1-04	5-1-04	5-1-04	5-1-04	5-1-04	5-1-04
CapKey		A	A	A	M	M	M				
SPRating	AAA	AAA	AAA	AAA	AA	A	A–	BBB+	BBB	BBB–	BB+
MoodyRating	Aaa	Aaa	Aaa	Aaa	Aa2	A2	A3	Baa1	Baa2	Baa3	Ba1
Size	45.6%	18.9%	8.9%	7.4%	6.1%	5.4%	1.5%	1.5%	1.2%	1.1%	0.7%
Coupon	0%	0%	0%	0%	0%	0%	0%	0%	0%	0%	0%
Margin	23 bp	12 bp	23 bp	49 bp	53 bp	120 bp	150 bp	200 bp	235 bp	375 bp	375 bp
Spread	23 bp	12 bp	23 bp	49 bp	53 bp	120 bp	150 bp	200 bp	235 bp	475 bp	875 bp
Benchmark	1mL	1mL	1mL	1mL	1mL	1mL	1mL	1mL	1mL	1mL	1mL
WALTarget		0.8	2.0	–1							
Underwriting	25 bp	25 bp	25 bp	25 bp	25 bp	25 bp	25 bp	25 bp	25 bp	25 bp	25 bp
Guarantee	T	T	T	T	F	F	F	F	F	F	F
PrimaryCollat	G1	G2	G2	G2							
Leg	L1	L1	L1	L1	L1	L1	L1	L1	L1	L1	L1

TABLE 4.3 Scalar Input Parameters to Liability Cash Flow Model

Parameter	Typical Value	Meaning
Freq	12	# payment periods per year
FirstPmtDate	25-Jun-04	Date of first bond coupon payment
SettleDate	26-May-04	Date of settle
CollatModel	S&P	"PSA," "Moodys," "S&P," "Fitch," etc.
Rating	BB+	Stress rating for selecting interest rate curve
SettleCollFlat	TRUE	Add accrued interest to bond expense
ResidEval	TRUE	Evaluate residual
StepDownOC	TRUE	Permit O/C step down
StepUpSpread	TRUE	Step up call spread
RunToCall	TRUE	Run to call (FALSE = run to maturity)
FullyFundedOC	TRUE	Init. and target O/C are pegged
CapsOn	TRUE	Int. rate caps
SwapsOn	FALSE	Int. rate swaps
WACReduction	1	Scale excess cash by this stress factor
CallPct	10.00%	If collat bal/org bal < callpct, then call
LossStepUp	0.00%	Percentage to stress O/C
ServicingRate	0.00%	Paid top of the waterfall (in addition to any fees specified in the replines)
TrusteeRate	0.00%	Paid top of the waterfall (in addition to any fees specified in the replines)
SuretyRate	0.05%	Paid top of the waterfall
OCFloor	0.50%	Minimum required O/C
InitOCPct$_{Leg}$	1.25%	Desired initial O/C for Leg. This parameter plus the Sizes of tranches in the Leg must sum to one.
TargetOCPct$_{Leg}$	1.25%	Dynamic target O/C for Leg
SeniorPostCallMult	2.0	After callable date, senior floating-rate bond margins get multiplied by this penalty.
SubPostCallMult	1.5	After callable date, subordinate floating-rate bond margins get multiplied by this penalty.
PostCallStepUp	0.50%	After callable date, fixed-rate bond coupons get increased by this penalty.
TargetSub$_{Senior}$	2.0	Multiplier for target O/C
OCPeriod	24	After this period, stress O/C
IOPeriod	26	IO active during these initial periods
StepPeriod	36	After this period O/C can step down

here. A bond to be sized in this manner must be a member of a multi-tranche block. If the target is positive it is interpreted as a WAL. A "−1" value indicates that any WAL is acceptable for this tranche such that all subsequent tranches in the block have zero allocation. See section 5.1.

- <u>Underwriting</u>: rate paid to the underwriter for securitization, on bond proceeds.
- <u>Guarantee</u>: Boolean indicates if tranche has guaranteed interest and principal payments.
- <u>PrimaryCollat</u>: string identifier representing the primary collateral group supporting this tranche. The tranche may be supported by other groups through cross-collateralization, as specified in the waterfall. If this field is *empty*, then the tranche is supported by *all* collateral groups available to the leg.
- <u>Leg</u>: string identifier representing the leg that contains this tranche. Every tranche can be a member of at most one leg. If this field is empty it means the tranche is not associated with any leg. The collateral supporting a leg is the set of groups indicated as PrimaryCollat in the leg's tranches.

Table 4.3 lists the model parameters shared by all the tranches. Rather than expound on these here, additional color will be given when the parameter is used.

Subsequent sections are presented in the order they appear in a typical waterfall. Unfortunately, not everything in the waterfall lends itself to this linear presentation (e.g., triggers). Triggers test for conditions that indicate if collateral is having difficulty meeting its obligations, or if otherwise healthy collateral is insufficient in size to protect the issued bonds. Triggers are introduced somewhat out of order in section 4.9. The over-collateralization (O/C) trigger is critical. Its cure is to pay down senior bonds until O/C grows sufficient, as discussed in section 4.5.

The first period is denoted as period one and ends on the *FirstPmtDate*. Initial balances are indexed at period zero, for example, CollBal(0).

4.3 EXPENSES

Recall that the collateral cash flow models, in conjunction with data supplied in the loan replines (see *ExpRate* field in Table 3.1), *already* pay certain (servicer and trustee) expenses on the collateral balance. For example, one might typically pay fees (in the collateral model) of 50 bps (servicer) + 2 bps (trustee). In addition to this, at the top of the liability waterfall, there is the option to pay *extra* expenses as follows.

First, the servicer can be paid an additional fee on the collateral balance. Also, the trustee and guarantor (surety provider) can be paid—the former for all tranches and the latter for guaranteed tranches. A swap counterparty may also need to be paid (see section 4.8.2). For the first period, an adjustment is made for the missing portion of collateral interest due to a short period. *AccrualPct* is the percentage of the first period *prior* to settlement. By convention, the *SuretyRate* is unadjusted for day count. $Bal_k(t)$ is the balance of tranche k, initially $(t = 0)$ derived from $Size_k$ (Table 4.2). Note that both the collateral and the bonds can be settled flat. Here, the collateral accrual is paid as a bond expense if settling the collateral flat.

The insurance premium is paid here in anticipation of possible cash draws should the insured (senior) bonds experience missing or late interest or principal. If a late payment is advanced by the insurer and subsequently recovered, recoveries are used to pay back the insurer. This is analogous to servicer advances in the collateral cash flow model. The details of repaying the insurer are not included in the models presented here. This level of detail is not necessary except under extremely high (over AAA rating) stress levels when the seniors experience cash flow irregularities.

$$\forall g \in Collat : Servicing_g(t) = CollBal_g(t-1) \times ServicingRate \tag{4.1}$$

$$\forall Leg \in Legs :$$

$$\forall k \in Leg :$$

$$AccrualPct_k = \min[1, (SettleDate - AccrualDate_k) \times Freq \div 360] \tag{4.2}$$

$$Adj(t) = \begin{cases} AccrualPct_k \times CollInt_{Leg}(t) & t = 1 \wedge SettleCollFlat \\ 0 & \text{otherwise} \end{cases} \tag{4.3}$$

$$SuretyExp_k(t) = \begin{cases} Bal_k(t-1) \times SuretyRate & k.Guarantee \\ 0 & \text{otherwise} \end{cases} \tag{4.4}$$

$$TrusteeExp_k(t) = Bal_k(t-1) \times TrusteeRate \tag{4.5}$$

$$BondExp_k(t) = TrusteeExp_k(t) + SuretyExp_k(t) \tag{4.6}$$

$$BondExp_{Leg}(t) = \sum_{k \in Leg} BondExp_k(t) + Adj(t) \tag{4.7}$$

$$Expense_{Leg}(t) = Servicing_{Leg}(t) + BondExp_{Leg}(t) + SwapExp_{Leg}(t) \tag{4.8}$$

The notation used here deserves comment. $Servicing_g(t)$ is the servicing expense of collateral group g (Equation 4.1). $Servicing_{Leg}(t)$, although

$$
\boxed{
\begin{array}{l}
\text{if failure} \rightarrow \text{terminate model} \\[4pt]
\forall g \in Collat : Servicing_g(t) \Leftarrow CollInt_g(t) \\[4pt]
\forall leg \in Legs : \\[4pt]
\quad \forall g \in Leg : BondExp_{Leg}(t) \times \left(\dfrac{CollInt_g(t)}{CollInt(t)} \right) \Leftarrow CollInt_g(t)
\end{array}
}
$$

FIGURE 4.5   Bond Expense Waterfall

not explicitly defined, is the total servicing expense of all collateral groups supporting *Leg* (Equation 4.8).

The above equations give a *declarative* explanation of amounts computed. A *procedural* explanation is also required of *who pays* and *how they pay*. Throughout this book, procedural waterfalls are enclosed in *boxes*. The procedural equations in Figure 4.5 specify that if a payment cannot be made in full, then the entire model fails. In other words, if there are insufficient funds to pay expenses, then bond holders cannot be paid.

First, servicing fees are paid. Servicing fees corresponding to each collateral group are paid from interest cash flows of that collateral group. Second, bond expenses are paid. The net expenses are allocated, pro rata, among the collateral groups. Cutting corners, only interest is used to pay these expenses because if the expenses exceed the available interest then things are so bad that termination is required.

The $\Leftarrow$ operator indicates payment from a cash source to an obligation. Without formal semantics for this operator, it suffices to treat it as a T-account. Every dollar paid is *debited* from the source (right-hand-side variable) and *credited* to the obligation (left-hand-side variable). If there are insufficient funds to pay the obligation, then the remaining obligation is a positive amount and the source becomes zero. Negative amounts never appear. Section 4.11 describes how such waterfalls are modeled in class architecture.

The reader's indulgence is sought for the somewhat sloppy notation. For example, the variable $CollInt_g(t)$ is used in many of the following declarative specifications of *what to pay*. Yet it is also used in many procedural (waterfall) specifications of *how and when to pay*. This requires a bastardized declarative reading of $CollInt_g(t)$: "the group g collateral interest of period t, *after previous sections of the waterfall have debited from it*."

4.4   INTEREST

Interest expense is paid next in the waterfall. Simply put, interest owed for a given tranche is the previous period's ending balance times the current coupon. However, there are several details. The bond may be fixed or float-ing. For a floating-rate bond, the coupon is the margin plus a benchmark index rate. The rate curve $Benchmark_k(t)$ is set appropriately depending on the use of the model.[3] For example, in pricing a structure a forward curve is used. For the purpose of generating a prospectus "decrement table," a flat curve is used.

Bonds that are callable have a penalty spread, $CallSpd$, added to their coupons. For fixed-rate bonds, this penalty is the $PostCallStepUp$, typically a value around 50 bps. For floating-rate bonds, the margin gets scaled up by either $SeniorPostCallMult$ (for senior bonds) or $SubPostCallMult$ (for subordinate bonds). Typically, the stepped-up margin can be up to twice the original margin. Note that one is subtracted from the multipliers in Equation 4.14 because a call *spread* is computed, to be *added* to the rate.

$\forall k \in Tranche$:

$$Base_k = \begin{cases} SettleDate & SettleFlat_k \\ AccrualDate_k & \text{otherwise} \end{cases} \tag{4.9}$$

$$PayDate'_k(t-1) = \begin{cases} Base_k & t = 1 \\ PayDate(t-1) & \text{otherwise} \end{cases} \tag{4.10}$$

$$Adj30_k(t) = Days360(PayDate'_k(t-1), PayDate(t)) \div 360 \tag{4.11}$$

$$AdjAct_k(t) = [PayDate(t) - PayDate'_k(t-1)] \div 360 \tag{4.12}$$

$$DayAdj_k(t) = \begin{cases} Adj30_k(t) & DayCount_k = 30/360 \\ AdjAct_k(t) & \text{otherwise} \end{cases} \tag{4.13}$$

$$CallSpd_k = \begin{cases} Margin_k \times & Type_k = Float \wedge k \in Senior \\ (SeniorPostCallMult - 1) & \\ Margin_k \times & Type_k = Float \wedge k \in Sub \\ (SubPostCallMult - 1) & \\ PostCallStepUp & Type_k = Fixed \end{cases} \tag{4.14}$$

$$CallAdj_k(t) = \begin{cases} CallSpd_k & Callable(t-1) \wedge k \in Bond \\ 0 & \text{otherwise} \end{cases} \tag{4.15}$$

---

[3] $Benchmark_k$ is defined in Table 4.2 as a *string* identifying the interest rate curve basis for a floating bond. In the shorthand notation above, $Benchmark_k(t)$ is the curve associated with that identifier. Similar shorthand is used throughout the text.

$$Coup_k(t) \quad = \begin{cases} Benchmark_k(t) + Margin_k & Type_k = Float \\ Coupon_k & \text{otherwise} \end{cases} \qquad (4.16)$$

$$RawRate_k(t) = [Coup_k(t) + CallAdj_k(t)] \times DayAdj_k(t) \qquad (4.17)$$

The bonds all settle on a settlement date $SettleDate$, and pay on a series of payment dates $PayDate(t)$. In addition, each bond starts to accrue interest on its accrual date $AccrualDate_k$. The settlement and payment dates must be ordered. Every accrual date must precede or be concurrent with the settlement date. The first period extends from the accrual date to the first payment date. If a bond "settles flat," then the interest accrued from the accrual date to the settlement date is not paid to the bond holder.

An "actual/360" day count convention means that the interest accrued over a period is based on the number of days in that period. A "30/360" day count convention means that the interest accrued over a period is based on the number of "30/360" days in that period. For example, from March 1, 2006, to April 15, 2006, these conventions give 45 and 44 days, respectively. Usually, deals have regular payment dates. All the deals discussed in this book have monthly periods.[4]

Ah, if things could only be so simple! In reality the rate is usually capped by available collateral interest. In a stressed scenario (with high interest rates), by capping each tranche's interest the available collateral, interest can be distributed fairly. Interest owed above the cap is paid back in later periods if there is excess cash. The details follow.

The raw rate computed above is capped by a *WAC cap* (also called the Available Funds Cap or AFC) and possibly a collateral *group WAC cap*. The 2004-HE2 prospectus (Morgan Stanley 2004a) definition follows[5]:

The "WAC Cap" means the weighted average of the mortgage rates for each mortgage loan (in each case, less the applicable Expense

---

[4] The most common mortgage structure has monthly periods with the settlement date one month prior to the first payment date. Assuming the deal settles flat, then "30/360" bonds have $Days360(PayDate_k'(t-1), PayDate(t)) \div 360 = 1 \div Freq$. The Excel built-in Days360(x,y) is the number of 30/360 days between dates x and y.

[5] Throughout the book, excerpts from prospectuses are given as examples of the legal language one encounters in actual deals. This gives only a taste of the complexity out there. The reader may be unsatisfied because often the excerpts will refer to "defined terms" for which no definitions are given (they are defined elsewhere in the prospectus and refer to other defined terms, etc.) For readers who want to further familiarize themselves with the legal specifications, reading a few prospectuses is highly recommended.

*Fee Rate) then in effect on the beginning of the related Due Period
on the mortgage loans (on an actual/360 basis) and, with respect to
the Class A-1 certificates only, as further reduced by the applicable
fee rate payable with respect to the premium due to the certificate
insurer in respect of the certificate insurance policy.*

*[The "Group I Loan Cap" means] the weighted average mort-
gage rate of the Group I mortgage loans then in effect on the beginning of the related Due Period, less the applicable Expense Fee
Rate and further reduced by a fee rate payable with respect to the
premium due to the certificate insurer for the certificate insurance
policy in respect of the Class A-1 certificates.*

For a leg in the structure, *Leg*, $WACcap_{Leg}(t)$ is the current collateral
interest divided by the collateral balance of the previous period, for *all* collateral associated with *Leg* (Equation 4.18). Tranches may have *primary* collateral groups, as noted in Table 4.2. For example, in 2004-HE2, A1 (called the
"Class A-1 Certificates") is associated with G1 collateral (called the "Group
I mortgage loans"). Thus in the A1 interest calculation a group WAC cap
based on G1, $WACcap_{G1}(t)$, is computed (Equation 4.19). The minimum of
the WAC cap and group WAC cap is calculated as $MinWACcap(t)$ (Equation 4.20).

Expenses are netted from the minimum WAC cap (Equation 4.21). Recall that expenses are modeled at two levels: collateral loans and tranches.
The collateral cash flows arriving at the liability model will already be net
any expenses specified within the mortgage loans (e.g., for guarantor and/or
trustee). Thus the WAC cap will already account for them. Additional expense (*SuretyFee*) can be declared for each tranche.[6] This additional expense
must be explicitly netted from the minimum WAC cap because it has already
been paid at the top of the waterfall and hence is no longer available to
support the interest obligation. Finally, the effective rate is the minimum of
the raw rate and the minimum WAC cap (Equation 4.22).

$\forall Leg \in Legs :$

$$WACcap_{Leg}(t) = CollInt_{Leg}(t) \div CollBal_{Leg}(t - 1) \tag{4.18}$$

$\forall g \in Leg :$

$$WACcap_g(t) = CollInt_g(t) \div CollBal_g(t - 1) \tag{4.19}$$

---

[6] The surety payment is made 30/360 by convention.

$\forall k \in Leg :$

$g = k.PrimaryCollat$

$$MinWACcap(t) = \begin{cases} WACcap_{Leg}(t) \times DayAdj_k(t) & g \text{ is empty} \\ \min[WACcap_{Leg}(t), & \text{otherwise} \\ \quad WACcap_g(t)] \times DayAdj_k(t) & \end{cases} \quad (4.20)$$

$$MinWACcap'(t) = \begin{cases} MinWACcap(t)- & k.Guarantee \\ \quad SuretyRate \times Adj30_k(t) & \\ MinWACcap(t) & \text{otherwise} \end{cases} \quad (4.21)$$

$$EffRate_k(t) = \min[RawRate_k(t), MinWACcap'(t)] \quad (4.22)$$

$$IntOwed_k(t) = Bal_k(t-1) \times EffRate_k(t) \quad (4.23)$$

$$UnCapIntOwed_k(t) = Bal_k(t-1) \times RawRate_k(t) \quad (4.24)$$

The interest owed is sometimes known as the Accrued Certificate Interest. The excess between the uncapped and capped interest owed is the Basis Risk Carry Forward Amount (BRCFA). The BRCFA is an obligation to the bond holders to be paid with extra cash at the bottom of the waterfall (see section 4.8.3). If the BRCFA cannot be repaid, it accumulates, accruing interest at the "raw" interest rate, as actual/360.

$\forall Leg \in Legs :$

$\forall k \in Leg :$

$$Excess_k(t) = \max[0, UnCapIntOwed_k(t) - IntOwed_k(t)] \quad (4.25)$$

$$UnpaidBRCFA_k(t) = BRCFA_k(t-1) \times [1 + RawRate_k(t)] \quad (4.26)$$

$$BRCFA_k(t) = Excess_k(t) + UnpaidBRCFA_k(t) \quad (4.27)$$

Procedurally, there are several options for specifying the interest waterfall. Four main templates are sketched in Figure 4.6. The simplest is sequential pay, where two or more tranches are paid, one after the other, from the same collateral group. Equally simple is parallel pay, where two or more tranches are paid from different groups. Next is cross-collateralized pay, which is similar to a parallel pay sequence followed by a second parallel pay sequence. The latter sequence reassigns the collateral groups to different

$$
\begin{array}{l}
\text{Sequential:} \\
\quad IntOwed_k(t) \Leftarrow CollInt_g(t) \\
\quad IntOwed_\ell(t) \Leftarrow CollInt_g(t) \\
\text{Parallel:} \\
\quad IntOwed_k(t) \Leftarrow CollInt_g(t) \\
\quad IntOwed_\ell(t) \Leftarrow CollInt_h(t) \\
\text{Cross-collateralized:} \\
\quad IntOwed_k(t) \Leftarrow CollInt_g(t) \\
\quad IntOwed_\ell(t) \Leftarrow CollInt_h(t) \\
\quad IntOwed_k(t) \Leftarrow CollInt_h(t) \\
\quad IntOwed_\ell(t) \Leftarrow CollInt_g(t) \\
\text{Pro-rata parallel}: \\
\quad IntOwed_k(t) \Leftarrow CollInt_g(t) \times Share_k \\
\quad IntOwed_\ell(t) \Leftarrow CollInt_g(t) \times Share_\ell \\
\quad Share_k + Share_\ell = 1
\end{array}
$$

FIGURE 4.6 Common Interest Waterfall Alternatives. This Assumes Two Tranches, k and ℓ, and Two Collateral Groups, g and h.

tranches. Consider the case with only two groups. Each tranche gets the opportunity to be paid from *both* groups, although it gets paid from its *primary* group first.

Finally there is pro rata parallel pay, which is similar to sequential pay with only a share $Share_j$ of the group applied to each tranche j. There are alternative means of computing the share, for example, the tranche interest owed as a percentage of total interest owed for all tranches associated with the group, or as a percentage of outstanding bond balance, and so on. The latter is the default assumption used in most prospectuses where it says to distribute "pro rata." Shorthand is introduced for pro rata pay, for example,

$$
IntOwed_k(t) \underset{Bal}{\Leftarrow} CollInt_g(t)
$$

The common templates shown in Figure 4.6 can be both extended by the number of tranches as well as combined into more complex waterfalls. For example one can combine cross-collateralized and pro rata parallel. Section 4.11 discusses these issues.

4.5 OVER-COLLATERALIZATION

A detailed specification is now given of how to cure under-collateralization. A leg in a structure is a set of tranches and their supporting collateral. A leg has an over-collateralization (O/C) target. If the current O/C does not meet the target, then additional cash is allocated to pay down senior bonds so that the O/C target is achieved. This is called *acceleration* or *turbo-amortization*. Conservatively, if the current O/C exceeds the target, then no adjustment is made.[7] Formally, the actions described in this section constitute a *cure* for an O/C *trigger event*. Triggers, their cures, and the "core" waterfall closely interact, so there is no best order to introduce these concepts. Since the first step in a principal distribution is likely to be adjustment of O/C, it is introduced here. Other triggers, because they might be thought of as rarer events, are delegated to section 4.9.

4.5.1 Current Subordinated Amount

Collateral interest is used to pay bond expenses and extra servicing (section 4.3), swap counterparty payments (section 4.8.2), and liability interest owed (section 4.4). An interest shortfall occurs when collateral interest is not sufficient to cover these obligations. In this case, the excess is zero. Excess cash is sometimes scaled by a WAC reduction penalty to be on the conservative side. The various rating agencies treat WAC reduction differently. For a given *Leg*:

$$Excess(t) = \min[0, CollInt_{Leg}(t) - Expense_{Leg}(t) - IntOwed_{Leg}(t)] \quad (4.28)$$

$$ReducedExcess(t) = WACReduction \times Excess(t) \quad (4.29)$$

For the remainder of the chapter, unless otherwise indicated, cash flow variables have an implicit "Leg" subscript. For example, $Excess(t)$ is shorthand for $Excess_{Leg}(t)$.

---

[7] Because bonds are issued in round lots, the final delivered collateral may have slightly more O/C than necessary. Should this be the case, the principal cash flows available to pay down bond principal in the *first* period is lessened by the excess O/C amount. The residual is credited with the excess. After the first period, there should never be too much O/C.

The O/C (or Subordinated Amount) for a given period is the collateral balance minus the bond balance in that period. O/C refers informally to either a percentage (of total collateral) or a dollar amount. In an ambiguous context, clarification will be given. The O/C amount can be forced to remain static during the initial years of a deal. At some point, given a set of rules explained below, O/C is allowed to "step down." The rationale behind this is that during the first few years extra enhancement is needed to protect the bond holders. Only after a certain point can this enhancement be safely removed should all other indicators be healthy.

Two equivalent definitions for O/C are now shown. In the first, assume that the previous period's bond balance is paid down by all collateral principal and prepayments of the current period (*CollPrin*) to arrive at the current period's bond balance. The collateral and bond balances are then netted. This is only an estimate—in reality, the bonds may pay down faster or slower depending on a few considerations. O/C as computed here is a baseline.

$$Bal'(t) = Bal(t - 1) - CollPrin(t) \qquad (4.30)$$

$$OC(t) = CollBal(t) - Bal'(t) \qquad (4.31)$$

An alternative derivation of baseline O/C is shown below. From basics we know that this period's collateral balance is equal to last period's collateral balance less current principal paid and losses realized.

$$CollBal(t) = CollBal(t - 1) - CollPrin(t) - CollLoss(t) \qquad (4.32)$$

Substituting Equations (4.32) and (4.31) into Equation (4.30) gives a new expression for O/C. It is last period's collateral balance less losses netted with last period's debt balance.[8]

$$
\begin{aligned}
OC(t) &= CollBal(t - 1) - CollPrin(t) - CollLoss(t) \\
&\quad - [Bal(t - 1) - CollPrin(t)] \\
&= CollBal(t - 1) - CollLoss(t) - Bal(t - 1)
\end{aligned}
$$

O/C can be a *negative* quantity. If negative, it indicates that the deal is under-collateralized. As shown below, this will cause greater *acceleration* of principal paydown to increase the O/C. Subordination targets (as percentage

---

[8] This expression can also used to solve for collateral loss given O/C: $CollLoss(t) = CollBal(t - 1) - Bal(t - 1) - OC(t)$.

of collateral) for each tranche k are defined from the initial O/C and structure allocation:

$$TargetSub_k = \left[\sum_{j<k} Bal_j(0) + OC(0) \right] \div CollBal(0) \qquad (4.33)$$

So far, *baseline* O/C has been defined, that is, the O/C resulting from paying down last period's bond balance with all of this period's collateral principal. The next question is: What additional pay down, if any, is needed to achieve the target O/C? This is the *acceleration*. But first O/C "step down" must be determined.

4.5.2 Stepdown Date

O/C protects the bond holders from loss. At a certain point, when the structure is safely on its way to amortizing down, the O/C can be released. O/C is one of the main sources of cash for the residual, and begins to release on the Stepdown Date. Thus the NIM and post-NIM values can be sensitive to the O/C stepdown.

O/C stepdown occurs if a set of conditions is satisfied. Stepdown is overridden with the *StepDownO/C* parameter (the rating agencies generally do not permit it when modeling). Stepdown can occur only after a threshold month, *Step Period*, and only if the Senior Enhancement Percentage is greater than twice the initial Senior Enhancement Percentage. Once O/C steps down, it remains so unless a trigger overrides it (section 4.9).

$$Threshold(t) = [t > StepPeriod] \vee [SeniorBal(t) = 0]$$

$$SeniorEnhPer(t) = [SubBal(t-1) + OC(t)] \div CollBal(t)$$

$$StepDown(t) = StepDownOC \wedge [\neg Stress] \wedge Threshold(t)$$

$$\wedge [SeniorEnhPer(t) \geq 2 \times SeniorEnhPer(0)] \qquad (4.34)$$

Recall that $\wedge$ and $\vee$ are logical AND and OR (Table 3.3). If the seniors get paid down quickly enough (prior to *StepPeriod*), for instance, in a highly stressed scenario with fast prepays, then O/C stepdown can proceed if the other conditions are met.

From the 2004-HE2 Prospectus (Morgan Stanley 2004a):

"Stepdown Date" means the later to occur of (i) the earlier to occur of (a) the distribution date in June 2007 and (b) the distribution date following the distribution date on which the aggregate

Class Certificate Balances of the Class A Certificates are reduced to zero and (ii) the first distribution date on which the Senior Enhancement Percentage (calculated for this purpose only after taking into account scheduled and unscheduled payments of principal on the mortgage loans on the last day of the related Due Period but prior to any application of the Principal Distribution Amount to the LIBOR Certificates on the applicable distribution date) is greater than or equal to 38%.

"Senior Enhancement Percentage" means, with respect to any distribution date, the percentage obtained by dividing (x) the sum of (i) the aggregate Class Certificate Balances of the Subordinated Certificates and (ii) the Subordinated Amount (in each case after taking into account the distributions of the related Principal Distribution Amount for that distribution date) by (y) the Current Maximum Amount for that distribution date.

Let's translate this. *StepPeriod* is the number of periods between June 1, 2007 and the Settlement Date of May 26, 2004, rounded *down*: $\lfloor 6/1/07 - 5/26/04 \rfloor = 36$ months. The initial Senior Enhancement Percentage, $SeniorEnhPer(0) = 38\% \div 2 = 19\%$.

4.5.3 Target Subordinated Amount

The *target* O/C is computed next (sometimes known as the Specified Subordinated Amount or the Over-collateralization Target Amount). If there has been no step down, and we are not using a stress scenario, then the target is the *original* O/C target. This parameter *InitOCTarget* is computed as a percentage, *TargetOCPct*, of the original collateral balance. For S&P stress, after some threshold month (e.g., *OCPeriod* = 24), additional O/C is required, specified in terms of a percentage *LossStepUp* of the original collateral balance.

If stepdown has occurred, the O/C target is the lesser of the original target and a new target *NewOCTarget* computed as a *higher* percentage of the *remaining* collateral balance. For example, *TargetOCPct* = 2% and *TargetSubMult* = 2, so that once the current balance is half the original balance the step down has an effect. In any case, a trigger event prevents the O/C from changing.[9] For example, a loss trigger is a warning that losses are accumulating at too dangerous a rate, so to moderate this, O/C cannot step

---

[9] Note that triggers can be updated at the end of the waterfall only, so last period's trigger values moderate this period's O/C.

down further (see section 4.9). The actual O/C cannot exceed the (previous period) collateral balance nor fall below a certain floor, *OCFloor*.

$$TriggerEvent(t) = LossTrigger(t-1) \lor DelinqTrigger(t-1) \qquad (4.35)$$

$$InitOCTarget = CollBal(0) \times TargetOCPct_{Leg} \qquad (4.36)$$

$$NewOCTarget = CollBal(t) \times TargetOCPct_{Leg} \times TargetSubMult \qquad (4.37)$$

$$StepUp(t) = t > OCPeriod \land Stress \qquad (4.38)$$

$$OCTarget'''(t) = \begin{cases} \min[InitOCTarget, NewOCTarget] & StepDown(t) \\ InitOCTarget + LossStepUp \times & StepUp(t) \\ \quad CollBal(0) & \\ InitOCTarget & \text{otherwise} \end{cases}$$

$$OCTarget''(t) = \begin{cases} OCTarget''(t-1) & TriggerEvent(t) \\ OCTarget'''(t) & \text{otherwise} \end{cases}$$

$$OCTarget'(t) = \min[CollBal(t-1), OCTarget''(t)]$$

$$OCTarget(t) = \max[OCFloor, OCTarget'(t)] \qquad (4.39)$$

The following is the floating leg O/C target definition from the 2005-3 CWABS Prospectus (Countrywide Home Loans 2004). In this deal there are two collateral groups (Loan Group 2 and Loan Group 3) supporting the floating leg. The O/C target amount is defined as a percentage here. It is 3.35% prior to step down and $2 \times 3.35\% = 6.70\%$ after step down, subject to an O/C floor of 0.50%.

"Adjustable Rate Over-collateralization Target Amount" means with respect to any Distribution Date (a) prior to the Adjustable Rate Stepdown Date, an amount equal to 3.35% of the sum of the aggregate Initial Cut-off Date Principal Balance of the Initial Mortgage Loans in Loan Group 2 and Loan Group 3 and the original Pre-Funded Amount in respect of Loan Group 2 and Loan Group 3 and (b) on or after the Adjustable Rate Stepdown Date, the greater of (i) an amount equal to 6.70% of the aggregate Stated Principal Balance of the Mortgage Loans in Loan Group 2 and Loan Group 3 for the current Distribution Date and (ii) the Adjustable Rate OC Floor; provided, however, that if an Adjustable Rate Trigger

Event is in effect on any Distribution Date, the Adjustable Rate Over-collateralization Target Amount will be the Adjustable Rate Over-collateralization Target Amount as in effect for the prior Distribution Date.

Figure 4.7 shows an example of an O/C target over time (for another deal), with and without the floor. The stepdown occurs in period 37 and the floor kicks in during period 69. The O/C adjustment is the final O/C target minus the current O/C amount. If the adjustment is negative then there is currently too much O/C. Usually, nothing is done in this case to be on the conservative side. A positive adjustment is called the "acceleration" and cannot exceed the reduced excess cash computed in Equation 4.29. Acceleration is sometimes known as the Extra Principal Distribution Amount.

$$OCAdj(t) = OCTarget(t) - OC(t) \tag{4.40}$$

$$Acceleration(t) = \max[0, \min[OCAdj(t), ReducedExcess(t)]] \tag{4.41}$$

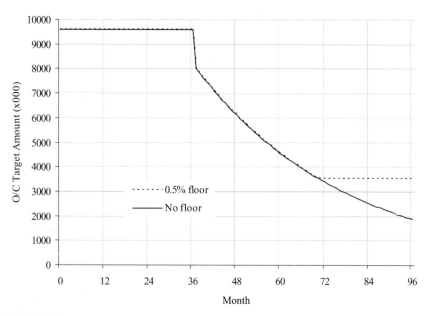

FIGURE 4.7 Example of O/C Target With and Without Floor. Stepdown Occurs in Period 37.

4.6 PRINCIPAL

4.6.1 Gross Principal Distributions

Collateral principal payments (recall this includes prepayments) must be used to pay down debt. The O/C adjustment may indicate that *additional* paydown is required, i.e., acceleration. The *aggregate* paydown to the debt is therefore collateral principal paid plus acceleration. The aggregate is often *distributed* between the senior and subordinate classes, as a whole. Seniors get priority, and leftovers are assigned to subordinates. Once the gross distribution is made, a finer-grain distribution to individual classes is made (see section 4.6.2). The general technique is sometimes called a "shifting interest mechanism" (e.g., Lucas 2006).

Prior to O/C stepdown, all principal is distributed to the seniors (none to subordinate tranches, unless the seniors totally pay down, i.e., their balances go to zero), similarly for S&P and Moody's stress scenarios. In these cases, the "optimal" senior balance is *zero*.

After O/C stepdown, an "optimal" senior balance, $SeniorOpt(t)$, is computed. The difference between the current and optimal balances, if positive, is distributed to the seniors. The optimal balance, $SubTarget'_{Senior}$, is computed in a similar way to how $NewOCTarget$ is computed for O/C allocation. For $SubTarget'_{Senior}$ the subordination target for seniors is scaled by $TargetSubMult$, the multiplier given in Table 4.2. $TargetSub_{Senior}$ is the total subordination to the seniors (including initial O/C) as a percentage of the original collateral (Equation 4.33). The resulting product is the "optimal" subordination to the seniors. This cannot be allowed to be less than $OCFloor$. The floored product is then subtracted from the current collateral balance to produce the optimal senior balance, which cannot be allowed to be greater than actual senior balance (Equation 4.42).

$$SubTarget'_{Senior}(t) = CollBal(t) \times TargetSubMult \times TargetSub_{Senior}$$

$$SubTarget_{Senior}(t) = \max[OCFloor, SubTarget'_{Senior}(t)]$$

$$SeniorOpt'(t) = \begin{cases} 0 & Stress \vee \neg\, StepDown(t) \\ CollBal(t) - SubTarget_{Senior}(t) & \text{otherwise} \end{cases}$$

$$SeniorOpt(t) = \max[0, \min[SeniorBal(t-1), SeniorOpt'(t)]] \tag{4.42}$$

Calculation of the optimal senior balance is illustrated in Figure 4.8. As previously noted, O/C is buried within $SubTarget_{Senior}(t)$. The gross principal

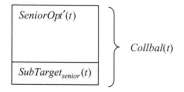

FIGURE 4.8 Sketch of How the Optimal Senior Balance is Computed After O/C Step Down

distribution between seniors and subordinates is calculated as follows. *Agg-BondPrin* is sometimes known as the Principal Distribution Amount.

$$AggBondPrin(t) = CollPrin(t) + Acceleration(t) \tag{4.43}$$

$$SeniorDist(t) = \min[SeniorBal(t-1) - SeniorOpt(t),$$
$$AggBondPrin(t)] \tag{4.44}$$

$$SubDist(t) = AggBondPrin(t) - SeniorDist(t) \tag{4.45}$$

Note the test if a stepdown has occurred in the definition above of $SeniorOpt'(t)$. Setting the optimal balance to zero forces the distribution to fully pay down seniors (if sufficient cash is available). In such a case, subordinate tranches get no distribution unless there is sufficient cash to completely pay down all seniors.

For a sample prospectus specification of a waterfall (for 2004-HE2) see Figure 4.14. The relevant section is (ii). Section (ii)(A) claims that prior to stepdown, subordinates can be paid down (sequentially) only after all seniors are fully paid down. Section (ii)(B) claims that after step down, subordinates can be paid down concurrently with seniors.

If the seniors are comprised of *blocks*, it will be necessary to *split* the aggregate senior principal distribution among collateral *groups*. For example, in 2004-HE2 the seniors are split between two blocks: "Class A-1 Certificates" (A1) and "Group II Class A Certificates" (A2,A3,A4), supported by collateral groups: Group-I (G1) and Group-II (G2) respectively. The aggregate senior distribution is split pro rata based on principal collateral cash flows. Other deals may split differently.

The allocation among senior blocks is formalized below. For each leg, for each collateral group supporting the seniors, a share of the aggregate senior distribution is computed.

$$\forall g \in Senior \; : \; SeniorDist_g(t) = SeniorDist(t) \times \frac{CollPrin_g(t)}{CollPrin(t)} \tag{4.46}$$

4.6.2 Detailed Principal Distributions

The senior/subordinate principal distribution computed in the previous section (*SeniorDist* and *SubDist*) are each further subdivided in this section. Because deals often specify a different priority of payments for seniors, principal payments to senior bonds are programmed in the deal's waterfall, as described in section 4.11. On the other hand, subordinate bonds (mezzanine and juniors) usually have the same payment priorities.

Before getting into the details of how to split up these distributions, it is helpful to look at the big picture. Within the overall waterfall, a principal waterfall (for residential mortgage deals) is typically laid out as follows (for each leg):

1. Compute the senior and subordinate distributions (as described in the previous section).
2. Pay down the senior bonds.
3. Recompute the senior bond balances.
4. Compute the split of the subordinate distributions (depends on senior balances).
5. Compute writedowns for all bonds (in reverse order).
6. Pay down the subordinate bonds.
7. Recover deferred interest and writedowns for all bonds (in forward order).

In some of these steps a distribution quantity is computed. In others that quantity is paid down. The order is critical—the steps are ordered by these dependencies. These steps are detailed in the following sections.

Senior Distributions For sequential seniors, principal distribution among seniors pays senior-most tranches first (A1, then A2, etc.). For senior tranches, the optimal balance is *zero*. Hence they are paid down entirely, in sequence. The current period's balance equals the previous balance less the principal paydown less writedowns (section 4.7).

$\forall k \in Senior :$

$$PrinDist_k(t) = \min[SeniorDist(t) - \sum_{j>k} PrinDist_j(t), Bal_k(t-1)] \quad (4.47)$$

$$Bal_k(t) = Bal_k(t-1) - PrinDist_k(t) - WriteDown_k(t) \quad (4.48)$$

The above equations do not express nonsequential seniors, that is, senior blocks that are paid pro rata. Such bonds are paid in a waterfall as described in section 4.11.

Subordinate Distributions Distribution of principal paydown among subordinate classes is performed next. Similar to the gross senior distribution, optimal balances for each subordinate class k are calculated from individual targets: $TargetSub_k$. In general, a given subordinate tranche k is sandwiched between tranches senior and subordinate to it. This is modeled in the following equations. Calculation of the optimal balance (subordinate class k) is illustrated in Figure 4.9.

$\forall k \in Sub:$

$$SubTarget'_k(t) = CollBal(t) \times TargetSub_k \times TargetSubMult \qquad (4.49)$$

$$SubTarget_k(t) = \max[OCFloor, SubTarget'_k(t)] \qquad (4.50)$$

$$OptBal'_k(t) = \begin{cases} CollBal(t) - [SeniorBal(t) + \quad StepDown(t) \\ \quad \sum_{j>k} Bal_j(t) + SubTarget_k(t)] \\ 0 \qquad\qquad\qquad\qquad\quad otherwise \end{cases} \qquad (4.51)$$

$$OptBal_k(t) = \max[0, \min[Bal_k(t-1), OptBal'_k(t)]] \qquad (4.52)$$

Note the test if a stepdown has occurred in the definition of $OptBal'_k(t)$ (Equation 4.51). Setting the optimal balance to zero forces sequential paydown of subordinates tranches prior to stepdown. As an example, review the waterfall language in the 2004-HE2 Prospectus (Figure 4.14: ii.A.c-i).

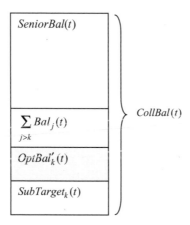

FIGURE 4.9 Sketch of How the Optimal Subordinate Balance Is Computed after O/C Step-down

After stepdown, subordinate tranches can be paid down concurrently, each with its own subdistribution.

Detailed principal distribution among subordinates pays senior-most tranches first (M1, then M2, etc.). Let's now attempt to achieve the optimal balance computed above. The paydowns cannot exceed the total subordinate distribution. The current period's balance is the previous balance minus the principal paydown minus any writedown due to losses (section 4.7).

$\forall k \in Sub:$

$PrinDist_k(t) =$

$$\min \left[SubDist(t) - \sum_{j > k} PrinDist_j(t), Bal_k(t-1) - OptBal_k(t) \right] \quad (4.53)$$

$$Bal_k(t) = Bal_k(t-1) - PrinDist_k(t) - WriteDown_k(t) \quad (4.54)$$

Reading the Prospectus   To put these equations in the context of typical prospectus language, consider 2004-HE2. The B1 principal distribution is defined in the prospectus as follows (Morgan Stanley 2004a):

> *"Class B1 Principal Distribution Amount" means, with respect to any distribution date, an amount equal to the excess of (x) the sum of (i) the aggregate Class Certificate Balances of the Class A Certificates (after taking into account the payment of the Class A Principal Distribution Amount on such distribution date), (ii) the Class Certificate Balance of the Class M-1 certificates (after taking into account the payment of the Class M-1 Principal Distribution Amount on such distribution date), (iii) the Class Certificate Balance of the Class M-2 certificates (after taking into account the payment of the Class M-2 Principal Distribution Amount on such distribution date), (iv) the Class Certificate Balance of the Class M-3 certificates (after taking into account the payment of the Class M-3 Principal Distribution Amount on such distribution date) and (v) the Class Certificate Balance of the Class B-1 certificates immediately prior to such distribution date over (y) the lesser of (A) approximately 91.20% of the Current Maximum Amount and (B) the excess, if any, of the Current Maximum Amount over approximately $3,302,841.*

This definition is equivalent to the mathematics given above, as is now shown. Starting with the math, let's derive the English. For class B1, Equation

(4.53) gives:

$$PrinDist_{B1}(t) =$$

$$\min\left[SubDist(t) - \sum_{j>B1} PrinDist_j(t), Bal_{B1}(t-1) - OptBal_{B1}(t)\right]$$

The prospectus definition gives the *optimal* distribution, given sufficient cash. Equation (4.53) gives the *actual* distribution, given the total subordinate distribution available. Remove the min, assuming sufficient cash:

$$PrinDist_{B1}(t) = Bal_{B1}(t-1) - OptBal_{B1}(t)$$

Substituting Equation (4.52):

$$\begin{aligned}
PrinDist_{B1}(t) &= Bal_{B1}(t-1) - \max[0, \min[Bal_k(t-1), OptBal'_{B1}(t)]] \\
&= \min[Bal_{B1}(t-1), Bal_{B1}(t-1) - \\
&\quad \min[Bal_k(t-1), OptBal'_{B1}(t)]] \\
&= \min[Bal_{B1}(t-1), \max[0, Bal_{B1}(t-1) - OptBal'_{B1}(t)]] \\
&= \max[0, Bal_{B1}(t-1) - OptBal'_{B1}(t)]
\end{aligned}$$

Substituting Equation (4.51):

$$PrinDist_{B1}(t) = \max\left[0, Bal_{B1}(t-1) - \left(CollBal(t) - \right.\right.$$

$$\left.\left.\left[SeniorBal(t) + \sum_{j>B1} Bal_j(t) + SubTarget_{B1}(t)\right]\right)\right]$$

$$= \max\left[0, SeniorBal(t) + \sum_{j>B1} Bal_j(t) + Bal_{B1}(t-1)\right.$$

$$\left.- \left(CollBal(t) - SubTarget_{B1}(t)\right)\right]$$

$$= \max[0, x - y]$$

where:

$$x = SeniorBal(t) + \sum_{j>B1} Bal_j(t) + Bal_{B1}(t-1)$$
$$y = CollBal(t) - SubTarget_{B1}(t)$$

Term x corresponds to the prospectus language: the three terms in x correspond to (i), (ii–iv), and (v). Term y needs to be expanded. Substituting Equations (4.49) and (4.50):

$$y = CollBal(t) - SubTarget_{B1}(t)$$
$$= CollBal(t) - \max\big[OCfloor, CollBal(t) \times TargetSub_{B1} \times$$
$$TargetSubMult\big]$$
$$= \min\big[CollBal(t) - OCfloor, CollBal(t) - CollBal(t) \times$$
$$TargetSub_{B1} \times TargetSubMult\big]$$
$$= \min\big[CollBal(t) - OCfloor, CollBal(t) \times (1 - TargetSub_{B1}$$
$$\times TargetSubMult)\big]$$
$$= \min[B, A]$$

where:

$$A = CollBal(t) \times \big(1 - TargetSub_{B1} \times TargetSubMult\big)$$
$$B = CollBal(t) - OCfloor$$

These match the prospectus given the following information. The Current Maximum Amount is $CollBal(t)$. In this deal $OCFloor = \$3.3MM$. As mentioned previously $TargetSubMult = 2$. The critical variable is the B1 subordination ratio $TargetSub_{B1} = 4.4\% = 1.25\% + 1.15\% + 0.75\% + 1.25\%$, corresponding to B2, B3, B4, and O/C respectively. Thus $A = CollBal(t) \times (1 - 4.4\% \times 2 = 91.2\%)$, just like the prospectus language. The results are summarized in Table 4.4. Other tranches can be matched up with the prospectus in a similar manner.

4.7 WRITEDOWNS AND RECOVERIES

Bond loss can be defined as total debt minus total assets. If there is loss, it must be *written down* (i.e., realized). Total writedown is distributed from *bottom to top* (e.g., first from B4, then from B3, etc.). Note that if the seniors are split into pro-rata blocks then writedowns need to be distributed among them, perhaps in a manner similar to how principal was distributed among them. Alternatively, some deals omit having seniors take write-downs—such a case would be performing so poorly that it might as well terminate.

TABLE 4.4   Mapping Formal Model into Legal Language of Prospectus (2004-HE2)

Mathematics	English
$PrinDist_{B1}(t) = \max[0, x - y]$	"Class B-1 Principal Distribution Amount" means, with respect to any distribution date, an amount equal to the excess of
$x = SeniorBal(t) +$	(x) the sum of (i) the aggregate Class Certificate Balances of the Class A Certificates (after taking into account the payment of the Class A Principal Distribution Amount on such distribution date),
$\sum_{j > B1} Bal_j(t) +$	(ii) the Class Certificate Balance of the Class M-1 certificates (after taking into account the payment of the Class M-1 Principal Distribution Amount on such distribution date), (iii) the Class Certificate Balance of the Class M-2 certificates (after taking into account the payment of the Class M-2 Principal Distribution Amount on such distribution date), (iv) the Class Certificate Balance of the Class M-3 certificates (after taking into account the payment of the Class M-3 Principal Distribution Amount on such distribution date), and
$Bal_{B1}(t - 1)$	(v) the Class Certificate Balance of the Class B-1 certificates immediately prior to such distribution date
$y = \min[A, B]$ $A = 91.2\% \times CollBal(t)$ $B = CollBal(t) - \$3.3MM$	over (y) the lesser of (A) approximately 91.20% of the Current Maximum Amount and (B) the excess, if any, of the Current Maximum Amount over approximately \$3,302,841.

$$Loss(t) = \max[0, \ Bal(t - 1) - AggBondPrin(t) - CollBal(t)] \tag{4.55}$$

$$CumLoss(t) = CumLoss(t - 1) + Loss(t) \tag{4.56}$$

$$\forall k \in Bond :$$

$$WriteDown_k(t) = \min[Bal_k(t - 1), \ Loss(t) - \sum_{j < k} WriteDown_j(t)] \tag{4.57}$$

Compare the bond loss expression $Loss(t)$ with that of collateral loss in Equation (3.23). These differ when there is O/C and/or excess interest to absorb collateral losses. $CumLoss(t)$ is computed for use in a loss trigger as defined in section 4.9.5. Note that *Bond* is a block that contains senior and subordinate tranches (see definitions in section 4.2).

Principal losses that have been written down, as well as interest shortfalls, can be *recovered* in future periods. In a given period, the cumulative principal paydown deferred is the deferred minus recovered amounts from the previous period plus new writedowns this period (Equation 4.58). Recoveries are paid from residuals. The recovered amount is the lesser of the cash available and the amount owed. For a given tranche, cash available is the initial residual less all recoveries made on more senior tranches. Target recovery is the deferred amount plus a non-negative adjustment $AccruedInt_k(t)$ for accrued interest on the deferred amount (Equation 4.59).

Among recoverable tranches, recoveries are made senior-most first (e.g., class M1, then M2, etc.). Recall that some deals don't distribute losses to seniors, so they don't recover for seniors either.

$\forall k \in Bond:$

$$DeferredInt'_k(t) = DeferredInt_k(t-1) + UnpaidIntAmt_k(t)$$

$$DeferredPrin_k(t) = DeferredPrin_k(t-1) + WriteDown_k(t) \tag{4.58}$$

$$AccruedInt_k(t) = Coupon_k \times [DeferredInt'_k(t-1) + DeferredPrin_k(t-1)]$$

$$DeferredInt_k(t) = DeferredInt'_k(t) + AccruedInt_k(t) \tag{4.59}$$

Restated, for a given tranche, deferred interest is the cumulative unpaid interest amount. Deferred principal is the cumulative writedown. Interest is accrued (at the coupon rate of the tranche) on all deferred interest and principal. The accrued interest is added to the deferred interest to comprise the interest owed. Each period, at this stage of the waterfall, the interest owed is paid from all remaining collateral cash flow. Any remaining cash flow is then used to pay deferred principal.

Procedurally, for each tranche in seniority order, deferred interest is paid first from all remaining collateral cash flows. Then deferred principal is paid from all remaining collateral cash flows. This is shown in Figure 4.10. Figure 4.11 gives the relevant section from the waterfall for 2004-HE2.

4.8   DERIVATIVES

Two types of derivatives commonly used to hedge basis risk in liability structures are *corridors* and *swaps*. Basis risk arises from potential differences between the duration of assets and liabilities due to interest rate volatility. In a typical deal, assets are comprised of fixed, floating, and hybrid mortgages.

$$\forall k \in Leg:$$
$$deferredInt_k(t) \Leftarrow CollInt_g(t)$$
$$deferredInt_k(t) \Leftarrow CollPrin_g(t)$$
$$deferredPrin_k(t) \Leftarrow CollInt_g(t)$$
$$deferredPrin_k(t) \Leftarrow CollPrin_g(t)$$

FIGURE 4.10 Deferred Interest and Principal Waterfall for Collateral Group g of Tranche k

Liabilities are comprised of fixed and floating tranches. Because of this complexity, it is difficult to map out interest rate sensitivities of both assets and liabilities as functions of time.

A corridor is a set of interest rate options. The options usually have decreasing notionals corresponding to the amortization schedule of the structure. Each option has a strike—if interest rates exceed the strike, then the counterparty pays the market rate less the strike, times the notional. The options usually have a ceiling or cap rate. If the market rate exceeds the cap, then only the cap less the strike, times the notional is paid. The corridor is paid for as an initial expense in the deal. Throughout the life of the deal, corridor cash can flow only into (never out from) the waterfall.

A swap also has a schedule of decreasing notionals and corresponding strikes. Each period two payments are made between the structure and the swap counterparty. The structure pays fixed and the counterparty pays floating. In other words, every period the structure pays the strike times the notional to the swap counterparty. This fixed payment is based on a 30/360 day count. Every period the counterparty pays the market rate times the notional times number of days in the period over 360. This floating payment

---

(iii) any amount remaining after the distributions in clauses (i) and (ii) above is required to be distributed in the following order of priority with respect to the certificates:

    (a)   to the certificate insurer, to the extent of any remaining reimbursements for prior, unreimbursed draws for either interest or principal, as well as other amounts owed to the certificate insurer;

    (b)   to the holders of the Class M-1 certificates, any Unpaid Interest Amounts for that class;

    (c)   to the holders of the Class M-1 certificates, any Unpaid Realized Loss Amounts for that class;

    (d)   to the holders of the Class M-2 certificates, any Unpaid Interest Amounts for that class;

    (e)   to the holders of the Class M-2 certificates, any Unpaid Realized Loss Amounts for that class;

    . . .

    (n)   to the holders of the Class B-4 certificates, any Unpaid Interest Amounts for that class;

    (o)   to the holders of the Class B-4 certificates, any Unpaid Realized Loss ounts for that class;

FIGURE 4.11 From "Distributions of Interest and Principal" in 2004-HE2 Prospectus

Source: Morgan Stanley 2004a.

is based on an actual/360-day count. The two payments are netted. Swaps have no up-front payment as do corridors.

The derivatives discussed here have fixed amortization schedules, estimated by the expected collateral amortization. If the estimate is inaccurate, the deal runs the risk of being over- or underhedged. This inefficiency can be removed with a *balance-guaranteed swap*. This type of swap does not have a static amortization schedule, but rather tracks the swap and collateral balances. This optionality comes at a cost.

The hedge counterparty gets repaid at the top of the waterfall. In other words, if the derivative would have the structure pay a counterparty, then this obligation *precedes* bond holder distributions, and is at the top of the waterfall near payment of other outside parties such as the servicer and guarantor (section 4.3). Payments *from* the hedge, however, are distributed *after* collateral cash flows have been distributed (i.e., near the end of the waterfall). For this reason, hedges are introduced near the end of this chapter.

4.8.1 Corridors

Corridors are also known as "cash corridors" or "caps." A corridor can be created to support any subset of tranches. For example, a structure may define A, M, B, and NIM corridors hedging the senior, mezzanine, and junior bonds, and NIMs, respectively. Recall from section 4.4 that tranches are limited in the interest they can pay the bond holders—the "WAC cap" puts a maximum limit on this payout. In any period for which interest is limited in this manner, the shortfall is known as the Basis Risk Carry-Forward Amount (BRCFA). Attempts are made in subsequent periods to pay back any BRCFA to the bond holders.

Caps (corresponding to issued bonds) pay cash into Excess Reserve Fund Accounts (ERFAs). Each period any nonzero BRCFA is paid down by the corresponding ERFA—more about this later. If the entire BRCFA cannot be eradicated, then the hedge is not complete and interest is deferred. During size allocation of the liability structure (Chapter 5), deferred interest is considered a structural failure. In other words, the subordination protecting the tranche that defers its interest payment is considered insufficient and the allocation is rejected. A larger subordination that does not defer interest is required.

A logical way to set corridor strikes for issued bonds is the difference between the gross coupon (WAC) of the collateral and the balance-weighted spread of the tranches in the class (e.g., A, M, or B). This should track the risk of exceeding the WAC cap. Such an estimate must be made under some scenario (e.g., the "Prosup" assumptions): zero loss, 100% prepay speed, run to call, O/C stepdown enabled, and static LIBOR. Assigning a ceiling rate will depend on how much cost reduction is required.

The corridor typically lasts for a few years until the seniors have sufficiently amortized. The corridor notional in a given period is the corresponding issued bond balance in that period. Thus the A corridor balance will decrease each period, whereas the M and B corridor balances will typically stay fixed (they will not start to amortize until the seniors completely pay down). A NIM corridor typically lasts a couple of years, the life of the NIM.

Let's look at an example to clarify how the strike is set. Consider the class M corridor. Recall from section 3.4.1 that $Rates(t)$ are the underlying interest rates for floating collateral. Recall from sections 4.2 and 4.4 that $Spread_k$ and $Benchmark_k(t)$ represent the spread and index rates of tranche k. To simplify things, assume that all collateral share the same interest rate index, as do all tranches within the class M corridor. The annual balance-weighted-average mezzanine spread is:

$$ReqSpread_M(t) = \sum_{k \in Mezz} Bal_k(t) \times Spread_k \div Bal_{Mezz}(t)$$

The gross WAC of the collateral is computed as the total interest divided by the total balance, annualized. This is effectively an index rate plus excess spread.

$$WAC(t) = \frac{CollInt(t)}{CollBal(t)} = Rates(t) + ExcessSpread(t)$$

The strike is set to the difference between these two quantities.

$$Strike_M(t) = WAC(t) - ReqSpread_M(t)$$

If the current benchmark rate exceeds the strike, the corridor pays cash. The difference between the actual liability rate $Benchmark_M(t)$ and the estimated asset rate $Rates(t)$ is basis risk gap. The difference between the required and excess spreads is the spread risk gap. By setting the strikes above, the corridor pays both gaps under the interest rate assumptions.

$$
\begin{aligned}
CorridorPays(t) &= \max[0, Benchmark_M(t) - Strike_M(t)] \\
&= \max[0, Benchmark_M(t) - WAC(t) + ReqSpread_M(t)] \\
&= \max[0, Benchmark_M(t) - Rates(t) - ExcessSpread(t) \\
&\quad + ReqSpread_M(t)] \\
&= \max[0, (Benchmark_M(t) - Rates(t)) + (ReqSpread_M(t) \\
&\quad - ExcessSpread(t))]
\end{aligned}
$$

The NIM corridor deserves special mention. Chapter 5 discusses how to optimally allocate the tranches in a structure—this is called sizing. The issued bonds are allocated first, followed by residual notes (e.g., NIMs). The NIM corridor balances must be generated *after* the issued bonds have been allocated by the sizing process, but *before* the NIM has been sized. That way, the corridor balances reflect the correctly allocated bond sizes. The corridor notional amounts are then passed into the NIM sizer, which dynamically determines if the options are struck, using the same forward rate curve used when modeling the NIM. This raises an interesting question about what constitutes the "best" NIM corridor.

Consider deriving *optimal* strike and cap rates, given the NIM corridor balances. The objective is to maximize the total present value of the corridor and NIM cash flows. As mentioned, a corridor is paid for up front—the price is computed to achieve zero net present value of the corridor itself. The NIM however is priced under a *different* stress scenario. Suppose an initial corridor is constructed that achieves a total present value (with NIM) of $100. Now consider a perturbation of the strikes and/or caps such that a new total present value of $101 is achieved. This extra $1 arises because two different interest rate curves are used in pricing the corridor and NIM. Essentially, the required NIM stress scenario is arbitraged by purchasing a corridor in the real market (priced under less stressful conditions). This concept can be applied to corridors of other classes also. This optimization is nonlinear and can be implemented, for example, by simulated annealing (section 3.2.2) or another method.

4.8.2 Swaps

Swaps are an alternative to corridors. Whereas corridors only pay out cash into the structure, swaps can make a net payment, $SwapExp(t)$, to the counterparty (usually this happens in early periods, or may not happen at all). Corridors inject their cash into the structure via the ERFA accounts and the ERFA waterfall that governs their priority of payments. ERFAs usually pay BRCFA obligations only, thus corridors are directed to pay the BRCFA of specific tranche groups. The swap counterparty is paid with a 30/360-day count. The deal structure is paid with an actual/360-day count.

The swap schedule is tailored to the collateral pool. The objective is to hedge basis risk stemming from fixed loans and the fixed portion of adjustable-rate mortgages (ARMs). Furthermore, the schedule should not extend past the estimated call date to avoid over hedging. Care must be taken to treat prefunded loans correctly. During prefunding, loan balance should not be included in the swap. In other words, prefunded loan balance is *cash money* and need not be hedged, until after the prefunding period when assets will have been purchased that *do* need to be hedged. Given the schedule, typically the swap rate is set to make the net present value of the swap equal to zero.

$$ok(t, Loan) = [[Loan.Type = ARM \wedge t < Loan.InitReset]$$
$$\vee \ Loan.Type = FRM] \wedge [Loan.PrefundPeriod < t < CallPeriod]$$
$$\forall \ell \in Collat.Loans$$
$$SwapSched(t) = \sum_{l|ok(t,l)} (1 - InitOC) \times CollBal_\ell(t)$$

Swaps can have a dedicated waterfall at the end of the general waterfall. Each deal may have different priority of swap payments, but generally they follow the same pattern. The waterfall indicates how the swap cash is directed to tranches. Highest priority is to pay the swap counterparty from collateral interest (hence this payment is placed at the top of the interest waterfall). If there are multiple collateral groups, the swap is paid pro rata by collateral group balance. Next in priority is to pay unpaid interest, then deferred principal, then BCRFA.

An easier way to model swaps is to add the swap cash flows to collateral cash flows, as interest. If there are multiple collateral groups, each with its own swap, then this is straightforward. If there are multiple collateral groups sharing some swap(s), then the swap cash flows must be distributed, probably pro rata by collateral balance. *Caution*: Injecting swap cash flows as collateral is only an approximation (and perhaps not an accurate one) if the legal specification indicates a swap waterfall.

4.8.3 Excess Reserve Fund Account

Staging accounts, reservoirs, and reserve funds (used interchangeably here) are placed between sources and uses of cash within the waterfall. Such accounts have rules stipulating where they get cash from, how they pay cash out (priority of payments in the waterfall), and what they do with any excess cash remaining after paying obligations in a given period. A reservoir likely denotes an account that accumulates excess cash, say from bond issuance or from excess spread. The purpose of creating such stages or buffers is to smooth out potential hiccups in bond holder cash flows. This is considered a form of *internal* credit enhancement. An example of a nonaccumulating account is now given.

The ERFA is primarily used for collecting corridor cash flows. However, it also collects residual cash flows from above it in the waterfall. The cash

(p)   to the Excess Reserve Fund Account, the amount of any Basis Risk Payment for that distribution date;

(q)   (i) from any Group II Class A Interest Rate Cap Payment on deposit in the Excess Reserve Fund Account with respect to that distribution date, an amount equal to any unpaid remaining Basis Risk Carry Forward Amount with respect to the Class A Certificates (other than the Class A-1 certificates) for that distribution date, allocated (a) first, between the Class A-2, Class A-3 and Class A-4 certificates *pro rata*, based upon their respective Class Certificate Balances and (b) second, any remaining amounts to the Class A-2, Class A-3 and Class A-4 certificates, *pro rata*, based on any Basis Risk Carry Forward Amounts remaining unpaid, in order to reimburse such unpaid amounts, (ii) from any Class M Interest Rate Cap Payment on deposit in the Excess Reserve Fund Account with respect to that distribution date, an amount equal to any unpaid remaining Basis Risk Carry Forward Amount with respect to the Class M certificates for that distribution date, allocated (a) first, among the Class M-1, Class M-2 and Class M-3 certificates *pro rata*, based upon their respective Class Certificate Balances and (b) second, any remaining amounts to the Class M-1, Class M-2 and Class M-3 certificates, *pro rata*, based on any Basis Risk Carry Forward Amounts remaining unpaid, in order to reimburse such unpaid amounts, and (iii) from any Class B Interest Rate Cap Payment on deposit in the Excess Reserve Fund Account with respect to that distribution date, an amount equal to any unpaid remaining Basis Risk Carry Forward Amount with respect to the Class B certificates for that distribution date, allocated (a) first, among the Class B-1, Class B-2, Class B-3 and Class B-4 certificates *pro rata*, based upon their respective Class Certificate Balances and (b) second, any remaining amounts to the Clss B-1, Class B-2, Class B-3 and Class B-4 certificates, *pro rata*, based on any Basis Risk Carry Forward Amounts remaining unpaid, in order to reimburse such unpaid amounts;

(r)   from funds on deposit in the Excess Reserve Fund Account (not including any Interest Rate Cap Payment included in that account) with respect to that distribution date, an amount equal to any unpaid Basis Risk Carry Forward Amount with respect to the LIBOR Certificates for that distribution date to the LIBOR Certificates in the same order and priority in which Accrued Certificate Interest is allocated among those classes of certificates;

FIGURE 4.12   From "Distributions of Interest and Principal" in the 2004-HE2 Prospectus
Source: Morgan Stanley 2004a.

from corridors is used to pay BRCFA obligations (section 4.4). Any excess cash is paid out the bottom of the waterfall to the deal's residual (section 4.10).

Consider 2004-HE2 as an example, with the relevant prospectus definition given in Figure 4.12. There are groups of dedicated corridors that feed the ERFA (these are called the Basis Risk Payment in Figure 4.12). For example, one group of corridors, if struck, adds cash to the ERFA, but that cash can be used *only* to pay the BRCFA obligations of certain tranches. Excess interest and principal collateral cash flows also feed the ERFA, for shared use across the bonds.

The shared portion is denoted as $ERFA_X$ and the dedicated portions as $ERFA_{Senior}$, $ERFA_{Mezz}$, and $ERFA_{Junior}$, corresponding to the options dedicated to seniors, mezzanine, and junior tranches, respectively. Each of these is referred to here as an *individual* account, simplifying the logic from the prospectus. For 2004-HE2 these options mature from one to 33 months after

$$\forall s \in Blk2: \quad BRCFA_s(t) \underset{Bal}{\Longleftarrow} ERFA_{Senior}(t)$$

$$\forall s \in Blk2: \quad BRCFA_s(t) \underset{BRCFA}{\Longleftarrow} ERFA_{Senior}(t)$$

$$\forall s \in Mezz: \quad BRCFA_s(t) \underset{Bal}{\Longleftarrow} ERFA_{Mezz}(t)$$

$$\forall s \in Mezz: \quad BRCFA_s(t) \underset{BRCFA}{\Longleftarrow} ERFA_{Mezz}(t)$$

$$\forall s \in Junior: \quad BRCFA_s(t) \underset{Bal}{\Longleftarrow} ERFA_{junior}(t)$$

$$\forall s \in Junior: \quad BRCFA_s(t) \underset{BRCFA}{\Longleftarrow} ERFA_{Junior}(t)$$

$$\forall s \in Senior: \quad BRCFA_s(t) \underset{Bal}{\Longleftarrow} ERFA_X(t)$$

$$\forall s \in Sub: \quad BRCFA_s(t) \Longleftarrow ERFA_X(t)$$

FIGURE 4.13 ERFA Waterfall Paying BRCFA Obligations for 2004-HE2, Where $Blk2 = (A2,A3,A4)$

the deal settles. Thus cash is injected into the ERFA for only a small fraction of the life of the deal.

The procedural use of the ERFA, for 2004-HE2, is given in Figure 4.13. Each tranche is potentially paid *three times*. The first distribution is from corridor cash flows and made pro rata by principal balance remaining. The second distribution is from corridor cash flows and made pro rata by BRCFA. The third distribution is from excess collateral cash flow. Distribution of the residual is made "... in the same order and priority in which Accrued Certificate Interest is allocated among those classes of certificates ... " Thus the seniors are paid pro rata on balance and then the subordinate bonds are paid sequentially. By rule (r) in Figure 4.12 A1 isn't paid anything until the end, hence the block $Blk2 = (A2,A3,A4)$ is necessary in Figure 4.13.

4.9 TRIGGERS

The structure can contain a number of *triggers* that affect the operation of the waterfall. Triggers can be placed in various locations after expenses are paid; hence, they are introduced here as a refinement of the general model already introduced. Triggers test for conditions that indicate the collateral is having difficulty meeting its obligations. For example, two common triggers test for delinquencies and losses—if these are on the rise, or they exceed some threshold, then bond holders may be at risk. Triggers can be used in cash flow specifications to take more conservative actions, and can be used to indicate a premature termination or "early amortization" of the structure if things look really bad. The cure for these triggers usually involves diversion of cash flows to more senior tranches.

In addition to these tests, CDOs with active management also have *quality tests*. Quality tests constrain any new assets purchased to fit within certain prespecified ranges. The mortgage structures discussed in Chapter 3 are actively managed only to the extent of purchasing assets during the prefunding period. In general, quality tests can constrain the diversity score, WAC, WAM, WAL, WARF, and so on.

4.9.1 Call Features

The liability structure can be *called* when the ratio of the current to original collateral balance is less than *CallPct* (see Table 4.3). Some deals may have a noncall period during which this cleanup call cannot be exercised.

$$Callable(t) = \frac{CollBal(t)}{CollBal(0)} < CallPct \tag{4.60}$$

$$Called(t) = Callable(t) \wedge RunToCall \tag{4.61}$$

If the model is run to call, the current collateral balance is paid down in the first period it is callable (counted as a "prepay" cash flow). Beyond this period, all liability cash flows are zero. Even if the model is run to maturity, once the bond is callable the coupon steps up.

4.9.2 Over-collateralization Test

An *O/C test* is also known as a *par value test*. In general, it can be defined for an individual tranche k (the reference bond). An O/C ratio is the current collateral balance over the current reference bond balance plus bond balance senior to the reference bond. If the ratio drops below a certain threshold, then the test fails. Shorthand denoting the O/C ratio over a group of tranches (e.g., the senior bonds) is shown below.

$$OCRatio_k(t) = \frac{CollBal(t)}{\sum_{j \le k} Bal_j(t)} \tag{4.62}$$

$$OCRatio_{Senior}(t) = \frac{CollBal(t)}{Bal_{Senior}(t)}$$

If an O/C test fails, then a remedy is performed—paydown of the bonds senior to the reference bond and the reference bond itself, until the ratio is in compliance. For example, consider a cash flow collateralized debt obligation (CDO) with two O/C tests for senior and mezzanine tranches. A likely interest waterfall proceeds as follows:

1. Pay senior interest.
2. Perform senior O/C test.
3. If senior O/C test fails, pay down seniors until test passes.
4. Pay mezzanine interest.
5. If mezzanine O/C test fails, pay down seniors (and mezzanine, if seniors fully paid down) until tests pass.
6. Pay subordinate interest, etc.

Within the principal waterfall of a cash flow CDO, similar tests and remedies are performed for any interest shortfalls. These tests and remedies have a higher priority than the usual principal payments. The higher the O/C ratio, the more severe the trigger and the greater the chance that cash flows are diverted from subordinate bonds. A variant of the O/C test is the *supplemental* O/C test, which has a more severe O/C ratio. Instead of cash flow diversion, the cure is *reinvestment* of excess cash flows. The supplemental and regular O/C tests are used in conjunction, as belt and suspenders.

In mortgage securitizations, the O/C test and cure are usually performed as defined in section 4.5. This is simpler than the general CDO O/C tests described above. First, there is typically only one O/C test in mortgage securitizations:

$$OCRatio_{Bond}(t) = \frac{CollBal(t)}{Bal_{Bond}(t)} = \frac{CollBal(t)}{\sum_{j < O/C} Bal_j(t)}$$

Second, if the mortgage O/C test determines that principal needs to be paid down, interest is paid first, then the O/C is cured (sometimes called a turbo-amortization or acceleration).

4.9.3 Interest Coverage Test

An *interest coverage (IC) test* can be defined for an individual tranche, k, or a group of tranches. An IC ratio is the current collateral interest cash flow over the current interest owed to the reference bond and all bonds senior to the reference bond. If the ratio drops below a certain threshold, then the test fails. Shorthand is used to denote the IC ratio over a group of tranches, for example, the senior bonds as shown below.

$$ICRatio_k(t) = \frac{CollInt(t)}{\sum\limits_{j \le k} IntOwed_j(t)} \tag{4.63}$$

$$ICRatio_{Senior}(t) = \frac{CollInt(t)}{IntOwed_{Senior}(t)}$$

These definitions are simplified—in reality, hedge contributions and costs, as well as other expenses must be accounted for to get an accurate estimation of the coverage. If an IC test fails, then a remedy is performed— the same remedy as for OC tests. In general, the OC and IC tests are referred to as *coverage tests*. The CDO waterfalls described in the last section can be generalized to performing both coverage tests at each step, and if either fails, then a remedy is required.

4.9.4 Delinquency Trigger

A typical delinquency trigger fires if the ratio of the three-month rolling daily average of 60+ day delinquent loans over the aggregate principal balance of the mortgage loans exceeds some fixed percentage, say 45%, of the prior period's senior enhancement percentage.

$$DelinqTrigger(t) =$$
$$\frac{[Delinq_{60+}(t-2) + Delinq_{60+}(t-1) + Delinq_{60+}(t)] \div 3}{CollBal(t-1)} > 45\% \tag{4.64}$$

This typical trigger has two parameters: the fixed percentage and the number of days delinquent. Unfortunately, the collateral model presented says nothing about delinquencies! In fact, the replines were simplified here by removing that information. One alternative is to collect that loan-level delinquency information so that 60+ day delinquency ratio can be computed. If this is not feasible, delinquencies can be modeled from losses, for example,

$$DelinqDelay = 18 \times Freq \div 12$$
$$Delinq_{60+}(t) = Delinq_{60+}(t-1) + (1 + CureRate) \times$$
$$[Loss(t + DelinqDelay) - Loss(t)]$$

For example, *CureRate* is 35% for 60+ day delinquent trigger and 15% for 90+ day delinquent triggers. The idea is that losses (defaults) 18 months

TABLE 4.5 Schedule Describing Loss Trigger Thresholds,
LossThreshold(t)

From	To	Cum loss
settle	2/2008	N/A
3/2008	2/2009	3.00%
3/2009	2/2010	4.75%
3/2010	2/2011	6.00%
3/2011	2/2012	6.50%
3/2012	maturity	6.75%

in the future predict delinquencies today. Since some of these delinquencies are cured, the number of defaults must be scaled upwards to account for those cured.

One use of this trigger (and the loss trigger discussed next) is to override the O/C stepdown (section 4.5.2). The O/C stepdown allows the overcollateralization to decrease under certain conditions. If either trigger has fired, even if those conditions exist, the O/C must remain at its present level.

4.9.5 Loss Trigger

A typical loss trigger fires if the cumulative realized losses divided by the total aggregate principal balance of the mortgage loans exceeds some percentage.

$$LossTrigger(t) = \frac{CumLoss(t)}{CollBal(t-1)} > LossThreshold(t) \qquad (4.65)$$

This is individually computed for the collateral groups supporting each leg. In other words, each leg must stand on its own with respect to this test, which makes sense since each leg is supported with different collateral. (In a case where two legs are cross-collateralized, the definition of the loss trigger might be more subtle.) Table 4.5 gives a typical loss trigger schedule. This trigger overrides the O/C step down, as discussed in the previous section.

4.10 RESIDUALS: NIMS AND POST-NIM

Structures have a residual; that is, the excess collateral interest and principal cash flows, as well as options cash flows (swaps, caps, etc.), after all issued bonds are paid what is owed them. The residual is defined as a tranche in the structure (e.g., "Class X"). In mortgage deals, Class X is assigned a balance that tracks the O/C amount. In addition, prepayment penalties are often segregated into another tranche (e.g., "Class P"). These are degenerate tranches because they are not purchased as securities, owed interest and principal, have meaningful balances, and so on. They are simply cash flows.

$$Res(t) = CollInt(t) + CollPrin(t) \qquad (4.66)$$

$$ClassX(t) = Res(t) + ERFA_X(t) + ERFA_{Senior}(t) + ERFA_{Mezz}(t)$$

$$+ERFA_{Junior}(t) + SwapCash(t) \qquad (4.67)$$

$$ClassP(t) = CollPPP(t) \qquad (4.68)$$

Additional bonds can be built atop these cash flows. Two types of such notes are examined next.

The deal residual (Class X) is used to pay additional notes subordinate to the "issued" bonds as defined in the deal prospectus. If these super-subordinate bonds are isolated from the deal, they have their own prospectus. For example, Figure 1.2 illustrates a deal with a NIM bond. For 2004-HE2, the "NIM trust" structure is laid out in Morgan Stanley (2004b). In general there might be a series of NIMs, each feeding its residual into the next. The final residual is packaged into what is known as a "post-NIM" bond or OTE (called "preferred shares" in CDOs). There are other possibilities, but these are the emphasis here.

All tranches (pre-NIM, NIM, and post-NIM) are modeled within the same framework because all are linked by cash flows. Thus input parameters describing the NIMs and OTE are required as in Table 4.2. Table 4.6 lists typical parameters for the NIM and post-NIM, omitting irrelevant fields.

NIM tranches are not included in the previously interest and principal waterfalls because they do not obey standard payment rules.

TABLE 4.6 Input Parameters Describing NIM and OTE Classes for 2004-HE2

Name	N1	OET
Desc	NIM	Post-NIM
Type	Fix	Fix
Size	7.6%	0%
Coupon	8.25%	0%
Guarantee	FALSE	FALSE
Leg	L1	L1

A NIM is sized as a percentage of the initial collateral balance. Each period the NIM holders are promised a fixed coupon (*NIMReinvRate*) paid from the deal residual. (Floating NIMs also exist.) Any remaining cash is used to pay down the NIM balance. However, it can happen that the incoming cash flow is insufficient to pay the interest due, in which case the missing interest is accrued. This missing interest is capitalized; that is, interest is owed on it as well as the NIM balance. Unlike standard tranches, repaying accrued interest has *higher priority* than paying down the principal on the NIM. After completely paying down the NIM, residual cash flows through to either another NIM or eventually an OTE.

The formulae below describe NIM payments declaratively. The set of residuals (*Res*) link the NIM chain. For the first NIM in the chain, $Res_1(t) = Class X(t)$. For the last NIM in the chain, $OTE(t) = Res_m(t)$.

$\forall k \in NIM :$

$$Bal_k(t) = \begin{cases} NIMPct_k \times CollBal(0) & t = 0 \\ Bal_k(t-1) - PrinPaid_k(t) & t > 0 \end{cases} \quad (4.69)$$

$$IntDue_k(t) = (AccruedInt(t-1) + Bal_k(t-1)) \times NIMReinvRate \quad (4.70)$$

$$IntPaid_k(t) = \min[IntDue_k(t), Res_k(t)] \quad (4.71)$$

$$AccruedInt_k(t) = AccruedInt_k(t-1) + IntDue_k(t) - IntPaid_k(t)$$
$$- AccruedIntPaid_k(t) \quad (4.72)$$

$$PrinPaid_k(t) = \min[Bal_k(t-1), Res_k(t) - IntPaid_k(t)$$
$$- AccruedIntPaid_k(t)] \quad (4.73)$$

$$AccruedIntPaid_k(t) = \min[AccruedInt_k(t-1),$$
$$Res_k(t) - IntPaid_k(t), Bal_k(t-1)] \quad (4.74)$$

$$Res_{k+1}(t) = Res_k(t) - IntPaid_k(t) - AccruedIntPaid_k(t) - PrinPaid_k(t)$$
$$(4.75)$$

It is easy to get lost in the details of the cash flows and lose sight of the big picture, so let's review the main motivation behind such an "arbitrage" structure. The residual investors (in general the equity/NIM/OTE investors) lever the structures, that is, effectively have the pre-NIM bond investors fund the deal. Hence, the residual investors aim to earn the positive excess spread as their return. The residual cash flows are generally "front loaded," that is, occur near settlement and have a short weighted-average life. Since the structure is healthy at settlement, there should be excess cash from the get-go. This "arbitrage" is not risk free—there is always the chance of negative returns on the residual pieces, as we shall see in Chapter 6. However, the structure is interesting because of the *nonrecourse* funding supplied by the pre-NIM bond investors—these investors have no claim on the residual investors, only on the assets.

4.11 CLASS ARCHITECTURE

This section describes two alternative architectures that encapsulate the priority of payments. The first alternative, called the *passive* approach, requires "custom" programming for a given deal. For example, if the deal requires two senior blocks that pay interest in a cross-collateralized manner, the modeler must translate that specification into code. The second alternative, called the *active* approach, builds a network of class objects that represents the priority of payments. Each period the network is "executed," causing its subcomponents (tranches in the structure) to get paid. The modeler needs only construct this network.

Throughout this section code snippets are given as illustrations. The 2004-HE2 and 2005-HE3 deals are used to show how actual priority of payments are implemented. The 2004-HE2 waterfall, as specified in the prospectus, is given in Figure 4.14. The two approaches are compared in Section 4.11.3.

4.11.1 Passive Approach

A parent Waterfall class is defined with the following interface:

```
Public Sub Init( _
    Legs As Collection, _
    Collat As Collection, _
    Debt As Structure, _
    CapsOn As Boolean, _
    SwapsOn As Boolean, _
    LossTriggers As Variant, _
    Swaps As Collection)
End Sub

Public Sub Destroy()
End Sub

Public Sub Interest(period As Integer)
End Sub
```

```
Public Sub Principal(period As Integer)
End Sub

Public Sub ERFA(period As Integer)
End Sub

Public Sub Swap(period As Integer)
End Sub
```

These methods are implemented in each child. Each child represents a different structure and is required to supply the main waterfall components specified here. Init initializes the Waterfall object and Destroy recycles it. Interest pays interest obligations to the bonds. Principal pays principal obligations to the bonds. ERFA (caps) pays BRCFA obligations to the bonds. Swap pays unpaid interest, BRCFA, and deferred principal.

Implicit in the class is that all collateral groups are available in aggregate to pay subordinate principal. Furthermore, all subordinate tranches are paid principal sequentially. Most structures are organized in this manner. The architecture can be modified to support other assumptions.

The 2004-HE2 child class has the following data members. G1 and G2 are two Collateral objects supporting the two senior blocks, Blk1 and Blk2. (Throughout this code, variables could have been named after Defined Terms in the prospectus to lend additional transparency to the implementation— shorter variables are used here simply to save space on the page.) Leg is a Leg object—in this structure there is only one leg. Debt is a Structure object. A key method of the Structure class is cash flow generation, a loop over each period invoking the various waterfall methods defined here. Swap is a Swap object. LossTriggers is a loss trigger schedule. CapsOn and SwapsOn are flags indicating whether caps and swaps are in use. Refer to section A.2 of Appendix A for a review of the built-in Collection class.

```
Dim Debt As Structure
Dim Leg As Leg
Dim Blk1 As Collection
Dim Blk2 As Collection
Dim G1 As Collateral
Dim G2 As Collateral
Dim LossTriggers As Variant
Dim CapsOn As Boolean
Dim SwapsOn as Boolean
Dim Swap As Swap
```

The child Init class is defined as follows. Note that the interface is more general than this child—for example, this child has only one leg, one swap, and so on. The interface is defined with collections to handle any number of these components. Blocks (Blk1 and Blk2) are new collections, to which senior tranches are added.

```
Public Sub Waterfall_Init(. . .)
    Legs As Collection, _
    Collat As Collection, _
    Debt_ As Structure, _
    CapsOn_ As Boolean, _
    SwapsOn_ As Boolean, _
    LossTriggers_ As Variant, _
    Swaps As Collection)

    Set Debt = Debt_
    Set Swap = Swaps.item(1)
    Set Leg = Legs.item(1)
    Set G1 = Collat("G1")
    Set G2 = Collat("G2")
    LossTriggers = LossTriggers_
    CapsOn = CapsOn_
    SwapsOn = SwapsOn_

    Set Blk1 = New Collection
    Blk1.Add Leg.Senior("A1")

    Set Blk2 = New Collection
    Blk2.Add Leg.Senior("A2")
    Blk2.Add Leg.Senior("A3")
    Blk2.Add Leg.Senior("A4")

    Leg.Collat.Add G1
    Leg.Collat.Add G2
End Sub
```

The Destroy method recycles the two block collections previously created. Nothing more needs to be cleaned up because this class references all the other objects.

```
Public Sub Waterfall_Destroy()
    Set Blk1 = Nothing
    Set Blk2 = Nothing
End Sub
```

Interest The Interest method for 2004-HE2 is given next. Prior to the execution of this waterfall, interest owed in the current period has already been computed and placed in the Tranche object (see section 4.4). Here, for the first time, we can see how priority of payments is programmed by the modeler. The waterfall corresponds to section (i) in Figure 4.14. Payment to the insurer (i)(a) is done elsewhere in the Structure class. Payments to seniors (i)(b) and to subordinates (i)(d)-(i)(j) are defined in the code below. Each piece of this code is explained below.

```
Public Sub Waterfall_Interest(period As Integer)

    Dim tranche As Tranche

    Leg.Senior("A1").PayInt period, G1, "seq"
    Debt.ProRataBal period-1, Blk2, G2.Bal(period)
    For Each tranche In Blk2
        tranche.PayInt period, G2, "par"
    Next

    Leg.Senior("A1").PayInt period, G2, "seq"
    Debt.ProRataBal period-1, Blk2, G1.Bal(period)
    For Each tranche In Blk2
        tranche.PayInt period, G1, "par"
    Next

    For Each tranche In Leg.Subord
        tranche.PayInt period, G1, "seq"
        tranche.PayInt period, G2, "seq"
    Next
End Sub
```

First tranche A1 is paid interest from collateral group G1:

```
Leg.Senior("A1").PayInt period, G1, "seq"
```

Table 4.7 summarizes the various class methods used in this section. These methods can be thought of as a high-level language for describing waterfalls. The PayInt method of the Tranche class is used to pay interest owed from a specified collateral group. The amount of interest owed is an internal data member of the A1 tranche object. A1 is not paid pro rata with any other tranche so the PayInt method distributes as much of G1 as is necessary, as indicated by the "seq" argument. Note that PayInt side-effects both the tranche and the collateral, debiting the collateral and crediting the tranche.

(i) <u>from the Interest Remittance Amount, in the following order of priority:</u>

    (a)   to the certificate insurer, its premium for that distribution date;

    (b)   concurrently, with equal priority of payment:

        (x)   payable solely from the Group I Interest Remittance Amount for that distribution date, to the holders of the Class A-1 certificates, the Accrued Certificate Interest and any Unpaid Interest Amounts for the Class A-1 certificates, and cross-collateralize from Group II.

        (y)   payable solely from the Group II Interest Remittance Amount for that distribution date, to the holders of the Group II Class A Certificates, *pro rata*, the Accrued Certificate Interest and any Unpaid Interest Amounts for the Group II Class A Certificates, and cross-collateralize from Group I; and

    (c)   payable from any remaining Interest Remittance Amounts, to the certificate insurer, reimbursement for prior unreimbursed interest draws;

    (d–j)   payable from any remaining Interest Remittance Amounts, to the Class M-1 certificates, the Accrued Certificate Interest for that class on that distribution date; (Similar for M2, M3, B1, B2, B3, and B4).

(ii) (A) on each distribution date (x) *before* the related Stepdown Date or (y) with respect to which a Trigger Event is in effect, to the holders of the class or classes of LIBOR Certificates then entitled to distributions of principal as set forth below, and to the certificate insurer, <u>an amount equal to the Principal Distribution Amount in the following order of priority</u>:

    (a)   to the Class A Certificates, allocated among the Class A Certificates as described [Figure 4.15] until the Certificate Principal Balances of those classes have been reduced to zero;

    (b)   to the certificate insurer, the amount of prior unreimbursed principal draws then owed;

    (c–i)   to the Class M-1 certificates, until the Certificate Principal Balance of that class has been reduced to zero; (Same for M2-B4).

(B) on each distribution date (x) *on and after* the related Stepdown Date and (y) as long as a Trigger Event is not in effect, to the holders of the class or classes of LIBOR Certificates then entitled to distribution of principal an amount equal to the Principal Distribution Amount in the following amounts and order of priority:

    (a)   to the Class A Certificates, the lesser of the Principal Distribution Amount and the Class A Principal Distribution Amount, allocated among the Class A Certificates as described elsewhere, until the Certificate Principal Balances of those classes have been reduced to zero;

    (b)   to the certificate insurer, the amount of prior unreimbursed principal draws then owed to it;

    (c–i)   to the Class M-1 certificates, the lesser of the remaining Principal Distribution Amount and the Class M-1 Principal Distribution Amount, until the Certificate Principal Balance of that class has been reduced to zero; (Same for M2-B4).

(iii) any amount remaining after the distributions in clauses (i) and (ii) above is required to be distributed in the following order of priority with respect to the certificates:

    (a)   to the certificate insurer, to the extent of any remaining reimbursements for prior, unreimbursed draws for either interest or principal, as well as other amounts owed to the certificate insurer;

    (b)   to the holders of the Class M-1 certificates, any Unpaid Interest Amounts for that class;

    (c)   to the holders of the Class M-1 certificates, any Unpaid Realized Loss Amounts for that class;

    (d–o)   similar for M2, M3, B1, B2, B3, and B4.

    (p)   to the Excess Reserve Fund Account, the amount of any Basis Risk Payment for that distribution date;

    (q)   (i) from any Group II Class A Interest Rate Cap Payment on deposit in the Excess Reserve Fund Account with respect to that distribution date, an amount equal to any unpaid remaining Basis Risk Carry Forward Amount with respect to the Class A Certificates (other than the Class A-1 certificates) for that distribution date, allocated (a) first, between the Class A-2, Class A-3 and Class A-4 certificates *pro rata*, based upon their respective Class Certificate Balances and (b) second, any remaining amounts to the Class A-2, Class A-3 and Class A-4 certificates, *pro rata*, based on any Basis Risk Carry Forward Amounts remaining unpaid, in order to reimburse such unpaid amounts, (ii) from any Class M Interest Rate Cap Payment on deposit in the Excess Reserve Fund Account with respect to that distribution date, an amount equal to any unpaid remaining Basis Risk Carry Forward Amount with respect to the Class M certificates for that distribution date, allocated (a) first, among the Class M-1, Class M-2 and Class M-3 certificates *pro rata*, based upon their respective Class Certificate Balances and (b) second, any remaining amounts to the Class M-1, Class M-2 and Class M-3 certificates, *pro rata*, based on any Basis Risk Carry Forward Amounts remaining unpaid, in order to reimburse such unpaid amounts, and (iii) from any Class B Interest Rate Cap Payment on deposit in the Excess Reserve Fund Account with respect to that distribution date, an amount equal to any unpaid remaining Basis Risk Carry Forward Amount with respect to the Class B certificates for that distribution date, allocated (a) first, among the Class B-1, Class B-2, Class B-3 and Class B-4 certificates *pro rata*, based upon their respective Class Certificate Balances and (b) second, any remaining amounts to the Class B-1, Class B-2, Class B-3 and Class B-4 certificates, *pro rata*, based on any Basis Risk Carry Forward Amounts remaining unpaid, in order to reimburse such unpaid amounts;

    (r)   from funds on deposit in the Excess Reserve Fund Account (not including any Interest Rate Cap Payment included in that account) with respect to that distribution date, an amount equal to any unpaid Basis Risk Carry Forward Amount with respect to the LIBOR Certificates for that distribution date to the LIBOR Certificates in the same order and priority in which Accrued Certificate Interest is allocated among those classes of certificates;

    (s)   to the Class X certificates, those amounts as described in the pooling and servicing agreement; and

    (t)   to the holders of the Class R certificates, any remaining amount.

FIGURE 4.14 Abridged Interest and Principal Waterfall for 2004-HE2
Source: Morgan Stanley 2004a.

TABLE 4.7 Sketch of Abstract Class Architecture Used in Waterfall

`Collat.Interest(Period)`	Property to access Collat's interest cash flow. `Collat.AllCash` is similar.
`ERFA(AcctId).Bal(Period)`	Balance of ERFA object indexed by AcctId, in Period.
`Leg.Debt`	Collection of all tranches in Leg. `Leg.Senior`, `Leg.Subord`, `Leg.Mezz`, and `Leg.Junior` are similar.
`Leg.ERFA`	Collection of all ERFAs in Leg.
`Leg.SeniorDist(` `GroupId,Period)`	Amount of senior principal distribution from collateral object indexed by GroupId.
`Leg.ShortOC(Period)`	Returns amount target O/C is greater than the actual O/C.
`Structure.ProRataBal(` `Period,Blk[,Amt])`	Assign pro-rata share *percentages* (by bond balance) to tranches in Blk. If Amt present, then pro rata share *amounts* also assigned to tranches by put property `Tranche.ProRataAmt(Val)`.
`Structure.ProRataBRCFA(` `Period,Blk[,Amt])`	Similar to ProRataBal, but by BRCFA outstanding.
`Structure.SeqPrinPay(` `Period,Distr,Blk,Collat)`	Executes `Tranche.SeqPrinPay(Period,Distr,Collat)` for each Tranche in Blk.
`Swap.Collat`	Underlying Collateral object in Swap.
`Tranche.Bal(Period)`	Property to access Tranche's balance. `Tranche.BRCFA` and `Tranche.PrimaryCollatBal` are similar.
`Tranche.PayBRCFA(` `Period,Collat,Type)`	Pay BRCFA owed by Tranche from Collat interest and principal in Period. Type is used to regulate pro rata payment as in `Tranche.PayInt`.
`Tranche.PayDeferPrin(` `Period,Collat)`	Pay deferred principal owed by Tranche from Collat interest and principal in Period. This uses all available collateral cash.
`Tranche.PayInt(` `Period,Collat,Type)`	Pay interest owed by Tranche from Collat interest in Period. If Type is "seq," then all Collat interest (in Period) is available for payment. If Type is "par," then the lesser of the Tranche's pro rata amount and Collat interest is available for payment.
`Tranche.ProRataAmt(Val)`	Property to access Tranche's pro rata distribution amount.
`Tranche.SeqPrinPay(` `Period,Distr,Collat)`	Pay principal owed by Tranche from Collat interest and principal in Period. This uses the lesser of Distr and available collateral cash.

Next, the pro-rata distribution among Blk2 tranches (A2,A3,A4) is computed and saved. Then each tranche in Blk2 is paid interest from collateral group G2:

```
Debt.ProRataBal period-1, Blk2, G2.Bal(period)
For Each tranche In Blk2
    tranche.PayInt period, G2, "par"
Next
```

The ProRataBal method of the Structure class is used when pro-rata shares among a block of tranches is needed. A family of related methods supports distribution by interest owed and the like. Distribution by bond balance is commonly used in structures. For each tranche in its second argument, this method computes the ratio of that tranche's balance to the total block balance. The shares are saved as data members ProRataShare and ProRataAmt inside the Tranche objects. Subsequent methods reference these to compute their payment.

Here, PayInt is given a "par" argument indicating that the previously computed pro-rata share amounts should be used. A tranche is paid the lesser of the pro-rata share amount and the interest owed. Next the cross-collateralization is performed by repeating the same code but *reversing* the collateral:

```
Leg.Senior("A1").PayInt period, G2, "seq"
Debt.ProRataBal period-1, Blk2, G1.Bal(period)
For Each tranche In Blk2
    tranche.PayInt period, G1, "par"
Next
```

Finally, the subordinate bond interest is paid from cash remaining in the two collateral groups:

```
For Each tranche In Leg.Subord
    tranche.PayInt period, G1, "seq"
    tranche.PayInt period, G2, "seq"
Next
```

Principal   The Waterfall Principal method for 2004-HE2 is given next, corresponding to Figure 4.15. Here, principal is paid to *senior* tranches only. Subordinate tranches are paid down in a manner specified elsewhere in the class. The rules governing subordinate tranche pay down are described in Figure 4.14 (ii)(A)(c-i) and (ii)(B)(c-i). Should these rules change from deal

All principal distributions to the holders of the Class A Certificates on any Distribution Date will be allocated between the Class A-1 certificates and the Group II Class A Certificates on a *pro rata* basis based on the Class A Principal Allocation Percentage for each such group on such Distribution Date. However, if the Class Certificate Balances of the Class A Certificates in either Class A Certificate Group are reduced to zero, then the remaining amount of principal distributions distributable to the Class A Certificates on that Distribution Date, and the amount of those principal distributions distributable on all subsequent Distribution Dates, will be distributed to the holders of the Class A Certificates in the other Class A Certificate Group remaining outstanding, until the Class Certificate Balances of the Class A Certificates in such Class A Certificate Group have been reduced to zero (with any remaining amounts of principal distributions allocable to the Class A Certificates distributed to the certificate insurer as reimbursement for unreimbursed draws under the certificate insurance policy for the Class A-1 Principal Parity Amounts). Any payments of principal to the Class A-1 certificates will be made first from payments relating to the Group I Mortgage Loans and any payments of principal to the Group II Class A Certificates will be made first from payments relating to the Group II Mortgage Loans.

The principal distribution to the Group II Class A Certificates will be allocated sequentially, first to the Class A-2 certificates until those certificates are reduced to zero, then to the Class A-3 certificates until those certificates are reduced to zero and then to the Class A-4 certificates until those certificates are reduced to zero. Notwithstanding the above, in the event that the Class Certificate Balances of all of the Subordinated Certificates and the principal balance of the Class X certificates have been reduced to zero, principal distributions to the Group II Class A Certificates are required to be distributed *pro rata*, to the Class A-2, Class A-3 and Class A-4 certificates.

FIGURE 4.15   Principal Waterfall for 2004-HE2
Source: Morgan Stanley 2004a.

to deal, then subordinate principal payments would also be implemented in this method. Each piece of this code is explained below.

```
Public Sub Waterfall_principal(Period As Integer)
    Dim Dist1 as Double
    Dim Dist2 as Double

    Dist1 = Leg.SeniorDist("G1", Period)
    Dist2 = Leg.SeniorDist("G2", Period)

    Dist1 = Debt.SeqPrinPay(Period, Dist1, Blk1, G1)
    Dist2 = Debt.SeqPrinPay(Period, Dist2, Blk2, G2)

    Dist1 = Debt.SeqPrinPay(Period, Dist1, Blk1, G2)
    Dist2 = Debt.SeqPrinPay(Period, Dist2, Blk2, G1)

    Dist2 = Debt.SeqPrinPay(Period, Dist2, Blk1, G1)
    Dist2 = Debt.SeqPrinPay(Period, Dist2, Blk1, G2)
    Dist1 = Debt.SeqPrinPay(Period, Dist1, Blk2, G2)
    Dist1 = Debt.SeqPrinPay(Period, Dist1, Blk2, G1)
End Sub
```

Previous to this part of the waterfall, the senior principal distribution was computed and split pro rata by collateral group (see discussion at the end of section 4.6.1). The SeniorDist method of the Leg object returns the pro rata share of the collateral group named in its first argument. Dist1 and Dist2 are the distributions for senior blocks Blk1 and Blk2, respectively.

```
Dist1 = Leg.SeniorDist("G1", Period)
Dist2 = Leg.SeniorDist("G2", Period)
```

The first block of bonds (A1) is paid down from G1 up to the amount Dist1. Similarly, the second block of bonds (A2,A3,A4) is paid down from G2 up to the amount Dist2. Each block is paid sequentially by the SeqPrinPay method of the Structure class. SeqPrinPay pays down the amount specified in the second argument *sequentially* in the tranches specified in the third argument, from the collateral group given in the fourth argument. Dist1 and Dist2 are updated with any remaining distribution that is not used. This can happen if the corresponding collateral runs out of cash that period.

```
Dist1 = Debt.SeqPrinPay(Period, Dist1, Blk1, G1)
Dist2 = Debt.SeqPrinPay(Period, Dist2, Blk2, G2)
```

The blocks are then cross-collateralized. G2 is used to pay the first block and G1 is used to pay the second block.

```
Dist1 = Debt.SeqPrinPay(Period, Dist1, Blk1, G2)
Dist2 = Debt.SeqPrinPay(Period, Dist2, Blk2, G1)
```

At this point, we are potentially not yet finished. The problem is that all of the distribution may not be spent, even though bonds are outstanding and collateral cash exists. The second sentence (underlined) in Figure 4.15 describes this situation. The following payments are added to fix this:

```
Dist2 = Debt.SeqPrinPay(Period, Dist2, Blk1, G1)
Dist2 = Debt.SeqPrinPay(Period, Dist2, Blk1, G2)
Dist1 = Debt.SeqPrinPay(Period, Dist1, Blk2, G2)
Dist1 = Debt.SeqPrinPay(Period, Dist1, Blk2, G1)
```

To see why these last four statements are needed, consider a degenerate case shown at the top of Table 4.8. By virtue of how pro rata distributions are made, such a lopsided situation cannot occur, but it helps to illustrate the problem. The figure shows these variables after each of the first five SeqPrin-Pay statements above. Note that the third payment changes nothing because G2 is zero. After the fourth payment the problem becomes apparent: A1 is outstanding, G1 has available cash, *and* Distr2 has remaining allocation.

TABLE 4.8   Degenerate Example of Payments in Senior Principal Waterfall

	Blk1	G1	Distr1	Blk2	G2	Distr2
Intial	100	100	1	40	1	50
After 1	99	99	0	40	1	50
After 2	99	99	0	39	0	49
After 3	99	99	0	39	0	49
After 4	99	60	0	0	0	10
After 5	89	50	0	0	0	0

The additional payments (5–8) ensure that the distributions will be used to the extent that bonds remain unpaid and collateral cash doesn't run out. After the fifth payment, both distributions have been completely used so no more pay downs are made.

Given a different set of initial conditions, any one of the last four payments would be needed, so all four are needed in general, although this is inefficient to execute every period. The prospectus says that once a block's balance goes to zero, its principal distribution should be assigned to the other block. If we had a method of attaching the distribution once for future periods, then the last four statements would not all be necessary. Without inventing an attachment method, the solution above does the cross-attachment every period just to be safe.

Two methods are used to define the waterfall: PayPrin and SeqPrinPay. The former method is similar to PayInt—it pays principal to a tranche from a collateral group. The amount to pay down is precomputed (see sections 4.6.1 and 4.6.2) and saved in a data member in the tranche. SeqPrinPay is equivalent to a sequence of PayPrin calls. For example,

```
Dist1 = Debt.SeqPrinPay(Period, Dist1, Blk2, G2)
```

is equivalent to:

```
Dist1 = A2.PayPrin(Period, Dist1, G2)
Dist1 = A3.PayPrin(Period, Dist1, G2)
Dist1 = A4.PayPrin(Period, Dist1, G2)
```

The reader may be bothered that paying interest and principal are not implemented symmetrically. Principal could have been paid by computing a distribution and saving it internal to the tranche, as was done for interest owed. The asymmetry arises in how pro rata payments are made differently for senior interest and principal. If a pro rata tranche owes $100 interest, no matter how complex the cross-collateralization may be, it pays only up to $100. Say two pro rata bonds with balances of $101 and $100 are assigned principal distributions of $100 and $101 respectively. The extra $1 of distribution from the latter should be used to pay down the former.

ERFA The Waterfall ERFA (Excess Reserve Fund Account) method for 2004-HE2 is given next, corresponding to (iii)(p-r) in Figure 4.14. Section (iii)(b-o) in the waterfall is executed elsewhere in the Structure class. Since the payment of short interest and deferred principal for the subordinate clauses is sequential, the user is not allowed flexibility there. The ERFA is more complex and requires user definition. The method PayBRCFA in the Tranche class pays the BRCFA from the specified ERFA (recall there are three ERFAs in 2004-HE2). Each is paid twice based on two different pro rata shares. The ProRataBRCFA method is used here as an alternative to ProRataBal already introduced.

```
Public Sub Waterfall_ERFA(period As Integer)
    Dim BalA As Double
    Dim BalM As Double
    Dim BalB As Double
    Dim BalX As Double
    Dim tranche As Tranche

    BalA = Leg.ERFA("A") .bal(period)
    BalM = Leg.ERFA("M") .bal(period)
    BalB = Leg.ERFA("B") .bal(period)
    BalX = Leg.ERFA("X") .bal(period)

    If options_on Then
        Debt.ProRataBal period-1, Blk2, BalA
        For Each tranche In Blk2
            tranche.PayBRCFA period, Leg.ERFA("A"), "par"
        Next

        Debt.ProRataBRCFA period-1, Blk2, BalA
        For Each tranche In Blk2
            tranche.PayBRCFA period, Leg.ERFA("A"), "par"
        Next

        Debt.ProRataBal period-1, Leg.Mezz, BalM
        For Each tranche In Leg.Mezz
            tranche.PayBRCFA period, Leg.ERFA("M"), "par"
        Next
```

```
        Debt.ProRataBRCFA period-1, Leg.Mezz, BalM
        For Each tranche In Leg.Mezz
            tranche.PayBRCFA period, Leg.ERFA("M"), "par"
        Next

        Debt.ProRataBal period-1, Leg.Junior, BalB
        For Each tranche In Leg.Junior
            tranche.PayBRCFA period, Leg.ERFA("B"), "par"
        Next

        Debt.ProRataBRCFA period-1, Leg.Junior, BalB
        For Each tranche In Leg.Junior
            tranche.PayBRCFA period, Leg.ERFA("B"), "par"
        Next
    End If

    Debt.ProRataBal period-1, Leg.Senior, BalX
    For Each tranche In Leg.Senior
        tranche.PayBRCFA period, Leg.ERFA("X"), "par"
    Next

    For Each tranche In Leg.Subord
        tranche.PayBRCFA period, Leg.ERFA("X"), "seq"
    Next
End Sub
```

Swaps The Waterfall Swap method for 2005-HE3 is given next, corresponding to the prospectus language (Morgan Stanley 2005) given in Figure 4.16. If a swap makes a net payment to the swap counterparty (i), the payment is made from collateral interest in the Interest waterfall. The following waterfall is for distributing cash from the swap into the structure. Each piece of this code is reviewed below.

```
Public Sub Waterfall_swap(period As Integer)
    Dim dist As Double
    Dim SwapPaymentAlloc As Double
    Dim tranche As Tranche

    If SwapsOn Then
        SwapPaymentAlloc = Swap.Collat.Interest(period)

        Debt.ProRataBal period-1, Leg.Senior
        For Each tranche In Leg.Debt
            tranche.PayInt period, Swap.Collat, "seq"
        Next
```

```
        dist = Leg.ShortOC(period)
        If dist>0 Then
            Debt.SeqPrinPay period, dist, Leg.Debt, Swap.Collat
    End If

        debt.pro_rata_bal period-1, Leg.debt, Swap.Bal(period)
        For Each tranche In Leg.senior
            tranche.payBRCFA period, Swap.Collat, "par"
        Next

        debt.pro_rata_bal period-1, Leg.debt, SwapPaymentAlloc
        For Each tranche In Leg.subord
            tranche.payBRCFA period, Swap.Collat, "par"
        Next

        Debt.ProRataBRCFA period-1, Leg.Debt, Swap.Bal(period)
        For Each tranche In Leg.Debt
            tranche.PayBRCFA period, Swap.Collat, "par"
        Next

        For Each tranche in Leg.Subord
            tranche.PayDeferPrin period, Swap.Collat
        Next
    End If
End Sub
```

All payments due under the Swap Agreement and any swap termination payment pursuant to the Swap Agreement will be deposited into the Swap Account, and allocated in the following order of priority, in each case after taking into account any payments made from Net Excess Monthly Cashflow:

(i)   to pay any net swap payment owed to the Swap Counterparty pursuant to the Swap Agreement;
(ii)   to pay any swap termination payment to the Swap Counterparty, to the extent the termination is not due to a default on the part of the Swap Counterparty;
(iii)   to the Class A-1, A-2, A-3 and A-4 Certificates, the Accrued Certificate Interest and the Unpaid Interest Shortfall for each class, on a pro rata basis, to the extent not yet paid;
(iv)   to the Class M-1, M-2, M-3, M-4, M-5, M-6, B-1, B-2, B-3, and B-4 Certificates, Accrued Certificate Interest and Unpaid Interest Shortfall for each class, sequentially and in that order, to the extent not yet paid;
(v)   to be paid as principal, in accordance with the principal distribution rules in effect for such Distribution Date, as needed to maintain the required overcollateralization;
(vi)   concurrently, to the Class A-1, A-2, A-3 and A-4 Certificates, any Basis Risk Carry Forward Amount for each such Class up to their respective Swap Payment Allocation, to the extent not yet paid;
(vii)   sequentially, to the Class M-1, M-2, M-3, M-4, M-5, M-6, B-1, B-2, B-3, and B-4 Certificates, any Basis Risk Carry Forward Amount for each such Class up to their respective Swap Payment Allocation, to the extent not yet paid;
(viii) concurrently to Class A Certificates, Class M Certificates, and Class B Certificates, any unpaid Basis Risk Carryforward Amount, pro rata based on need;
(ix)   sequentially to the Class M-1, M-2, M-3, M-4, M-5, M-6, B-1, B-2, B-3, and B-4 Certificates the allocated unreimbursed realized loss amount, to the extent not yet paid;
(x)   to pay any swap termination payment due to the Swap Counterparty, to the extent the termination is due to a default on the part of the Swap Counterparty; and
(xi)   all remaining amounts to the holder of the Class X Certificate.

FIGURE 4.16 Swap Payment Priority for 2005-HE3
Source: Morgan Stanley 2005.

The Swap Payment Allocation is the cash available from the swap *prior* to any payments. Each tranche has a pro rata share of the Swap Payment Allocation based on its bond balance. The Swap class has a Collateral data member for its accounts. Cash available from the swap to pay the structure is kept as Interest in this Collateral object.

```
SwapPaymentAlloc = Swap.Collat.Interest(period)
```

The highest priority is paying deferred interest (iii)–(iv). This is paid pro rata by bond balance. The pro rata distribution made in the Interest waterfall is based on senior blocks, each paid by a different collateral group and then cross-collateralized (2005-HE3 is similar to 2004-HE2 in this regard). In contrast, the swap distribution is pro rata across all senior bonds.

```
Debt.ProRataBal period-1, Leg.Senior
For Each tranche In Leg.Debt
    tranche.PayInt period, Swap.Collat, "seq"
Next
```

The next highest priority is paying principal to the extent that the O/C target has not been achieved (v). The ShortOC method in the Leg class returns the difference between the target and actual O/C amounts.

```
dist = Leg.ShortOC(Period)
If dist>0 Then
    Debt.SeqPrinPay Period, dist, Leg.Debt, Swap.Collat
End If
```

The BRCFA is paid next (vi)–(viii). First available cash is distributed to the seniors pro rata by balance.

```
debt.pro_rata_bal period-1, Leg.debt, Swap.Bal(period)
For Each tranche In Leg.senior
    tranche.payBRCFA period, Swap.Collat, "par"
Next
```

Then available cash is distributed sequentially to the subordinates, each capped by its individual Swap Payment Allocation. These caps are implemented in the same manner as a pro rata distribution.

```
Debt.pro_rata_bal period-1, Leg.Debt, SwapPaymentAlloc
For Each tranche In Leg.Subord
    tranche.payBRCFA period, Swap.Collat, "par"
Next
```

Then available cash is distributed to all bonds pro rata by need.

```
Debt.ProRataBRCFA period-1, Leg.Debt, Swap.Bal(period)
For Each tranche In Leg.Debt
    tranche.PayBRCFA period, Swap.Collat, "par"
Next
```

Next, any deferred principal is paid (referred to as Unreimbursed Realized Loss Amount in rule ix). The method PayDeferPrin in the Tranche class is similar to PayBRCFA, PayInt, and the like.

```
For Each tranche in Leg.Subord
    tranche.PayDeferPrin Period, Swap.Collat
Next
```

Any cash remaining is added to ERFA(X) in rule (xi)—this is implemented in the Structure class (section 4.10). Swap termination payments (ii and x) are not modeled here.

4.11.2 Active Approach

Two new classes are needed to implement the active approach: Distribution and Node classes. The Distribution class is trivial:

```
Public amt As Double
```

It consists only of a public data member. It is effectively a global value that can be shared by other objects.

The parent Node class is defined with the following interface. The Init method initializes the object. The Info method returns information from the object. The Pay method instructs the object to make a payment to a specified account.

```
Public Sub Init( _
    collat As Variant, _
    DistrType As Variant, _
    tranche As Variant)
End Sub

Public Function Info( _
    what As String, _
    period As Integer) As Double
End Function
```

```
Public Function Pay( _
    what As String, _
    period As Integer, _
    Optional share As Double) As Double
End Function
```

These methods will become clear when the child Node classes are introduced next. Three child classes represent leaf, parallel, and sequential nodes.

Leaf Node   The Leaf child class is defined with the following data members:

```
Dim cash As Collateral
Dim tranche As Tranche
Dim distr As Distribution
```

A leaf node consists of a tranche and a source of cash (a Collateral object). Note that the cash source may differ from the primary collateral group of the tranche. For example, a swap may supply the cash source for the nodes specifying a swap waterfall. The third data member above is a Distribution object. To initialize a leaf node, these three data members are initialized.

```
Public Sub Node_Init( _
    cash_ As Variant, _
    distr_ As Variant, _
    tranche_ As Variant)

    Set cash = cash_
    Set tranche = tranche_
    Set distr = distr_
End Sub
```

The Info method returns the information requested. For example, if the parameter what = "bal", then the tranche's balance is returned. This method can be extended to service other requests.

```
Public Function Node_Info( _
    what As String, _
    period As Integer) As Double

    Select Case what
        Case "bal"
            Node_Info = tranche.Bal(period)
```

```
          Case "BRCFA"
               Node_Info = tranche.BRCFA(period)
          Case "collat"
               Node_Info = tranche.PrimaryCollatBal(period)
     End Select
End Function
```

The Pay method causes the tranche to attempt a cash payment to a specified account. For example, if the parameter what = "int", then the tranche attempts to pay any unpaid interest obligation (*IntOwed* in section 4.4) from the leaf node's cash source, up to a maximum share amount. Similarly, principal and BRCFA can be paid. This method can be extended to pay other obligations. The principal payment case is interesting. If the global distribution share amount (distr) exists, it is used. Otherwise, the optional input parameter for share amount is used. In essence, distr is a global variable, and will be shared by other nodes. By modifying distr here, other nodes see the updated value. This allows complex priority of payments, as shown later in this section for a principal waterfall.

```
Public Function Node_Pay( _
     what As String, _
     period As Integer, _
     Optional share As Double) As Double

     Select Case what
          Case "int"
               tranche.proRataAmt = share
               Node_Pay = tranche.PayInt(period, cash, "par")

          Case "prin"
               If distr Is Nothing Then
                    Node_Pay = tranche.SeqPrinPay(period, _
                         share, cash)
               Else
                    distr.amt = tranche.SeqPrinPay(period, _
                         distr.amt, cash)
               End If

          Case "BRCFA"
               tranche.proRataAmt = share
               Node_Pay = tranche.PayBRCFA(period, cash, "par")
     End Select
End Function
```

Parallel Node   A Parallel child node consists of the following data members:

```
Dim nodes As Collection
Dim nbranches As Integer
Dim distr() As Double
Dim DistrType As String
Dim cash As collateral
```

The collection of nodes represents branches from this node. (Think of the network as a downward-branching tree.) There are nbranches number of subnodes, each with a distribution amount representing a pro rata share. DistrType indicates the type of pro rata distribution (e.g., by bond balance). Finally cash is the cash source shared by all subnodes. The public Node methods are now defined. The initialization method simply assigns values to the data members.

```
Public Sub Node_Init( _
    cash_ As Variant, _
    DistrType_ As Variant, _
    nodes_ As Variant)

    Set collat = cash_
    Set nodes = nodes_
    nbranches = nodes.count
    ReDim distr(1 To nbranches) As Double
    DistrType = DistrType_
End Sub
```

The Info method returns the sum total of the requested information across all subnodes.

```
Public Function Node_Info( _
    what As String, _
    period As Integer) As Double
    Dim item As Node
    Dim sum As Double

    For Each item In nodes
        sum = sum + item.Info(what, period)
    Next

    Node_Info = sum
End Function
```

The Pay method forces all subnodes to attempt payment, capped by pro rata distributions. The distributions are computed with the Distribute method.

```
Public Function Node_Pay( _
    what As String, _
    period As Integer, _
    Optional share As Double) As Double

    Dim i As Integer
    Dim item As Node

    Distribute DistrType, what, period

    For Each item In nodes
        i = i + 1
        item.Pay what, period, distr(i)
    Next
End Function
```

To compute the pro rata distribution, the distribution type is requested from each subnode. For example, if distributing pro rata by bond balance, then DistrType = "bal" and each subnode is queried for its total bond balance. These are summed and pro rata shares are computed. The distribution amount is calculated as the pro rata share of the node's cash source. The method can be extended to other pro rata types.

```
Private Sub Distribute( _
    DistrType As String, _
    what As String, _
    period As Integer)

    Dim i As Integer
    Dim item As Node
    Dim share as Double
    Dim sum As Double
    ReDim Bal(1 To nbranches) As Double

    For Each item In nodes
        i = i + 1
        Select Case DistrType
            Case "bal"
                Bal(i) = item.Info(DistrType, period - 1)
            Case "BRCFA"
                Bal(i) = item.Info(DistrType, period)
```

```
                 Case "collat"
                     Bal(i) = item.Info(DistrType, period - 1)
              End Select
              sum = sum + Bal(i)
         Next

         For i = 1 To nbranches
              If sum > 0 Then
                   share = Bal(i) / sum
                   If what = "prin" then
                        distr(i) = collat.AllCash(period) * share
                   Else
                        distr(i) = collat.Interest(period) * share
                   End If
              Else
                   distr(i) = 0
              End If
         Next
    End Sub
```

Sequential Node   A Sequential node child consists of the following data members:

```
Dim nodes As Collection
Dim DistrType As String
```

The subnodes are similar to those in a Parallel node. In this case, they do not get pro-rata distributions, but rather sequential distributions. There are two types of sequential distributions: threaded and nonthreaded, as indicated by the DistrType member. This distinction will become clear below. Initialization is similar to that of other children.

```
Public Sub Node_Init( _
    NotUsed As Variant, _
    Distrtype_ As Variant, _
    nodes_ As Variant)

    Set nodes = nodes_
    DistrType = Distrtype_
End Sub
```

The Info method is quite similar to that in the Parallel node, except when collateral ("collat") information is requested. In this case, simplified code is presented where it is assumed that all subnodes share the same primary collateral group. In more complex structures, it may be necessary to take the union of the primary collateral groups of the subnodes.

```
Public Function Node_Info( _
    what As String, _
    period As Integer) As Double

    Dim item As node
    Dim sum As Double

    If what = "collat" Then
        Node_info = nodes.item(1).Info(what, period)
    Else
        For Each item In nodes
            sum = sum + item.Info(what, period)
        Next

        Node_info = sum
    End If
End Function
```

The Pay method forces each subnode to attempt payment, capped by a share amount. If the distribution type is "seq" then payment is threaded; that is, each time payment is made, the original share is decreased. If the distribution type is not "seq", then payment is not capped by share (this is implemented by setting the share amount to a very large number). In either case, the payment is always capped by available cash sourcing the node.

```
Public Function Node_Pay( _
    what As String, _
    period As Integer, _
    Optional share As Double) As Double

    Dim item As Node

    For Each item In nodes
        If DistrType <> "seq" Then share = 100000000000
        share = item.Pay(what, period, share)
    Next
    Node_Pay = share
End Function
```

Putting It All Together   Now that the building blocks have been defined, how do we create a waterfall? The idea is to build a network of Node objects and then instruct the root of the network to pay an obligation. For example, suppose we have a very simple structure with two tranches paid interest pro rata by bond balance. The following code sequence shows how to create a network modeling this.

```
Dim Node1 as New Node_Parallel
Dim Node2 as New Node_Leaf
Dim Node3 as New Node_Leaf
Dim Distr as New Distribution
Dim Coll as New Collection

Coll.add Node2
Coll.add Node3

Node2.Node_Init Distr, Cash, Bond1
Node3.Node_Init Distr, Cash, Bond2
Node1.Node_Init Cash, "bal", Coll
```

This code assumes that the structure consists of Bond1 and Bond2 (Tranche objects), with Cash (a Collateral object) supporting the structure. Three Node objects are instantiated. The leaf nodes are added to a collection, Coll. The three Nodes are initialized. In this case, the Distr variable is a placeholder that is not used by the network, but is required by the interface as defined. Once the network is created, it can be queried:

```
Node1.Pay "int", period, 0
```

This instructs the network to pay any as-yet-unpaid interest from cash, in a pro rata manner. Bond1 and Bond2 each receive at most a pro rata share of Cash for this period. This statement can be placed inside the main waterfall loop, attempting payment every period. Although it was slightly painful creating the network, invoking it is quite simple.

Once the Node class has been debugged and verified, errors can be introduced only by specifying a bad network, that is , a network that does not correspond to the intended structure. To help alleviate this risk, the network can be built by software. Ideally, the modeler specifies the network at a very high level, such as drawing a flowchart in a graphical user interface. Software then translates this input to a network of Nodes. Although such software is beyond the scope of this book, the following makes the technique a bit more palatable.

Networks can be built from tools that help construct sequential and parallel nodes. A few tools are introduced here and used to construct the entire waterfall for 2005-HE3. These tools can be thought of as members of a network construction class. The Leaf method builds a leaf node and is used solely by the other tools.

```
Private Function Leaf( _
    distr As Distribution, _
    cash As Collateral, _
    tranche As Tranche) As Node

    Dim leaf1 As New Node_Leaf

    leaf1.Node_Init cash, distr, tranche
    Set Leaf = leaf1
End Function
```

The Seq method builds a sequential node with up to eight predefined sub-nodes of any type.

```
Public Function Seq( _
    n1 As Node, _
    Optional n2 As Node, _
    Optional n3 As Node, _
    . . .
    Optional n8 As Node) As Node

    Dim coll As New Collection
    Dim seq1 As New Node_Sequential
    Dim distr As Distribution

    coll.add n1
    If Not(n2 Is Nothing) Then coll.add n2
    If Not(n3 Is Nothing) Then coll.add n3
    . . .
    If Not(n8 Is Nothing) Then coll.add n8

    seq1.Node_Init distr, "", coll
    Set Seq = seq1
End Function
```

The Seq_ method is a specialization of the previous method. Here, a sequential node is built with only Leaf subnodes. These subnodes are generated from a collection of tranches.

```
Private Function Seq_( _
    DistrType As String, _
    collat As Collateral, _
    tranches As Collection, _
    Optional distr As Distribution) As Node

    Dim coll As New Collection
    Dim tranche As Tranche
    Dim seq1 As New Node_Sequential

    For Each tranche In tranches
        coll.add Leaf(distr, collat, tranche)
    Next

    seq1.Node_Init distr, DistrType, coll
    Set Seq_ = seq1
End Function
```

The Par and Par_ methods are similar to the Seq and Seq_ methods, but for parallel rather than sequential nodes.

```
Private Function Par( _
    DistrType As String, _
    collat As Collateral, _
    n1 As Node, _
    Optional n2 As Node, _
    . . .
    Optional n8 As Node) As Node

    Dim coll As New Collection
    Dim par1 As New Node_Parallel

    coll.add n1
    If Not(n2 Is Nothing) Then coll.add n2
    . . .
    If Not(n8 Is Nothing) Then coll.add n8

    par1.Node_Init collat, DistrType, coll
    Set Par = par1
End Function

Private Function Par_( _
    DistrType As String, _
```

```
        collat As Collateral, _
        tranches As Collection) As Node
        Dim coll As New Collection
        Dim distr As New Distribution
        Dim tranche As Tranche
        Dim par1 As New Node_Parallel

        For Each tranche In tranches
            coll.add Leaf(distr, collat, tranche)
        Next

        par1.Node_Init collat, DistrType, coll
        Set Par_ = par1
End Function
```

Given these tools it is easier to specify a network without error. Consider the 2004-HE2 structure, modified with a swap. The Waterfall class introduced in the previous section is redefined here with the active approach. The following data members are added:

```
Dim d1 as Distribution
Dim d2 as Distribution
Dim InNetwork as Node
Dim PrinNetwork as Node
Dim ERFANetwork as Node
Dim SwapIntNetwork as Node
Dim SwapPrinNetwork as Node
Dim SwapBRCFA1Network as Node
Dim SwapBRCFA2Network as Node
```

As in the previous section, assume that Blk1 and Blk2 are the two senior bond blocks for parallel distribution from collateral groups G1 and G2, respectively. Variables d1 and d2 are two Distribution objects needed to thread the sequential principal payments. The other new data members are active networks corresponding to each waterfall, as defined at the bottom of the previous Waterfall_Init:

```
Set IntNetwork = Seq( _
    Seq_("", G1, Blk1), _
    Seq_("bal", G2, Blk2), _
    Seq_("", G2, Blk1), _
    Seq_("bal", G1, Blk2), _
    Seq_("", G1, Leg.Subord), _
    Seq_("", G2, Leg.Subord))
```

```
Set PrinNetwork = Seq( _
    Seq_("seq", G1, Blk1, d1), _
    Seq_("seq", G2, Blk2, d2), _
    Seq_("seq", G2, Blk1, d1), _
    Seq_("seq", G1, Blk2, d2), _
    Seq_("seq", G1, Blk1, d2), _
    Seq_("seq", G2, Blk2, d1), _
    Seq_("seq", G2, Blk1, d2), _
    Seq_("seq", G1, Blk2, d1))

Set ERFANetwork = Seq( _
    Par_("bal", ERFACollat, Leg.Senior), _
    Seq_("", ERFACollat, Leg.Subord))

Set SwapIntNetwork = Seq( _
    Par_("bal", SwapCollat, Leg.Senior), _
    Seq_("", SwapCollat, Leg.Subord))

Set SwapPrinNetwork = Seq( _
    Par("collat", SwapCollat, _
        Seq_("seq", SwapCollat, Blk1), _
        Seq_("seq", SwapCollat, Blk2)), _
    Seq_("", SwapCollat, Leg.Subord))

Set SwapBRCFA1Network = Par_("bal", SwapCollat, Leg.Debt)

Set SwapBRCFA2Network = Par_("BRCFA", SwapCollat, Leg.Debt)
```

ERFACollat and SwapCollat are other sources of cash: from the ERFA "X" account and the swap, respectively. The remaining four methods in the Waterfall interface are defined as follows. For example, interest is paid by calling the IntNetwork object's Pay method with the "int" string. This causes the request to trickle down the network. More exciting is how senior principal is paid. The two global Distribution variables d1 and d2 are initialized to the two collateral group balances. The PrinNetwork Pay method call causes the update of these two variables as the various nodes in the network are executed, effectively communicating the remaining cash that can be applied in priority order. The swap waterfall is unique in that it requires the execution of multiple networks. This is because the swap essentially mimics the previous sections of the waterfall using swap cash rather than collateral cash.

```
Public Sub Waterfall_Interest(period As Integer)
    IntNetwork.Pay "int", period
End Sub
```

```
Public Sub Waterfall_Principal(period As Integer)
    d1 = Leg.SeniorDist("G1", period)
    d2 = Leg.SeniorDist("G2", period)
    PrinNetwork.Pay "prin", period
End Sub

Public Sub Waterfall_ERFA(period As Integer)
    ERFANetwork.Pay "BRCFA", period
End Sub

Public Sub Waterfall_Swap(period As Integer)
    SwapIntNetwork.Pay "int", period
    SwapPrinNetwork.Pay "prin", period
    SwapBRCFA1Network.Pay "BRCFA", period
    SwapBRCFA2Network.Pay "BRCFA", period
End Sub
```

4.11.3 Comparison

The passive approach is entirely flexible because code can be written for any waterfall, no matter how arbitrary. The active approach is less flexible because the network has been defined over only common waterfall operations, such as sequential and pro rata pay. If something really strange is needed, it will likely not be expressible in the Node class.

However, the active approach has some strong advantages. First, the active network is simpler to model. For example, 2005-HE3 requires only 46 lines of VBA (above) compared to a few hundred for the passive approach. Furthermore, 29 lines of VBA are used to create the network, which can be avoided. The active network does not need to be coded, but in fact can be translated from textual user input, say in the form of a table. This takes the "programming" out of it, although it places a burden on the modeler to understand how the syntax and semantics of the textual input "language." This is done to a limited degree in interface of S&P's SPIRE model (Standard & Poor's 2005b). The active networks described here are general, but with generality comes a curse. Users may specify syntactically correct waterfalls that have no practical meaning. One can control this by imposing constraints on the active network.

4.12 *DOING IT IN EXCEL:* DATA TABLES

The asset and liability models introduced involve a set of assets and a set of bonds, each of which must be iterated through to produce cash flows. Excel, although great for laying out a cash flow model, is weak when it comes to iteration. One option is to *copy* the model formulae for each iteration; for example, if you have 10 bonds, then copy the interest, principal, and prepayment cash flow formulae 10 times. This is how most spreadsheet-based CDO models are built. The models are usually built for several tranches to be sure that they can accommodate larger structures in the future. Given that there are limited columns in a sheet (256), and many interesting flows for each tranche, one quickly runs out of space. To handle this, modelers often write fantastically complex formulae, packing in as much as possible (there is actually a limit to the number of characters in a formula—I won't tell you what it is to dissuade you from going there!).

Another option is to define user functions to encapsulate much of the "heavy lifting" in code, while still exploiting the spreadsheet's ability to display data intuitively. A third option, for sufficiently simple tasks, is data tables. A data table is the spreadsheet equivalent of single- or double-nested iteration in a programming language. In VBA a single iterator data table would be roughly equivalent to:

```
Dim inputs As Variant
Dim outputs As Variant
Dim I As Long

inputs = Array(1.7, 2.6, -3.4, ..., 11.2)

For I = 1 to Ubound(inputs)
    outputs(I) = F(inputs(I))
Next
```

Here, the data table inputs that are fed into the function F, one at a time via iterator I. To better explain how data tables are built, let's consider an example. Suppose you are planning to buy a house and are shopping for a tax-deductible mortgage. Further, say you have the luxury of having sufficient cash. In fact, suppose you plan to "arb" the mortgage, that is, reinvest the loan at higher rates. Assuming you will pay back the loan in five years, which product is best?

First, a cash flow model is built that evaluates a single mortgage. Second, a data table is built that operates on the initial cash flow model. Figure 4.17 shows the control sheet containing scalar inputs describing a mortgage. Whenever possible, named ranges are used, clarifying subsequent references. The ranges are named: term (actual term of the mortgage in periods), mrate (yearly mortgage rate), pts (points purchased), irate (yearly reinvestment rate), prepay (number of periods intended for paying down the loan), size

	A	B	C	D
1		**INPUTS**		
2				
3	term	360	# periods in loan	
4	mrate	4.38%	mortgage rate	
5	pts	4.000	points	
6	irate	5.50%	reinv rate	
7	prepay	180	# periods in prepay	
8	size	100,000	loan amt	=CFs!$I$63
9	tax_rate	45%	tax rate	
10	freq	12	periods per year	
11	salary	120,000	annual salary	=CFs!$D$63
12	maint	1,028	monthly maintenance	
13	mtg_fee	1,500	upfront mortgage fee	
14				=B15-B16
15		358,403	asset value at 5 years	
16		73,626	liability value at 5 years	
17	value	284,777	net value	

FIGURE 4.17 "Control" Sheet: Model Inputs Describing Single Mortgage (Range Names are Listed in Column A)

(initial balance), tax_rate (annual tax rate), freq (number of periods per year), salary (fixed yearly salary), maint (maintenance due each period—for New York City apartments!), mtg_fee (one-time fee for mortgage). Unfortunately, since it is difficult to *display* range names, names are used only sparingly in this book.

These inputs are used in formulae in the CFs sheet (Figure 4.18) to model the cash flows of the mortgage. CFs formulae are highlighted in comments that are attached to their cells. These cells are copied down in each column. Note that two Excel built-ins are used: IPMT and PPMT which compute the interest and principal payments in a standard mortgage. The advantage of working out the cash flow model on a spreadsheet is the facility of debugging.

First the interest and principal payments are computed from the original loan balance. This allows principal to be paid down faster or slower than the actual term of the mortgage. Salary is needed for computing taxes. Total income less deductions is gross income plus interest earned on the reinvested loan balance less mortgage interest paid (which is tax exempt). This simple model has a flat tax rate. The new balance is the previous ending balance less mortgage interest and principal paid less maintenance paid less taxes paid plus gross income plus reinvested interest earned. Unfortunately there is no way to name these variables because each row refers to different cells.

The formulae in row 4 (corresponding to period one) can be selected and dragged down 360 times to complete the cash flow model. By copying

	A	B	C	D	E	F	G	H	I	J	K
1		mortgage	mortgage	loan	gross	int	total inc	income	asset		
2	period	interest	principal	balance	income	earned	less deduct	tax	balance		
3				100,000					94,500		=size-pts/100* size - mtg_fee
4	1	(365)	(394)	99,606	10,000	433	10,069	4,531	98,616		
5	2	(364)	(395)	99,210	10,000	452	10,088	4,540	102,741		=I3+C4+E4-maint+ B4+F4-H4
6	3	(364)	(397)	98,814	10,000	471	10,107	4,548	106,875		
7	4	(363)	(398)	98,415	10,000	490	10,127	4,557	111,018		
8	5	(363)	(400)	98,015	10,000	509	10,146	4,566	115,171		=G4*tax_rate
9	6	(362)	(401)	97,614	10,000	528	10,166	4,575	119,332		
10	7	(362)	(403)	97,211	10,000	547	10,185	4,583	123,504		=E4+F4+B4
11	8	(361)	(404)	96,807	10,000	566	10,205	4,592	127,684		
12	9	(361)	(406)	96,402	10,000	585	10,225	4,601	131,874		
13	10	(360)	(407)	95,994	10,000	604	10,244	4,610	136,073		=I3*irate/freq
14	11	(360)	(409)	95,586	10,000	624	10,264	4,619	140,282		
15	12	(359)	(410)	95,176	10,000	643	10,284	4,628	144,500		=salary/freq
16	13	(359)	(412)	94,764	10,000	662	10,304	4,637	148,727		
17	14	(358)	(413)	94,351	10,000	682	10,324	4,646	152,964		=D3+C4
18	15	(358)	(415)	93,936	10,000	701	10,344	4,655	157,210		
19	16	(357)	(416)	93,520	10,000	721	10,364	4,664	161,466		
20	17	(357)	(418)	93,102	10,000	740	10,384	4,673	165,732		=PPMT(mrate/freq, $A4,prepay,size)
21	18	(356)	(419)	92,683	10,000	760	10,404	4,682	170,006		
57	54	(336)	(478)	76,530	10,000	1,493	11,157	5,021	330,403		
58	55	(335)	(480)	76,050	10,000	1,514	11,179	5,031	335,044		=IPMT(mrate/freq, $A4,term,size)
59	56	(335)	(481)	75,569	10,000	1,536	11,201	5,040	339,695		
60	57	(334)	(483)	75,086	10,000	1,557	11,223	5,050	344,357		
61	58	(334)	(485)	74,601	10,000	1,578	11,245	5,060	349,029		
62	59	(333)	(487)	74,114	10,000	1,600	11,267	5,070	353,711		
63	60	(332)	(488)	73,626	10,000	1,621	11,289	5,080	358,403		

FIGURE 4.18 "CFs" Sheet: Cash Flows for Mortgage Reinvestment; Months 1–23 and 54–60 Shown

the row, each unanchored variable will automatically be reset. For example, if one copies cell G4 to cell G5, the formula is transformed from "=E4+F4+B4" to "=E5+F5+B5." Either the row or column can be "anchored" by adding a "$" prefix. For a given loan, the net value of the investment at five years is asset value (CFs!I63) less the liability value (CFs!D63). These formulae are shown at the bottom of Figure 4.17.

There are a number of loan products to choose from: fixed or floating rates, ARMs with different initial reset periods, different maturities, points, etc. Let's simplify the problem and assume the universe of possible loans in Figure 4.19. The objective is to analyze all these loans in combination with varying reinvestment rates, prepayment rates, and initial loan balances. To make this concrete, suppose reinvestment rates vary from 5.5% to 7.5% by 0.5%, prepayment term is either 15 or 30 years, and loan balance is either zero, $100,000, $150,000, or $200,000. Zero loan balance is considered as a baseline. Since there are twenty 30-year loans, eight 15-year loans, five reinvestment rates, two prepayment terms, and four loan balances, there are $960 = (20 \times 5 \times 2 \times 4) + (8 \times 5 \times 4)$ valid combinations. The idea is to plug each of these input combinations into the cash flow model, one at a time, and collect the results. This is automated with an Excel data table.

	A	B	C	D
1	type	term	rate	points
2	5/1 ARM	30	4.38%	4.000
3	5/1 ARM	30	4.50%	3.625
4	5/1 ARM	30	4.63%	3.250
5	5/1 ARM	30	4.75%	2.875
6	5/1 ARM	30	4.88%	2.625
7	5/1 ARM	30	5.00%	2.250
8	5/1 ARM	30	5.13%	1.875
9	5/1 ARM	30	5.25%	1.500
10	5/1 ARM	30	5.38%	1.250
11	5/1 ARM	30	5.50%	0.875
12	5/1 ARM	30	5.63%	0.625
13	5/1 ARM	30	5.75%	0.250
14	5/1 ARM	30	5.88%	0.000
15	15 yr fix	15	4.88%	3.750
16	15 yr fix	15	5.00%	3.375
17	15 yr fix	15	5.13%	2.875
18	15 yr fix	15	5.25%	2.375
19	15 yr fix	15	5.38%	1.875
20	15 yr fix	15	5.50%	1.250
21	15 yr fix	15	5.63%	0.750
22	15 yr fix	15	5.75%	0.375
23	30 yr fix	30	5.38%	3.625
24	30 yr fix	30	5.50%	3.000
25	30 yr fix	30	5.63%	2.500
26	30 yr fix	30	5.75%	1.875
27	30 yr fix	30	5.88%	1.375
28	30 yr fix	30	6.00%	0.750
29	30 yr fix	30	6.13%	0.375
30				

FIGURE 4.19   "Loans" Sheet: Universe of Prime Mortgages Considered to Purchase

Figure 4.20 shows a portion of the 960 combinations. Each row is a combination, showing the model inputs in columns B:H. For now assume that all 960 combinations were typed in by hand (more about this later). The data table is constructed in the grey area. Before explaining how that works, first refer to Figure 4.21 showing a revised "control" sheet. The new control sheet references its input values from the "table" sheet. It uses the VLOOKUP built-in. VLOOKUP(k,d,c,FALSE) searches for the first instance of the *exact* value k in the first column of data range d and returns the corresponding value in column c. It is essentially a lookup function where the keys can be in any order. The input key k in this case is table!$I$1, shown with the value 1 in Figure 4.20. This cell is a critical part of the data table. Note that by changing the value in cell table!$I$1, the inputs to the model change, as do the cash flows (in CFs), as does the output (cell control!B17).

	type	term	mtg rate	pts	reinv rate	prepay yrs	loan size	I	J	delta
								1	284,777	
0	5/1 ARM	30	4.375%	4.000	5.50%	15	-		287,537	
1	5/1 ARM	30	4.375%	4.000	5.50%	15	100,000	1	284,777	(2,760)
2	5/1 ARM	30	4.375%	4.000	5.50%	15	150,000	2	283,397	(4,140)
3	5/1 ARM	30	4.375%	4.000	5.50%	15	200,000	3	282,017	(5,520)
4	5/1 ARM	30	4.375%	4.000	5.50%	30	-	4	287,537	-
5	5/1 ARM	30	4.375%	4.000	5.50%	30	100,000	5	286,082	(1,455)
6	5/1 ARM	30	4.375%	4.000	5.50%	30	150,000	6	285,354	(2,183)
7	5/1 ARM	30	4.375%	4.000	5.50%	30	200,000	7	284,626	(2,911)
8	5/1 ARM	30	4.375%	4.000	6.00%	15	-	8	289,523	-
9	5/1 ARM	30	4.375%	4.000	6.00%	15	100,000	9	288,027	(1,496)
10	5/1 ARM	30				15	150,000	10	287,279	(2,244)
11	5/1 ARM	30				15	200,000	11	286,531	(2,992)
12	5/1 ARM	30				30	-	12	289,523	-
13	5/1 ARM	30				30	100,000	13	288,457	(66)
14	5/1 ARM	30				30	150,000	14	289,423	(99)
15	5/1 ARM	30				30	200,000	15	289,390	(133)
16	5/1 ARM	30	4.375%	4.000	6.50%	15	-	16	291,526	-
17	5/1 ARM	30	4.375%	4.000	6.50%	15	100,000	17	291,313	(213)
18	5/1 ARM	30	4.375%	4.000	6.50%	15	150,000	18	291,206	(320)
19	5/1 ARM	30	4.375%	4.000	6.50%	15	200,000	19	291,400	(427)
20	5/1 ARM	30	4.375%	4.000	6.50%	30	-	20	291,526	-
21	5/1 ARM	30	4.375%	4.000	6.50%	30	100,000	21	292,868	1,342
22	5/1 ARM	30	4.375%	4.000	6.50%	30	150,000	22	293,540	2,014
23	5/1 ARM	30	4.375%	4.000	6.50%	30	200,000	23	294,211	2,685
24	5/1 ARM	30	4.375%	4.000	7.00%	15	-	24	293,647	-
25	5/1 ARM	30	4.375%	4.000	7.00%	15	100,000	25	294,635	1,088
26	5/1 ARM	30	4.375%	4.000	7.00%	15	150,000	26	295,179	1,632
27	5/1 ARM	30	4.375%	4.000	7.00%	15	200,000	27	295,823	2,176
28	5/1 ARM	30	4.375%	4.000	7.00%	30	-	28	295,647	
29	5/1 ARM	30	4.375%	4.000	7.00%	30	100,000	29	296,919	2,771
30	5/1 ARM	30	4.375%	4.000	7.00%	30	150,000	30	297,704	4,156

(L column, boxed: = value)

Table dialog box (overlaying rows):
Row input cell: [ ]
Column input cell: $I$1
[OK] [Cancel]

FIGURE 4.20 "Table" Sheet: Setting up 960 Combinations and Data Table (Shaded)

	A	B	C	D
1		**INPUTS**		
2				
3	term	360	# periods in loan	
4	mrate	4.38%	mortgage rate	
5	pts	4.000	points	=VLOOKUP(table!$I$1, table!$A:$H, 3, FALSE)*freq
6	irate	5.50%	reinv rate	
7	prepay	180	# periods in prepay	
8	size	100,000	loan amt	
9	tax_rate	45%	tax rate	
10	freq	12	periods per year	
11	salary	120,000	annual salary	=VLOOKUP(table!$I$1, table!$A:$H, 8, FALSE)
12	maint	1,028	monthly maintenance	
13	mtg_fee	1,500	upfront mortgage fee	
14				
15		358,403	asset value at 5 years	
16		73,626	liability value at 5 years	
17	value	284,777	net value	

FIGURE 4.21 Revised "Control" Sheet: Model Inputs Lookup Values From "Table" Sheet

In this case the data table is an array with two columns. The left column holds a sequence of inputs and the right column will hold their corresponding outputs. The top right cell of the data table is special. The top of the right column references where the outputs are found. The value of this reference is copied into each cell in the right column, one at a time. Basically the data table is an iteration construct.

In this instance, the top right cell (table!J1) is assigned to "= value" thus the data table captures the cash flow model result from the "control" sheet (control!B17). The data table is initially created by dragging over cells table!I1:J961 and selecting Data→Table, as shown in Figure 4.20. A choice box pops up. This is how the iterated input is assigned. In this case, $I$1 is entered as the column input because iteration proceeds along the (right) column. The iteration can be linked to any cell on this sheet—$I$1 was chosen just because it is easy to spot.

When the workbook is recalculated the data table will compute its values. The iteration is hidden—all one sees is an hour-glass cursor during the 960 evaluations of the cash flow model. When finished, the computed values will be in the right column of the data table. A few more points are in order. First, the net value of mortgage in year five is not a sufficient indicator of how good the arbitrage is. It must be compared to not borrowing at all, that is, earning an annual salary, paying taxes, and so on. The rightmost column K in Figure 4.20 ("delta") nets each data table result against the corresponding no-debt result to get the value of the arb. Second, one can summarize the results several ways. Each reinvestment assumption implies a loan that maximizes the arb, etc. To visualize these results, one can record a macro that sorts the "table" sheet by column K. Third, the most difficult part of the whole exercise has been swept under the rug, so to speak. The 960 combinations need to be generated, not typed in. Two ways that come to mind are: writing a VBA macro of nested loops that populate this data, or building formulae in Excel to do the job (this is left as an exercise for the reader).

4.13 EXERCISES

4.1. Implement a Tranche class that can accommodate senior, mezzanine, and subordinate bonds that are either fixed or floating.

4.2. Modify the Tranche class in Exercise 4.1 to accommodate NAS bonds. Non-Accelerating Senior (NAS) bonds have a fixed principal payment schedule. Usually, this schedule has no principal payments for the first few years. The bonds pay interest on their balance as do standard bonds. NAS bonds are a type of senior bond and thus their principal

TABLE 4.9 NAS Shift as Function of Month

From	To	NAS shift
0	36	0%
37	60	45%
61	72	80%
73	84	100%
85	360	300%

payment has higher priority than subordinate bonds. Among the senior bonds, principal is distributed to the NAS bonds first according to their schedules. This mechanism lowers the investor's risk of having excessive prepayments shorten the life of the bond and decreasing its value.

Table 4.9 gives an example of a NAS schedule. The percentage of the senior distribution allocated to the NAS is the shift factor times the ratio of the NAS balance to the total senior balance. Notice that initially the example NAS gets no principal pay downs for the first three years. After seven years the NAS gets three times its pro rata share.

4.3. Extend the NAS class in Exercise 4.2 to accommodate PAC bonds. Planned Amortization Class (PAC) bonds are similar to NAS bonds except that their amortization schedule is in dollars, not senior share. They have higher priority for principal payments than other bonds.

4.4. Modify the Tranche class in Exercise 4.1 to accommodate IO and PO bonds. An interest-only (IO) bond pays interest but not principal. Generally, an IO is linked to one or more other bonds from which it derives its "balance." The IO pays interest on this effective balance. A principal-only (PO) bond pays no interest, but does pay principal on its balance. A popular combination of these is an "IO/PO split"—an IO linked to a PO. IOs and POs speculate on prepayments. If prepayments are low, then outstanding balances remain high, and interest flows into an IO increasing its value. Thus IO value increases when interest rates increase. If prepayments are high, then principal flows early into a PO increasing its value.

4.5. Modify the Tranche class in Exercise 4.1 to accommodate Z bonds. Z bonds are linked to one or more bonds. Until these bonds are fully paid down, the Z bond receives no interest or principal payments. Normally, a low-priority bond would not receive principal payments until the bonds above it in sequential priority are fully paid down.

But such bonds would still receive interest in a timely manner. Because Z bonds don't pay interest either, the bonds *negatively amortize*; that is, the interest that was not paid is capitalized.

4.6. Design a class architecture to support legs, blocks, and collateral groups, as well as tranches.

4.7. Implement the "passive" architecture described in section 4.11.1 for one child similar to 2004-HE2, without caps or swaps.

4.8. Improve your solution to Exercise 4.7 by inventing a way to cross-collateralize the principal waterfall more efficiently than that described in section 4.11.1.

4.9. Implement the "active" architecture described in section 4.11.2 for one child similar to 2004-HE2, without caps or swaps.

4.10. Design and build a user interface for your solution to Exercise 4.9 to allow a modeler to give a high-level, declarative specification of the priority of payments. From the input, automatically generate the active network.

CHAPTER 5

Sizing the Structure

Order is heaven's first law, and this confessed,
Some are, and must be, greater than the rest...
                                                    —Alexander Pope

In the liability waterfall model previously introduced, bond allocations and spreads were given as inputs. Spreads are determined by the market. For example, there is a general consensus among traders as to the bid-ask spreads of A-rated bonds backed by diversified pools of subprime mortgages (or other assets). However, the *optimal* size or number of bonds of each rating in a new structure (called the allocation) is not obvious.

Where did each bond's rating come from? The rating is granted by an agency if the bond passes certain requirements specific to that rating and asset class. Key to the requirements is a credit enhancement constraint. This constraint may state that for a bond to be granted a certain rating, the bonds *subordinate* to it must absorb all losses of principal and all deferrals of interest over the life of the bond, given some particular assumption of asset losses, prepayments, and other characteristics. To get a higher rating, assumed asset losses need to be higher, among other things. For a given asset type, the agencies present the market with mappings between ratings and stress assumptions. The mappings are not equivalent among the agencies, so it can be that over periods of time one rating agency is more binding than another; that is, one agency is more conservative and its mappings require more credit enhancement for the "same" rating.

The key question is posed: What is the *optimal* bond allocation, given a structure, an asset portfolio, and a set of rating agency criteria? Let's analyze the problem from the view of the securitizer, that is, someone selling the bonds. In this case optimal means allocating the structure at *least cost* to the seller. Minimal cost is minimal average coupon, or in the usual case of floating bonds, minimal spread. Another way to view the optimal is maximum price, because by minimizing the issued coupons, residual cash flows increase, increasing the value of the structure.

Consider an extreme: It is cheaper to issue all AAA bonds with low spreads than BBB bonds with high spreads. On the margin, it is better *for the issuer* to reallocate one dollar of a given bond into any more senior bond, all other things being equal. Thus the optimal allocation essentially places every dollar as high in the structure as it can go while still retaining enough credit enhancement for each bond to achieve its target rating.

Like the portfolio optimization problem discussed in section 3.2, this new problem is *combinatorial* because of the possible explosion in the number of possible paths through the waterfalls for every change in allocation. The problem, however, is *nonlinear* because of the discrete decisions made in the waterfalls, e.g., changing the allocation just a bit may shift when the overcollateralization (O/C) steps down. Nonlinearities rule out a mathematical programming solution such as that described in section 3.2.1. Randomized search (e.g., simulated annealing in section 3.2.2) is possible. However, is there a smarter way to search for an optimum?

The search space is well behaved—a distinct advantage. A bond is *admissible* under a given rating, agency, and allocation if it passes the eligibility criteria for that rating by that agency. If a bond is admissible, it will remain admissible with additional credit enhancement. If a bond is inadmissible, it will remain inadmissible with reduced credit enhancement. Thus one can find an optimal allocation by finding a series of optimal suballocations.

Figure 5.1 illustrates sizing the structure. There two distinct optimizations performed to size the structure, noted next to the senior and subordinate tranches. *These optimizations can proceed in either order and are repeated until convergence.* Each senior tranche is successively sized in order to achieve its target weighted average life (*WALTarget* in section 4.2). Each subordinate tranche is successively sized in order to minimize its size. Whereas senior tranches are sized senior-most first, subordinate tranches are sized subordinate-most first. Following this, the NIMs are sized, given the derived allocation for the bonds senior to it. At this stage the OTE can be priced.

In actuality, sizing is more complex than described above because of several concerns.

- There are competing collateral models to evaluate the structure: the structurer and the rating agencies may have different collateral models. Rating agency models are used, in parallel, for subordinate sizing. For each tranche, the agency results are combined, picking the worst case.

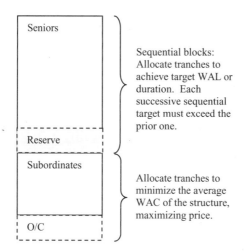

FIGURE 5.1 Overview of Sizing a Structure (Not Drawn to Scale)

- When sizing senior bonds for WAL, there must be at least one senior bond that is not allocated yet. This *reserved* bond is used as a plug during subordinate sizing. For example, if an optimal subordinate bond allocation requires a *reduction* of $100,000, then this reserved senior bond is *increased* by $100,000.
- For a given rating agency (collateral) model, sizing the subordinate tranches depends on the *initial* allocations. Put another way, if a bond is admissible, it will not necessarily remain admissible if more senior bonds are reallocated. Thus resizing the subordinate tranches a *second* time, with initialization from the results of the *first* sizing, can result in *different* allocations. Because tranches are sized in a certain order (junior-most first), sizing B_k can effect the *subsequent* sizing of $B_{j<k}$. Reallocations redistribute the cash available to interest and principal payments; hence, tranche sizes can fluctuate over multiple resizings. In practice, sizes quickly converge. In rare cases, the algorithm does not converge and in fact oscillates between alternative stable states.
- Related to the previous point, allocating the senior bonds can result in a different cost structure that will redistribute the cash available to interest and principal payments, hence affecting subordinate admissibility. Therefore, after senior sizing, subordinate sizing must be redone. Subordinate sizing can result in a different plug allocation for the (senior) reserved bond. One must check whether the plug goes below zero; that is, the senior and subordinate optima are inconsistent. All in all, the

senior and subordinate optimizations must iterate until convergence or failure.

- On top of all this, seniors are not the only bonds that can be partitioned to achieve WAL targets. Any other sequence of like-rated bonds can be partitioned in a similar manner.

- Different stress assumptions are used in sizing the issued ("pre-NIM") bonds than are used in sizing the NIMs, and different assumptions yet again in pricing the OTE ("post-NIM"). Keeping track of all these assumptions is a challenge. In addition, there are dependencies between sizing the pre-NIM, NIMs, and post-NIM. Each derived allocation from the previous stage must be fed into sizing the next stage.

- A "cash corridor" may be required to price the NIMs (see section 4.8.1). This NIM corridor is defined by pairs of high and low struck options. Should interest rates fall above the low strike, the options pay out, based on the total debt balance. The debt balance must be determined for the allocation fed into the NIM sizer. Thus the NIM corridor can be derived only between sizing the bonds and sizing the NIMs.

The algorithms and their behaviors are detailed next.

5.1 SENIOR SIZING

A block of sequential tranches that have the same rating can be allocated according to criteria other than minimization of coupon. Their coupons will vary, even though they have the same rating, because they are paid sequentially and therefore have different durations and hence risk. The purpose of issuing a *block* of such bonds is to offer a *selection of durations* to the market. Minimizing coupon will result in the issuance of only the first bond with the shortest duration and the lowest coupon. That would defeat the whole idea.

This idea is usually implemented for senior bonds since they constitute the majority of the issuance. Thus, in the following, this technique is referred to as "senior sizing," although it could be performed elsewhere in the structure. Furthermore, although duration better represents risk, here weighted-average life (WAL) is targeted because it is simpler to compute.

Consider 2004-HE2 with two senior blocks: (A1) and (A2,A3,A4). The first block consists of only one bond, so there is no flexibility in redistributing the collateral cash flows. Only the latter block can be sized in this manner. Before the formal algorithm is defined, let's look at the results of sizing this block, as shown in Table 5.1.

The key idea behind the algorithm is that an amortization schedule (i.e., schedule of principal payments) determines the WAL. The distribution of

TABLE 5.1 Example of Senior Sizing for 2004-HE2. WAL Targets are 0.4 and 0.9 Years for A2 and A3 Respectively

Period	Tranche	Weight	Prin CF	Running WAL	Target	Balance
1	A2	0.081	4,904,471	0.081	0.40	4,904,471
2	A2	0.164	5,248,489	0.124	0.40	10,152,960
3	A2	0.247	5,589,822	0.168	0.40	15,742,782
4	A2	0.331	5,928,619	0.212	0.40	21,671,401
5	A2	0.414	5,862,860	0.255	0.40	27,534,262
6	A2	0.497	5,799,081	0.297	0.40	33,333,342
7	A2	0.581	5,736,935	0.339	0.40	39,070,278
8	A2	0.664	5,676,083	0.380	0.40	44,746,360
9	A2	0.747	2,571,045	0.400	0.40	47,317,405
9	A3	0.081	3,045,548	0.081	0.50	3,045,548
10	A3	0.164	5,556,922	0.134	0.50	8,602,470
11	A3	0.247	5,491,595	0.178	0.50	14,094,065
12	A3	0.331	5,423,546	0.221	0.50	19,517,612
13	A3	0.414	5,308,577	0.262	0.50	24,826,189
14	A3	0.497	5,190,341	0.303	0.50	30,016,530
15	A3	0.581	5,070,620	0.343	0.50	35,087,151
16	A3	0.664	4,949,743	0.383	0.50	40,036,893
17	A3	0.747	4,831,634	0.422	0.50	44,868,528
18	A3	0.831	4,716,328	0.461	0.50	49,584,856
19	A3	0.914	4,603,759	0.499	0.50	54,188,615
20	A3	0.997	91,015	0.500	0.50	54,370,645

principal payments to a block determines the WAL of that block as a whole. To customize the WAL of the first tranche in the block, the schedule can be shortened: Apply only those payments that generate the target WAL. The sum of these paydowns equals the initial balance that achieves the target WAL for that tranche. Subsequent payments are allocated to the next tranche, and so on. Each tranche must have *increasing* target WALs. However, it may be impossible to satisfy all targets with the given amortization schedule.

Table 5.1 shows the principal cash flows allocated toward satisfying the target WAL of A2, the first tranche in the block. The weights are the cumulative number of years corresponding to each successive period. It takes nine periods to achieve the target WAL of 0.40 years. However, nine *full* periods would go over the target to 0.42 years. Thus only a fraction of the principal cash flow in period nine can be used for A2, and the remainder goes to A3, as shown in gray. A3 achieves its relative target WAL of 0.50 by period 20 (the actual target is 0.9 = 0.4 + 0.5). Again, only a fraction of the principal cash flow in period 20 is needed for A3—the rest goes to

A4, and so on. WAL is computed from a series of principal cash flows, $P(t)$, and cumulative time in years, $w(t)$. WAL_n is the weighted-average life accounting for cash flows through period n. WAL_{target} is achieved with cash flows through some period n plus an additional amount C (a fraction of the next cash flow $P(n+1)$).

$$WAL_n = \frac{\sum_{t=1}^{n} w(t)P(t)}{\sum_{t=1}^{n} P(t)} \tag{5.1}$$

$$WAL_{target} = \frac{\sum_{t=1}^{n} w(t)P(t) + w(n+1)C}{\sum_{t=1}^{n} P(t) + C} \tag{5.2}$$

Equation (5.2) can be solved for C as follows:

$$WAL_{target} \times \left[\sum_{t=1}^{n} P(t) + C \right] = \sum_{t=1}^{n} w(t)P(t) + w(n+1)C$$

$$WAL_{target} \times \left[\sum_{t=1}^{n} P(t) + C \right] - w(n+1)C = \sum_{t=1}^{n} w(t)P(t)$$

$$WAL_{target} \times \sum_{t=1}^{n} P(t) + WAL_{target} \times C - w(n+1)C = \sum_{t=1}^{n} w(t)P(t)$$

$$C \times [WAL_{target} - w(n+1)] = \sum_{t=1}^{n} w(t)P(t) - WAL_{target} \times \sum_{t=1}^{n} P(t)$$

$$C = \frac{\sum_{t=1}^{n} w(t)P(t) - WAL_{target} \times \sum_{t=1}^{n} P(t)}{WAL_{target} - w(n+1)} \tag{5.3}$$

This is the key to the algorithm: how to interpolate between two principal payments to derive the precise target WAL. The rest of the algorithm has no surprises so it is left to the reader to develop. Rather than WAL, duration can also be targeted. Effective duration will require the computation of three principal cash flows (shock up, shock down, and neutral) and their discounting. Because of the nonlinearity of discounting, the right spot to split a cash flow to achieve a target duration is not obvious. Search techniques can be used to allocate by duration.

5.2 SUBORDINATE SIZING

Before getting into the formal algorithm for finding the optimal subordinate allocation, consider an example first. Table 5.2 shows two alternative allocations for a typical mortgage deal. This structure has one senior bond and a swap. The deal is analyzed with spot LIBOR at 5.13%. The unoptimized allocation has a 101.3608 dollar price. (Price is computed as total proceeds less expenses divided by collateral balance, shown as OTE balance.) By optimizing, 0.3% of the allocation moves from B3 to A1 (O/C remains the same), generating additional proceeds (in NIM and OTE) by reducing the average coupon, that is, increasing the excess spread. Price increases by 1.36 bps to 101.3744. The second allocation is optimal in the sense that any additional migration upwards for increased price will be judged inadmissible by some agency for these ratings. Alternatively, the second allocation is not optimal if ratings are changed.

A few things to note about this example. The bonds don't change their prices between these allocations. A1 to B3 are sold at par (gross proceeds are equal to balance). B4 is below par because its margin is capped. NIM is slightly below par and the OTE is priced far below par to achieve a certain yield. Furthermore, the sum of the proceeds from A1 to B4 is the same, $1.142 billion. The extra 1.36 bps profit appears entirely in the NIM and OTE. Because 30 bps was moved from a bond paying 205 bps to a bond paying 19 bps, the second allocation is cheaper. A back-of-the-envelope estimate of the savings is:

$$(2.05\% \times 4.86 - 0.19\% \times 2.32) \times 0.30\% = 2.9 \text{ bps}$$

where A1 and B3 WAL are 2.32 and 4.86 years, respectively. The error in this estimate is due to the timing of cash flows.

Let's look at this abstractly. Suppose you purchase $100 notional of assets at a purchase price of 101%. The plan is to securitize this in a structure comprised of $98 in bonds with $2 of O/C. The bonds are sold, resulting in $98 in proceeds. So far, you have lost $3 on this transaction: one dollar because you paid above par for the assets and $2 because of the assets locked up as O/C. Consider the NIMs and OTE as one residual cash flow. The residual is highly discounted, say on average around 25%. Suppose the residual cash flow is $10 with WAL around six years. This comes from both

TABLE 5.2 Example of Sizing a Typical Structure. Total Collateral is $1.173 Billion and O/C = 2.25%. All Allocations are as Percentage of Initial Collateral

Tranche	Rating	Margin	Allocation	Unoptimized Balance	Unoptimized Gross Proceeds	Optimized Allocation	Optimized Balance	Optimized Gross Proceeds
A1	AAA	0.19%	77.90%	914,077,933	914,077,933	78.20%	917,598,130	917,598,130
M1	AA+	0.31%	3.85%	45,175,867	45,175,867	3.85%	45,175,867	45,175,867
M2	AA	0.34%	3.35%	39,308,871	39,308,871	3.35%	39,308,871	39,308,871
M3	AA–	0.35%	2.00%	23,467,983	23,467,983	2.00%	23,467,983	23,467,983
M4	A+	0.42%	1.80%	21,121,185	21,121,185	1.80%	21,121,185	21,121,185
M5	A	0.46%	1.75%	20,534,485	20,534,485	1.75%	20,534,485	20,534,485
M6	A–	0.53%	1.60%	18,774,386	18,774,386	1.60%	18,774,386	18,774,386
B1	BBB+	1.05%	1.55%	18,187,687	18,187,687	1.55%	18,187,687	18,187,687
B2	BBB	1.15%	1.35%	15,840,888	15,840,889	1.35%	15,840,888	15,840,889
B3	BBB–	2.05%	1.30%	15,254,189	15,254,189	1.00%	11,733,991	11,733,991
B4	BB+	2.40%	1.00%	11,733,991	10,274,847	1.00%	11,733,991	10,274,847
NIM				45,298,765	44,880,414		45,391,869	44,974,557
OTE				1,173,399,143	7,087,087		1,173,399,143	7,152,759
					1,193,985,822			1,194,145,638
			Expenses		4,618,797			4,618,797
			Net proceeds		1,189,367,026			1,189,526,841
			Price		101.3608%			101.37744%

excess spread and $2 of released O/C. The $10 is severely discounted, say to a $5 present value. Let's account for the present value of the structure: $98 − $101 + $5 = $2. That is a postage stamp–sized summary of the securitization business.

Now let's consider optimizing the allocation. First consider a shift in the bond allocation with no change in O/C. $98 of bonds is still sold in the new allocation. The only thing that changes is there is now more excess spread. Thus the residual cash flow increases, say from $10 to $11. It is still heavily discounted, say to $5.5. Thus the structure is now worth $98 − $101 + $5.5 = $2.5.

What happens if O/C is decreased? Suppose $99 of bonds are sold in the new allocation with $1 of O/C. All other things being equal, the one thing that changes is there is now less O/C to be released to the residual. Suppose the residual cash flow is thus $9 over the lifetime of the structure. Say the $9 is discounted to $4.5. Accounting for the present value of structure: $99 − $101 + $4.5 = $2.5. The $1 change in O/C translated into +$1 of new par bonds issued and −$0.5 change in discounted residual value. This is a trade-off we should make all day long, or at least until O/C disappears. Another way to view this is as follows. O/C can be considered a "virtual" bond with a large spread because it feeds the residual. Thus, O/C should be minimized for the same reason B3 is minimized: moving allocation from O/C upward makes the structure more cost effective.

The sizing algorithm is now described top-down, given the functions *SizeAgency* and *SizeBonds* in Figures 5.2 and 5.3. *SizeAgency* has the following input parameters: *Agency* is the rating agency, *Tranches* is the set of issued bonds, and *Curves* is the set of interest rate curves. First, for every tranche, collateral cash flows stressed at the agency rating are generated (2–4). Second, the bonds are structured multiple times to converge on a stable allocation (5–7). Ordered set *RevTranches* holds the tranches, in reverse order, prepended with O/C (more details about this in the next section). *SizeBonds* is repeated until it converges: each subsequent run uses the final allocation from the previous run. Credit enhancements are computed for each rating (8–11). *SizeAgency* produces a set of bond allocations and credit enhancements as its output. These values are embedded in *Tranches*.

SizeAgency is executed for *each* rating agency of interest. The enhancements from each are combined in the following manner. Starting at the seniormost tranche and moving downwards, the maximum enhancement among all agencies for that tranche is chosen. The allocation assigned to that tranche is the *difference* between this enhancement and the last enhancement (i.e., the enhancement corresponding to the tranche just above). For the seniormost bond, the "last" enhancement is 100%. The combined allocation is

	SizeAgency(Agency, Tranches, Curves)
1	$AgencyCurves = Curves(Agency)$
2	$\forall\, q \in Tranches$
3	$r = q.rating(Agency)$
4	$CFs_{Agency}(r) = Collat_{Agency}(r, AgencyCurves(r))$
5	$RevTranches = (O/C_{init}, O/C_{targ}, rev(Tranches.Sub))$
6	*Repeat until convergence*
7	$SizeBonds(CFs_{Agency}(r), AgencyCurves, RevTranches)$
8	$sum = 0$
9	$\forall\, q \in Tranches$
10	$q.enh = q.alloc + sum$
11	$sum = sum + q.enh$

FIGURE 5.2 Algorithm for Sizing Subordinate Tranches for a Single Rating Agency (Non–Fully Funded)

	SizeBonds(CFs, Curves, Tranches)
1	$MinAlloc = 0$
2	$MinDeltaAlloc = 5$ bps
3	$nsteps = 8$
4	$\forall q \in Tranches$
5	$LastOK = 100\%$
6	$step = MinDeltaAlloc \times 2^{nsteps}$
7	$AllocPct = q.alloc$
8	$\forall i \in [0..nsteps+1]$
9	$eval\ bond\ model(CFs(q.rating),\ Curves(q.rating))$
10	$ok = TRUE$
11	$\forall p \in Tranches \mid p > q$
12	$ok = ok \land timely(p.Int) \land p.DeferredPrin(M) = 0$
13	if ok then $LastOK = min(LastOK, AllocPct)$
14	if $i = nsteps$ then
15	if $LastOK=100\%$ then ERROR else $AllocPct = LastOK$
16	else
17	if ok then
18	$step = min(step, AllocPct/2)$
19	$AllocPct = max(MinAlloc, AllocPct - step)$
20	else
21	$AllocPct = min(LastOK, AllocPct + step)$
22	$AllocPct = int(AllocPct / MinDeltaAlloc) \times MinDeltaAlloc$
23	$AllocChg = AllocPct - q.Alloc$
24	$A1.Alloc = A1.Alloc - AllocChg$
25	$q.Alloc = AllocPct$
26	$step = step/2$

FIGURE 5.3 Core Algorithm for Sizing Subordinate Tranches (Binary Search Version—Simplified)

then evaluated to ensure that it is acceptable for all agencies. We shall see in the next section why this check is necessary.

Subordinate tranches are sized with the core algorithm sketched in Figure 5.3. *SizeBonds* has the following input parameters: *CFs* are a set of collateral cash flows stressed at each tranche rating, *Curves* is the set of interest rate curves, *Tranches* is a reverse-ordered set of subordinate tranches. Other parameters are: *MinAlloc* is the minimum allocation size,[1] *MinDeltaAlloc* is the smallest increment for adjusting allocation, and *nsteps* is the maximum number of iterations used to size each tranche.

The algorithm is essentially a binary search, guessing each allocation, tranche by tranche, and incrementally improving upon its guesses. *SizeBonds* produces a set of tranche allocations as its output. These values are embedded in *Tranches*.

Each tranche is sized, starting with O/C, from the bottom up (4). The tranche currently being sized is called the *pivot*. A *step* starts out large (6), and then decreases in size as the search proceeds. The initial pivot allocation is the last allocation assigned to that tranche (7). A search for a new optimal tranche allocation is conducted over at most *nsteps*+2 iterations (8). For each iteration, the bond structure is reevaluated; that is, the liability cash flows are generated (9). The appropriately stressed collateral cash flows and interest rate curve are selected to evaluate the bond model. For example, the most subordinate bond B4 in Table 5.2 is rated BB+. Thus the BB+ stressed collateral cash flows and forward interest rate curve are used for sizing O/C. Similarly, the BBB− stressed collateral cash flows and forward interest rate curve are used for sizing B4, and so on. Recall from Chapter 3 that Standard & Poor's (S&P) interest rate curves are stressed by rating, but Moody's are not.

To determine the admissibility of the allocation, tranches senior to the pivot must receive timely interest and experience no unrecovered deferred principal in the last period *M* (11–12). A few notes are in order. First, unrecovered deferred principal accumulates from period to period, so a zero value in the last period indicates no principal cash owed. Second, rating agencies define admissibility constraints differently, as summarized in Table 5.3. Third, Moody's requires what is called an Internal Rate of Return (IRR) test. The actual yields of tranches senior to the pivot are compared to their target yields. A target yield is computed from the actual cash flows with the addition of unrecovered deferred principal in the last period. The allocation is admissible if the actual and target yields are within a certain tolerance (e.g., 1 bp).

---

[1] This has been simplified—in reality, different tranches may be required to have different minimum allocations.

TABLE 5.3 Conditions that Must be Met for an Allocation to be Admissible

	S&P	Moody's
Short interest	Not allowed in any period	Not allowed in any period
BRCFA	Don't care	Not allowed in any period
Deferred principal	Not allowed in any period	Not allowed in last period
		IRR test must pass

If a new minimum allocation is found, it is saved in *LastOK* (13). On the last iteration, if no admissible allocation was found, the search fails (15). Otherwise the search returns *LastOK* as the minimum admissible allocation. For all other iterations, if the current allocation is admissible then it is decreased (18–19). If the current allocation is not admissible then it is increased (21). Adjustments must be made when the allocation is near zero (18), less than the minimum required allocation (19), greater than the last admissible solution (21), and not a whole multiple of *MinDeltaAlloc* (22).

The difference between the previous and new pivot allocations (23) must be reallocated to some senior tranche or tranches. As a simplification the difference is assigned here to tranche A1 (24). In reality, for a structure with multiple senior blocks supported by different collateral groups, the difference may be distributed among the blocks in some manner. Furthermore, senior sizing may need to be redone if subordinate sizing reallocates a senior tranche that has not been *reserved* for that purpose.

Finally the derived allocation is reassigned to the tranche (25) in preparation for the next evaluation of the model (9). The *step* size changes by a factor of two each iteration (26), constituting the binary search. As discussed in a later section, other searches are possible and may be more efficient under certain conditions.

5.2.1 Fully Funded versus Non–Fully Funded

There are two ways to size a structure: fully or non–fully funded. This is not related prefunding the assets or funded synthetics—it refers to O/C management. A fully funded structure must initially be over-collateralized as specified by the target O/C (*TargetOCPct$_{Leg}$* in section 4.2). A non–fully funded structure can initially have little or no extra collateral, but rather build it up over time to eventually attain the target O/C. Sizing a fully funded structure is simpler. The first "tranche" to minimize is the target O/C. At each sizing step, initial and target O/C amounts must be kept equal. The ordered set in line (5) in Figure 5.2 is modified as follows:

$$RevTranches = (O/C_{\text{targ}}, rev\,(Tranches.Sub))$$

For a non–fully funded structure, first initial O/C is minimized, followed by target O/C. Initial O/C is constrained only to be less than or equal to target O/C. Prior to minimizing initial O/C, the target O/C is increased by 5%, a suitably large number. Under normal conditions, a non–fully funded structure will have zero initial O/C. However, under stressed conditions (e.g., low asset WAC or high bond spreads) the minimal initial O/C is not zero.

$$RevTranches = (O/C_{\text{init}}, O/C_{\text{targ}}, rev\,(Tranches.Sub))$$

Table 5.4 shows a partial trace of the previous example structure, fully funded. Each row in the table represents a different structure allocation and its evaluation. The target O/C is minimized first to 0.85%. Then the B4

TABLE 5.4 Partial Trace of Sizing Fully Funded Structure

Tranche	Rating	AllocPct	LastOK	Timely int	Timely prin	ok	step
Target O/C	BB+	1.350%	1.35%	TRUE	TRUE	TRUE	0.675%
Target O/C	BB+	0.700%	1.35%	TRUE	FALSE	FALSE	0.338%
Target O/C	BB+	1.050%	1.05%	TRUE	TRUE	TRUE	0.169%
Target O/C	BB+	0.900%	0.90%	TRUE	TRUE	TRUE	0.084%
Target O/C	BB+	0.800%	0.90%	FALSE	FALSE	FALSE	0.042%
Target O/C	BB+	0.850%	0.85%	TRUE	TRUE	TRUE	0.021%
B4	BBB−	1.000%	1.00%	TRUE	TRUE	TRUE	0.500%
B4	BBB−	0.500%	1.00%	TRUE	FALSE	FALSE	0.250%
B4	BBB−	0.750%	1.00%	TRUE	FALSE	FALSE	0.125%
B4	BBB−	0.900%	0.90%	TRUE	TRUE	TRUE	0.063%
B4	BBB−	0.850%	0.85%	TRUE	TRUE	TRUE	0.031%
B4	BBB−	0.800%	0.80%	TRUE	TRUE	TRUE	0.016%
B3	BBB	0.600%	100.00%	TRUE	FALSE	FALSE	12.800%
B3	BBB	13.400%	13.40%	TRUE	TRUE	TRUE	6.400%
B3	BBB	7.000%	7.00%	TRUE	TRUE	TRUE	3.200%
B3	BBB	3.800%	3.80%	TRUE	TRUE	TRUE	1.600%
B3	BBB	2.200%	2.20%	TRUE	TRUE	TRUE	0.800%
B3	BBB	1.400%	1.40%	TRUE	TRUE	TRUE	0.400%
B3	BBB	1.000%	1.40%	TRUE	FALSE	FALSE	0.200%
B3	BBB	1.200%	1.20%	TRUE	TRUE	TRUE	0.100%
B3	BBB	1.100%	1.10%	TRUE	TRUE	TRUE	0.050%
B3	BBB	1.050%	1.05%	TRUE	TRUE	TRUE	0.025%

and B3 tranches are minimized to 0.80% and 1.05% respectively. The pivot allocation (AllocPct), the last valid allocation (LastOK) and the allocation's admissibility (ok) are shown. The step size given is either added or subtracted from the current pivot allocation to produce the next allocation. Note the initial step size is 5 bps $\times 2^8 = 12.8\%$ by default. However, if the allocation is admissible, then step size cannot exceed half the pivot allocation (Figure 5.3, line 18). Thus the initial step size when minimizing O/C and B4 is less than 12.8%.

As described the algorithm will step 10 times per pivot tranche. This trace was generated from a more complex implementation that could exit the iteration early. Only in the case of B3 were 10 iterations needed. In the case of B3, the final allocation of 1.05% may not be a true minimum. Recall that for each agency, this algorithm is repeated until convergence, so if the first B3 allocation is not optimal, subsequent runs will find the optimum. This illustrates how binary search can be inefficient. Although the first B3 allocation of 0.60% wasn't too far from optimal, the search took a giant step higher. Then it took several iterations to cut back that estimate.

Table 5.5 shows a partial trace of a non–fully funded structure. This is the previous example structure, but stressed by adding 200 bps to each issued bond margin. This forces the minimal initial O/C to be nonzero. The target O/C and other tranches also require much higher allocations than in the nonstressed case.

Convergence is not guaranteed—the algorithm can oscillate. Table 5.6 shows an allocation over eight iterations as it oscillates. Oscillation occurs because a tranche is allocated in minimal increments of 5 bps. If this constraint is relaxed, speed of convergence increases in degenerate cases. For example Table 5.6 will slowly converge within 10 iterations.

5.3   OPTIMIZATIONS AND COMPLEXITY

The algorithms described in the previous section can be made to run faster. The required modifications are sketched here.

- Binary search is not efficient if the initial allocation is close to the final result. The first guess the binary search makes is farthest from the initial allocation. It then tightens its guess in subsequent steps. Thus to move one sizing increment from the initial guess, it may require several guesses. In this scenario simple stepwise (incremental) search is better.

  Sizing repeats until convergence. It is best to use binary search for the first sizing because the initial allocation may not be close to the

TABLE 5.5 Partial Trace of Sizing Non–Fully Funded Structure

Tranche	Rating	AllocPct	LastOK	Timely int	Timely prin	ok	step
Init O/C	BB+	1.350%	1.35%	TRUE	TRUE	TRUE	0.675%
Init O/C	BB+	0.700%	1.35%	FALSE	TRUE	FALSE	0.338%
Init O/C	BB+	1.050%	1.05%	TRUE	TRUE	TRUE	0.169%
Init O/C	BB+	0.900%	1.05%	FALSE	TRUE	FALSE	0.084%
Init O/C	BB+	1.000%	1.05%	FALSE	TRUE	FALSE	0.042%
Target O/C	BB+	6.350%	6.35%	TRUE	TRUE	TRUE	3.175%
Target O/C	BB+	3.200%	6.35%	FALSE	TRUE	FALSE	1.588%
Target O/C	BB+	4.800%	4.80%	TRUE	TRUE	TRUE	0.794%
Target O/C	BB+	4.000%	4.00%	TRUE	TRUE	TRUE	0.397%
Target O/C	BB+	3.600%	3.60%	TRUE	TRUE	TRUE	0.198%
Target O/C	BB+	3.400%	3.40%	TRUE	TRUE	TRUE	0.099%
Target O/C	BB+	3.300%	3.40%	FALSE	TRUE	FALSE	0.050%
Target O/C	BB+	3.350%	3.40%	FALSE	TRUE	FALSE	0.025%
B4	BBB−	1.000%	100.00%	FALSE	FALSE	FALSE	12.800%
B4	BBB−	13.800%	13.80%	TRUE	TRUE	TRUE	6.400%
B4	BBB−	7.400%	7.40%	TRUE	TRUE	TRUE	3.200%
B4	BBB−	4.200%	4.20%	TRUE	TRUE	TRUE	1.600%
B4	BBB−	2.600%	4.20%	FALSE	TRUE	FALSE	0.800%
B4	BBB−	3.400%	3.40%	TRUE	TRUE	TRUE	0.400%
B4	BBB−	3.000%	3.00%	TRUE	TRUE	TRUE	0.200%
B4	BBB−	2.800%	3.00%	FALSE	TRUE	FALSE	0.100%
B4	BBB−	2.900%	2.90%	TRUE	TRUE	TRUE	0.050%
B4	BBB−	2.850%	2.85%	TRUE	TRUE	TRUE	0.025%

TABLE 5.6 Eight Sizing Iterations Under S&P Rules for a Degenerate Portfolio That Causes Oscillation. The Portfolio Consists of a Single Fixed-Coupon Loan That is a Mismatch Against the Floating Liabilities.

	1	2	3	4	5	6	7	8
A1	78.90%	78.90%	78.90%	78.90%	78.90%	78.90%	78.90%	78.90%
M1	6.15%	6.10%	6.10%	6.10%	6.10%	6.10%	6.10%	6.10%
M2	4.60%	4.65%	4.65%	4.65%	4.65%	4.65%	4.65%	4.65%
M3	0.05%	0.20%	0.15%	0.15%	0.15%	0.15%	0.15%	0.15%
B1	2.80%	2.80%	2.85%	2.85%	2.85%	2.85%	2.85%	2.85%
B2	0.05%	0.15%	0.10%	0.15%	0.10%	0.15%	0.10%	0.15%
B3	0.05%	0.20%	0.15%	0.15%	0.15%	0.15%	0.15%	0.15%
B4	2.45%	1.75%	2.10%	1.90%	2.05%	1.95%	2.05%	1.95%
O/C	4.95%	5.25%	5.00%	5.15%	5.05%	5.10%	5.05%	5.10%

solution. However, it is best to use stepwise search for subsequent sizings because these should be closer to their input allocations (coming from previous sizings). In practice this hybrid search method proves to be faster than pure binary or pure stepwise search. For example, for a given asset portfolio and structure, pure binary search required 207 steps (i.e., sizings) to converge, averaging 8.6 steps per tranche. The hybrid search required 147 steps averaging 6.1 steps per tranche.

- Root-finding methods (e.g., Press 1992) more sophisticated than binary search fail because of the nature of admissibility. If a solution is inadmissible, the liability cash flows will contain some missed interest and/or principal payments. However, there is no metric with which to differentiate admissible solutions—they have no late interest or principal payments. Total missing interest plus principal as a function of allocation size therefore has a *discontinuity* at the minimum solution. Root-finding methods cannot deal with such a discontinuity.

- A good initial allocation increases the speed of binary search. One idea for estimating a good initial allocation is by empirical study. This makes sense if the takeout structure is stable over time. Suppose one ran thousands of replines with different loan characteristics and priced each one for the takeout structure. Imagine categorizing these prices, and their corresponding allocations, in a multidimensional database indexed by the loan characteristics. Given a portfolio with certain average loan characteristics, one could index the database and retrieve the allocation as an initial guess. To keep the database size practical, binning is required over the dimensions. The database would necessarily have to be regenerated when interest rate, prepay, default, or recovery characteristics change significantly.

- In the algorithm previously described, the cash flow model does not make use of the knowledge *that it is being executed within the sizer*. This information is potentially valuable. For example, S&P rejects an allocation that causes principal to be deferred in any period, even if that principal is repaid in a subsequent period. Thus, if the model knows it is doing an S&P sizing, it can terminate as soon as it sees deferred principal. The model exits from that period straight back to the sizer, which rejects the allocation. This saves evaluating the full number of periods in the model.

In practice this optimization does speed up evaluation. However, it must be used with caution. For example, quickly exiting the model if *interest* is not paid in a timely manner is not practical in a VBA implementation of mine. It requires a test at the bottom of the waterfall that checks every tranche to determine if any unpaid interest remains. The cost of repeating this test every period outweighs the savings should the test allow a quick exit. However, with judicious recoding or in another programming language it may produce speedups.

- The stepwise search previously discussed can be inefficient when the initial allocation is far from the solution. If step size is *doubled*, then the *number* of steps should be approximately cut in *half*. This idea requires an extra step at the end to narrow the solution back within the required accuracy. Practically, this optimization is a mixed bag. Sometimes it runs faster and sometimes slower than pure stepwise search. The problem is with the required extra step. There are cases where simple stepwise search finds a tranche allocation in *two* steps. In this scenario, doubling the step size will find the allocation in *three* steps. So if there are enough of these cases, the added overhead of doubling step size detracts from its gains.

- All these optimizations involve a trade-off between the overhead of testing for an optimization and the savings from the optimization. Increasing the speed of the cash flow model is a pure play—it will always lead to faster sizing. However, finding speed optimizations in the model becomes increasingly difficult as the complexity of the model increases. As features are added to the model it becomes increasingly important to have a transparent implementation. Usually, transparency is at odds with speed.

Sizing a structure is a heavy computational burden on the model. There are two distinct modes of sizing a structure: portfolio-level and loan-level, as illustrated in Figure 5.4. Portfolio-level sizing supports the liability structure with the entire loan portfolio (all replines belong to a single portfolio). Loan-level sizing treats each repline as if it were a self-contained portfolio supporting the entire liability structure.

In each mode, asset cash flows are generated (2–6) and fed to the liability model (7–11). The structure is sized until it convergences to an optimal allocation (7). Each such run "locally" optimizes each subordinate bond, from the bottom up (8). To optimize a given bond requires a search for the minimum bond size (9). To determine if a given bond size is admissible requires iterating the liability cash flow model over the amortization schedule (10–11).

This figure has been simplified as follows. First, senior sizing is ignored. Second, the repeated searches for the minimum tranche size can use different search techniques, as discussed above. Third, each rating agency does not generate asset cash flows in the same manner. Fourth, the innermost loop (10–11) can exit early as previously discussed.

1	*for each portfolio*
2	*for each rating agency*
3	*for each tranche rating*
4	*for each repline*
5	*for each period*
6	*generate asset CFs*
7	*do until converged*
8	*for each subordinate tranche*
9	*while searching for optimal tranche size*
10	*for each period*
11	*generate liability CFs*

FIGURE 5.4   Sizing Complexity (Stylized). Portfolio-Level Sizing has a Single Portfolio Filled with All Replines. Loan-Level Sizing Has Many Portfolios, Each Consisting of One Repline.

5.4   EXAMPLE OF SIZING

The sizing algorithms are now illustrated in the context of a hypothetical deal. The deal was assumed to be fully funded, that is, the initial and target O/C amounts are equal. The deal has four senior tranches supported by two collateral groups (A1 is solely supported by one group). First, senior sizing was performed. To drive the senior sizing, target WALs are 0.8 years for A2 and 2.2 years for A3. Second, subordinate sizing was performed with both S&P and Moody's collateral models. Subordinate sizing converged after four iterations.

Table 5.7 summarizes the sizing results. The initial allocation prior to any sizing is shown on the left. The junior sizing results for each rating agency is then listed, with the same senior sizing results. To achieve the target WALs, allocation was shifted from A2 to A4. The S&P and Moody's subordinate results are dissimilar. Although Moody's has the higher required O/C of 2%, S&P has higher credit enhancements for other bonds. For example, the seniors require 22.3% enhancement by S&P and only 16.65% by Moody's.

The lower right columns in Table 5.7 combine the two rating agency results. A simple algorithm is used: the maximum of each tranche's minimum required enhancement by each agency is chosen (column "Max enhance"). Differences between successive enhancements are the allocations (column "Subord alloc"). The senior allocation is prepended to the subordinate allocation by taking the slack from A4, being the most expensive senior bond (column "Final alloc").

The astute reader will cry foul. Although each step seems logical, is the result? The minimum 2% Moody's O/C assumed for instance a 5.6% M1

TABLE 5.7 Sample Sizing. Each Rating Agency's Converged Allocation is Shown in "Alloc 4" Columns. The Combined Allocation is in the Lower Right.

S&P

Class	Initial	Rating	Alloc 1	Alloc 2	Alloc 3	Alloc 4	Enhance
A1	45.68	AAA	42.38	42.38	42.38	42.38	
A2	18.92	AAA	15.19	15.19	15.19	15.19	
A3	8.98	AAA	8.87	8.87	8.87	8.87	
A4	7.42	AAA	11.26	11.26	11.26	11.26	22.30
M1	6.10	AA	10.05	10.20	10.20	10.20	12.10
M2	5.50	A	4.65	4.70	4.70	4.70	7.40
M3	1.50	A−	1.00	1.00	1.00	1.00	6.40
B1	1.50	BBB+	1.05	1.00	1.00	1.00	5.40
B2	1.25	BBB	0.85	0.90	0.95	0.90	4.50
B3	1.15	BBB−	0.75	1.00	0.85	0.95	3.55
B4	0.75	BB+	2.50	2.00	2.15	2.10	1.45
O/C	1.25		1.45	1.50	1.45	1.45	

Moodys

Class	Initial	Rating	Alloc 1	Alloc 2	Alloc 3	Alloc 4	Enhance	Max enhance	Subord alloc	Final alloc
A1	45.68	Aaa	48.03	48.03	48.03	48.03			77.70	48.03
A2	18.92	Aaa	15.19	15.19	15.19	15.19				15.19
A3	8.98	Aaa	8.87	8.87	8.87	8.87				8.87
A4	7.42	Aaa	11.26	11.26	11.26	11.26	16.65	22.30		5.61
M1	6.10	Aa2	5.80	5.60	5.60	5.60	11.05	12.10	10.20	10.20
M2	5.50	A2	4.45	4.40	4.40	4.40	6.65	7.40	4.70	4.70
M3	1.50	A3	1.15	1.15	1.15	1.15	5.50	6.40	1.00	1.00
B1	1.50	Baa1	1.05	1.10	1.10	1.05	4.45	5.40	1.00	1.00
B2	1.25	Baa2	1.00	0.95	0.85	0.95	3.50	4.50	0.90	0.90
B3	1.15	Baa3	0.15	0.50	0.50	0.50	3.00	3.55	0.95	0.95
B4	0.75	Ba1	1.00	1.00	1.00	1.00	2.00	2.00	1.55	1.55
O/C	1.25		2.05	1.95	2.05	2.00	2.00			2.00

allocation. The final allocation has a 10.2% M1 allocation. The worry is that S&P's relatively high senior enhancement requirement sucks more cash from the combined allocation than is anticipated by the minimum Moody's 2% O/C. It could be that the final allocation no longer satisfies Moody's.

This example was purposely chosen to illustrate this quirky problem. Luckily, it can happen only when the agencies are significantly pulling the allocation in different directions. Recent stricter evaluation of second liens by S&P (Standard and Poor's 2006) has evened out the agencies. Most deals in the market do not exhibit such unbalanced behavior, and the simple combining algorithm is sufficient. Finding a solution to the general problem is left as an exercise for the reader!

Notice that in this example each subordinate tranche has a unique rating. The ratings are also ordered. Subordinate sizing works only if the tranches have unique and ordered ratings. If either of these criteria is not met, the sizing algorithm will produce strange results. For example, if multiple consecutive tranches have the *same* rating, the algorithm will derive a positive allocation for the most senior (cheaper) tranche and *minimum* allocation (*MinAlloc*) for the more junior (expensive) tranches. There is no distinguishing characteristic to steer the sizer to a different conclusion. In practice, multiple tranches can have the same ratings. In this case the allocation among them is determined with different criteria.

5.5 NIM AND OTE SIZING

One complication of sizing a structure is that the NIM and OTE stress assumptions will likely differ from those of the issued bonds. The key differences are summarized in Table 5.8 and Table 5.9. Although there are alternatives, the methodology presented here is a good base. In broad strokes, sizing pre-NIM (issued) bonds uses prepayment and interest rate curves specific to both repline and rating agency. For example, when sizing bonds under S&P BBB rating stresses, generating the collateral cash flow for an ARM loan requires an S&P ARM prepayment curve and a BBB interest rate curve. Pricing NIM and OTE notes uses the standard PSA model, hence the modeler has flexibility in specifying the prepayment and interest rate curves.

The prepayment curve is stressed by a multiplier. For sizing the issued bonds, this multiplier is one. Higher stresses are often used for NIM and OTE notes. No losses are assumed when sizing the issued bonds. Higher cumulative losses, with an appropriate distribution over time, are often used for NIM and OTE notes. All the tranches are run to maturity rather than to call date. Issued bonds and the OTE are usually modeled with O/C step down enabled, though NIMs are not.

TABLE 5.8 Differences in Stress Assumptions for Tranche Sizing

	Pre-NIM (issued bonds)	NIMs	Post-NIM (OTE)
Prepay curve	Repline and agency specific	Repline specific	Repline specific
Repline rates	See Table 5.9	Dynamic fwd 6mL curve	Dynamic fwd 6mL curve
Tranche rates	See Table 5.9	Dynamic fwd 1mL curve	Dynamic fwd 1mL curve
Prepay speed	100%	Use appropriate stress	Use appropriate stress
Loss	0%	Use appropriate stress	Use appropriate stress
Run to maturity	TRUE	TRUE	TRUE
O/C stepdown	TRUE	FALSE	TRUE
Yield	Market specific	Market specific	Market specific (very high)
Price	Par except for some subordinate tranches	Below par	Far below par
Sizing method	Algorithms given in previous sections	Keep changing NIM size until target yield is achieved, assuming pre-NIM derived allocations	Price OTE with target yield, using CFs assuming pre-NIM and NIM derived allocations

TABLE 5.9 Differences in Interest Rate Assumptions for Pre-NIM Tranche Sizing

Tranche	Asset/Liability	Agency	What to use for interest rates?
Senior	Repline		Static
	Tranche		Static
Subord	Repline	S&P	S&P curve, rating and repline specific
		Moodys	Moody's curve
	Tranche	S&P	S&P curve, rating specific
		Moodys	Moody's curve

Issued bonds are generally priced at par except for subordinate floating bonds with capped coupons that price under par. NIMs can be sized to achieve both a price (around par) and yield. However, NIMs can also be sized by rating agency constraints, achieving whatever prices correspond to their yields. The OTE is priced to achieve a target yield. Being very risky, OTE yields are high and therefore prices are far below par.

The NIM and OTE tranches receive residual cash flows from the junior-most issued bond. There can be more than one NIM, usually paid down sequentially. Because the NIMs and OTE are at the bottom of the waterfall, their values are highly sensitive to assumptions in the model. For example, consider a deal with a single senior pass-through (class A1) versus another deal with multiple senior tranches. Assume the total senior allocations of both deals are equal. Seniors are split for a variety of reasons, for example, to help sell bonds to desired WAL targets. In addition, a primary reason to split the seniors is to increase the economic value of the NIM and post-NIM. Thus given the market-clearing spreads of the split senior tranches, one would expect to see the OTE price *increase* compared to the original single-class senior deal. By tranching the seniors, cost is lowered and thus residual is increased.

NIMs can be sized different ways. When the rating agencies run the show they impose constraints on the NIM sizes. When the NIMs are not rated, rating agency input is not required. If there is one NIM, a possible objective is to find the size that achieves the market yield for a given price. Usually this price is around par. This can be done with binary search reasonably efficiently. It is interesting to note that because NIM yield as a function of size can be discontinuous, Newton-Raphson will not work. Figure 5.5 plots NIM yield versus size for a typical structure, and the degenerate behavior of Newton-Raphson search. The target yield is 6.74% shown with a dotted line.

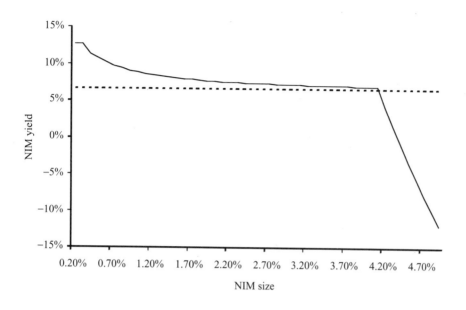

	alloc	yield	error
1	2.00%	7.58%	0.83%
2	3.52%	7.06%	0.31%
3	5.04%	−16.70%	−23.45%
4	3.75%	7.02%	0.27%
5	5.14%	−18.37%	−25.12%
6	3.71%	7.02%	0.27%
7	5.08%	−17.38%	−24.13%
8	3.73%	7.02%	0.27%
9	5.11%	−17.83%	−24.58%
10	3.73%	7.02%	0.27%
11	5.11%	−17.83%	−24.58%

FIGURE 5.5 Example of Newton-Raphson Getting into Trouble Sizing a NIM. Eleven Steps of the Search are Shown on the Left with Oscillating Errors.

	SizeNIMs(Agency, NIMs, Curves)
1	AgencyCurves = Curves(Agency)
2	$\forall\, q \in$ NIMs
3	$r = q.rating(Agency)$
4	$CFs_{Agency}(r) = Collat_{Agency}(AgencyCurves(r))$
5	eval bond model($CFs_{Agency}(r)$, AgencyCurves(r))
6	Allocs = gen all NIM allocations over certain ranges
7	$\forall\, alloc \in$ Allocs
8	alloc.ok = TRUE
9	$\forall\, q \in$ NIMs
10	eval NIM model(alloc, q.Residual)
11	alloc.ok = alloc.ok $\wedge$ q.Bal(ThresholdPeriod) = 0

FIGURE 5.6 Algorithm for Determining Feasible NIMs Allocations under a Rating Agency's Constraints

If there are multiple NIMs, a possible objective is to find the size that minimizes cost or maximizes value of all the NIMs given their yields (leaving price unconstrained). For sizing rated NIMs, the different agencies have different rules. Let's review S&P's requirements to get the overall flavor. S&P specifies that each NIM must be modeled with inputs stressed to the level of their assigned rating. So if the first NIM is to be rated BBB+, then a BBB+ interest rate curve must be used. Prepayment curves appropriate to NIM stresses (and specialized for different collateral types) must be used. Furthermore, a time limit is specified such that all NIMs must pay down fully prior to that period. So it is much like sizing subordinate bonds with the addition of a hard amortization deadline, say around five years.

Figure 5.6 sketches an algorithm for determining if multiple NIM allocations are feasible under constraints. *SizeNIMs* is a function that takes three inputs: *Agency* is the rating agency, *NIMs* is the NIM tranches, and *Curves* is the set of interest rate curves. For each NIM the collateral model is run for interest rates corresponding to that NIM's rating (1–4). The collateral cash flows and interest rates are used to evaluate the bond model (5). The key output of the bond model in this case is the pre-NIM residual cash flow. Next, a set of NIM allocations is generated with no regard to feasibility by the rating agency (6). For example, given three NIMs this set might have $51 \times 11 \times 11 = 6{,}171$ allocations and look like:

$$[0\%..5\%] \times [0\%..1\%] \times [0\%..1\%] = \{(0.0\%, 0.0\%, 0.0\%),$$

$$(0.0\%, 0.0\%, 0.1\%), (0.0\%, 0.0\%, 0.2\%), \dots, (5.0\%, 1.0\%, 1.0\%)\}$$

TABLE 5.10 Various NIM Tranches in the Market and Their Average Ratings, Coupons, and Sizes

	# bonds	Rating	Coupon	% of NIMs	% of Collateral
N1	32	BBB	5.8%	79.1%	2.8%
N2	29	BB+	7.0%	11.3%	0.4%
N3	18	BB	6.1%	11.5%	0.4%
N4	7	BB	7.5%	19.2%	1.0%

This brute force approach can be taken because evaluation of the full bond model, which is expensive, occurs only *once* for each NIM. Evaluation of the NIM model occurs thousands of times but is cheap to execute. For each such allocation, for each NIM, a NIM cash flow model is evaluated (7–10). The model is fed the pre-NIM residual associated with each NIM's rating (10). An allocation is feasible if each NIM, under its rating-induced residual, pays down prior to the threshold period (11).

Now that each allocation's feasibility has been determined, one can find the optimal allocation given an objective function. For example, to minimize cost, choose the feasible allocation with the least coupon, that is, the most N1, followed by the most N2, and so on. Alternatively, to maximize value, choose the feasible allocation with the greatest present value. The present value can be calculated assuming a cash flow scenario (e.g., that of Table 5.8), different from the ones used for determining feasibility. This optimization is further discussed in section 5.7.

So, how do the NIMs get allocated in reality? Table 5.10 shows the average sizes of 86 NIMs sampled from settled deals in the market. The column "% of NIMs" giving the allocation breakdown among the NIMs does not add up to 100% because not all structures have four NIMs.

5.6 CLASS ARCHITECTURE

5.6.1 Inheritance Revisited

In this and previous chapters, various search algorithms were introduced. For example, this chapter discussed how to optimize bond allocation with the objective of realizing target WAL or minimizing average WAC. NIM allocation was also discussed: searching for a yield given a price, and minimizing cost under rating agency constraints. Section 3.2 discussed searching for an optimal loan portfolio under constraints. Section 3.6 discussed how to search for an effective loss coverage that achieves a target loss coverage in the Moody's collateral model. Section B.3 of Appendix B reviews the traditional search problem of deriving a yield from a given bond price (and its cash flows). Section B.5 of Appendix B describes a bootstrapping method for deriving hazard rates from credit default swap (CDS) spreads. These various search problems are summarized in Table 5.11.

Weak inheritance proves helpful here as in section 3.8. Consider how to implement subordinate sizing as described above. One problem glossed over in Figure 5.3 is that different agencies can have different admissibility criteria. Let's sketch an architecture for this. Five classes are used: Functional and Search (as defined in section 3.8), Sizer (a general class that contains the algorithms described in this section), SPEval, and MoodysEval. The latter two classes are necessary stubs as explained below.

The Sizer class will contain the following three public methods. SPEval and MoodysEval (code not shown) run the bond cash flow model and evaluate the cash flows according to the appropriate admissibility criteria. SizeBonds instantiates a Search object for doing the heavy lifting.

```
Public Function SPEval(params As Variant) As Variant
    <run liability model and check if cash flows admissible by S&P>
End Function

Public Function MoodysEval(params As Variant) As Variant
    <run liability model and check if cash flows admissible by Moodys>
End Function

Public Function SizeBonds( _
    Agency As String,
    params As Variant, ...)

    Dim Search As New Search

    If Agency = "S&P" Then
        Dim f As New SPEval
        Set f.Sizer = Me
        SizeBonds = Search.BinarySearch(f, params, ...)
        Set f = Nothing
    ElseIf Agency = "Moodys" Then
        Dim g As New MoodysEval
        Set g.Sizer = Me
        SizeBonds = Search.BinarySearch(g, params, ...)
        Set g = Nothing
    End If

    Set Search = Nothing
End Sub
```

TABLE 5.11 Summary of Search Algorithms Used in This Book

Problem	Input	Output	Solution	Refer to
Find optimal loan portfolio under certain constraints.	Loan universe	Loan portfolio	Zero-one program simulated annealing	Section 3.2
Find effective loss coverage (LC) to achieve target LC in Moody's.	Target LC	Collateral cash flows	Interpolation search	Section 3.6.2
Find bond allocation among same-rated block of sequential bonds, to achieve target WALs.	Target WALs	Bond allocations	Split amort. schedule	Section 5.1
Find bond allocation to achieve minimum average WAC.	Bond ratings	Bond allocations	Binary search Incremental search	Section 5.2
Find NIM allocation to achieve yield and price.	Yield & price	Bond allocations	Binary search	Section 5.5
Find NIM allocation to achieve minimum WAC.	Threshold period	Bond allocations	Brute-force search	Figure 5.6
Find yield, given bond price.	Bond price Bond cash flows	Bond yield	Newton-Raphson	Figure B.2
Find hazard rates, given CDS spread term structure.	CDS spreads	Hazard rates	Newton-Raphson	Appendix B.5

Assume that the core algorithm outlined in Figure 5.3 is implemented as a public method BinarySearch in the Search class. Based loosely on InterpolationSearch in section 3.8, BinarySearch is passed a Functional object (CoreFunction) and various parameters packaged together (params). For simplicity, the inputs (cash flows, curves and tranches) and outputs (a new allocation) of the search are both encapsulated in params.

```
Public Sub BinarySearch( _
    CoreFunction As Functional, _
    params As Variant,...)
    . . .
    Out_ = CoreFunction.Eval(params)
    . . .
End Sub
```

Recall that every search procedure needs an evaluation function, called the Eval method in the Functional class. *We cannot make Sizer inherit from Functional because more than one evaluation function is needed.* Stated another way, if Sizer inherits from Functional, it must abide by the Functional interface that requires one public Eval function. This Eval method is to be used by the Search class to evaluate some aspect of the Functional object. In the application here, Sizer needs at least two Eval functions: one for each rating agency. The Functional interface calls for one Eval not two or more. What to do?

The idea is to define two stub classes that are Functional. Let's name them SPEval and MoodysEval to show their close relationship with Sizer methods of the same names. The SPEval class is defined as follows. The Sizer object is passed in so that the appropriate evaluation function can be used here. To reuse Functional as it was previously defined, a public data member for Sizer was included. A safer way to implement this is with a Let Property.

```
Implements Functional

Public Sizer As Sizer

Public Function Functional_Eval ( _
    params As Variant) As Variant
    Functional_Eval = Sizer.SPEval(params)
End Function
```

The MoodysEval class is defined similarly.

```
Implements Functional

Public Sizer As Sizer

Public Function Functional_Eval ( _
    params As Variant) As Variant
    Functional_Eval = Sizer.MoodysEval(params)
End Function
```

Let's review how this all works. A Sizer object is instantiated when sizing is to be performed. Its SizeBonds method is invoked. First, it instantiates a new Search object. Then, depending on the rating agency, either an SPEval or MoodysEval object will be briefly instantiated. Suppose it is S&P, the key code in SizeBonds is repeated below:

```
Dim f As New SPEval
Set f.Sizer = Me
SizeBonds = Search.BinarySearch(f, params, ...)
Set f = Nothing
```

Like a mayfly, the SPEval object lives only long enough to do the search. It attaches the Sizer ("Me" above) to itself (as the public Sizer member) and passes itself to the Search object. The Search object then invokes the Eval method from it. It may look inelegant on first or second glance, but is quite powerful.

5.6.2 Odds and Ends

Figure 5.7 summarizes, in broad strokes, one possible architecture of the models presented in this text. The dotted boxes represent inheritance. Overall execution of the models is managed by the Sizer class, getting its inputs through a GUI (Graphical User Interface) class. There are various modes of operation of the actual implementation, e.g., evaluating benchmarks for verification, running batch jobs for daily pricing, searching, etc. The Structure class represents a deal with assets (CollatModel) and liabilities (Waterfall, Leg, and Tranche classes). Structure generates bond cash flows by invoking both Leg and Waterfall objects. Legs encapsulate "standard" waterfall rules and Waterfall objects encapsulate deal-specific rules.

It is up to the model builder where to place rules. For example, if one usually models deals with the same O/C management rules, then O/C management should be done in the Leg. If one does deals with varying senior structures, then the priority of payments for seniors should be done in the Waterfall. It is interesting to note that the agencies are child classes for assets

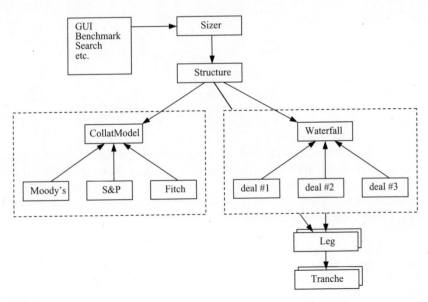

FIGURE 5.7 Sketch of Overall Model Architecture (From 30,000 Feet)

but not liabilities. As discussed in Chapter 3, this choice reflects that agencies differ most in the stresses they impose upon the collateral model. By the time collateral cash flows are generated, the agencies all agree (more or less) on how liabilities should be modeled. If there are any differences of opinion among the agencies on the liability side, they are parameterized.

Modeling is essentially abstraction and simplification while producing an accurate estimate of some aspect of reality. For example, in the implementation of the models described here, cash flows are scheduled period by period. In reality, a period has finer granularity with asset and liability payments not occurring at the same time. The assets themselves don't all pay at the same time. The intricacies of managing payments (performed by the servicer and trustee) are swept under the rug. This is a good abstraction—a microscopic view of cash flow does not lead to a more accurate estimate of bond value.

Notes about good implementation practice:

- Segregate data inputs and assumptions from structural logic. Market data needs to be segregated from deal data. For example, a LIBOR curve is market data, whereas the prepayment curve is a deal assumption. Each rating agency makes different assumptions, so these must be clearly organized. The model has various assumptions (tranche information, etc.), including stress scenarios (e.g., NIMs are stressed differently

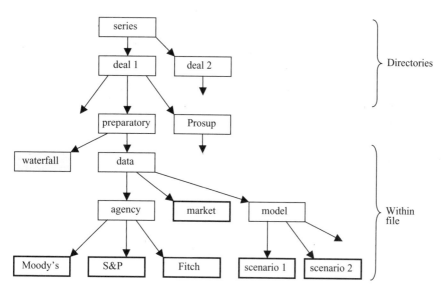

FIGURE 5.8 Deal Management Hierarchy

than the issued bonds). There are often multiple views of the same deal, for example, the preliminary structure as it is being designed and the structure as described in the prospectus. Each deal is likely a member in a series of similar deals (the "shelf"), and hence all should be given a uniform representation. Figure 5.8 sketches a hierarchy. Packaging a deal view into an Excel file can facilitate management. The file encapsulates all the assumptions made in a given view and can be easily transferred between counterparties. The exception in Figure 5.8 is the "waterfall" specification, which is a coded class within the model implementation itself. It is possible to include the waterfall specification *in the deal view* for the active waterfall model described in section 4.11.3.

- Output can also be managed within the deal files discussed above. Standard output reports might be components of a deal file. It is important to include benchmarking, calibration, and valuation outputs in a uniform way across all deals. For example, once a deal is settled, it should become a model benchmark. The cash flows corresponding to certain scenarios are saved in the deal file. All future releases of the model must pass a benchmark test. In this test, each deal with saved results is reevaluated on the new model, and the old and new cash flows are compared. As the number of benchmarks increases, the probability increases that passing the benchmark suite implies that the new model has no new bugs. As assumptions change from deal to deal, the benchmarking process remains valid because those assumptions are encapsulated in each deal file.

5.7 *DOING IT IN EXCEL*: SOLVER

Sizing the tranches is a nonlinear optimization problem—small changes in the allocation can alter cash flows in a discontinuous fashion. In a trivial sense, the optimizations run under linear constraints because each allocation must lie between 0% and 100% inclusive, and all allocations must add up to 100% (by convention in this book, all percentages are of the initial collateral balance). The Excel Solver is a useful tool for solving such problems. If one were to implement the models described in the previous chapters in a spreadsheet, the Solver could be best used for subordinate and NIM sizing.

For subordinates, a macro would be needed to loop through a succession of Solver calls, one per tranche, from subordinate to senior, each one evaluating the model to determine if constraints are met. The key constraint is that the total deferred interest and principal for all tranches senior to this tranche is zero. The objective is to minimize the allocation of this tranche. Then this entire procedure would be repeated until convergence and repeated again for each rating agency.

For NIM allocation under S&P constraints, each NIM is stressed in accordance with its rating. A NIM allocation is feasible if it amortizes down within an allotted period of time, given those stresses. The NIMs are valued, however, under a different, shared scenario. Thus feasibility and optimality are measured on two different scales. This makes NIM allocation tricky.

Consider a two-tier NIM, N1 and N2, as summarized at the top right of Figure 5.9. N1 has a fixed coupon of 6% equal to its market yield. N2 has a coupon of 7% with a yield of 9%. The OTE has a 30% yield. Currently, the allocations assigned to the NIMs are 3% and 0.5% respectively. The total collateral is $1B. The pre-NIM residual (column B), computed from modeling all the issued bonds (under Table 5.8 OTE stress), is given as the input to this NIM model. Since N1 is priced at par, its present value is $30MM. N2 is below par and its present value is less than its initial balance of $5MM. The OTE is deeply discounted at 30% and has a present value of around $8.6MM.

The formulae shown for each cell are copied up and down each column, except for period 0 which holds the initial conditions. If there is sufficient residual cash feeding the NIMs (column B), then interest is paid concurrently (columns C and D). If there is insufficient cash then interest may be deferred—this is not modeled here because the optimization does not consider such scenarios (they are inferior). NIM principal is paid sequentially. First N1 gets paid down as much as is possible (column F). Thus in Figure 5.9 N1 amortizes until period 21, while N2 pays only interest. As each NIM pays down, its successive NIM is allowed to pay principal. In this case, N2 amortizes from period 22 to 28 (column I). When all NIMs are paid down, any remaining

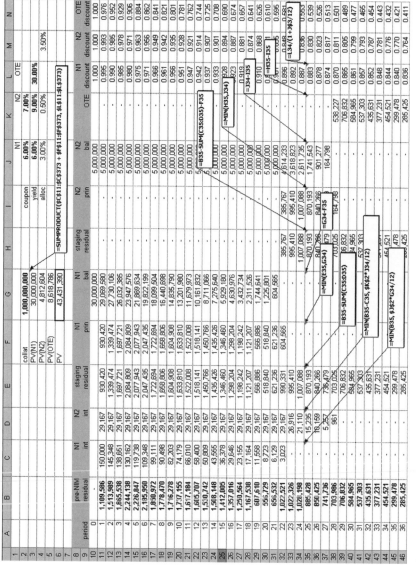

FIGURE 5.9 Simplified Model of Two NIMs in Excel (No Deferred Interest)

residual goes to the OTE. Discount factors are computed and the present values are computed as shown for N1 (cell G3).

Now we are ready to use the Solver to find the allocation (cells J4 and K4) that maximize the total present value (cell G6) under certain constraints. Let's start with constraints that each NIM must totally pay down by period 360, each individual allocation must be greater than or equal to 0%, and the total NIM allocation must be less than or equal to 100%. Figure 5.10 shows the Solver window for setting up constraints and other controls for the optimization. The objective function's value goes in the "target" cell—in this case $G$6. A number of independent variables can be modified, in this case $J$4:$K$4. The (linear) constraints themselves are entered in a drop-down window in a self-explanatory manner.

When the "Solve" button is hit, a search algorithm runs for a bit and another window pops up indicating whether a solution is found. In this case, the solution is N1 = 13.59% and N2 = 0%. By overwriting cells J4:K4 with this allocation, the spreadsheet shows that N1 amortizes all the way to period 360, starving N2 and OTE. This gives the maximum value of $135MM. The solution is valid, although unintended. Without more constraints, N2 and OTE's high discount factors will preclude them from getting any allocation. In any case, the rating agencies will not allow a NIM to mature past a few years at best.

As previously noted, an entirely different set of stresses is used by S&P for instance to determine if a given NIM allocation is feasible, that is, amortizes within a certain period. For each NIM, another pre-NIM residual generated

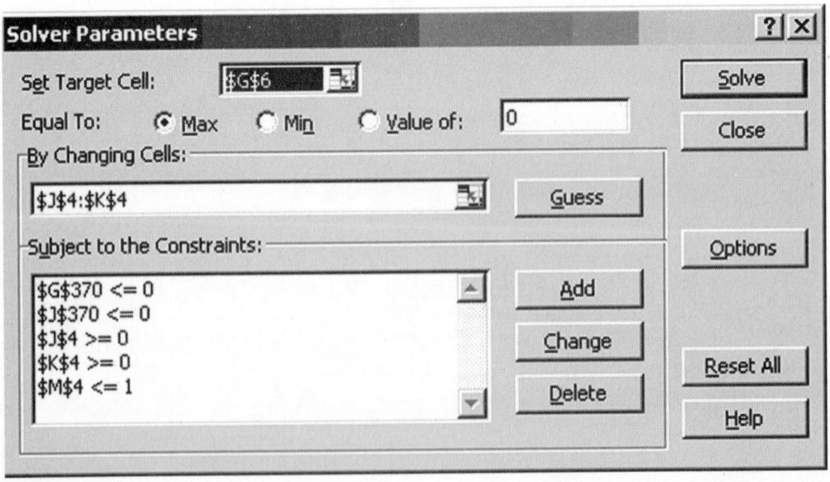

FIGURE 5.10 Setting Up Constraints in Solver

under its rated stress is needed. For this example, suppose N1 and N2 were to be rated BBB+ and BBB− by S&P. Two new "feasibility" residuals would be generated to go along with the previous "valuation" residual in Figure 5.9. Each residual would have its own cash flow model identical to that in Figure 5.9. Unfortunately, all Solver inputs must reside on the same sheet, so the two new cash flows must join the third. The N1-stressed model is shown in Figure 5.11. Note that the incoming residuals (column B) are significantly different. The N2-stressed model is similar. Both of these models take their allocations from that in Figure 5.9.

Suppose that N1 is to be constrained to amortize by 18 months. To implement this, the first constraint in Figure 5.10 is changed to $V$28 <= 0. N2 is constrained in a similar manner. If we constrain N2 to amortize by 23 months and resolve, the answer becomes 2.91% N1 and 0.60% N2 for a present value (including OTE) of $43MM. It should be noted that the Solver is a bit squirrelly, that is, it can produce slightly different results given different initial guesses for the independent variables. This is a concern if getting the absolute optimum solution is critical.

5.8 EXERCISES

5.1. A *decrement table* is an amortization table for each tranche in a structure, for a series of prepayment stresses. Thus the table has three dimensions: time (usually in years) vs. tranche vs. prepay speed. Each entry in the table is a percentage of outstanding bond balances. The first row of the table, at settlement or year zero, is 100% for each tranche. A PSA collateral cash flow model is used, assuming zero loss. Extend your full asset/liability model to create and display a decrement table for a given series of speeds.

5.2. Generalize the decrement tables previously described. Allow the user to specify the three dimensions. For instance: year vs. tranche vs. speed would display differently than year vs. speed vs. tranche. Alternatively, one could specify year vs. tranche vs. loss.

5.3. Create a table of weighted-average life (WAL) for each tranche as a function of prepay speed. Show two WALs for each tranche: to maturity and to call.

5.4. A *cash cap table* shows the effective interest rates for each tranche, for each period, under a given set of assumptions. Thus the table has two dimensions: time (usually in years) vs. tranche. Each entry in the table is an annualized effective interest rate: interest paid plus the BRCFA paid divided by the previous period balance for that tranche. This

period	pre-NIM residual	N1 int	N2 int	staging residual	N1 prin	N1 bal	staging residual	N2 prin	N2 bal	OTE	N1 discount	N2 discount	OTE discount
0						29,078,481			5,984,396		1.000	1.000	1.000
1	2,179,922	145,392	34,909	1,999,621	1,999,621	27,078,860	-	-	5,984,396	-	0.995	0.993	0.976
2	2,039,566	135,394	34,909	1,869,263	1,869,263	25,209,598	-	-	5,984,396	-	0.990	0.985	0.952
3	2,147,326	126,048	34,909	1,986,369	1,986,369	23,223,229	-	-	5,984,396	-	0.985	0.978	0.929
4	2,141,152	116,116	34,909	1,990,127	1,990,127	21,233,102	-	-	5,984,396	-	0.980	0.971	0.906
5	2,014,637	106,166	34,909	1,873,563	1,873,563	19,369,539	-	-	5,984,396	-	0.975	0.963	0.884
6	2,110,642	96,798	34,909	1,978,936	1,978,936	17,380,604	-	-	5,984,396	-	0.971	0.956	0.862
7	1,825,899	86,903	34,909	1,704,087	1,704,087	15,676,517	-	-	5,984,396	-	0.966	0.949	0.841
8	1,910,892	78,383	34,909	1,797,600	1,797,600	13,878,917	-	-	5,984,396	-	0.961	0.942	0.821
9	1,874,888	69,395	34,909	1,770,585	1,770,585	12,108,332	-	-	5,984,396	-	0.956	0.935	0.801
10	1,515,954	60,542	34,909	1,420,503	1,420,503	10,687,829	-	-	5,984,396	-	0.951	0.928	0.781
11	1,751,195	53,439	34,909	1,662,847	1,662,847	9,024,982	-	-	5,984,396	-	0.947	0.921	0.762
12	1,375,710	45,125	34,909	1,295,676	1,295,676	7,729,306	-	-	5,984,396	-	0.942	0.914	0.744
13	1,606,533	38,647	34,909	1,532,978	1,532,978	6,196,328	-	-	5,984,396	-	0.937	0.907	0.725
14	1,437,280	30,982	34,909	1,371,389	1,371,389	4,824,939	-	-	5,984,396	-	0.933	0.901	0.708
15	1,456,216	24,125	34,909	1,397,182	1,397,182	3,427,757	-	-	5,984,396	-	0.928	0.894	0.690
16	1,403,082	17,139	34,909	1,351,035	1,351,035	2,076,722	-	-	5,984,396	-	0.923	0.887	0.674
17	1,190,227	10,384	34,909	1,144,935	1,144,935	931,788	-	-	5,984,396	-	0.919	0.881	0.657
18	971,453	4,659	34,908	931,885	931,788		98	98	5,984,298		0.914	0.874	0.641
19	1,006,806	-	34,908	971,898			971,898	971,898	5,012,400		0.910	0.868	0.626
20	1,058,203	-	29,239	1,028,964			1,028,964	1,028,964	3,983,436	-	0.905	0.861	0.610
21	1,044,161	-	23,237	1,020,924	-		1,020,924	1,020,924	2,962,511		0.901	0.855	0.595
22	1,053,875	-	17,281	1,036,594			1,036,594	1,036,594	1,925,918		0.896	0.848	0.581
23	1,086,901	-	11,235	1,075,666			1,075,666	1,075,666	850,251		0.892	0.842	0.567
24	645,003	-	4,960	640,043			640,043	640,043	210,208		0.887	0.836	0.553
25	889,414	-	1,226	888,188			888,188	210,208		677,980	0.883	0.830	0.539
26	825,604	-	-	825,604			825,604			825,604	0.878	0.823	0.526
27	850,850	-	-	850,850			850,850			850,850	0.874	0.817	0.513
28	915,740	-	-	915,740			915,740			915,740	0.870	0.811	0.501
29	918,057	-	-	918,057			918,057			918,057	0.865	0.805	0.489
30	223,278	-	-	223,278			223,278			223,278	0.861	0.799	0.477

FIGURE 5.11 N1 BBB+ Stressed Residual Cash Flows

rate must be adjusted by the appropriate day count. Make the same assumptions as for decrement tables *except* that market rates are 20% flat. This places severe stress on the structure because the WAC caps all trigger and limit interest payouts to bonds. The BRCFA accounts fill up and there isn't enough cash to pay them down. As a result many nuances of the liability waterfall get exercised. Unless the rules are modeled correctly, this table cannot be generated precisely. Extend your model to generate this table.

5.5. An example of a *price/yield table* is shown in Table 5.12. For a given tranche, a price, and a set of loss and prepay speed assumptions, the table shows the yields and other various statistics. The table can be extended/shrunk by specifying different losses and speeds. The PSA collateral cash flow model is used. An additional way to generate the table is to specify the yield and generate the prices. Extend your model to generate this type of table.

5.6. A price/yield table can be reconfigured by specifying different inputs and outputs. For example, Table 5.13 has two inputs: tranches vs. losses, and three outputs: WAL, yield, and price. Generalize your previous implementation to allow rearranging these parameters. Out of the three inputs (tranches, losses, CPR), one must be held constant and the others varied.

5.7. Implement the senior sizing algorithm as described in section 5.1.

5.8. Implement the subordinate sizing algorithm (section 5.2) for a given rating agency. Modify the search to achieve better performance.

TABLE 5.12 Typical Price/Yield Table (Loss vs. Prepayment Rate)

		100% CPR	120% CPR
0% Loss	Avg Life	4.31	3.35
	First Pay	25-Mar-08	25-May-07
	Last Pay	25-Mar-09	25-Feb-08
	Window	46–58	36–45
	Yield	1.637%	1.637%
	Price	100.00	100.00
5% Loss	Avg Life	4.05	3.20
	First Pay	25-Jan-08	25-Apr-07
	Last Pay	25-Nov-08	25-Dec-07
	Window	44–54	35–43
	Yield	1.637%	1.637%
	Price	100.00	100.00

TABLE 5.13   Price/Yield Table (Tranche vs. Loss Rate)

		0% Loss	5% Loss	10% Loss
A1	Avg Life	1.67	1.64	1.61
	Yield	1.336%	1.336%	1.336%
	Price	100.00	100.00	100.00
M1	Avg Life	4.31	4.05	3.95
	Yield	1.637%	1.637%	1.637%
	Price	100.00	100.00	100.00
B1	Avg Life	7.06	6.50	7.23
	Yield	3.336%	3.324%	3.452%
	Price	100.00	100.00	100.00

5.9. Develop an algorithm for combing subordinate allocations among different agencies. Ensure that the resulting solution is both admissible (for all agencies) and optimal, even when rating agency requirements are unbalanced. See the discussion in section 5.4.

5.10. Design and implement a NIM sizing algorithm for multiple NIMs for a *set of agencies*. Research Moody's and Fitch approaches to rating NIMs. How can the individual rating agency optima be combined into a global optimum that is admissible for all agencies?

5.11. List eight instances of simplification of assumptions in the models presented in this book, similar to the one given in section 5.6.2 about pay periods. For four of the simplifications, argue that abstraction is justified given other noise in the model. For four of the simplifications, argue that the abstraction is not justified and give an alternative, more accurate representation.

5.12. Implement senior sizing with duration targets. This will require searching for the right balance (principal cash flow) that will achieve a given duration for each successive tranche.

5.13. Consider the process involved in pricing a bid. Calls for bids arrive at the trading desk at irregular intervals. A bid pool of collateral loans is given. The desk's open position is the loan portfolio already on the books, ready for the next securitization. To evaluate a bid, two breakeven prices are computed.

   a. What is the pool price that achieves the same *dollar* profit in both the open and blended positions ("dollar arb")?

   b. What is the pool price that achieves the same *percentage* dollar profit in both the open and blended positions ("arb")?

   Implement a method for evaluating bids.

CHAPTER 6

Analysis

Get the habit of analysis—analysis will in time enable synthesis to become your habit of mind.

—Frank Lloyd Wright

6.1 RISK FACTORS

In this section the risks affecting returns on a securitized structure are reviewed. The primary example is mortgage securitization, but many of these concepts apply to various types of asset-backed securities.

6.1.1 Prefunding

- For a prefunded deal, if the prefunded amount is not fully spent by the prefunding deadline, say three months after settlement, then the excess prefunding cash is effectively a prepayment that pays down the bonds. This will shorten the bonds and may lessen their yield. In general, if a bond is purchased at a premium and pays down faster than anticipated, then the yield will be lower than anticipated.
- When prefunding assets, the assets purchased may differ slightly from the characteristics stipulated in the the prospectus. This difference should be small and not impact the performance of the deal. A similar risk is inherent in an actively managed collateralized debt obligation (CDO).

6.1.2 Prepayments

- A prepayment option is the ability of a borrower to pay down his loan faster than the scheduled amortization. Various ABS loans have prepayment risk to different degrees: mortgages, student loans, auto loans, and

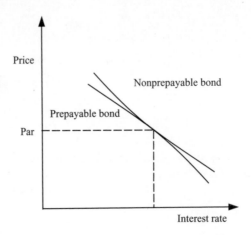

FIGURE 6.1   Sensitivity of Mortgage Bond Price to Interest Rates

the like. In general, prepayment risk is the relative devaluation of a prepayable bond compared to a nonprepayable bond. Consider a par bond. Interest rates ↓→ prepayments ↑→ excess cash needs to be reinvested at lower rates. Interest rates ↑→ prepayments ↓→ weighted-average life (WAL) ↑→ cash stuck in low-yield investment. In both cases, a prepayable bond's value decreases relative to that of a nonprepayble bond, all other things being equal. This is negative convexity, as illustrated in Figure 6.1.

- Another way to look at the economics of prepayments is the same reasoning given under "Prefunding" above. If a bond is purchased at a premium and pays down faster than anticipated then the yield will be lower than anticipated. If a bond is purchased at a discount and pays down slower than anticipated then the yield will also be lower than anticipated. These are sometimes called contraction and extension risks.
- For mortgages, prepayments can generally be discouraged by charging a prepayment penalty. However, the inverse relationship between prepayment penalty and prepayment rate is not guaranteed. Prepayment penalty cash flows contribute directly to the residual, not the issued bonds.
- Prepayment rates are a function of market interest rates. For fixed-rate loans if the market rate decreases below the loan's fixed rate then the probability of that loan's prepayment increases. If the market rate increases above the loan's fixed rate then the probability of that loan's prepayment decreases. During their fixed-rate period, hybrid adjustable-rate mortgage (ARM) loans act like fixed-rate loans with respect to

prepayment rates. Also, upon its first reset, an ARM has a greater probability of defaulting should market rates have increased beyond the loan's initial fixed rate ("reset shock").

6.1.3 Buybacks and Cleanup Calls

- Prepayments can also emanate from an originator making a required buyback of loans. Typical buyback protection lasts for one month after purchase and obligates the originator to repurchase a defaulting loan. After the protection period, the originator may be obligated to repurchase fraudulent loans, for example, misrepresented documentation or violation of the Racketeer-Influenced Corrupt Organization Act (RICO). Such buybacks are effectively prepayments and have the same economics.
- Total prepayment can occur due to a "cleanup" call of the bonds at par. The purpose of a call option on the bonds is to prevent the situation, for a highly amortized structure, where servicing costs exceed income. A typical call option is struck when the collateral balance is less than 10% of its initial value. For mortgages, Net Interest Margin (NIM) economics are sensitive to residual cash flows. In this regard, a NIM holder may wish *not* to exercise the call option in order to keep cash trickling into the NIM. The rating agencies, should they have rated the NIM, may also wish to keep cash flowing to prevent a possible NIM downgrade. Servicers however may wish to exercise the call because they are not breaking even. These counterparties negotiate a call-rights hierarchy before settlement. The prospectus will specify who has the first right to call, the second right to call, etc.
- In general, certain CDOs can be called without meeting any "cleanup" criteria. The residual holder or asset manager owns the option and may exercise in order to structure a new deal under tighter spreads. Investors are at risk that should spreads decline, their bonds may be called, and they will need to reinvest at lower spreads. If the call is at a premium then exercising the option is discouraged.

6.1.4 Defaults

- If defaults increase beyond what is anticipated, realized loss will likely also increase, resulting in lower yield than is anticipated. All forms of credit enhancement in the structure may be insufficient to protect a given bond: overcollateralization (O/C), excess spread, swaps, caps or other options, and recovery on defaults. Not only may the yield decrease, but the rating may also be affected if the agencies reevaluate the bond. A downgrade in rating will result in decreased value of the bond.

- Should a default occur and subsequent recovery, the cash recovered is in effect an "involuntary" prepayment and the economics are the same as given previously for "voluntary" prepayments.

- Defaults are estimated assuming some *correlation* or interrelatedness among the assets. If the correlation differs from this assumption, realized defaults will differ. The sensitivity of a tranche's value to correlation depends on its seniority. Senior tranches are relatively insensitive to correlation because they have so much credit enhancement to protect them. However, as correlation among assets increases, the senior tranches will see a decrease in value. Junior tranches are sensitive to correlation because they are first in line to absorb losses. As correlation increases, the equity tranche will see an *increase* in value (all other things being equal). This effect is explained in Chapter 7 for synthetic credit indexes. The cash structures described in previous chapters have correlation assumptions hidden within their default rate assumptions.

- O/C protects the structure by absorbing losses. Anytime the structure needs to accelerate principal payments to get into O/C compliance is effectively a prepayment to the bond holders, and the economics are equivalent. Acceleration will be required when excess spread is insufficient to maintain O/C. There are many reasons why excess spread may become insufficient. Effective prepayments (voluntary or involuntary) reduce the amount of collateral and its ability to generate interest. The gap between the average liability and asset coupons (i.e., basis risk) can increase and be insufficiently hedged by swaps, caps, and the like.

- Priority of payments makes the sensitivities of subordinate bonds greater than those of senior bonds. For example, the subordinates are usually paid principal *only after* seniors are fully paid down, or perhaps sooner than that if/when the O/C steps down (section 4.6.1). Thus the subordinates have longer WAL and greater duration. Thus changes in interest and prepayment rates will more greatly affect the value of subordinate bonds. With no step down, sensitivities increase monotonically from the first mezzanine bond to the junior-most bond and have increasing spreads (and decreasing ratings) to match. With step down, all the subordinate bonds start to pay down in unison and their durations are approximately equal. See section B.4 of Appendix B for an example of this effect.

- Servicers are generally obligated to advance for delinquent and defaulted collateral until a loss is realized and bonds are written down. Once a bond is written down, no interest or principal distribution will be made corresponding to that written down amount—these cash flows are lost. Recoveries from defaults will revert back to the servicers to the extent they advanced cash. However, servicers can deem a defaulted asset to be unrecoverable and thereby not advance any cash at all.

6.1.5 Interest Rates

- Basis risk is the potential gap between liability and asset rates. Due to the intricacy of hybrid ARMs, there are a few ways in which mortgage loans can gap from issued bonds. ARMs have fixed rates for an initial period, after which they typically float on six-month LIBOR (floating bonds usually float on one-month LIBOR). ARMs also have caps that their effective rates cannot exceed. If there is a hedge against basis risk, say in the form of an interest rate swap, a related risk occurs. If the swap is placed low in the waterfall, its cash infusion may not be put to the same use as if it were at the top of the waterfall (where interest is normally paid).
- If the swap schedule does not match the actual bond amortization then the hedge is imperfect. Prepayments more than anticipated will lead to the swap schedule extending beyond the actual bond amortization schedule. This can result in net swap payments to the swap counterparty if interest rates decrease, reducing cash from the deal. Caps can be affected in a similar way, although caps are paid up front.
- Assets with high weighted-average coupon (WAC) are more likely to be prepaid than assets with low WAC. Thus excess spread is more sensitive to prepayment rate if WAC is unevenly distributed among the assets.
- The WAC cap or AFC (Available Funds Cap) is a limit on the interest that can be paid out to issued bonds (section 4.4). The remainder (the BRCFA) may be distributed, but its priority order in the waterfall is rerouted. Thus there is the risk that should the WAC cap hit, the cash (that should go to paying the BRCFA) is usurped for paying principal.

6.1.6 Spreads

- Subordinate tranches are more sensitive to changes in underlying asset spreads than are senior tranches. This applies to structures with bonds or CDS as assets. For example, a synthetic structure based on CDS assets will have an equity tranche with higher spread duration (called the "delta" in Chapter 7) than is its mezzanine and senior tranches. This sensitivity drops off quickly as one moves up the capital structure.

- Equity tranches have negative spread convexity whereas more senior tranches have positive spread convexity. Again, this applies to structures with bonds or CDS as assets. This perhaps nonintuitive behavior is explained in Chapter 7.

6.1.7 Miscellaneous

- Timing of cash flows will affect bond yields. As previously noted, subordinate bonds are most sensitive to timing (i.e., delays in cash flows). The more subordinate, the more sensitive. Delinquencies and defaults can delay cash flows to the extent that bond yield decreases, and yet the bond itself may not realize any losses.
- If recovery rates (or loss severities) differ from those assumed, realized losses will differ and hence value. The models described here make the gross assumption that each asset has a static recovery rate.
- Assets of various types have specific risks associated with them. Risks associated with mortgage loans include high loan-to-value (LTV), high WAC, and second liens, all with increased probability of loss. Payment shocks can result from balloon payments, interest-only periods, and option ARMs that allow negative amortization. When payments gap, delinquency and defaults increase. Borrowers holding such loans may attempt to refinance their debt prior to the payment step up. However, in adverse markets, refinancing may become difficult, resulting in more losses.
- Various counterparties upon whom the structure relies may default in their obligations. These include the servicer, originator, and swap counterparty.

6.1.8 Residual Sensitivities

- Notes built from residual cash flows (NIMs and Owner's Trust Equities [OTEs]) are sensitive to the same factors as subordinate bonds, and to a greater magnitude. When losses increase beyond what is anticipated, NIM yields decrease below anticipated levels. When interest rates increase beyond what is anticipated, the interest gap between collateral and bonds may suck up excess spread, starving the residual. Since NIMs are usually short lived (with WAL around one year), they are extremely sensitive to basis risk during the fixed period of ARM collateral. When they extend, their yield declines.
- Basis risk is a serious enough concern that some structures include a cash corridor devoted solely to the NIM (section 4.8.1). The corridor helps hedge against basis risk, but may be imperfect.

TABLE 6.1   Simple Liability Structure: Four Floating Tranches

Name	A1	M1	M2	B1
Desc	Senior	Mezz	Mezz	Sub
Type	Float	Float	Float	Float
SettleFlat	FALSE	FALSE	FALSE	FALSE
DayCount	act/360	act/360	act/360	act/360
SP Rating	AAA	AA	A	BBB
Margin	25 bp	80 bp	140 bp	250 bp
Benchmark	1mL	1mL	1mL	1mL
Size	80.75%	6.50%	5.00%	5.75%

6.2   MEZZANINE AND SUBORDINATE CLASSES

Schorin and Mehra (2005) is a great resource for the empirical characteristics of subprime mortgage structures. In this section and the next, benchmarks from Schorin and Mehra are rerun on the models introduced here. One can analyze any number of asset pools and structures. Because the focus of this book is modeling, it is best to analyze known benchmarks so that the reader can cross reference the results. Three studies are analyzed here: a four-tranche structure, a seven-tranche structure, and a NIM structure.

First consider a structure with four classes: A1, M1, M2, and B1. The collateral is a single 2/28 ARM repline.[1] The base case studied has both prepayments and losses. The liability structure is floating and summarized in Table 6.1, implying 2% O/C. Figure 6.2 shows the interest rate, prepayment, and loss assumptions.

Thirteen scenarios were examined in which these input curves were combined (not all combinations were run). All scenarios assume that the structure runs to maturity with no O/C stepdown. This implies that the coupon will step up to 1.5 times its value once a bond is callable (known as the *SeniorPostCallMult* and *SubPostCallMult* parameters in section 4.2). O/C stepdown could be disabled by a delinquency trigger firing, for example.

---

[1] The initial WAC is 8.6% with an initial two-year reset to LIBOR + 6.3%. The loan resets every six months after that. The initial periodic cap is 3% and the periodic cap is 1%. The life floor is 8.9% and the life cap is 15%. There is no aging, no balloon, no IO period, and no prepayment penalty. The maturity is 30 years. We assume that one-month and six-month LIBOR are equal in this section.

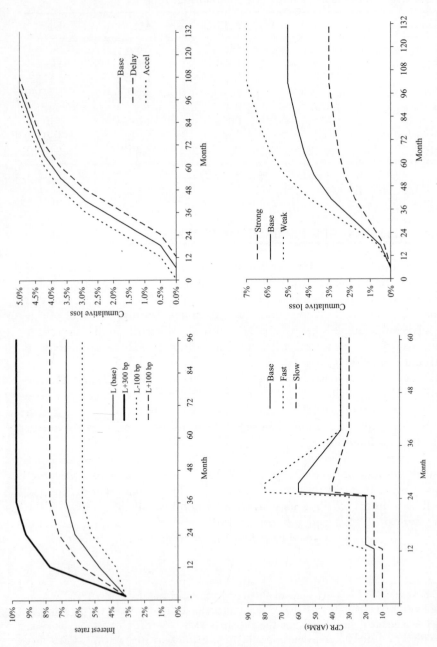

FIGURE 6.2 Interest Rate, Prepay, and Loss Curves Used in First Study

Source: Schorin and Mehra 2005.

TABLE 6.2 Discount Margins and WAL for Stress Scenarios

	Rates	Prepay	Loss	DM M1	DM M2	DM B1	WAL M1	WAL M2	WAL B1
1	base	base	base	80	141	272	4.36	5.30	6.93
2	L−100	base	base	80	141	273	4.36	5.29	6.92
3	L+100	base	base	80	141	262	4.37	5.30	6.94
4	L+300	base	base	60	112	226	4.53	5.59	7.93
5	base	fast	base	80	142	282	3.12	4.02	5.88
6	base	slow	base	80	141	269	5.76	6.92	8.98
7	L−100	fast	base	80	143	284	3.12	4.02	5.90
8	L+100	slow	base	64	114	219	5.76	6.93	8.99
9	L+300	slow	base	64	114	219	5.77	6.93	9.01
10	base	base	weak	80	142	274	4.29	5.22	6.94
11	base	base	strong	80	141	271	4.46	5.43	7.14
12	base	base	delay	80	141	271	4.36	5.27	6.88
13	base	base	accel	80	142	272	4.38	5.33	6.99

Table 6.2 summarizes the results for the scenarios. The tranches show stability for all these stresses, indicating that the mechanisms of disabling O/C stepdown and enabling margin step up are sufficient in these cases to satisfy the bond holders. These results are similar to, but do not exactly match, those of Schorin and Mehra (2005), perhaps due to slightly different interest rate assumptions. The largest differences among the results are in scenarios 4, 8, and 9, where Schorin and Mehra (2005) report M1 discount margins of 68, 80, and 80 respectively.

For fast and slow prepayments the WAL contracts and extends as expected. The B1 discount margin actually *increases* for fast prepayments because although the WAL *decreases*, its tail *increases* (with the 1.5 times margin step up for a portion of this).

A more complex structure with seven tranches (A1, M1, M2, M3, B1, B2, B3) is now examined. Table 6.3 summarizes the structure. The collateral is different than in the previous example—now 78% floating ARMs and 22% fixed loans.[2] Fixed-rate loan prepayment rates are given in Figure 6.3. Interest rate assumptions are given in Figure 6.4. Floating-rate loan

---

[2] The initial WAC is 7.5% for ARMs, resetting to LIBOR + 5.6%. All other ARM parameters are the same as in the previous example. The fixed-rate loans have a 7.5% WAC.

TABLE 6.3 Simple Liability Structure: Seven Floating Tranches

Name	A1	M1	M2	M3	B1	B2	B3
Desc	Senior	Mezz	Mezz	Mezz	Sub	Sub	Sub
Type	Float	Float	Float	Float	Float	Float	Float
SettleFlat	FALSE	FALSE	FALSE	FALSE	FALSE	FALSE	FALSE
DayCount	act/360	act/360	act/360	act/360	act/360	act/360	act/360
SP Rating	AAA	AA	A	A−	BBB+	BBB	BBB−
Margin	41bp	65bp	165bp	195bp	305bp	375bp	375bp
Benchmark	1mL	1mL	1mL	1mL	1mL	1mL	1mL
Size	80.50%	6.40%	5.25%	1.75%	1.50%	1.05%	1.30%

prepayment rates and base loss curves are given in Figure 6.2. Loss curves are *scaled* in the following study.

We continue to assume that the structure runs to maturity with no O/C stepdown, implying a subordinate postcall margin multiplier of 1.5. Discount margin and WAL are plotted against cumulative loss, varying from 0% to 20% loss.

Figure 6.5 summarizes how performance varies with loss. As loss increases from zero, the performance is stable for some range before it begins to degrade. For each tranche the discount margin drops suddenly for a certain

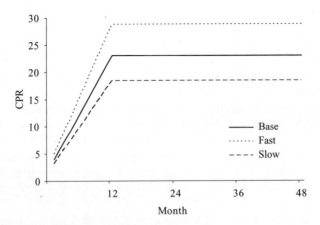

FIGURE 6.3 Prepayment Curves for Fixed-Rate Loans
Source: Schorin and Mehra 2005.

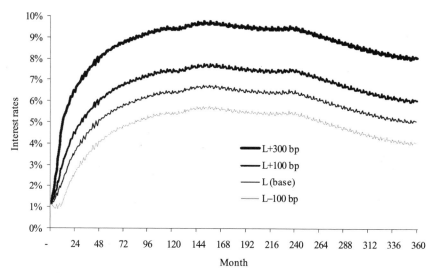

FIGURE 6.4 Rate Curves Used in Second Study
Source: Schorin and Mehra 2005.

loss. WAL also starts to extend, although not as precipitously for higher rated bonds.

Table 6.4 presents performance results from a different view. Three breakeven loss rates are analyzed. "First write down" is the loss rate at which the tranche first experiences writedowns (i.e., for a loss rate lower than this), no losses are realized. "DM = 0" is the loss rate at which the discount margin first goes to zero. "Next higher rated tranche outperforms" is the loss rate at which the tranche just senior to this tranche first has a higher discount margin than this tranche.[3]

All these measures consistently show that fast prepayments lower performance whereas slow prepayments increase performance, except for the highest AA rated mezzanine tranche. With the +300 bps rate shock, performance degrades even further. Over all tranches for each metric shown, the breakeven loss decreases (going from +0 to +300 bps) by 1.1% to 3.8% (except for M1 again). Rising interest rates and fast prepayment don't make sense together in realistic economic markets, but may be useful in stress analysis.

---

[3] To generate such breakeven losses, it is easiest to use brute force: evaluate the model for 250 losses: 0%, 0.1%, ..., 24.9%, 25% and pick the breakevens from this data.

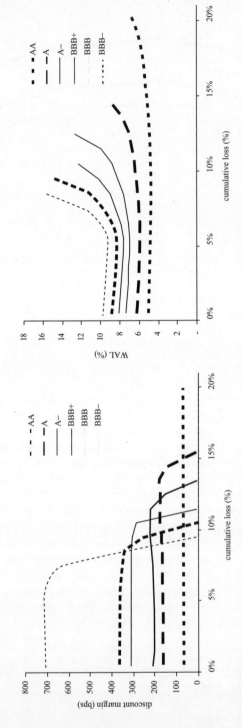

FIGURE 6.5 Discount Margin and WAL as Functions of Cumulative Loss for Each Tranche. WAL Curves are Cut Off Once the Discount Margin Goes Negative.

TABLE 6.4 Loss Rates to Hit Various Performance Breaks. Base, Fast and Slow Refer to Prepayment Rates. The Lower Group of Results has Interest Rates Shocked +300 bps.

LIBOR + 0 bps		First write down			DM = 0			Next higher rated tranche outperforms		
		Base	Fast	Slow	Base	Fast	Slow	Base	Fast	Slow
M1	AA	20.0%	20.5%	21.9%	20.6%	21.0%	22.6%			
M2	A	13.8%	12.4%	16.2%	14.9%	13.5%	17.6%	14.5%	13.1%	17.1%
M3	A−	11.9%	10.1%	14.3%	12.4%	10.6%	14.9%	12.0%	10.2%	14.4%
B1	BBB+	10.2%	8.3%	12.7%	10.9%	8.9%	13.4%	10.4%	8.5%	12.9%
B2	BBB	8.9%	7.0%	11.5%	9.5%	7.5%	12.1%	9.0%	7.0%	11.6%
B3	BBB−	7.4%	5.5%	10.1%	8.4%	6.5%	11.1%	8.0%	6.1%	10.7%

LIBOR + 300 bps		First write down			DM = 0			Next higher rated tranche outperforms		
		Base	Fast	Slow	Base	Fast	Slow	Base	Fast	Slow
M1	AA	16.7%	17.1%	18.5%	17.2%	17.5%	25.0%			
M2	A	11.2%	10.0%	13.0%	12.2%	10.9%	14.2%	11.7%	10.6%	13.7%
M3	A−	9.3%	8.1%	11.1%	9.7%	8.4%	11.6%	8.6%	7.6%	11.0%
B1	BBB+	7.7%	6.5%	9.5%	8.2%	6.9%	10.0%	7.8%	6.5%	9.6%
B2	BBB	6.7%	5.5%	8.4%	7.0%	5.7%	8.8%	5.4%	4.2%	7.8%
B3	BBB−	5.6%	4.4%	7.3%	6.2%	5.0%	8.0%	6.0%	4.8%	7.8%

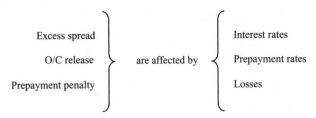

FIGURE 6.6   Key Influences on NIM Value

6.3   NIM CLASSES

NIM notes, being leveraged off the end of the structure, are sensitive to several parameters. As discussed in section 6.1, cash flow into the residual depends on excess spread and O/C (and its release), which are affected by interest and prepayment rates. In addition, prepayment penalties contribute to the residual. This is diagrammed in Figure 6.6. NIMs in general can be fixed- or floating-rate notes, but fixed-rate notes will be the focus here. They can be targeted to various ratings around BBB, or perhaps not rated if privately held. In either case, sufficiently stressful input assumptions must be made in their analysis (see section 5.5).

Excess spread and prepayment penalties are the main contributors to residual cash flows. Excess spread comes from O/C as well as the fact that the collateral has a higher WAC than the bonds. O/C is released after the *StepPeriod* (section 4.2), usually three years, and after the seniors are paid down. This can be delayed if performance triggers fire. In any case, a typical NIM is shorter lived than three years, so it won't get any benefit from this cash. For an OTE or a NIM that lives longer (for instance, in a chain of NIMs), O/C release will contribute to its value.

Figure 6.7 illustrates the main NIM performance sensitivities for a simple structure. The structure has the same issued bonds (A1–B3) as previously with a single NIM. The same curves are used. The NIM is sized as 6.81% of the collateral with a 10.21% fixed coupon. The collateral is all 2/28 ARMs, although 85% of the loans have a prepayment penalty.[4] The five graphs in Figure 6.7 are now described, in order. The graphs plot the amortization schedule of the NIM vs. perturbation of various parameters. In each graph, the bold curve is the base scenario (5% loss in this case).

---

[4] The ARM parameters are the same as in the first example in section 6.2 (8.6% initial WAC, etc.). The prepayment penalty period is 24 months with a penalty of six months' interest on 80% of the prepaid balance (denoted as "24 IP 4.8" in the notation of section 3.1).

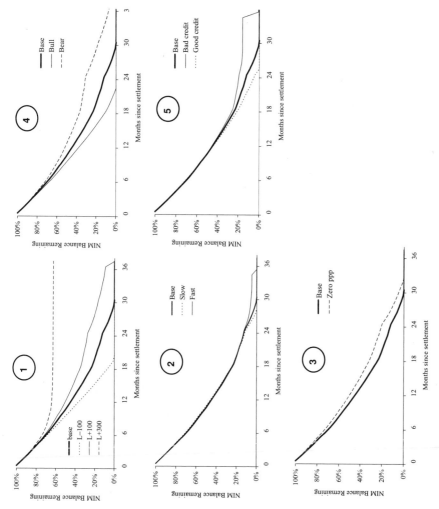

FIGURE 6.7 NIM Sensitivities Demonstrated in Sample Structure

The first graph compares interest rates shocked up and down. Increasing rates extends the NIM because it is starved for cash during the two years when the ARMs are not resetting. The effect can be extreme, as shown for +300 bps when the NIM stops getting any cash at all. As discussed earlier in this chapter, this can be eliminated by introducing a cash corridor for the NIM.

The second graph shows the effects of fast and slow prepayment rates. Performance doesn't change much. Increasing prepayments both increases prepayment penalties and decreases excess interest. These opposite effects balance for much of the schedule. Eventually the lack of excess interest extends the NIM out a few periods. Decreasing prepayments also has both effects in reverse.

The third graph emphasizes the effect of prepayment penalty. Here the base case (with penalty) is compared to collateral with no penalty ("zero ppp"). Without penalties, residual cash flow decreases and the NIM extends. The effect does not appear to be large. However, note that prepayment penalties effect prepayment rates as a regulator. If prepayment penalties were zero, prepayment rates would likely be higher and the NIM would extend farther.

The fourth graph compares strong and weak economic markets. The strong market is −100 bps rate shock with fast prepayments. The weak market is +100 bps rate shock with slow prepayments. These combinations grossly represent alternative economic environments. As one might expect, the weak market extends the NIM and the strong market shortens it. Since prepayment rates themselves don't affect the NIM much, as seen in the second graph, the primary factor is the interest rate shock.

The fifth graph compares good credit collateral (3% cumulative loss) versus bad credit collateral (7% loss). Recall that the base case is 5% loss. Increasing loss by a few percent has a similar effect to shocking rates by +100 bps. The timing of losses has a similar effect: accelerating the loss extends the NIM because it reduces residual cash flow. Delaying the loss shortens the NIM (see Schorin and Mehra 2005).

Table 6.5 shows a price-to-yield table generated for the NIM. The table assumes a par price and the base scenario described above. The grey square highlights the base case—the reason the yield is not equal to the 10.21% coupon is that these are bond-equivalent yields by convention. The table shows that within this range the NIM is insensitive to loss and prepayment perturbations. The yield was impacted by the 8% loss on the bottom row.

6.4 PUTTING IT ALL TOGETHER

Price is computed by deriving an "optimal" takeout structure for the securitization, one with the lowest average WAC and still meeting the agency

TABLE 6.5 Price-to-Yield Table for NIM. "Mod Dur" Is Discount Spread Duration. First and Last Pay are Given in Months.

		0% CPR	50% CPR	100% CPR	150% CPR
0% Loss	Yield	10.464%	10.465%	10.465%	10.466%
	Avg Life	0.91	0.90	0.88	0.87
	Mod Dur	0.83	0.82	0.81	0.79
	First Pay	1	1	1	1
	Last Pay	23	23	23	23
2% Loss	Yield	10.463%	10.464%	10.464%	10.464%
	Avg Life	0.95	0.93	0.92	0.91
	Mod Dur	0.86	0.85	0.84	0.83
	First Pay	1	1	1	1
	Last Pay	25	25	25	26
4% Loss	Yield	10.462%	10.462%	10.462%	10.462%
	Avg Life	0.99	0.98	0.97	0.98
	Mod Dur	0.90	0.89	0.88	0.88
	First Pay	1	1	1	1
	Last Pay	26	26	27	31
5% Loss	Yield	10.461%	10.461%	10.461%	10.461%
	Avg Life	1.02	1.01	1.00	1.02
	Mod Dur	0.92	0.91	0.90	0.92
	First Pay	1	1	1	1
	Last Pay	27	27	30	31
6% Loss	Yield	10.460%	10.460%	10.460%	10.460%
	Avg Life	1.05	1.04	1.06	1.07
	Mod Dur	0.94	0.93	0.95	0.95
	First Pay	1	1	1	1
	Last Pay	28	29	37	31
8% Loss	Yield	10.458%	10.458%	9.633%	5.177%
	Avg Life	1.12	1.13	1.20	1.06
	Mod Dur	1.00	1.01	1.07	1.00
	First Pay	1	1	1	1
	Last Pay	30	34	50	31

rating requirements. A key part of the agency requirements are loss assumptions (and to a lesser degree, prepayment assumptions). The loss coverages (i.e., the expected losses) for each target bond rating are baked into the price—cash flows are penalized by applying these losses.

Consider two alternative portfolios. The first has a bit worse credit quality and/or higher LTV than the second. This makes the first more risky. To compensate for this, the first has a bit higher WAC than the second. The higher risk translates into higher expected loss (as confirmed by rating agency or internal business models). For each portfolio, the loss and coupon are mixed (among other things) to get a price. Either portfolio might have the higher price, or they could be equal.

The profitability of a pool will depend on how low a bid can be made. Consider the case where the more risky pool can be successfully bid lower than its model price, say by 2 points. Suppose the less risky pool can be bid lower than its model price by only 1 point. Such is the case when the market discounts risky assets more heavily, that is, general risk aversion. No matter what the relative prices, one must decide if the higher spread on the risky pool is worth it in the context of other pools in the securitization mix.

6.5 EXERCISES

6.1. Model a structure with tranches issued at each rating, from AAA to BBB−. Redo the studies presented in this chapter to calibrate your model.

6.2. Study the effect of prepayment curve shape on bond performance. The curves used in this chapter all peaked at the initial reset, e.g., at month 24 for 2/28 ARMs. The base prepayment curve jumped from 20% to 60% and then ramped down to 35%. Consider a peak that rises prior to the initial reset. Consider different fixed-rate loan prepayment curves also.

6.3. Consider losses that are distributed differently in time than those presented here. How does the loss distribution affect bond performance?

6.4. Study the performance of a chain of two NIMs, as a function of the stresses discussed in this chapter.

CHAPTER 7

Stochastic Models

Inveniemus viam aut faciemus. (We will find a way, or we will make one.)

—Hannibal

7.1 STATIC VERSUS STOCHASTIC

Previous chapters describe a *static* asset-backed security (ABS) model for deriving the price of a portfolio of loans given interest rates, prepayments, losses, and recoveries. These are in reality stochastic variables; that is, their future values are functions of probabilistic events. The simplest static model takes one interest rate curve, one prepayment curve, one default curve, and one recovery curve. Each curve represents one view of its variable over time— it may be the expectation, a stressful scenario, or something else.

The static model evolved to use alternative curves in certain cases. For example, each bond of a different rating uses a different interest rate curve to derive its collateral cash flows. Hybrid adjustable-rate mortgage (ARM) loans having different initial resets use different prepay curves. First liens and second liens use different loss curves, and so on. These evolved static models are intended to give more accurate results. For example, an ARM that first resets in two years will have a flurry of prepayments around two years. An ARM that first resets in five years will effectively delay that peak of prepayments to around five years. Fundamentally, however, use of a finite number of values to represent a stochastic variable, rather than its entire distribution, is an approximation.

To help understand the approximation, consider the simple case of a single stochastic input variable. For mortgages this is reasonable—prepayments and losses are often modeled deterministically from interest rates. Let's call this input variable r with distribution or density $P(r)$. Price is a function $f(r)$.

The variable r is a vector not a scalar—it is often called a path variable. By definition (e.g., Drake 1967) the mean price is:

$$E(f) = \int f(r)P(r)dr \tag{7.1}$$

Higher-order moments could also be calculated with similar integrations. The integrals are rarely amenable to analytical solution (just imagine the complexity of $f(r)$ from previous chapters!). Compare this to a simple static model where the mean price is approximated as $f(r_1)$. If there is any price convexity, then $E(f) \neq f(r_1)$ by Jensen's Inequality (e.g., Weisstein 2006). We can see this by writing price as a Taylor expansion:

$$f(r) = f(r_0) + (r - r_0) \times \left.\frac{df}{dr}\right|_{r=r_0} + \frac{1}{2}(r - r_0)^2 \times \left.\frac{d^2 f}{dr^2}\right|_{r=r_0} + \cdots \tag{7.2}$$

Introducing more concise notation, let $f'(r_0) = df/dr|_{r=r_0}$:

$$f(r) = f(r_0) + (r - r_0)f'(r_0) + \frac{1}{2}(r - r_0)^2 f''(r_0) + \cdots \tag{7.3}$$

Substituting Equation (7.3) into Equation (7.1):

$$
\begin{aligned}
E(f) &= \int f(r)P(r)dr \\
&= \int f(r_0)P(r)dr + \int (r - r_0)f'(r_0)P(r)dr \\
&\quad + \frac{1}{2}\int (r - r_0)^2 f''(r_0)P(r)dr + \cdots \\
&= f(r_0)\int P(r)dr + f'(r_0)\int (r - r_0)P(r)dr \\
&\quad + \frac{1}{2}f''(r_0)\int (r - r_0)^2 P(r)dr + \cdots \\
&= f(r_0) + f'(r_0) \times \left(\int r P(r)dr - \int r_0 P(r)dr \right) \\
&\quad + \frac{1}{2}f''(r_0)\int (r - r_0)^2 P(r)dr + \cdots \\
&= f(r_0) + f'(r_0) \times (E(r) - r_0) + \frac{1}{2}f''(r_0) \times E[(r - r_0)^2] + \cdots
\end{aligned}
$$

Making the simplifying assumption that $r_0 = E(r)$ eliminates the second term:

$$E(f) = f(r_0) + f'(r_0) \times (E(r) - r_0) + \frac{1}{2} f''(r_0) \times E[(r - r_0)^2] + \cdots$$

$$= f(r_0) + \frac{1}{2} f''(r_0) \times E[(r - E(r))^2] + \cdots$$

$$= f(r_0) + \frac{1}{2} f''(r_0) \times Var(r) + \cdots \tag{7.4}$$

The new second term is price convexity, showing that even the price at the risk-free rate r_0 is not exactly the mean price.

Suppose we want to compute the mean price *exactly*, or to our best ability in evaluating the expectation integral (Equation (7.1)). One common technique is *Monte Carlo* simulation. Monte Carlo simulation is effectively an approximation of an integral by sampling. Each of the thousands of samples is called a *path*. For each stochastic variable, a different value is generated for each path, sampling the distribution of that variable.[1] If these variables are meant to be correlated then a sophisticated model will account for this by correlating the underlying distributions.

In the simple case of one stochastic variable, as discussed above, each path uses a different forward rate curve, and other variables are derived from that. Each path will potentially result in different bond cash flows and be discounted differently, and hence have a different price. The average of these prices is an *estimate* of the mean of the theoretical price distribution. Such a sample mean improves in accuracy as the number of samples increases. So the more paths executed, the more accurate the estimate. Figure 7.1 illustrates the relationship between the static and stochastic models.

Given this stochastic model, one can construct a value r with which to subsequently approximate the price expectation as $f(r)$. This may seem circular, but consider that evaluation of the stochastic model is costly. If it can be used just once to derive the best estimate of the stochastic variable, then pricing other assets can use the static model.

We know $E(f)$ exactly from the stochastic model for some asset portfolio. We search over all values r such that $f(r) \approx E(f)$. This is the calibration phase and is done periodically as interest rates change. Alternatively, if the single stochastic input variable represents time to default, it can be backfitted in a similar manner. If stochastic model evaluation is sufficiently fast, $E(f)$ can be estimated by Monte Carlo simulation every time.

---

[1] We are abstracting since r is a function of time. Think of a "sample" as a time series. In actuality, the series is constructed from random samples.

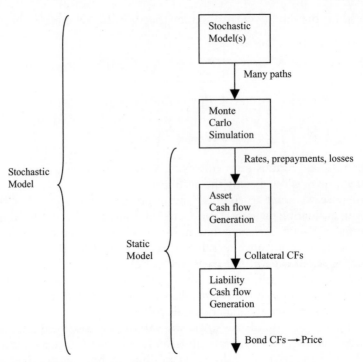

FIGURE 7.1 Static and Stochastic Models

7.2 LOSS MODEL

The stylized stochastic simulation sketched in Figure 7.1 feeds a large number of paths (corresponding to stochastic variables) into the static cash flow model. An alternative organization is to produce probability distributions for these variables and then sample the distributions within the cash flow model. An empirical distribution is built as a histogram that is then translated into a cumulative distribution that can be sampled. In this section, three techniques are described for modeling asset defaults. The first derives an estimation of the probability of default from a ratings transition matrix. The second derives an estimation of the probability of default from asset spread. The third derives an estimation of the probability of the time to default.

7.2.1 Probability of Default from Transition Matrix

For many asset types, ratings transition matrices based on historical data have been created (e.g., Ahmed et al. 2004; Carty 1997). Table 7.1 gives a

TABLE 7.1 Typical (Annual) Ratings Transition Matrix (Blend from Various Agencies). Each Row Sums to 100%.

	AAA	AA+	AA	AA-	A+	A	A-	BBB+	BBB	BBB-	BB+	BB	BB-	B+	B	B-	CCC	Def
AAA	91.15%	4.22%	3.26%	0.53%	0.21%	0.27%	0.21%	0.00%	0.05%	0.00%	0.00%	0.05%	0.05%	0.00%	0.00%	0.00%	0.00%	0.00%
AA+	2.77%	83.89%	9.56%	2.52%	0.25%	0.50%	0.00%	0.00%	0.38%	0.00%	0.00%	0.00%	0.00%	0.13%	0.00%	0.00%	0.00%	0.00%
AA	0.68%	1.28%	84.86%	7.59%	2.67%	1.60%	0.32%	0.54%	0.11%	0.11%	0.04%	0.04%	0.04%	0.04%	0.00%	0.04%	0.04%	0.00%
AA-	0.00%	0.09%	3.72%	81.64%	9.62%	3.72%	0.56%	0.28%	0.14%	0.00%	0.00%	0.00%	0.00%	0.00%	0.23%	0.00%	0.00%	0.00%
A+	0.00%	0.03%	0.95%	4.65%	81.68%	8.22%	2.78%	0.54%	0.35%	0.16%	0.13%	0.19%	0.00%	0.16%	0.10%	0.00%	0.03%	0.03%
A	0.08%	0.02%	0.53%	0.66%	5.14%	82.40%	5.57%	3.24%	1.07%	0.35%	0.21%	0.27%	0.00%	0.23%	0.00%	0.00%	0.00%	0.04%
A-	0.16%	0.04%	0.12%	0.31%	1.09%	8.76%	77.31%	6.90%	3.18%	0.74%	0.23%	0.50%	0.19%	0.27%	0.04%	0.04%	0.00%	0.08%
BBB+	0.00%	0.00%	0.09%	0.14%	0.60%	2.67%	8.28%	74.06%	8.78%	3.31%	0.51%	0.32%	0.14%	0.46%	0.37%	0.00%	0.14%	0.14%
BBB	0.04%	0.04%	0.04%	0.25%	0.36%	1.01%	2.38%	7.22%	78.46%	5.13%	2.17%	1.12%	0.69%	0.51%	0.36%	0.00%	0.00%	0.22%
BBB-	0.06%	0.00%	0.12%	0.23%	0.12%	0.75%	0.58%	2.42%	9.79%	73.21%	5.93%	3.34%	1.27%	0.81%	0.40%	0.46%	0.29%	0.23%
BB+	0.09%	0.00%	0.00%	0.00%	0.00%	0.53%	0.26%	0.97%	3.98%	13.63%	66.64%	4.87%	3.89%	2.48%	1.24%	0.18%	0.71%	0.53%
BB	0.00%	0.00%	0.13%	0.00%	0.07%	0.39%	0.20%	0.33%	1.64%	5.39%	7.29%	70.77%	7.03%	3.29%	1.18%	0.85%	0.59%	0.85%
BB-	0.00%	0.00%	0.00%	0.05%	0.10%	0.05%	0.25%	0.35%	0.40%	1.26%	3.78%	9.17%	69.68%	8.06%	2.77%	1.56%	1.16%	1.36%
B+	0.00%	0.04%	0.00%	0.07%	0.00%	0.04%	0.22%	0.11%	0.18%	0.18%	0.48%	2.38%	6.30%	77.96%	5.16%	2.45%	1.79%	2.64%
B	0.00%	0.00%	0.08%	0.00%	0.00%	0.16%	0.23%	0.00%	0.23%	0.08%	0.47%	1.09%	2.87%	7.92%	69.17%	3.26%	5.67%	8.77%
B-	0.00%	0.00%	0.00%	0.00%	0.20%	0.00%	0.00%	0.20%	0.00%	0.59%	0.39%	0.59%	0.98%	4.91%	5.89%	65.22%	9.63%	11.40%
CCC	0.19%	0.00%	0.00%	0.00%	0.38%	0.00%	0.00%	0.19%	0.57%	0.19%	0.38%	0.76%	1.51%	3.03%	4.73%	3.78%	61.98%	22.31%
Def	0.00%	0.00%	0.00%	0.00%	0.00%	0.00%	0.00%	0.00%	0.00%	0.00%	0.00%	0.00%	0.00%	0.00%	0.00%	0.00%	0.00%	100.00%

typical matrix based on a blend of different agencies, over some historical period, for corporate bonds. For example, the probability of a BBB+ credit transitioning to a BBB credit in the next year is 8.78%. The probability of a BBB+ credit defaulting over the next year is 0.14%. Such matrices have been constructed for corporates, ABSs, collateralized debt obligations (CDOs), and others. If an appropriate matrix is unavailable for the asset type(s) being structured, perhaps a stressed matrix of a similar type can act as a placeholder. There are various ways to stress such a matrix. The simplest stress is to increase the probabilities of default and to remove the excess probability from the other transitions on a pro rata basis, but other methods are possible.

Given a rating transitions matrix, asset credits can be transitioned through the matrix, once per period, tracking their progress. If a credit hits the default state, it remains defaulted. This is essentially a Markov chain process (e.g., Drake 1967; Schonbucher 2003) with default as an absorbing state. One can avoid the mathematics of an analytical solution and estimate the result by using a transition matrix *within* a Monte Carlo simulation. The simulation produces an empirical estimation of the default distribution, as well as the probability distribution of reaching any rating, in n periods.

Let G be an annual ratings transition matrix. The matrix is the conditional annualized probability of transitioning from rating g_1 to rating g_2.

$$G(g_1, g_2) = \Pr(g_2 \text{ in one year} \mid g_1 \text{ initially}) \qquad (7.5)$$

The square of the matrix is the conditional probability over two years, and so on. In general:

$$G^n(g_1, g_2) = \Pr(g_2 \text{ in year } k + n \mid g_1 \text{ in year } k) \qquad (7.6)$$

The process is time invariant; that is, the model assumes the same annual matrix is in effect this year as next year. Semiannual, quarterly, and other granularity transition matrices are possible. For example, one can transform an annual matrix into a semiannual matrix by decomposing the annual matrix G into its eigenvectors S and eigenvalues Λ (e.g., Strang 1995):

$$G = S\Lambda S^{-1}$$
$$S^{-1}GS = \Lambda$$
$$\Lambda^n = (S^{-1}GS)(S^{-1}GS)\cdots$$
$$\Lambda^n = S^{-1}G^n S$$
$$G^n = S\Lambda^n S^{-1}$$

where n can be set to $1/2$, $1/4$, etc. The "trick" is that Λ^n is easy to calculate because Λ is diagonal. The hard part is to *find* S and Λ, but software packages are available, for example, Numerical Algorithms Group (www.nag.co.uk).

Some probabilities in Table 7.1 are zero because of sparse historical data. For instance, BB cannot transition to AA+ in one year. However, BB can transition to AA+ in *two* years by moving through an intermediate state (e.g., AA). Sampling a ratings transition matrix requires the generation of a cumulative probability matrix.

$$C(g_1, g_2) = \sum_{h \geq g_2} G(g_1, h) \tag{7.7}$$

Thus, for instance, C(AA+,AAA) = 2.77% and C(AA+,AA+) = 2.77% + 83.89% = 86.66%. To sample this matrix, given the *current* rating g_1 and a uniform $(0,1)$ random number U, the *next* period's rating is:

$$\max[g_2 \mid U \leq C(g_1, g_2)]$$

The default probabilities from successive transition matrices, G^n, can be combined into a default table, D:

$$D(g, n) = G^n(g, Def)$$

Often, an "equivalent" annual default rate $\tilde{D}(g)$ is constructed by choosing a year k (say five) and finding what probability when accumulated over k years would result in the k-year default rate. This smooths the data, removing zero annual probabilities of default.

$$\tilde{D}(g) = 1 - \sqrt[k]{1 - D(g, k)}$$

These computations are further discussed in section 7.6. See Schonbucher (2003) for an extensive discussion of transition matrix models.

7.2.2 Probability of Default from Spread

Let's shift our focus to modeling defaults without dependence on historical data as above. A "classic" way to model bond defaults is as a function of stochastic spreads. This is considered a "risk neutral" model because it presupposes no particular risk appetites. Consider N bonds, independent and identically distributed with respect to credit default, the only risk they are exposed to. These are zero-coupon bonds that mature exactly in one period.

The risk-free interest rate over this period is r. Let Q be the probability of default, that is, $N \times Q$ bonds are expected to default out of N bonds. Suppose the recovery rate is R. Thus we expect to receive $(1 - Q)N + QNR$, which discounted back to today is worth $[(1 - Q)N + QNR]/(1 + r)$. Now suppose the bond has spread s over the risk-free rate. This spread is the excess yield that an investor must receive to be exposed to the bond's default risk. Define spread *multiplicatively*.[2] Then N (risky) bonds are worth $N/[(1 + r)(1 + s)]$ today. Equating these two:

$$\frac{(1 - Q)N + QNR}{1 + r} = \frac{N}{(1 + r)(1 + s)} \tag{7.8}$$

Simplifying,

$$Q = \frac{s}{(1 + s)(1 - R)} = \frac{h}{1 + s} \tag{7.9}$$

where h is:

$$h = \frac{s}{1 - R} \tag{7.10}$$

seen to be the *hazard rate* under certain approximations (e.g., section B.5 of Appendix B). A Monte Carlo simulation can evolve spreads by one of several interest rate models, and in each period the probability of default can be estimated with the spread. Alternatively, a static spread curve can be given so that the same probability of default is used, for a given period, in *every* path.

For a given period, a uniform $(0,1)$ random number U is generated. If $U < Q$ then the asset defaults, otherwise it survives. Equivalently, if $U < 1 - Q$ then the asset survives, otherwise it defaults. This is seen to be a Bernoulli distribution with two outcomes: survival and default (Figure 7.2). Like any other distribution, it is sampled by using its cumulative distribution, in this case a step function.

7.2.3 Probability of Time to Default

Consider a discrete Markov process representing an asset that can evolve towards a *default* barrier. Let q_t be the *conditional* probability of defaulting

---

[2] Multiplicative spread can be used by the following approximation. For small Δt, $(1 + r\Delta t)(1 + s\Delta t) = 1 + (r + s)\Delta t + rs\Delta t^2 \approx 1 + (r + s)\Delta t$.

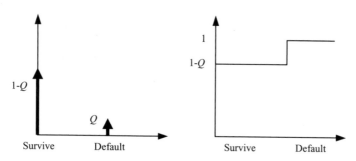

FIGURE 7.2 Bernoulli Probability Density Function (Left) and Its Cumulative Density Function (Right)

in period t (given the asset survived up to t). The *cumulative* probability P_i of surviving until period i is:

$$P_i = \prod_{t=1}^{i} (1 - q_t) \tag{7.11}$$

The *marginal* probability Q_i of surviving through period $i - 1$ and then *defaulting* in period i is:

$$
\begin{aligned}
Q_i &= \prod_{t=1}^{i-1} (1 - q_t)\, q_i \\
&= \prod_{t=1}^{i-1} (1 - q_t)\, (1 - (1 - q_i)) \\
&= \prod_{t=1}^{i-1} (1 - q_t) - \prod_{t=1}^{i} (1 - q_t) \\
&= P_{i-1} - P_i \tag{7.12}
\end{aligned}
$$

An alternative presentation is in terms of *hazard rate* h_i which is the ratio of the conditional probability of default to the conditional probability of survival (e.g., Larson and Marx 1986; Weisstein 2006).

$$h_i = \frac{q_i}{1 - q_i} \tag{7.13}$$

Rearranging:

$$1 - q_i = \frac{1}{1 + h_i} \tag{7.14}$$

Substituting Equation (7.14) into Equation (7.11):

$$P_i = \prod_{t=1}^{i} (1 - q_t)$$

$$= \prod_{t=1}^{i} \frac{1}{1 + h_t} \tag{7.15}$$

For homogeneous credits with *constant* spread, the hazard rate is constant h, hence:

$$P_t = (1 + h)^{-t} \tag{7.16}$$

Another expression for the hazard rate is derived for credit default swaps (CDSs) in section B.5 of Appendix B. This estimate for hazard rate matches that in Equation (7.10). See also Schonbucher (2003) for a discussion of hazard rate.

P_t is computed with either Equation (7.15) or Equation (7.16) depending on the spread assumptions. For a given credit, a uniform $(0,1)$ random number U is generated. For a given period t, if $U < P_t$ then the asset survives, otherwise the asset defaults. This is equivalent to saying that $P^{-1}(U) = t_{default}$. Note that Equation (7.16) can be transformed:

$$P_t = (1 + h)^{-t} = \left(1 + \frac{q}{1 - q}\right)^{-t} = (1 - q)^t = p^t \tag{7.17}$$

where p is the conditional probability of surviving. This is perhaps an obvious result that the cumulative probability of surviving to period t is equal to the conditional probability of survival raised to the t-th power. One can compute hazard rate from spread or from the effective annual default rate, $\tilde{D}$ (section 7.2.1). In summary, the probability of the time to default, as derived here, is also a "risk-neutral" model like the model in the previous section. Although these both take market spreads, representing market consensus, and convert them into defaults, they do so in ways that are too "literal" in some sense. Since market participants have non-neutral risk tolerances, these models are biased on the conservative side.

7.3 GAUSSIAN COPULA

Correlation is a measure of how two or more random variables change value in sync. Uncorrelated variables move independently and perfectly correlated

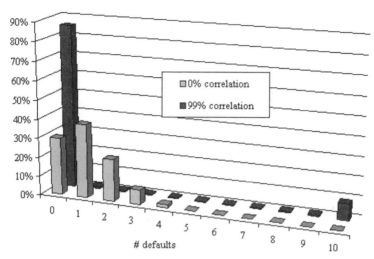

FIGURE 7.3 Probability Distributions of Number of Defaults in One Year for 10 B–
Assets for 0% and 99% Correlation

variables share the same values. In the context of credit markets, an asset
can be modeled with a random variable whose value represents the credit
quality of the asset, where one extreme is default. Thus uncorrelated assets
default independently and perfectly correlated assets default together. More
generally, uncorrelated assets transition through their ratings independently
and perfectly correlated assets share the same ratings. Consider 10 B– rated
assets assuming the one-year transition matrix given in Table 7.1. An estimate of the probability mass function (PMF) for the number of defaults
experienced in one year is given in Figure 7.3. With near-perfect correlation
the distribution has two peaks at 0 and 10, that is, almost all the time either
no assets default or all assets default. With zero correlation the distribution
is fairly smooth with a flat tail. If we were betting on how many defaults
will occur (for instance, if we were buying the equity tranche of a CDO)
then correlation would be important information to know! For the equity
tranche, the higher the correlation, the less chance of default.

There are at least two popular methods of incorporating correlation
among assets. One method is to *compress* the number of assets to reflect
correlation among them. The Moody's diversity score is a popular way to
estimate this compression (e.g., Cifuentes 2004). Modeling correlation with
compression makes intuitive sense. Consider a portfolio of 10 similar loans,
each $10MM, transitioning through a ratings matrix. Compare this to a
portfolio of two similar loans, each $50MM. The latter portfolio is more
correlated than the former. It is equivalent to a portfolio of 10 loans split

into two groups of five, where each group transitions through the matrix together (i.e., are perfectly correlated). An advantage of compression is that if you don't agree with the Moody's diversity score, you can pick your own compression number. Risk managers like this feature, often arguing that no portfolio can be uncorrelated to the extent of greater than say 10 or 15 independent factors.

A second way to incorporate correlation is with a *copula*. The basic idea behind the Gaussian copula method is that it is quite easy to compute correlated *normal* random variables, but not particularly easy to compute correlated non-normal random variables, for example, uniform random variables. The "trick" of the copula is to sample a group of uncorrelated normal random variables, correlate them (in normal space), then translate the correlated variables back into a desired non-normal space. Before formalizing this a bit more, let's briefly review normal distributions.

Consider $X_i \sim N(\mu, \sigma^2)$ and $Z_i \sim N(0, 1)$, then

$$Z_i = \frac{X_i - \mu}{\sigma} \tag{7.18}$$

$$X_i = \sigma Z_i + \mu \tag{7.19}$$

where μ is the mean and σ^2 is the variance of the normal distribution. This shows how to transform univariant (i.e., single variable) normal X_i and *standard* normal Z_i random variables (e.g., Larson and Marx 1986). Assuming zero mean, Equation (7.19) can be written

$$X_i = \sqrt{\sigma^2} Z_i \tag{7.20}$$

to emphasize the structure of the transformation for the univariant normal. Note that variance in the univariant case corresponds to a correlation matrix Σ in the multivariant case. The Cholesky decomposition is analogous to the square root of a matrix; for example, the decomposition R of the correlation matrix Σ is defined (e.g., Weisstein 2006) such that

$$\Sigma = RR^T \tag{7.21}$$

where R^T is the transpose of matrix R. The multivariant normal and standard normal can be transformed in a similar manner to the univariant case in Equation (7.20) (given here without proof):

$$X = RZ \tag{7.22}$$

In other words, multivariant normal X correlated by Σ is the product of the Cholesky decomposition of Σ and Z the multivariant standard normal.[3]

Let's consider an example with two variables (assets) to make this concrete. Let U_1 and U_2 be two *independent* uniform random variables. These are converted to independent standard normals:

$$Z_1 = \Phi^{-1}(U_1)$$
$$Z_2 = \Phi^{-1}(U_2)$$

where Φ^{-1} is the inverse standard normal cumulative distribution. In other words Z_1 and Z_2 are two *independent* random samples from the standard normal distribution Φ, i.e., $Z_i \sim N(0, 1)$.

Suppose we want to correlate these two variables by the correlation coefficient ρ. Create the correlation matrix Σ:

$$\Sigma = \begin{pmatrix} 1 & \rho \\ \rho & 1 \end{pmatrix}$$

The Cholesky decomposition is computed (see Press 1992 for the general calculation):

$$\Sigma = RR^T$$
$$\begin{pmatrix} 1 & \rho \\ \rho & 1 \end{pmatrix} = \begin{pmatrix} r_{11} & 0 \\ r_{21} & r_{22} \end{pmatrix} \begin{pmatrix} r_{11} & r_{21} \\ 0 & r_{22} \end{pmatrix}$$
$$1 = r_{11}^2$$
$$\rho = r_{11}r_{21}$$
$$1 = r_{21}^2 + r_{22}^2$$

Solving for r_{ij} the decomposition for this simple matrix is:

$$R = \begin{pmatrix} r_{11} & 0 \\ r_{21} & r_{22} \end{pmatrix} = \begin{pmatrix} 1 & 0 \\ \rho & \sqrt{1 - \rho^2} \end{pmatrix}$$

---

[3] Cholesky decomposition is preferred to eigenvector/eigenvalue decomposition for computing the "square root" of a square matrix because it is easier to compute and results in a triangular matrix R. The product RZ is easy to interpret because R is triangular—each correlated random variable is related to prior random variables and introduces a new random component. See Exercise (7.12) for another way to generate correlated variables.

Multiplying the Cholesky decomposition by two independent standard normal random samples gives two correlated normal random samples:

$$X = RZ$$
$$\begin{pmatrix} X_1 \\ X_2 \end{pmatrix} = \begin{pmatrix} 1 & 0 \\ \rho & \sqrt{1 - \rho^2} \end{pmatrix} \begin{pmatrix} Z_1 \\ Z_2 \end{pmatrix} = \begin{pmatrix} Z_1 \\ \rho Z_1 + \sqrt{1 - \rho^2} \times Z_2 \end{pmatrix}$$

This can be verified against the bivariate normal (e.g., Weisstein 2006). Now the correlated normals are translated back into uniform space: $\Phi(X_1)$ and $\Phi(X_2)$ are the correlated *uniform* random samples. Figure 7.4 illustrates the sampling, where the steps are:

1. Sample U(0,1) to get U_i.
2. Map samples onto standard normal to get $Z_i = \Phi^{-1}(X_i)$.
3. Map Z_i into correlated normals X_i by the Cholesky.
4. Map X_i into correlated uniform samples by $\Phi(X_i)$.
5. Map correlated uniform samples into cumulative target distribution.

The final step uses the sample to model default. Figure 7.4 illustrates a cumulative Bernoulli distribution corresponding to modeling default events as in sections 7.2.1 and 7.2.2. Alternatively, the cumulative probability distribution of survival (Equation (7.17)) can be used as in section 7.2.3, to derive the time to default.

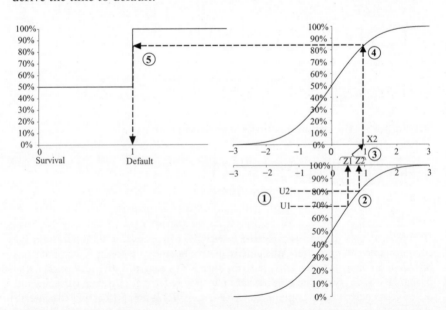

FIGURE 7.4 Mapping Uncorrelated Uniform Random Variables onto Default Events with the Gaussian Copula

A few comments are in order about this technique:

- The correlation coefficient of the uniform correlated samples is a function of ρ not ρ itself. Thus one can adjust ρ (the input correlation) to achieve a target correlation.
- Although the correlation matrix Σ is decomposed above, other derivations of this technique decompose the covariance matrix, to the same effect.
- Although the normal distribution is used here, hence the name Gaussian copula, other distributions can be used (Schonbucher 2003; Li and Skarabot 2003).
- In practice, the copula boils down to a "one factor" model in standard use by Wall Street firms when modeling synthetic indexes (see Exercise 7.12). To cure the deficiencies of the one-factor model, non-copula multi-factor models have been proposed (e.g., Hull, 2006 and Longstaff, 2006).

7.4 MONTE CARLO SIMULATION

Three alternative collateral models are sketched in Figures 7.5 through 7.7. These Monte Carlo algorithms have similar structures, but differ in how defaults are modeled. The models are simplified here (compared to section 3.4) to focus on correlation issues. Noticeably absent from these core computations are interest, principal, and prepayment cash flows. Only loss is tracked. This simplified model is appropriate for fixed-rate assets, for example, synthetic credit indexes discussed in section 7.5.

In Figure 7.5, for instance, the core simulation loops over all paths (1), all periods (2), and all assets (5). It is the asset transitions that are correlated, and hence a set of correlated random variables is generated for the assets (4). Default is an absorbing state, so that once defaulted, always defaulted (6–8). Otherwise, the next transition is calculated with the random sample corresponding to the asset (10). If the next transition is to default, a loss is computed (11–14).

Figure 7.6 illustrates modeling (instantaneous) default via spread rather than transition matrix. A probability of default is computed (3) as per Equation (7.9). The spread can be taken from a static curve supplied for each credit, or can be dynamically evolved by a stochastic spread model (e.g., Schonbucher 2003). Alternatively, the initial rating g can be translated to an effective annual default rate $\tilde{D}(g)$. The correlated random samples are generated as before (5), but are used differently. Here, the random sample corresponding to an asset is compared to the probability of default (11).

Figure 7.7 illustrates modeling *time to default* rather than default itself. The key difference is that now the cumulative probability of survival is

```
1   for all Paths
2      for all Periods
3          Losses(Path, Period) = 0
4          Rands = m correlated uniform random samples (where m = # Assets)
5          for all Assets
6              LastRating = Assets(Asset).Rating(Period-1)
7              if LastRating = DefaultState then
8                  NewRating = DefaultState
9              else
10                 NextRating = TransMatrix(LastRating, Rands(Asset))
11                 if NextRating = DefaultState then
12                     NewRating = DefaultState
13                     Loss = (1 - RecoverRate) x Assets(Asset).Notional
14                     Losses(Path, Period) = Losses(Path, Period) + Loss
15                 else
16                     NewRating = NextRating
17                 end if
18             end if
19             Assets(Asset).Rating(Period) = NewRating
```

FIGURE 7.5   Monte Carlo with Transition Matrix (Simplified)

computed (4–5) as per Equations (7.10) and (7.15). The correlated random sample corresponding to the asset is compared to the cumulative probability of survival (12). Note that Figure 7.7 uses spread to derive hazard rate. A simpler alternative is to use the effective annual default rate of the initial rating $\tilde{D}(g) = q$ as per Equation (7.17).

A key question is: how many paths are necessary? Variance of results generally decreases as the square root of the number of paths. For example,

```
1   for all Paths
2      for all Periods
3          ProbDef = Spread(Period) / (1+Spread(Period)) / (1−RecoverRate)
4          Losses(Path, Period) = 0
5          Rands = m correlated uniform random samples (where m = # Assets)
6          for all Assets
7              LastRating = Assets(Asset).Rating(Period-1)
8              if LastRating = DefaultState then
9                  NewRating = DefaultState
10             else
11                 if Rands(Asset) < ProbDef then
12                     NewRating = DefaultState
13                     Loss = (1 - RecoverRate) x Assets(Asset).Notional
14                     Losses(Path, Period) = Losses(Path, Period) + Loss
15                 else
16                     NewRating = LastRating
17                 end if
18             end if
19             Assets(Asset).Rating(Period) = NewRating
```

FIGURE 7.6   Monte Carlo with Instantaneous Probability of Default (via Spread)

```
1   for all Paths
2       Rands = m correlated uniform random samples (where m = # Assets)
3       for all Periods
4           HazardRate = Spread(Period)/(1-RecoverRate)
5           CumProbSurvival(Period) = CumProbSurvival(Period-1)/(1+HazardRate)

6           Losses(Path, Period) = 0
7           For all Assets
8               LastRating = Assets(Asset).Rating(Period-1)
9               if LastRating = DefaultState then
10                  NewRating = DefaultState
11              else
12                  if Rands (Asset) > CumProbSurvival(Period) then
13                      NewRating = DefaultState
14                      Loss = (1 – RecoverRate) x Assets(Asset).Notional
15                      Losses(Path, Period) = Losses(Path, Period) + Loss
16                  else
17                      NewRating = LastRating
18                  end if
19              end if
20              Assets(Asset).Rating(Period) = NewRating
```

FIGURE 7.7   Monte Carlo with Cumulative Probability of Survival (via Spread)

should the number of paths be increased by four times, the variance in results will decrease by half. This is an important consideration when estimating duration, for example. A slight perturbation in an input variable will create a change in the output. If the difference between the original and new outputs is less than the variance, the results are suspect. Stratified sampling is a technique of producing less paths in the Monte Carlo simulation, yet not increasing the variance.

Monte Carlo simulation is a rich area in financial engineering. There are different techniques for random number generation, path generation for different types of stochastic variables, and various efficiency techniques for speeding up the algorithm while retaining accuracy. These issues are beyond the scope of this book, although the interested reader might consult Glasserman (2003) and Dupire (1998). To illustrate Monte Carlo simulation in action, the next section discusses how to value synthetic (corporate) credit indexes.

7.5   SYNTHETIC CREDIT INDEXES

Synthetic deals were introduced in section 1.3. The assets are not sold into a trust, as in "cash" deals, rather CDSs are used to synthetically mimic cash flow behavior. ABS collateral can require extensive cash flow analysis for optimizing the synthetic structure, the same as for a "cash" deal. In this section, we consider corporate collateral. A corporate credit is fundamentally simpler than say a mortgage. A corporate credit is traded at a specific rating and spread. Individual mortgages (and other ABS collateral) are not traded—they have no rating or spread. The corporate credit spread allows one to model default directly, as will be shown in this section. Furthermore, corporate bonds don't prepay or amortize, facilitating the modeling of their cash flows. Synthetic corporate structures have no waterfalls or triggers, vastly simplifying the model.[4]

A synthetic credit index consists of assets and liabilities. On the asset side are a set or "basket" of credits (usually 100 or 125). On the liability side are a set of contiguous tranches for example, 0% to 3%, 3% to 7%, etc. Investors in a tranche (going long in the tranche) sell credit protection associated with that tranche. The investor must pay out any losses infringing on the tranche. As mentioned in section 1.3, there are also bespoke tranches that can be customized in numerous ways, a topic beyond the scope of this book.

For example, consider 100 credits. If 10 credits default recovering 60%, the total loss is $(10/100) \times (1 - 60\%) = 4\%$. The 0–3% tranche investor pays the full 3% and the 3–7% investor pays the remaining 1%. We say, for example, that the 0–3% tranche *attaches* at 0% and *detaches* at 3%. *Caution:* The first tranche absorbs losses up to 3% *of the original notional*, the second tranche up to 7%, and so on.

Now consider a simple example with four credits, 50% survival probability, and 0% recovery. In the absence of correlation, this is analogous to flipping a fair coin four times, where heads you survive and tails you default. The probability mass function of pool loss is shown in Figure 7.8. This is the standard binomial distribution. Pool loss is the total number of losses in the entire structure (e.g., the 0–100% tranche). Since there is no recovery, a 25% pool loss is equivalent to one credit defaulting. Similarly, a 50% pool loss is equivalent to two credits defaulting, and so on.

With respect to this distribution, investors are generally interested in the *mean* loss. The mean pool loss is 50%:

$$50\% = 0\% \times 6.25\% + 25\% \times 25\% + 50\% \times 37.5\% +$$

$$75\% \times 25\% + 100\% \times 6.25\%$$

Let's assume the pool notional is \$4 or \$1 per credit ($N_{credit} = 1$). The expected pool loss is thus \$2.

---

[4] In 2006, synthetic ABS indexes (ABX) started trading. Their assets are tranches issued from subprime securitizations, with all the characteristics discussed in this book. Modeling an ABS index is thus more complex than the corporate indexes described in this chapter.

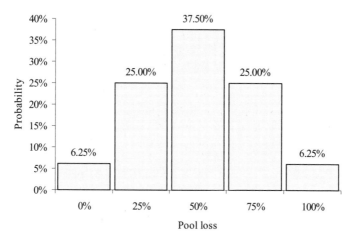

FIGURE 7.8 Probability Mass Function of Loss (Binomial Distribution): Four Credits, 0% Correlation, 50% Survival Probability, and 0% Recovery

7.5.1 Loss-Lets

Mean tranche losses are computed in a similar manner, but caution is required. Consider a 0–50% tranche for this example. The tranche notional is $50\% \times \$4 = \$2$. The mean tranche loss is 40.6% computed as follows:

$$40.625\% = 0\% \times 6.25\% + 25\% \times 25\% + 50\% \times 37.5\% +$$
$$50\% \times 25\% + 50\% \times 6.25\%$$

In absolute terms, the expected loss is $40.625\% \times \$4 = \$1.625$. The investor is liable only for losses to the tranche. So if losses *exceed* the tranche, the investor's loss is *capped*. Note that the mean tranche loss is not equal to any particular mass beneath the pool loss distribution. An erroneous guess is that the mean tranche loss in this case is $\$2.5 = (25\% + 37.5\%) \times \$4$.

Generalizing what was done to compute a tranche loss, the concept of a "loss-let" is now introduced. This is the loss associated with a one-credit-wide tranche. A structure with one-credit-wide tranches is called an *Nth-to-default* structure. There are four loss-lets associated with the example given above. Each attaches when another credit defaults. For example, the first loss-let is the probability that one or more credit defaults.

$$P_{\geq 1} = 25\% + 37.5\% + 25\% + 6.25\% = 93.75\%$$

Similarly:

$$P_{\geq 2} = 37.5\% + 25\% + 6.25\% = 68.75\%$$
$$P_{\geq 3} = 25\% + 6.25\% = 31.25\%$$
$$P_{\geq 4} = 6.25\%$$

Loss-lets can be added to compute the mean tranche loss of a larger tranche. For example, let's revisit the 0–50% tranche. The tranche encompasses one or two credits defaulting, thus the mean tranche loss is:

$$\$1 \times P_{\geq 1} + \$1 \times P_{\geq 2} = \$0.9375 + \$0.6875 = \$1.625$$

Thus it checks with the prior calculation. Similarly, a 25–75% tranche has a mean loss of

$$\$1 \times P_{\geq 2} + \$1 \times P_{\geq 3} = \$0.6875 + \$0.3125 = \$1$$

Recall that the 25–75% tranche investor pays for the second and third losses, not the first loss (covered by the 0–25% tranche). In general:

$$E[loss(i; j)] = \sum_{k=i}^{j} P_{\geq k} \times N_{credit} \qquad (7.23)$$

Finally, note that the mean pool loss is simply the sum of all the loss-lets:

$$E[loss(1; 4)] = \$1 \times P_{\geq 1} + \$1 \times P_{\geq 2} + \$1 \times P_{\geq 3} + \$1 \times P_{\geq 4}$$
$$= \$1 \times (93.75\% + 68.75\% + 31.25\% + 6.25\%) = \$2$$

The pool loss *distribution* can be computed a variety of ways. Generally these methods use a copula to account for correlations among credits. Should one use Monte Carlo simulation, the distribution is rendered as a large set of path losses. This is not formally a probability mass function (PMF) because should we run more paths, we would likely get different loss values. The path losses are *binned* at fine-enough granularities so that errors are acceptable. The Monte Carlo simulations sketched in section 7.4 are appropriate to modeling synthetic fixed-rate credits. Recall from Figures 7.5 through 7.7 that interest, principal, and prepayment cash flows are absent—only losses are calculated. In actuality, interest cash flow can be derived from losses, as we shall see later in this section. A Gaussian copula Monte Carlo simulator was written based on correlating time to default, as summarized in Figure 7.7. This synthetic credit index model is used in the remainder of this chapter.

Consider an example with 100 credits, 70 bps spread per credit, five years maturity, 8% correlation between credits, 30% recovery rate, and 0%

TABLE 7.2 Binned Probability Mass Function of Loss: 100 Credits, $1B Notional, 70 bps Spread, 5 Years, 8% Correlation, 30% Recovery, 0% Risk-free Rate, 50,000 Paths

Pool Loss $MM	% loss	Pr(loss)	Cum Pr(loss)	Pool Loss $MM	% loss	Pr(loss)	Cum Pr(loss)
—	0.00%	5.42%	5.42%	126	12.60%	0.21%	99.43%
7	0.70%	10.56%	15.99%	133	13.30%	0.18%	99.60%
14	1.40%	13.24%	29.22%	140	14.00%	0.10%	99.71%
21	2.10%	13.40%	42.62%	147	14.70%	0.09%	99.79%
28	2.80%	12.14%	54.76%	154	15.40%	0.05%	99.85%
35	3.50%	10.54%	65.30%	161	16.10%	0.03%	99.88%
42	4.20%	8.36%	73.66%	168	16.80%	0.03%	99.91%
49	4.90%	6.52%	80.18%	175	17.50%	0.02%	99.93%
56	5.60%	5.21%	85.39%	182	18.20%	0.02%	99.95%
63	6.30%	3.78%	89.16%	189	18.90%	0.01%	99.96%
70	7.00%	2.89%	92.05%	196	19.60%	0.01%	99.97%
77	7.70%	2.18%	94.24%	203	20.30%	0.01%	99.98%
84	8.40%	1.62%	95.85%	210	21.00%	0.01%	99.99%
91	9.10%	1.18%	97.04%	217	21.70%	0.01%	99.99%
98	9.80%	0.83%	97.87%	238	23.80%	0.00%	100.00%
105	10.50%	0.59%	98.46%	245	24.50%	0.00%	100.00%
112	11.20%	0.47%	98.93%	273	27.30%	0.00%	100.00%
119	11.90%	0.29%	99.22%				

risk-free rate. Suppose the pool notional is $1B or $10MM per credit. A pool loss distribution, estimated from 50,000 paths, is shown in Table 7.2.

The simple definition of loss-let given earlier no longer applies when the bucket widths are irregular and/or do not correspond to a single credit's notional amount. In this example, a credit amounts to $N_{credit} = \$10MM$, yet the first bucket comprises $7MM with probability mass of 10.56%. The loss-let computation is generalized as follows. Let ℓ_i and ℓ_{i+1} be attachment and detachment points (given as a percentage of pool notional).[5] Let $\pi(\ell)$ be the probability density function of loss.

$$\hat{P}_{\geq \ell_i} = \left(\frac{1}{2} \int_{\ell_i}^{\ell_{i+1}} \pi(\ell) d\ell + \int_{\ell_{i+1}}^{100\%} \pi(\ell) d\ell \right) \times (\ell_{i+1} - \ell_i) \qquad (7.24)$$

---

[5] Throughout this chapter, contiguous tranches are assumed to simplify the exposition. This can be generalized to discontinuous and overlapping tranches with some extra work.

The factor of $1/2$ for the first mass is necessary because some assumption must be made for the distribution of mass *within* the bucket. Given no other information it is assumed that all the mass is centered within the bucket, that is, equivalent to uniformly distributing the mass across the bucket.

The continuous form of the loss-let is discretized as follows:

$$\hat{P}_{\geq \ell_i} = \frac{m_{\ell_i}}{2} + P_{\geq \ell_{i+1}}$$

$$= \frac{m_{\ell_i}}{2} + \sum_{k=i+1}^{N} m_{\ell_k} \qquad (7.25)$$

where m_{ℓ_i} is the mass in bucket attaching at ℓ_i and detaching at ℓ_{i+1}. N is the final bucket number. It is conceptually easier to use equal-size buckets in the PMF. However, the buckets must be small enough to reduce the estimation error. Table 7.3 shows the pool loss distribution with bucket size of $1MM or 10 bps of the $1B pool notional (only the first 70 buckets are shown). Because of the previous assumptions of a fixed 30% recovery rate and 0% risk-free rate, there is no dispersion around the losses. The probability mass is clumped at points.

Consider the mean loss of the 3–7% tranche. The simulation generated an estimate of 24.26% of the $40MM tranche notional. To estimate the mean loss with loss-lets, sum buckets #31 to 70 inclusive in Table 7.3 ("loss-lets" column). The sum of the loss-lets is 0.943% of the $1B pool notional, equivalent to 23.58% of the tranche notional. The error between these two estimates is entirely due to the factor of $1/2$ in the loss-let formula. This error can be decreased by increasing the number of buckets. For instance, if the bucket size is reduced by $1/2$ then the error is likewise reduced by $1/2$.

If the factor of $1/2$ causes loss-lets to diverge from simulated results, why define them in this manner? The reason is that should recovery be stochastic and/or should we have a nonzero interest-rate curve for the risk-free rate, losses will be dispersed among the buckets. In this case, the $1/2$ will not introduce a biased error; that is, errors will likely cancel out. In summary, a loss-let table is nothing more than tabulated loss probabilities facilitating the quick estimation of tranche losses across any attachment and detachment points. If one's simulator is fast enough, or an analytic solution is possible, then such a shortcut is not needed.

7.5.2 Analysis

Producing a loss distribution is the core of the synthetic index model. However, there is a bit more computation to convert loss to value. Because the synthetic corporate index is built upon corporate swaps, the valuation is fundamentally different (and simpler) than for cash assets. Figure 7.9 illustrates the cash flows of a CDS: the premium and contingency legs.

TABLE 7.3 Loss-Let table for 100 credits, $1B notional, 5 years, 70 bps spread, 8% correlation, 30% recovery, 0% risk-free rate, 100,000 paths. Only 70 loss-lets shown

Pool Loss ($MM)	% Loss	Pr(loss)	Cum Pr(loss)	Loss-Lets	Pool Loss ($MM)	% Loss	Pr(loss)	Cum Pr(loss)	Loss-Lets
—	0.00%	5.639%	5.64%						
1	0.10%	0.000%	5.64%	0.0944%	36	3.60%	0.000%	65.53%	0.0345%
2	0.20%	0.000%	5.64%	0.0944%	37	3.70%	0.000%	65.53%	0.0345%
3	0.30%	0.000%	5.64%	0.0944%	38	3.80%	0.000%	65.53%	0.0345%
4	0.40%	0.000%	5.64%	0.0944%	39	3.90%	0.000%	65.53%	0.0345%
5	0.50%	0.000%	5.64%	0.0944%	40	4.00%	0.000%	65.53%	0.0345%
6	0.60%	0.000%	5.64%	0.0944%	41	4.10%	0.000%	65.53%	0.0345%
7	0.70%	10.508%	16.15%	0.0891%	42	4.20%	8.319%	73.85%	0.0303%
8	0.80%	0.000%	16.15%	0.0839%	43	4.30%	0.000%	73.85%	0.0262%
9	0.90%	0.000%	16.15%	0.0839%	44	4.40%	0.000%	73.85%	0.0262%
10	1.00%	0.000%	16.15%	0.0839%	45	4.50%	0.000%	73.85%	0.0262%
11	1.10%	0.000%	16.15%	0.0839%	46	4.60%	0.000%	73.85%	0.0262%
12	1.20%	0.000%	16.15%	0.0839%	47	4.70%	0.000%	73.85%	0.0262%
13	1.30%	0.000%	16.15%	0.0839%	48	4.80%	0.000%	73.85%	0.0262%
14	1.40%	13.237%	29.38%	0.0772%	49	4.90%	6.604%	80.45%	0.0229%
15	1.50%	0.000%	29.38%	0.0706%	50	5.00%	0.000%	80.45%	0.0196%
16	1.60%	0.000%	29.38%	0.0706%	51	5.10%	0.000%	80.45%	0.0196%
17	1.70%	0.000%	29.38%	0.0706%	52	5.20%	0.000%	80.45%	0.0196%
18	1.80%	0.000%	29.38%	0.0706%	53	5.30%	0.000%	80.45%	0.0196%
19	1.90%	0.000%	29.38%	0.0706%	54	5.40%	0.000%	80.45%	0.0196%
20	2.00%	0.000%	29.38%	0.0706%	55	5.50%	0.000%	80.45%	0.0196%
21	2.10%	13.458%	42.84%	0.0639%	56	5.60%	5.131%	85.58%	0.0170%
22	2.20%	0.000%	42.84%	0.0572%	57	5.70%	0.000%	85.58%	0.0144%
23	2.30%	0.000%	42.84%	0.0572%	58	5.80%	0.000%	85.58%	0.0144%
24	2.40%	0.000%	42.84%	0.0572%	59	5.90%	0.000%	85.58%	0.0144%
25	2.50%	0.000%	42.84%	0.0572%	60	6.00%	0.000%	85.58%	0.0144%
26	2.60%	0.000%	42.84%	0.0572%	61	6.10%	0.000%	85.58%	0.0144%
27	2.70%	0.000%	42.84%	0.0572%	62	6.20%	0.000%	85.58%	0.0144%
28	2.80%	12.220%	55.06%	0.0510%	63	6.30%	3.828%	89.41%	0.0125%
29	2.90%	0.000%	55.06%	0.0449%	64	6.40%	0.000%	89.41%	0.0106%
30	3.00%	0.000%	55.06%	0.0449%	65	6.50%	0.000%	89.41%	0.0106%
31	3.10%	0.000%	55.06%	0.0449%	66	6.60%	0.000%	89.41%	0.0106%
32	3.20%	0.000%	55.06%	0.0449%	67	6.70%	0.000%	89.41%	0.0106%
33	3.30%	0.000%	55.06%	0.0449%	68	6.80%	0.000%	89.41%	0.0106%
34	3.40%	0.000%	55.06%	0.0449%	69	6.90%	0.000%	89.41%	0.0106%
35	3.50%	10.464%	65.53%	0.0397%	70	7.00%	2.754%	92.16%	0.0092%

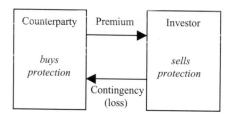

FIGURE 7.9 Corporate Credit Default Swap Cash Flows

The premium leg has cash flows based on paying an annual premium (coupon) on the outstanding notional balance of the tranche. The loss leg has cash flows based on paying a nonrecoverable loss amount impinging on the tranche. The premium cash flow corresponds to interest cash flow in previous chapters. *Principal and prepayment cash flows are noticeably absent.* The Monte Carlo simulation produces raw loss data $Loss(t, p)$ tallied by path p and period t. This raw data is in effect the empirical loss distribution, and from it statistical moments can be computed.

For a given path p, for a given period T, cumulative loss is computed from the loss distribution.

$$CumLoss(T, p) = \sum_{t=1}^{T} Loss(t, p) \tag{7.26}$$

For a given tranche with attachment point ℓ_i and detachment point ℓ_{i+1}, premium and loss cash flows are computed from cumulative loss. The undiscounted premium is the notional amount remaining in the tranche after cumulative losses are absorbed. The premium *rate* is accounted for later.

$$Prem_{\ell_i}(T, p) = \min[\max[0, \ell_{i+1} - CumLoss(T, p)], \ell_{i+1} - \ell_i] \tag{7.27}$$

For a given period, loss absorbed is the difference between the premiums on successive periods (since there is no prinicipal paydown, any change in premium is due to loss).

$$Loss_{\ell_i}(T, p) = Prem_{\ell_i}(T - 1, p) - Prem_{\ell_i}(T, p) \tag{7.28}$$

To calculate present values, these cash flows are discounted over some interest rate curve—the discount factors are $Disc(t)$. The premium present value is scaled by a basis point and called $PV01$—this is the value per one bps of annualized premium rate. These are stated as fractions of tranche notional.

$$PV01_{\ell_i}(p) = 1 \text{ bps} \times \frac{1}{\ell_{i+1} - \ell_i} \times \sum_{t=1}^{T} Prem_{\ell_i}(t, p) \times Disc(t) \tag{7.29}$$

$$PVLoss_{\ell_i}(p) = \frac{1}{\ell_{i+1} - \ell_i} \times \sum_{t=1}^{T} Loss_{\ell_i}(t, p) \times Disc(t) \tag{7.30}$$

This empirical data can be used to compute moments. The sample means are show below, for n paths.

$$\overline{PVO1}_{\ell_i} = \frac{1}{n} \sum_{p=1}^{n} PVO1_{\ell_i}(p) \tag{7.31}$$

$$\overline{PVLoss}_{\ell_i} = \frac{1}{n} \sum_{p=1}^{n} PVLoss_{\ell_i}(p) \tag{7.32}$$

The tranche present value is the net of the leg present values. Here we account for the premium rate, $Premium_{\ell_i}$. The factor of 10,000 undoes the 1 bps in Equation (7.29).

$$\overline{PV}_{\ell_i} = UpFront + \overline{PVO1}_{\ell_i} \times Premium_{\ell_i} \times 10000 - \overline{PVLoss}_{\ell_i} \tag{7.33}$$

Par Premium (Breakeven Spread) The par premium is the premium that prices the swap at par (i.e., with zero net present value). Equity (i.e., the tranche attaching at 0%) spread is currently quoted by the market as a fixed coupon *with a variable up-front fee*. Thus for equity the up-front fee is derived rather than spread. For certain indexes, other tranches are also quoted this way.

$$UpFront = \begin{cases} \overline{PVLoss}_{\ell_i} - \overline{PVO1}_{\ell_i} \times Coupon_{\ell_i} \times 10000 & \ell_i \text{ has upfront} \\ 0 & \text{otherwise} \end{cases} \tag{7.34}$$

$$ParPremium_{\ell_i} = \begin{cases} Coupon_{\ell_i} & \ell_i \text{ has upfront} \\ \overline{PVLoss}_{\ell_i} \div \left(\overline{PVO1}_{\ell_i} \times 10000\right) & \text{otherwise} \end{cases} \tag{7.35}$$

The simulator mentioned in the previous section was compared to an analytic model, for the January 22, 2004, TRAC-X marks quoted from a broker/dealer on that day. Actually, TRAC-X is an old index that isn't used anymore. As of the writing of this book, the U.S. market revolves around the Dow Jones CDX (www.djindexes.com/mdsidx/index.cfm?event=cdx) and the European market around iTRAXX (www.itraxx.com). These come in various flavors: investment grade, high yield, and so on. Markit is somewhat of an industry standard for collecting and calculating marks for the underlying credits (www.markit.com). The empirical results given in this section are for investment grade, but the modeling technique is general.

TABLE 7.4 Synthetic Credit Index Model Input Parameters (Values Shown for 7–10% Tranche)

Input Parameter	Value	Explanation
# credits	100	asset entities (uniform notionals)
Maturity	5	all assets have this maturity (in years)
InterestRate	3.4%	market rate (flat curve assumed)
MktCreditSpread	0.545%	spread on each asset
RecoveryRate	36%	recovery percentage
Correlation[6]	17.18%	correlation of default time between two assets
ℓ_i	7%	attachment point of tranche of interest
ℓ_{i+1}	10%	detachment point of tranche of interest
UpFront	0%	up-front fee as % of tranche notional
Premium$_{\ell_i}$	1.02%	premium paid (p.a.) to tranche investor (quarterly)

More paths are required to calibrate higher tranches than lower tranches because fewer losses hit these higher tranches. To accurately measure the frequency of these rare events, more trials are required. Since the accuracy of a Monte Carlo simulation improves roughly as the square root of the number of paths, significant increases in paths are necessary. For simplicity the number of paths was kept constant for all tranches.

The static input parameters of the TRAC-X calibration are: 100 credits of equal size, five-year maturity, 3.4% interest rate, 54.5 bps credit spread, 36% recovery rate, as summarized in Table 7.4. These parameters are shared among all the tranches. The last five input parameters in Table 7.4 are specific to the given tranche. The analytic model ran quarterly whereas the simulation ran annually. The rates and spreads are static, and all credits have the same spread for this calibration.

The key outputs of the model for the 7–10% tranche follow (these values are rounded). By Equation (7.35) the tranche's par premium is seen to be 1.02%.

$$\overline{PV01}_{7\%} = 0.048\%$$
$$\overline{PVLoss}_{7\%} = 4.882\%$$
$$ParPremium_{\ell_i} = \overline{PVLoss}_{\ell_i} \div \left(\overline{PV01}_{\ell_i} \times 10000\right) = 1.02\%$$

Relative-Value (Rich-Cheap) Analysis Table 7.5 compares the par premiums for each both bid and ask correlations (dealer marks) for each tranche. Both

---

[6]Unless otherwise stated, all correlations stated in this chapter are "compound" correlations, as opposed to "base" correlations defined later in this section.

TABLE 7.5 TRAC-X Calibration Results, January 22, 2004, Par Premiums. 40,000 Paths Used for Simulation.

Attach	Detach	Bid/Ask	Dealer Corr	Dealer Par Prem.	Analytic Par Prem.	MC Par Prem.	MC-Dealer	Analytic-Dealer	Dealer vs. Models
0%	3%	Bid	22.90%	5% + 36.3%	33.27%	33.29%	−301 bp	−303 bp	Cheap
		Ask	16.72%	5% + 41.5%	38.48%	38.58%	−292 bp	−302 bp	Cheap
3%	7%	Bid	5.98%	302 bp	288 bp	289 bp	−13 bp	−14 bp	Cheap
		Ask	14.29%	360 bp	353 bp	355 bp	−5 bp	−7 bp	Cheap
7%	10%	Bid	17.18%	102 bp	102 bp	101 bp	−1 bp	0 bp	Fair
		Ask	21.22%	123 bp	123 bp	122 bp	−1 bp	0 bp	Fair
10%	15%	Bid	23.00%	47 bp	50 bp	48 bp	+1 bp	+3 bp	Rich
		Ask	28.76%	65 bp	68 bp	67 bp	+2 bp	+3 bp	Rich
15%	30%	Bid	27.82%	10 bp	11 bp	12 bp	+2 bp	+1 bp	Rich
		Ask	33.24%	16 bp	19 bp	18 bp	+2 bp	+3 bp	Rich

the Monte Carlo simulation model and the analytic model are compared against the "market" quotes given by the broker/dealer on that day. The error of these models is highest for the equity tranche. Errors are likely introduced by different input assumptions (e.g., recovery).

Convention is such that bid spreads are *lower* than ask (offer) spreads. In other words, the bid spread is the premium that the dealer wishes to pay when buying protection on the tranche. The offer spread is the premium that the dealer wishes to receive when selling protection on the tranche. Typically, investors sell protection, so the bid spread is of primary relevance, as are bid correlations, that is, correlations imputed from bid spreads.

This market data can be used to calibrate the models. For example, assuming 3.4% interest rate and 36% recovery rate, the 7–10% tranche bid of 102 bps and corresponding correlation of 17.18% are calibrated in the models: they produce a fair price (Tranche PV = 0.002% for the analytic solution, i.e., close to zero). However, these same assumptions do not calibrate the other tranches. For example, given the same assumptions with a correlation of 23%, the implied premium for the 10–15% tranche is 50 bps (48 bps for the Monte Carlo). As an investor wanting to buy the tranche (i.e., sell protection on the tranche), the dealer's quote is *rich*: The investor would rather receive 50 bps (or 48 bps) than 47 bps. Evaluations of all tranches in the model, using the 7–10% tranche as the "fair" baseline, are summarized in the last column of Table 7.5.

Given a neutral view on the market, there is no reason to favor any of the tranches as the baseline ("fair value") with which to calibrate the others. One should instead find a pair of tranches, one rich and one cheap, and trade them both. This is a form of "arbitrage": Selling the rich and buying the cheap will hopefully result in a profit. For this index for this day, nothing was particularly rich—the senior three tranches seemed to be fairly priced. Because no two model signals clearly disagree with the dealer in both directions, there is no trading opportunity.

Table 7.6 compares the mean present values of the swap legs for the Monte Carlo simulator and the analytic model. There is close correspondence between these models. The simulator has an added advantage that it is more flexible: The model can be modified and still solved in the same manner. For example, we could add stochastic sampling of recovery rates from a distribution. It is unlikely that an analytic solution can easily be found for this extension. Of course the analytic solver is much faster.

Consider another structure with equity (0–20%), mezzanine (20–40%), and senior (40–100%) tranches. The underlying 100 credits have equal spreads of 2.3%. Assume a five-year maturity, a flat interest rate curve of 1%, and a 45% recovery rate. Figure 7.10 illustrates how par premium varies with correlation. Fifty thousand paths were used in this simulation. Equity spread

TABLE 7.6 PV of Swap Legs for Both Models in TRAC-X Calibration. 40,000 Paths Used for Simulation. PV Stated as % of Total Notional.

Attach	Detach	Bid/Ask	Dealer Corr	MC E(PVLoss)	Analytic E(PVLoss)	MC E(PV01)	Analytic E(PV01)	MC Stdev(PVLoss)
0%	3%	Bid	22.90%	47.99%	48.94%	0.029%	0.031%	22.86%
		Ask	16.72%	52.58%	53.52%	0.028%	0.030%	21.26%
3%	7%	Bid	5.98%	12.37%	12.63%	0.043%	0.044%	9.77%
		Ask	14.29%	0.00%	15.14%	0.042%	0.043%	12.07%
7%	10%	Bid	17.18%	4.46%	4.59%	0.044%	0.045%	4.26%
		Ask	21.22%	5.38%	5.53%	0.044%	0.045%	5.10%
10%	15%	Bid	23.01%	2.16%	2.27%	0.045%	0.045%	2.11%
		Ask	28.76%	2.97%	3.09%	0.045%	0.045%	2.89%
15%	30%	Bid	27.82%	0.53%	0.52%	0.045%	0.046%	0.53%
		Ask	33.24%	0.83%	0.85%	0.045%	0.046%	0.82%

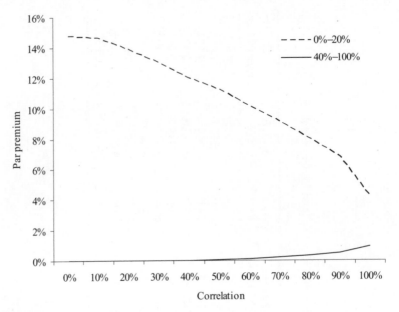

FIGURE 7.10 Equity and Senior Transches: Par Premium vs. Correlation; 5 Years, 230 bps Spread 1% Interest Rates, 45% Recovery Rate, 50,000 Paths

decreases with increasing correlation (and its value increases). Senior spread increases with increasing correlation (and its value decreases).

As stated in Equation (7.35), par premium is a function of loss and hence correlation. Alternatively, given the market premium, one can solve for correlation—this is called the *implied* correlation. Although not shown in Figure 7.10, mezzanine tranche premium may not be monotonic in correlation. As a result, implied correlation is not always well defined, i.e., the same premium can correspond to two correlations. To fix this problem, "base" correlations are quoted. Base correlations are implied correlations of equity tranches of varying detachment points, for example, 0–3%, 0–7%, 0–10%, and so on.

7.5.3 Hedging

In a synthetic deal, suppose the investor sells protection to the dealer/structurer. Depending on the tranche purchased by the investor, the investor is either long or short correlation; that is, the value of the investment will either increase or decrease with increasing correlation.

For equity (synthetic) in general:

↑correlation → ↓ loss → ↑ value → ↓ value of protection → ↑ "investor" value

↑correlation →   ↑ "investor" value: "investor" is long correlation

protection seller has bought correlation ↔ protection buyer has sold correlation

investor has bought correlation ↔ dealer has sold correlation

dealer hedge is to buy correlation

The view from the senior tranche is the opposite. For senior (synthetic) in general:

↓correlation → ↓ loss → ↑ value → ↓ value of protection → ↑ "investor" value

↓correlation → ↑ "investor" value: "investor" is short correlation

protection seller has sold correlation ↔ protection buyer has bought correlation

investor has sold correlation ↔ dealer has bought correlation

dealer hedge is to sell correlation

For the mezzanine things are not so simple—it can act as either equity or senior debt, depending on attachment and width. Correlation is just one of several factors that the investment may be sensitive to and for which hedges are sought. In the following we focus on credit spread rather than correlation, but the reasoning is similar.

Let's revisit the TRAC-X calibration discussed in the previous section. Five perturbations of the 7–10% tranche are presented in Table 7.7. The

TABLE 7.7 Five Sensitivities or Durations of the Synthetic Structure (7–10% Tranche in TRAC-X Calibration). PV Stated as % of Total Notional.

	Scenario	$\overline{PV}_{7\%}$	Difference (w/ Base)	-Difference ÷ $\overline{PV01}_{7\%}$
	Base	−0.019%		
1	$MktCreditSpread$ +1 bp	−0.209%	−0.190%	4.2
2	$RecoveryRate$ +10%	0.353%	0.372%	−8.2
3	$Correlation$ +5%	−1.167%	−1.148%	25.3
4	$Correlation$ −5%	1.431%	1.451%	−31.9
5	$InterestRate$ +1%	0.029%	0.048%	−1.1

tranche present value is shown for each. Differences are computed with respect to a baseline. The difference is also displayed as a multiple of the PV01, that is, the sensitivity of premium value to a one-bps shock to premium rate. For example, in the third row correlation is increased by 5% and the tranche decreases in value by 1.148% to -1.167%. This tranche, being senior to equity, is not "long correlation" as we would expect equity to be. This sensitivity is 25 times higher than the PV01 sensitivity.

An investor (buyer of the tranche or seller of protection) wishes to hedge its investment against decreasing value. This can happen when credit spreads *widen* or when correlation *increases* (for nonequity tranches)—these result in *lower* tranche value. To hedge against this decline in value, the investor wishes to buy protection.

One possible hedge ratio is the amount of protection the investor should buy to offset the decline in tranche value should credit spreads increase by Δ, for example, one bps. This is sometimes called the "tranche delta" and is the *negative* of the *MktCreditSpread* perturbation difference in Table 7.7.

$$TrancheDelta_{\ell_i} = \frac{\overline{PV}_{\ell_i}(MktCreditSpread) - \overline{PV}_{\ell_i}(MktCreditSpread + \Delta)}{\Delta}$$

$$(7.36)$$

The sensitivity of the value of the entire index to a perturbation in credit spreads is:

$$DV01 = \frac{\overline{PV}_{0\%-100\%}(MktCreditSpread) - \overline{PV}_{0\%-100\%}(MktCreditSpread + \Delta)}{\Delta}$$

$$(7.37)$$

The *DV01* is invariant under changes in the number of credits and correlation. This is because the sensitivity is over the whole basket. In other words, looking at the behavior of the entire set of tranches, it hardly matters how the assets are split: Their diversity is irrelevant because every loss is felt by some tranche.

The hedge ratio is the tranche sensitivity normalized to the sensitivity of the entire index, as if they both had the same notional. The terminology used here is not universal; sometimes the hedge ratio is called the "delta" or the "leverage."

$$HedgeRatio_{\ell_i} = -\frac{TrancheDelta_{\ell_i} \div (\ell_{i+1} - \ell_i)}{DV01}$$

$$(7.38)$$

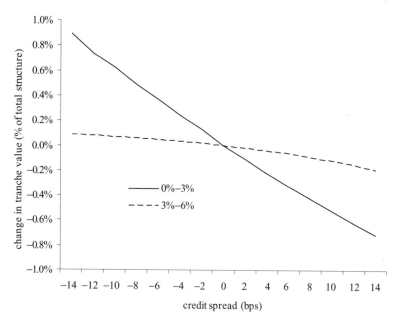

FIGURE 7.11 Equity and Mezzanine Tranches: How Value Changes with Credit Spread; 5 Years, 100 Credits, 40 bps Spread (Centered at "0"), 3% Interest Rates, 40% Recovery, 0% Correlation, 50,000 Paths

For the TRAC-X example, for the 7–10% tranche, the 1.02% premium is fair; that is, the dealer's quote (bid side) and the model produce the same premium for the correlation assumption of 17.18%. For $\Delta = 1$ bps, $Tranche Delta_{7\%-10\%} \div (10\% - 7\%) = 19$ bps and $DV01 = 4.5$ bps. In other words, the entire index loses 4.5 bps in value for each one bps increase in spread. The tranche is thus $19/4.5 = 4$ times more sensitive to a one bps shock than the entire basket.

Figure 7.11 illustrates how tranche value varies with credit spread. The five-year structure has 100 underlying credits each with 40 bps spread. We assume a flat interest rate curve of 3%, 40% recovery rate, and 0% correlation. Fifty thousand paths were used in the simulation. Equity value is much more sensitive to changes in spread than mezzanine (and senior) tranches. The slope at any point represents the hedge ratio.

Figure 7.12 illustrates how hedge ratio varies with attachment point. The five-year structure has 100 underlying credits each with 35 bps spread. We assume a flat interest rate curve of 3%, 40% recovery and 0% correlation. Two hundred thousand paths were used in the simulation.

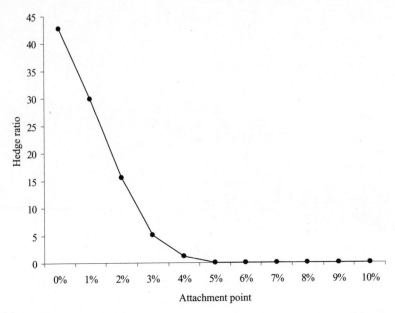

FIGURE 7.12 Tranches Hedge Ratio vs. Attachment Point for Tranches of 3% Width; 5 Years, 100 Credits, 35 bps Spread, 3% Interest Rates, 40% Recovery, 0% Correlation, 200,000 Paths

Hedge ratio can be computed with respect to the change in *one particular* underlying credit spread, as opposed to *all* underlying spreads as above. This is called a "credit delta." This allows one to hedge against specific credits. Hedges based on tranche and credit deltas are first-order approximations that ignore lower-order terms, notably convexity. Spread convexity (or gamma) differs in sign depending on the tranche. For senior in general:

$\uparrow$ spread $\rightarrow \uparrow$ Prob(default) $\rightarrow \uparrow$ sensitivity to spread (delta) $\rightarrow$ +convexity

For equity in general:

$\uparrow$ spread $\rightarrow \uparrow$ Prob(default) $\rightarrow \downarrow$ sensitivity to spread (delta) $\rightarrow$ −convexity

The subtle difference here is that the senior tranche becomes a bit closer, but still far from default, so it becomes *more* sensitive to additional spread changes. The equity becomes very close to default so that it becomes *less* sensitive to additional spread changes.

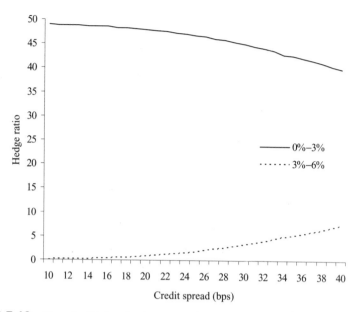

FIGURE 7.13 Tranche Hedge Ratio vs. Credit Spread for Equity and Mezzanine Tranches; 5 Years, 100 Credits, 5% Interest Rates, 40% Recovery, 0% Correlation, 200,000 Paths

Figure 7.13 illustrates this point with a plot of hedge ratio vs. credit spread. The five-year structure has 100 underlying credits. We assume a flat interest rate curve of 3%, 40% recovery and 0% correlation. Two hundred thousand paths were used in the simulation. As spreads increase, the equity hedge ratio decreases and the mezzanine hedge ratio increases. Thus convexity is negative for equity and positive for the mezzanine.

These sections only scratch the surface of synthetic credit indexes and structures. The structures described can be made more flexible in practice. For example, floating premiums can be offered, active management of credits is possible (with dynamic addition and removal of credits), a full structure is not necessary—bespokes are customized tranches sold on their own, portfolios with both long and *short* credits are possible, noncontiguous (overlapping) tranches are possible, and even "cash" structure-like triggers can be incorporated. Furthermore, hedging can be more complicated than discussed, e.g., when considering options to buy/sell tranches, CDOs built from underlying bespokes, and combinations of bespokes with other types of derivatives. See Bank of America (2004), Chaplin (2005), and Mahadevan (2006a,b) for further discussion.

7.6 *DOING IT IN EXCEL*

Building a Monte Carlo Simulator

Excel provides limited ability to manipulate matrices. To compute a two-year transition matrix from a one-year matrix requires simply multiplying the two matrices. Figure 7.14 shows how this can be done in Excel with the MMULT built-in. MMULT multiplies the two matrices represented by its arguments. In this case, the matrices are square: "trans" is the named range corresponding to B2:S19. The probabilities in the matrix are scaled by 100 so the product must be scaled by 1/100. A named range is used so that multiple copies of the second matrix can be made in a downward direction within the spreadsheet. This will produce a three-year matrix, a four-year matrix, and so on.

Every cell in the second matrix has the formula: {=MMULT(B2:S19, trans)/100}. The brackets are created, after all the cells are populated and selected, by the key sequence CTRL-SHIFT-ENTER. This is the infamous sequence for creating an "array" construct within Excel. The array construct binds together its component cells into a higher-order object. For example, a data table (section 4.12) is also an "array" object. Array objects cannot be piecewise modified—one can only clear the entire array and recreate it. Other matrix built-ins are TRANSPOSE and MINVERSE.

Figure 7.15 shows how a default table is created from transition matrices. Assume the previous matrices are located on the "transition table" sheet. Using the OFFSET built-in, the last column of each matrix is dropped into this table. OFFSET(A,R,C) references the cell R rows and C columns offset from cell A. Every cell in this table has a similar formula to that shown in cell C18—the formulae are simply copied to populate the table. In so doing, the row and column indicies (column A and row 1) are used to compute the R and C offsets needed. Figure 7.16 shows a "loss table" generated from the default table, assuming a static 33% recovery rate. Each entry is simply (1–33%) × default. Column G in Figure 7.15 could be used to compute the effective annual default rates to drive a Monte Carlo simulation as in Figure 7.6 or Figure 7.7. This is left for Exercise 7.11.

Let's look at how a Monte Carlo simulator can be built around correlated sampling of the transition matrix. The transition matrix in Figure 7.14 must first be used to compute cumulative transition probabilities. This is done by simply adding each successive probability to the sum preceding it, from left to right in Figure 7.17. Cumulative probabilities are used to transition from one state to the next as shown in Figure 7.18. MATCH(x,y,1) is a built-in that returns the index of the *closest* match of x within range y (if the last argument is "0" then an *exact* match is sought). First, the initial state is mapped into

FIGURE 7.14 Transition Matrix for One and Two Years (Sheet "transition table").

One Year

	AAA	AA+	AA	AA-	A+	A	A-	BBB+	BBB	BBB-	BB+	BB	BB-	B+	B	B-	CCC	Def
AAA	91.15	4.22	3.26	0.53	0.21	0.27	0.21		0.05			0.05	0.05	0.13				
AA+	2.77	83.89	9.56	2.52	0.25	0.50			0.38		0.04			0.04				
AA	0.68	1.28	84.86	7.59	2.67	1.60	0.32	0.54	0.11	0.11		0.04	0.04	0.04	0.23	0.04	0.04	
AA-		0.09	3.72	81.64	9.62	3.72	0.56	0.28	0.14						0.10			
A+		0.03	0.95	4.65	81.68	8.22	2.78	0.54	0.35	0.16	0.13	0.19		0.16	0.04			0.03
A	0.08	0.02	0.53	0.66	5.14	82.40	5.57	3.24	1.07	0.35	0.21	0.27	0.23	0.23	0.37			0.04
A-	0.16	0.04	0.12	0.31	1.09	8.76	77.31	6.90	3.18	0.74	0.23	0.50	0.23	0.27	0.36			0.08
BBB+			0.09	0.14	0.60	2.67	8.28	74.06	8.78	3.31	0.51	0.32	0.14	0.46	0.40			0.14
BBB	0.04	0.04	0.04	0.25	0.36	1.01	2.38	7.22	78.46	5.13	2.17	1.12	0.69	0.51	0.14			0.22
BBB-	0.06		0.12	0.23	0.12	0.75	0.58	2.42	9.79	73.21	5.93	3.34	1.27	0.81	0.40	0.18	0.29	0.23
BB+	0.09					0.53	0.26	0.97	3.98	13.63	66.64	4.87	3.89	2.48	1.18	0.18	0.71	0.53
BB			0.13		0.07	0.39	0.20	0.33	1.64	5.39	7.29	70.77	7.03	3.29	1.18	0.85	0.59	0.85
BB-				0.05	0.10	0.05	0.25	0.35	0.40	1.26	3.78	9.17	69.68	8.06	2.77	1.56	1.16	1.36
B+		0.04		0.07		0.04	0.22	0.11	0.18	0.18	0.48	2.38	6.30	77.96	5.16	2.45	1.79	2.64
B			0.08			0.16	0.23		0.23	0.08	0.47	1.09	2.87	7.92	69.17	3.26	5.67	8.77
B-					0.20			0.20		0.59	0.39	0.59	0.98	4.91	5.89	65.22	9.63	11.40
CCC	0.19				0.38			0.19	0.57	0.19	0.38	0.76	1.51	3.03	4.73	3.78	61.98	22.31
Def																		100.00

Two Years

	AAA	AA+	AA	AA-	A+	A	A-	BBB+	BBB	BBB-	BB+	BB	BB-	B+	B	B-	CCC	Def
AAA	83.22	7.43	6.17	1.28	0.53	0.60	0.39	0.05	0.12	0.01	0.01	0.09	0.09	0.01	0.00	0.00	0.00	0.00
AA+	4.91	70.62	16.32	4.93	0.94	1.11	0.09	0.10	0.64	0.03	0.01	0.01	0.02	0.22	0.01	0.01	0.01	0.00
AA	1.23	2.20	72.48	12.81	5.27	3.23	0.77	0.98	0.29	0.22	0.08	0.09	0.08	0.09	0.03	0.06	0.07	0.02
AA-	0.03	0.20	6.31	67.41	16.01	7.01	1.40	0.68	0.34	0.05	0.03	0.04	0.02	0.05	0.36	0.01	0.02	0.03
A+	0.02	0.07	1.81	7.73	67.65	13.94	4.96	1.35	0.82	0.36	0.25	0.04	0.02	0.24	0.01	0.01	0.06	0.08
A	0.15	0.05	0.98	1.39	8.59	68.95	9.34	5.57	2.25	0.80	0.42	0.21	0.04	0.44	0.02	0.02	0.02	0.10
A-	0.28	0.08	0.28	0.63	2.27	14.32	60.95	10.99	5.75	1.60	0.55	0.89	0.46	0.54	0.13	0.08	0.03	0.19
BBB+	0.02	0.01	0.19	0.33	1.21	5.08	12.93	56.22	14.03	5.49	1.16	0.78	0.41	0.87	0.62	0.05	0.24	0.36
BBB	0.08	0.07	0.11	0.46	0.73	2.12	4.41	11.36	62.90	8.41	3.61	2.07	1.31	1.06	0.67	0.07	0.08	0.49
BBB-	0.11	0.01	0.22	0.41	0.31	1.45	1.38	2.05	15.38	55.19	8.82	5.36	2.42	1.71	0.85	0.74	0.55	0.67
BB+	0.15	0.01	0.03	0.05	0.08	1.01	0.69	0.86	7.31	19.62	45.83	7.63	6.05	4.33	2.09	0.53	1.16	1.37
BB	0.01	0.00	0.21	0.04	0.16	0.73	0.46	0.66	3.35	8.95	10.67	51.38	10.50	5.85	2.21	1.45	1.14	2.02
BB-	0.01	0.00	0.02	0.09	0.18	0.19	0.47	0.24	1.08	2.87	5.97	13.35	49.98	12.64	4.57	2.53	2.06	3.30
B+	0.01	0.06	0.01	0.12	0.03	0.12	0.39	0.08	0.42	0.58	1.16	4.23	9.69	61.96	8.03	3.86	3.12	5.94
B	0.01	0.00	0.13	0.02	0.05	0.28	0.38	0.08	0.45	0.33	0.91	2.07	4.70	12.27	48.82	4.84	7.93	16.73
B-	0.02	0.00	0.01	0.01	0.33	0.04	0.05	0.33	0.18	0.95	0.72	1.19	2.01	7.90	8.67	43.24	12.69	21.65
CCC	0.29	0.01	0.02	0.02	0.56	0.06	0.07	0.33	0.89	0.44	0.68	1.33	2.43	4.96	6.64	5.07	39.13	37.10
Def	0.00	0.00	0.00	0.00	0.00	0.00	0.00	0.00	0.00	0.00	0.00	0.00	0.00	0.00	0.00	0.00	0.00	100.00

{=MMULT(B2:S19,trans)/100}

FIGURE 7.14 Transition Matrix for One and Two Years (Sheet "transition table"). Probabilities in %, e.g., Pr(A in 1 Year | AAA Today) = 0.27%.

	A	B	C (1)	D (2)	E (3)	F (4)	G (5)	H (6)	I (7)
1			1	2	3	4	5	6	7
2	1	AAA	0.00	0.00	0.01	0.01	0.03	0.05	0.08
3	2	AA+	0.00	0.00	0.02	0.04	0.07	0.11	0.17
4	3	AA	0.00	0.02	0.05	0.11	0.17	0.26	0.35
5	4	AA-	0.00	0.03	0.07	0.14	0.23	0.34	0.47
6	5	A+	0.03	0.08	0.16	0.26	0.39	0.53	0.71
7	6	A	0.04	0.10	0.18	0.30	0.45	0.64	0.87
8	7	A-	0.08	0.19	0.33	0.52	0.75	1.03	1.35
9	8	BBB+	0.14	0.36	0.65	1.00	1.41	1.87	2.38
10	9	BBB	0.22	0.49	0.84	1.27	1.78	2.37	3.03
11	10	BBB-	0.23	0.67	1.30	2.06	2.94	3.92	4.97
12	11	BB+	0.53	1.37	2.44	3.69	5.05	6.50	8.01
13	12	BB	0.85	2.02	3.46	5.09	6.87	8.73	10.66
14	13	BB-	1.36	3.30				13.50	16.15
15	14	B+	2.64	5.94				20.86	24.38
16	15	B	8.77	16.73				39.61	43.52
17	16	B-	11.4	21.65				48.78	52.89
18	17	CCC	22.31	37.10	47.17	54.24	59.36	63.19	66.15
19	18	Def	100.00	100.00	100.00	100.00	100.00	100.00	100.00

=OFFSET(
'transition table'!$A$1,
$A18+(C$1-1)*19,
18)

FIGURE 7.15 Cumulative Default Table Generated from Set of Transition Matrices. Probabilities in %, e.g., Pr(Def in 5 years | A today) = 0.45%.

	A	B (1)	C (2)	D (3)	E (4)	F (5)	G (6)	H (7)
1		1	2	3	4	5	6	7
2	AAA	0.00	0.00	0.00	0.01	0.02	0.03	0.05
3	AA+	0.00	0.00	0.01	0.03	0.05	0.08	0.11
4	AA	0.00	0.01	0.04	0.07	0.12	0.17	0.24
5	AA-	0.00	0.02	0.05	0.10	0.16	0.23	0.32
6	A+	0.02	0.06	0.11	0.18	0.26	0.36	0.47
7	A	0.03	0.07	0.12	0.20	0.30	0.43	0.58
8	A-	0.05	0.13	0.22	0.35	0.50	0.69	0.91
9	BBB+	0.09	0.24	0.44	0.67	0.94	1.25	1.59
10	BBB	0.15	0.33	0.56	0.85	1.19	1.59	2.03
11	BBB-	0.15	0.45	0.87	1.38	1.97	2.63	3.33
12	BB+	0.36	0.92	1.64	2.47	3.38	4.36	5.37
13	BB	0.57	1.35	2.31	3.41	4.60	5.85	7.14
14	BB-	0.91	2.21	3.77	5.47	7.25	9.04	10.82
15	B+	1.77	3.98	6.43	8.97	11.51	13.97	16.33
16	B	5.88	11.21	15.91	19.99	23.51	26.54	29.16
17	B-	7.64	14.51	20.38	25.29	29.34	32.68	35.44
18	CCC	14.95	24.85	31.60	36.34	39.77	42.34	44.32
19	Def	67.00	67.00	67.00	67.00	67.00	67.00	67.00

FIGURE 7.16 Cumulative Loss Table at 33% Recovery, Generated from Previous Default Table

		C	D	E	F	G	H	I	J	K	L	M	N	O	P	Q	R	S	T
		AAA	AA+	AA	AA-	A+	A	A-	BBB+	BBB	BBB-	BB+	BB	BB-	B+	B	B-	CCC	Def
23																			
24 AAA	0	91.15	95.37	98.63	99.16	99.37	99.64	99.85	99.85	99.90	99.90	99.90	99.95	100.00	100.00	100.00	100.00	100.00	100.00
25 AA+	0	2.77	86.66	96.22	98.74	98.99	99.49	99.49	99.49	99.87	99.87	99.87	99.87	99.87	100.00	100.00	100.00	100.00	100.00
26 AA	0	0.68	1.96	86.82	94.41	97.08	98.68	99.00	99.54	99.65	99.76	99.80	99.84	99.77	99.92	99.92	99.96	100.00	100.00
27 AA-	0	-	0.09	3.81	85.45	95.07	98.79	99.35	99.63	99.77	99.77	99.77	99.77	99.68	99.77	100.00	100.00	100.00	100.00
28 A+	0	0.08	0.03	0.98	5.63	87.31	95.53	98.31	98.85	99.20	99.36	99.49	99.68	99.73	99.84	99.94	99.94	99.97	100.00
29 A	0	0.16	0.10	0.63	1.29	6.43	88.83	94.40	98.86	99.20	99.06	99.27	99.34	99.57	99.96	99.96	99.96	99.96	100.00
30 A-	0	-	0.20	0.32	0.63	1.72	10.48	87.79	97.64	98.71	98.61	99.06	99.34	98.89	99.84	99.88	99.92	99.92	100.00
31 BBB+	0	0.04	-	0.09	0.23	0.83	3.50	11.78	85.83	94.61	97.92	98.43	98.75	98.89	99.35	99.72	99.72	99.86	100.00
32 BBB	0	0.06	0.08	0.12	0.37	0.73	1.74	4.12	11.34	89.80	94.93	97.10	98.22	98.91	99.42	99.78	99.78	99.78	100.00
33 BBB-	0	0.09	0.06	0.18	0.41	0.53	1.28	1.86	4.28	14.07	87.27	93.20	96.54	97.81	98.62	99.02	99.48	99.77	100.00
34 BB+	0	-	0.09	0.09	0.09	0.09	0.62	0.88	1.85	5.83	19.46	86.10	90.97	94.86	97.34	98.58	98.76	99.47	100.00
35 BB	0	-	-	0.13	0.13	0.20	0.59	0.79	1.12	2.76	8.15	15.44	86.21	93.24	96.53	97.71	98.56	99.15	100.00
36 BB-	0	-	-	-	0.05	0.15	0.20	0.45	0.80	1.20	2.46	6.24	15.41	85.09	93.15	95.92	97.48	98.64	100.00
37 B+	0	-	0.04	0.04	0.11	0.11	0.15	0.37	0.48	0.66	0.84	1.32	3.70	10.00	87.96	93.12	95.57	97.36	100.00
38 B	0	-	-	0.08	0.08	0.08	0.24	0.47	0.40	0.70	0.78	1.25	2.34	5.21	13.13	82.30	85.56	91.23	100.00
39 B-	0	-	-	-	-	0.20	0.20	0.20	0.40	-	0.99	1.38	1.97	2.95	7.86	13.75	78.97	88.60	100.00
40 CCC	0	0.19	0.19	0.19	0.19	0.57	0.57	0.57	0.76	1.33	1.52	1.90	2.66	4.17	7.20	11.93	15.71	77.69	100.00
41 Def	0	-	-	-	-	-	-	-	-	-	-	-	-	-	-	-	-	-	100.00

FIGURE 7.17 Cumulative Transition Probabilities (Sheet "trans")

	A	B	C	D	E	F	G	H	I	J	K
1	asset	type	rand	start	start index	next index	next				
2	1	x	0.9984	AA	3	13	BB-	=OFFSET(ratings, F4-1, 0, 1, 1)			
3	2	x	0.9599	A	6	8	BBB+				
4	3	x	0.3201	A+	5	5	A+				
5	4	y	0.3976	BBB+	8	8	BBB+	=MATCH(			
6	5	y	0.6036	AA-	4	4	AA-	C4*100,			
7	6	y	0.7283	A+	5	5	A+	OFFSET(trans!$A$23, E4, 1, 1, 19),			
8	7	y	0.7954	A	6	6	A	1)			
9	8	x	0.4348	AA-	4	4	AA-				
10	9	x	0.9993	A+	5	15	B	=MATCH($D4, ratings, 0)			
11	10	x	0.8632	A	6	6	A				

FIGURE 7.18　Transitioning 10 Assets from One State to Next

an index with an exact match, as shown in cell E2. Ratings (cells A24:A41 in Figure 7.17) are a named range "ratings." Second, OFFSET is used to return the row of Figure 7.17 corresponding to the initial state. This row is used as an argument to another MATCH for looking up the random sample, as shown in cell F2. Uncorrelated uniform random numbers are generated in column C, to be readdressed below. Finally, another OFFSET is used to return the string representation of the next state, as shown in cell G2.

The formulae in Figure 7.18 have been combined in Figure 7.19 as shown for a typical cell C11. Each cell is similar, with its own random sample from

	A	B	C	D	E	F	G	H
1	asset	year 0	year 1	year 2	year 3	year 4	year 5	year 6
2	1	AA	AA	AA-	AA-	AA-	AA-	AA-
3	2	A	A	A	A	A	A	A
4	3	A+	A+	A+	AA-	AA-	AA-	A+
5	4	BBB+	BBB	BBB	BBB+	BBB+	BBB+	A
6	5	AA-	AA-	AA-	AA-	AA-	AA-	AA-
7	6	A+	A+	A+	A+	A+	A	A
8	7	B	B	B	B	B	B	B
9	8	AA-	A+	A+	A+	A+	A+	A
10	9	A+	A+	A+	A+	A+	A+	A+
11	10	A	A	AA	AA	AA	AA	AA
12								
13					=OFFSET(ratings,			
14					MATCH(RAND()*100,			
15					OFFSET(trans!$A$23,			
16					MATCH(B11,ratings,0),			
17					1, 1, 19),			
18					1)-1,			
19					0,1,1)			

FIGURE 7.19　Transitioning 10 Assets over 6 Years

		C	D	E	F	G	H	I	J	K	L			O	P
1		x	x	x	y	y	y	y	x	x	x				
2		1	2	3	4	5	6	7	8	9	10				
3	x 1	1.0	0.3	0.3	0.1	0.1	0.1	0.1	0.3	0.3	0.3				
4	x 2	0.3	1.0	0.3	0.1	0.1	0.1	0.1	0.3	0.3	0.3				corr
5	x 3	0.3	0.3	1.0	0.1	0.1	0.1	0.1	0.3	0.3	0.3			within group	0.3
6	y 4	0.1	0.1	0.1	1.0	0.3	0.3	0.3	0.1	0.1	0.1			outside group	0.1
7	y 5	0.1	0.1	0.1	0.3	1.0	0.3	0.3	0.1	0.1	0.1	correlations			
8	y 6	0.1	0.1	0.1	0.3	0.3	1.0	0.3	0.1	0.1	0.1				
9	y 7	0.1	0.1	0.1	0.3	0.3	0.3	1.0	0.1	0.1	0.1				
10	x 8	0.3	0.3	0.3	0.1	0.1	0.1	0.1	1.0	0.3	0.3				
11	x 9	0.3	0.3	0.3	0.1	0.1	0.1	0.1	0.3	1.0	0.3				
12	x 10	0.3	0.3	0.3	0.1	0.1	0.1	0.1	0.3	0.3	1.0				

		C	D	E	F	G	H	I	J	K	L	
14		1	2	3	4	5	6	7	8	9	10	
15	1	1.00	0.00	0.00	0.00	0.00	0.00	0.00	0.00	0.00	0.00	
16	2	0.30	0.95	0.00	0.00	0.00	0.00	0.00	0.00	0.00	0.00	
17	3	0.30	0.22	0.93	0.00	0.00	0.00	0.00	0.00	0.00	0.00	
18	4	0.10	0.07	0.06	0.99	0.00	0.00	0.00	0.00	0.00	0.00	
19	5	0.10	0.07	0.06	0.28	0.95	0.00	0.00	0.00	0.00	0.00	
20	6	0.10	0.07	0.06	0.28	0.21	0.93	0.00	0.00	0.00	0.00	Cholesky decomposition
21	7	0.10	0.07	0.06	0.28	0.21	0.17	0.91	0.00	0.00	0.00	
22	8	0.30	0.22	0.17	0.04	0.03	0.03	0.02	0.91	0.00	0.00	
23	9	0.30	0.22	0.17	0.04	0.03	0.03	0.02	0.14	0.90	0.00	
24	10	0.30	0.22	0.17	0.04	0.03	0.03	0.02	0.14	0.12	0.89	

`{=computeCholesky($C$3:$L$12)}`

FIGURE 7.20 Correlations among Assets and Their Cholesky Decomposition; the Bottom Matrix is Named "cholesky."

the RAND built-in. RAND returns a uniform sample over $(0,1)$, so it is scaled by 100 for the lookup in the cumulative probability table. Writing such a dense formula is not recommended if you want anyone else to understand and potentially modify your spreadsheet. In this case, however, it cannot be helped because the model is to be extended in two dimensions: assets and years.

Now let's consider how to generate *correlated* ratings transitions. Figure 7.20 shows a possible correlation matrix assuming assets in the same group are correlated at 30% and those in different groups at 10%. Groups might represent corporate industry sectors or ABS classes for example. The asset groups assigned in Figure 7.18 (column B) automatically create the top matrix in Figure 7.20. Then the Cholesky decomposition is performed in the lower matrix in Figure 7.20. A user-defined function was written for this. Note that every cell in lower matrix has the same formula as in cell G20. The entire matrix is an array construct, as indicated by the curly brackets. It was created by selecting all its cells and typing CTRL-SHIFT-ENTER (just as for MMULT). Alternatively, Cholesky could be implemented within the spreadsheet itself.

Figure 7.21 shows the steps involved in generating correlated uniform samples from uncorrelated uniforms, as per the discussion of the Gaussian copula in Section 7.3. Steps 2 and 4 use NORMSINV and NORMSDIST built-ins for the standard normal distribution. Step 3 multiplies the Cholesky matrix by each vector of normal samples in step 2.

To tie up the example, reconsider Figure 7.19. Each cell is driven by an uncorrelated random number. Replace each instance of RAND() in these formulae with a reference to the final matrix of uniform correlated samples in Figure 7.21, resulting in a correlated simulation path. Note that in this example, ratings transitions and hence default events are correlated, not *time* to default. The model is wrapped up with a simple macro that iterates over a number of paths, collecting default statistics.

```
Public Sub monte()
    Dim defs(1 To 6) As Long
    Dim i As Integer
    Dim npaths As Long
    Dim path As Long
    Dim tally(0 To 10, 1 To 6) As Long

    npaths = Range("npaths")
    For path = 1 To npaths
        Calculate
        For i = 1 To 6
            defs(i) = Range("state").Cells(i)
        Next
        For i = 6 To 2 Step -1
            defs(i) = defs(i) - defs(i - 1)
        Next
        For i = 1 To 6
            tally(defs(i), i) = tally(defs(i), i) + 1
        Next
    Next
    Range("tally") = tally
End Sub
```

The loop primarily recalculates the spreadsheet, forcing new random samples. The rest of the loop collects default statistics from a named range "state." This is the number of defaults in each year for a given path. The results are tallied and output. Although this is a toy example, one can still

	A	B	C	D	E	F	G	H	I	J	K	L	M	N	O
1		year 1	year 2	year 3	year 4	year 5	year 6			year 1	year 2	year 3	year 4	year 5	year 6
2		**1. uniform**								**3. correlated normals**					
3	1	0.306	0.348	0.183	0.120	0.008	0.887		1	-0.506	-0.392	-0.905	-1.174	-2.417	1.210
4	2	0.129	0.479	0.911	0.390	0.169	0.387		2	-1.233	0.168	1.012	-0.618	-1.640	0.090
5	3	0.251	0.572	0.962	0.071	0.484	0.009		3	-1.025	0.040	1.672	-1.774	-0.973	-1.896
6	4	0.227	0.956	=RAND()	0.960	0.023	0.834		4	-0.915	1.654	{=MMULT(cholesky, B$15:B$24)}			0.925
7	5	0.811	0.602	0.723	0.851	0.167	0.657		5	0.450	0.695	0.115	0.869		0.622
8	6	0.879	0.177	0.889	0.657	0.551	0.399		6	0.882	-0.352	0.779	0.463	-0.968	0.088
9	7	0.101	0.041	0.078	0.456	0.509	0.601		7	-1.163	-1.232	-1.000	0.274	-1.043	0.514
10	8	0.869	0.570	0.512	0.817	0.834	0.121		8	0.499	0.085	0.121	-1.836	-0.177	-1.120
11	9	0.313	0.464	0.598	0.058	0.884	0.882		9	-0.800	-0.133	0.318	0.509	0.152	0.843
12	10	0.626	0.461		0.896	0.457	0.927		10	-0.135	-0.150			-0.878	1.215
13															
14		**2. inverse standard normal**								**4. correlated uniforms**					
15	1	-0.506	-0.392	-0.905	-1.174	-2.417	1.210		1	0.306	0.348	0.183	0.120	0.008	0.887
16	2	-1.133	-0.053	1.346	-0.279	-0.960	-0.286		2	0.109	0.433	0.844	0.268	0.050	0.536
17	3	-0.672	0.182	1.775	-1.466	-0.040	-2.366		3	0.153	0.516	0.953	0.038	0.165	0.029
18	4	-0.749	1.703	=NORMSINV(B3)		-1.999	0.971		4	0.180	0.951	=NORMSDIST(J3)		0.011	0.823
19	5	0.880	0.257	0.592		-0.965	0.404		5	0.674	0.757	0.546	0.807	0.036	0.733
20	6	1.169	-0.926	1.221	0.403	0.127	-0.255		6	0.811	0.363	0.782	0.678	0.166	0.535
21	7	-1.276	-1.739	-1.421	-0.111	0.023	0.256		7	0.122	0.109	0.159	0.608	0.148	0.696
22	8	1.121	0.177	0.031	0.904	0.970	-1.170		8	0.691	0.534	0.548	0.033	0.430	0.131
23	9	-0.486	-0.091	0.031	-1.573	1.197	1.183		9	0.212	0.447	0.548	0.694	0.560	0.800
24	10	0.322	-0.099	0.249	1.257	-0.109	1.452		10	0.446	0.440	0.625		0.190	0.888

FIGURE 7.21 Four Steps to Create Correlated Uniform Random Samples

277

observe the effect of correlation—in fact, this model was used (with 50,000 paths) to generate the distributions shown in Figure 7.3. These distributions show how high correlation produces a "fatter" tail. The assets move together more often thus increasing the frequency of extreme events.

Binomial Expansion Technique (BET) Moody's developed a static model for evaluating the risk of CDO-like securitizations called the Binomial Expansion Technique (Cifuentes 1996). Although this model is no longer used much (Moody's has moved to a Monte Carlo based approached as outlined in Xie and Witt 2005), it deserves study. The first innovative simplification of the model is to transform a set of correlated assets into a smaller, compressed set of independent assets, using the Moody's diversity score. For the math behind calculating a diversity score the interested reader is referred to Cifuentes (2004) and Dullmann (2006). The second key simplification of the model is to assume the same average default rate for each asset. A set of independent, identically distributed (IID) assets with constant marginal probability of default means that the joint distribution of default (i.e., the probability distribution of total default summed across all assets) is the binomial distribution (e.g., Drake 1967). Risk managers like this model because it is intuitive and one can quickly estimate Value-at-Risk (VaR). For example, the 99% VaR is the 99% quantile of the binomial distribution.

Let's sketch out an implementation of the BET. Start with a transition matrix based Monte Carlo simulator such as described earlier in this section. Either the original portfolio of correlated assets, or a compressed set of independent assets, can be simulated. For each path in the simulation, for each period in the path, a new set of N ratings is attained for the asset portfolio. This set of ratings has an average rating, for example, using the Moody's Weighted-Average Rating Factor (WARF). The WARF is an exponential scale ranging from 1 (Aaa) to 10,000 (default) indicating a ten-year average default rate (in basis points). The balance-weighted average WARF of the portfolio is the WARF of the average rating. The annual historical average default rate Q of this average rating is used in the binomial distribution.

Binomial(N, Q) is computed (e.g., Drake 1967):

$$\Pr(k \text{ defaults}) = \binom{N}{k} Q^k (1 - Q)^{N-k}$$

For a given liability structure, the attachment point of each tranche is known (i.e., the bond allocation is fixed). The loss corresponding to each defaulting asset is known. These losses can be distributed over the tranches from most subordinate to most senior.

Note that for each period in a path, new defaults may occur. If so, the size of the subordinate tranche(s) will change because losses are absorbed by the structure. Furthermore, the diversity score will decrease by the number of new defaults. Be sure to make these necessary modifications to the BET inputs each period.

Let's do a small example in Excel. Consider a $100MM structure with three tranches: classes A (90%), B (6%), and C (4%). Suppose the average rating of the portfolio is B+, the diversity score is 54.5, and the recovery rate is 33%. Looking up B+ in Figure 7.15, the one-year default rate is 2.64%. Figure 7.22 shows the BET cash flow. In this spreadsheet, the named ranges are: TrancheBsize ($6MM), TrancheCsize ($4MM), notional ($100MM), recovery_rate (33%), and diversity (54.5). The Excel builtin-in BINOMDIST(s,N,Q,0) returns point s in the distribution Binomial(N, Q). The formulae for tranche losses (columns E and F) are rather difficult. Note placement of anchors ("$") in the cell references to understand how the formulae copy down. For example, the formula in cell E4 is $E$2:E3, which becomes $E$2:E4 in cell E5. This range grows as the formula migrates downwards, allowing the loss to be calculated as the cumulative gross loss minus the total loss absorbed already.

Key outputs of the spreadsheet are the expected loss experienced by each tranche and its implied rating. For example the tranche B expected loss is calculated by:

```
= SUMPRODUCT($B$2:$B$80, $I$2:$I$80)
```

Thus the tranche B mean loss is 0.9%. This can be looked up in Figure 7.16 (with MATCH and OFFSET built-ins) to get an implied rating, in this case BB− for year one.

If this spreadsheet were placed within a simulation, each period for each path the diversity score, average rating, and default probability could change. By recalculating the sheet, a new expected loss and implied rating is produced. Combined over all paths, loss and ratings distributions can be constructed.

7.7 EXERCISES

7.1. Consider the synthetic credit index structure described by the loss-lets in Table 7.3. Should there be a single default, the 3–7% tranche effectively becomes a 2.3% to 6.3% tranche (recall 1% loss rate × 70% loss severity = 0.7% loss coverage). What is the mean loss of

Number of Defaults	Default Probability	Cumulative Default Probability	Cumulative Gross Loss	Tranche C Loss	Tranche B Loss	Tranche C Loss %	Tranche B Loss %	Tranche C Cum Loss	Tranche B Cum Loss
0	0.642%	0.642%							
1	3.398%	4.040%	1,229,358	1,229,358	-	30.734%	0.000%	1,229,358	-
2	8.824%	12.864%	2,458,716	1,229,358	-	30.734%	0.000%	2,458,716	-
3	14.988%	27.852%	3,688,073	1,229,358	-	30.734%	0.000%	3,688,073	-
4	18.726%	46.577%	4,917,431	311,927	917,431	7.798%	15.291%	4,000,000	917,431
5	18.350%	64.927%	6,146,789	-	1,229,358	0.000%	20.489%	4,000,000	2,146,789
6	14.685%	79.612%	7,376,147	-	1,229,358	0.000%	20.489%	4,000,000	3,376,147
7	9.867%	89.479%	8,605,505	-	1,229,358	0.000%	20.489%	4,000,000	4,605,505
8	5.681%	95.160%	9,834,862	-	1,229,396	0.000%	20.489%	4,000,000	5,834,862
9	2.845%	98.005%	11,064,220	-	165,138	0.000%	2.752%	4,000,000	6,000,000
10	1.255%	99.260%	12,293,578	-	-	0.000%	0.000%	4,000,000	6,000,000
11	0.492%	99.752%	13,522,936	-	-	0.000%	0.000%	4,000,000	6,000,000
12	0.173%	99.924%	14,752,294	-	-	0.000%	0.000%	4,000,000	6,000,000
13	0.055%	99.979%	15,981,651	-	-	0.000%	0.000%	4,000,000	6,000,000
14	0.016%	99.995%	17,211,009	-	-	0.000%	0.000%	4,000,000	6,000,000
15	0.004%	99.999%	18,440,367	-	-	0.000%	0.000%	4,000,000	6,000,000
16	0.001%	100.000%	19,669,725	-	-	0.000%	0.000%	4,000,000	6,000,000
17	0.000%	100.000%	20,899,083	-	-	0.000%	0.000%	4,000,000	6,000,000
18	0.000%	100.000%	22,128,440	-	-	0.000%	0.000%	4,000,000	6,000,000
19	0.000%	100.000%	23,357,798	-	-	0.000%	0.000%	4,000,000	6,000,000
20	0.000%	100.000%	24,587,156	-	-	0.000%	0.000%	4,000,000	6,000,000
21	0.000%	100.000%	25,816,514	-	-	0.000%	0.000%	4,000,000	6,000,000
22	0.000%	100.000%	27,045,872	-	-	0.000%	0.000%	4,000,000	6,000,000
23	0.000%	100.000%	28,275,229	-	-	0.000%	0.000%	4,000,000	6,000,000
24	0.000%	100.000%	29,504,587	-	-	0.000%	0.000%	4,000,000	6,000,000
25	0.000%	100.000%	30,733,945	-	-	0.000%	0.000%	4,000,000	6,000,000
26	0.000%	100.000%	31,963,303	-	-	0.000%	0.000%	4,000,000	6,000,000
27	0.000%	100.000%	33,192,661	-	-	0.000%	0.000%	4,000,000	6,000,000
28	0.000%	100.000%	34,422,018	-	-	0.000%	0.000%	4,000,000	6,000,000
29	0.000%	100.000%	35,651,376	-	-	0.000%	0.000%	4,000,000	6,000,000
30	0.000%	100.000%	36,880,734	-	-	0.000%	0.000%	4,000,000	6,000,000
31	0.000%	100.000%	38,110,092	-	-	0.000%	0.000%	4,000,000	6,000,000
32	0.000%	100.000%	39,339,450	-	-	0.000%	0.000%	4,000,000	6,000,000
33	0.000%	100.000%	40,568,807	-	-	0.000%	0.000%	4,000,000	6,000,000
34	0.000%	100.000%	41,798,165	-	-	0.000%	0.000%	4,000,000	6,000,000
35	0.000%	100.000%	43,027,523	-	-	0.000%	0.000%	4,000,000	6,000,000

Formula callouts:

- Tranche B Cum Loss: `=L3+F4`
- Tranche C Cum Loss: `=K3+E4`
- Tranche B Loss %: `=F4/TrancheBsize`
- Tranche C Loss %: `=E4/TrancheCsize`
- Tranche B Loss: `=MAX(MIN(D4-SUM($E$2:$E$70)-SUM($F$2:F3),TrancheBsize-SUM($F$2:F3)),0)`
- Tranche C Loss: `=MIN(D4-SUM($E$2:E3),TrancheCsize-SUM($E$2:E3))`
- Cumulative Gross Loss: `=MIN(notional,(A4*notional/diversity)*(1-recovery_rate))`
- Cumulative Default Probability: `=C3+B4`
- Default Probability: `=IF(A4>diversity,0,BINOMDIST(A4,INT(diversity),DefProb,0))`

FIGURE 7.22 Binomial Expansion Technique (BET) in Excel (Tranche A Hidden)

this new tranche, and how is it related to the previous mean? Give an intuitive explanation of your result. Be careful!

7.2. Implement Cholesky decomposition as a user-defined function and in spreadsheet formulae.

7.3. Implement the Gaussian copula as a user-defined function and in spreadsheet formulae.

7.4. Research pseudo-random number generation and implement a function that is better than the RAND (Excel) and Rnd (VBA) built-ins. A better generator has a longer cycle before it repeats. Demonstrate that your cycle is longer.

7.5. Extend the Monte Carlo example given in Excel here with more assets. Assume that loss occurs in the same year as default. Sample a Beta distribution (e.g., Weisstein 2006) for recovery. Generate estimates of loss distributions.

7.6. Research the Moody's diversity score and implement as a user-defined function and in spreadsheet formulae.

7.7. Package your functions from Exercises 7.2 through 7.6 into a Monte Carlo class architecture.

7.8. Implement the static cash flow model underlying the Moody's BET model as described in section 7.6 as a spreadsheet in Excel.

7.9. Wrap the BET model in Exercise 7.8 in a Monte Carlo simulator. Generate loss and implied rating distributions. Use either a diversity score calculator or a Gaussian copula to model correlation among the assets. Use the class architecture designed in Exercise 7.7 to elegantly implement dynamic BET.

7.10. From doing the previous exercises you will note several public methods that would be nice to have in a Monte Carlo class. For example, methods for manipulating histograms, calculating quantiles and moments, calculating the joint distribution from two marginal distributions, and so on. Extend your class with some of these methods and illustrate their use in BET (Exercise 7.9).

7.11. Compare two stochastic models for synthetic credit indexes. In the first model, a random variable represents *a default* of an asset (section 7.2.2). Assume annual periods, constant recovery rate, and constant equal correlation among assets. In the second model, a random variable represents the *time to default* of an asset (section 7.2.3). In both models use the initial asset rating to derive an effective annual default rate. Implement both models with Monte Carlo simulation. Assume a portfolio of 100 credits: 5 AAA, 10 AA, 30 A, 45 BBB, 5 BB, and 5 B. Assume the liability structure has attachment points at 0%, 3%, 7%, 10%, 20%, and 30%. Estimate the probability distributions of losses after one and five years. Compare the means and standard deviations of these two distributions. Compare the percentage of mass in the tail beyond 3% loss. Explain why the distributions differ.

7.12. Recall from section 7.3 that with a general correlation matrix in two variables, $X_1 = Z_1$ and $X_2 = \rho Z_1 + \sqrt{1 - \rho^2} \times Z_2$. Extending this to more assets, each successive correlated random variable is a function of *all the previous* (uncorrelated) variables. Different correlation coefficients can be accommodated in the correlation matrix Σ. However, if we restrict all assets to share the same correlation coefficient ρ, then the matrix is degenerate. This can be exploited by introducing a new independent random variable Y unassociated with the assets (sometimes this is called the "market" variable). It turns out that $X_i = \sqrt{\rho} \times Y + \sqrt{1 - \rho} \times Z_i$, i.e., each correlated variable is a function of the market variable and its own uncorrelated variable. This is called the "one factor" model and is used extensively by Wall Street firms to model synthetic indexes. Prove this result by showing that the covariance of any two correlated random variables is a function of ρ. Recall that $\text{cov}(X_1, X_2) = E[(X_1 - \mu_1)(X_2 - \mu_2)]$ and that for any two independent random variables, $E[Z_1 Z_2] = 0$.

7.13. Given a set of n random variables, a covariance matrix M is an $n \times n$ matrix where $M(i, j) = \text{cov}(Z_i, Z_j)$. Recall that $\text{cov}(Z_i, Z_j) = \sigma_i \sigma_j \rho_{ij}$, where σ_i is the standard deviation of asset i and ρ_{ij} is the correlation coefficient of assets i and j. Consider the set of n assets, with defaults modeled by n random variables with binomial distributions. Recall that for a binomial process with probability P, the variance is $P \times (1 - P)$. For example, flipping a fair coin a number of times constitutes a binomial process with $P = 50\%$. Suppose every asset shares the same correlation coefficient ρ. Build the covariance matrix. The sum of all elements of this matrix is the variance of the total number of defaults. Derive an expression for, and plot, the standard deviation of the total number of defaults as a function of different correlation coefficients (from 0% to 100%) for different numbers of assets (1, 10, 100, 1000). What conclusions can you draw?

7.14. Use the synthetic credit index model developed in Exercise 7.11 to redo Figure 7.10 under the assumptions given. Compute par premiums for different correlations (0% to 100% by 10%) for senior (40–100%), mezzanine (20–40%), and equity (0–20%) tranches.

7.15. Use the synthetic credit index model developed in Exercise 7.11 to redo Figure 7.11 under the assumptions given. For *three* tranches 0–3%, 3–6% and 6–9%, plot *change* in tranche value vs. *change* in average market credit spread. The slopes of these plots are the tranche deltas.

7.16. Use the synthetic credit index model developed in Exercise 7.11 to redo Figure 7.12 under the assumptions given. Plot tranche hedge ratio vs.

attachment point (0% to 10% by 1%), again assuming tranches with 3% width.

7.17. Use the synthetic credit index model developed in Exercise 7.11 to redo Figure 7.13 under the assumptions given. Plot tranche hedge ratio vs. credit spread (10 bps to 40 bps) for the 0–3% and 3–6% tranches.

7.18. Introduce a term in Equation B.6 in Appendix B for the partial premium payment made in a CDS in the period when the underlying reference defaults. This term is small but is included in the "street model" for CDS. Then derive the par swap premium, also known as the breakeven spread.

7.19. Extend Exercise 7.11 to account for hedges on individual credits. Consider a simple model that any of the credits can be insured against loss; that is, the hedge is perfect and costless. Thus, when simulating these credits, a possible default has 100% recovery. Consider two alternative hedges for the original portfolio in Exercise 7.11—with BB credits hedged and with B credits hedged. Estimate the loss distributions of these two new portfolios and compare to the originals. Comment on the effectiveness of the hedges.

Excel and VBA

Premature optimization is the root of all evil (or at least most of it) in programming.

—Donald Knuth

The competent programmer is fully aware of the limited size of his own skull. He therefore approaches his task with full humility, and avoids clever tricks like the plague.

—Edsger Dijkstra

This appendix summarizes a number of years of hard-earned experience in using Excel and VBA. It is meant as a compendium of advice rather than a programming manual. For precise system and language semantics, please refer to online help facilities, Internet user interest group discussions, modeling books (e.g., Gottfried 1996, Benninga 2000, and Jackson and Staunton 2001), and programming texts. Some of my suggestions are personal and as such can be disputed. However, Excel can be notoriously nonmodular if used in a haphazard manner. Most of these "rules" force the modeler to abide by a stricter methodology to avoid common pitfalls.

Migration is key to model development in Excel. One typical migration path is as follows:

Pure spreadsheet model.
↓
Spreadsheet model with recorded macros for common operations.
↓
Spreadsheet model with user-written VBA macros (perhaps modified recorded macros) and functions.
↓

"Hollowed out" model with most computation in VBA, the spreadsheet used primarily for I/O and data archive.

↓

"Hollowed out" model with interface to Access or other database for data management.

↓

"Hollowed out" model with VBA code linked to compiled VBA libraries.

↓

"Hollowed out" model with VBA code linked to compiled C++ libraries.

↓

Model with hardened user interface.

The migration is driven by the increasing need for flexibility, speed, and storage capacity. As the model proves its utility, users demand more features and flexibility that naturally tend to slow it down. For example, deliver a model that prices a security and users will realize they want to price a portfolio by repeated invocations. Modify the model to price a portfolio and users will realize they want to hedge a portfolio, and so on.

Initially a slow, limited model is delivered quickly. The bottlenecks are migrated to interpreted VBA code. As the model gets bogged down with heavier tasks, the interpreted VBA bottlenecks (e.g., cash flow generator) are migrated to compiled VBA libraries. Again, as this solution gets bogged down, the compiled VBA bottlenecks (e.g., random number generator) are migrated to C++ libraries.

A.1 SPREADSHEET STYLE

1. Names can be assigned to ranges in a workbook. A name is assigned under Insert→Name→Define. Names aid in modular programming because they can be referred to directly in VBA. For example, suppose a range is named "1mLIBOR." Corresponding VBA code that inputs this data is

```
Dim LIBOR1m As Variant
LIBOR1m = Range("1mLIBOR")
```

If this range is cut and pasted somewhere else in the spreadsheet, the above code continues to work. Names should be assigned to *every* input range in a workbook application. One should avoid code like:

```
LIBOR1m = Range("A1:B360")
```

2. Names can get out of hand. A name is often created, then its range removed. The name will still exist in the name registry under Insert→Name→Define. All broken references in this directory should be removed. Names can also be assigned to a range that is no longer referenced by any other cell or VBA code. Such names should be removed. To check if a named range is referenced by other cells, use: Tools→Formula Auditing→Trace Dependents. To check if a name is referenced in VBA code, go to the VBA editor and search over all modules for that string. Unused and broken names should be removed to lessen the chance that future developers will be puzzled by the extraneous information.

3. Named ranges used for VBA inputs and outputs should be colored in a consistent manner to remind developers what they are. A common error is for an unassuming developer to delete or modify the shape of a range (say by deleting rows or columns), thereby causing an error. VBA uses of the named range should not depend on its particular dimensions (one should use the functions: Lbound and Ubound, and the range methods: Rows.Count and Columns.Count), but just to be safe, coloring named ranges helps.

4. Named ranges used for VBA inputs are sourced by user-supplied data, static data, and dynamically linked data (from other workbooks, live feeds, etc.). These three data input sources should be clarified by coloring their typefaces differently. For example, use blue typeface for user inputs and green for links (usually market data).

5. Data and control, inputs and outputs should be clearly presented. For example, a "control panel" of macros for running various tasks might be lumped together on a control sheet. User inputs, market data inputs, and model outputs should all be on separate sheets. It should be no mystery, even to someone who is looking at the application for the first time, where things are and what they mean. Rarely should a spreadsheet cell be used as both input and output.

6. Work in progress should never simply be hidden (by hiding the sheets) for later developers to discover.

7. Data should always be laid out in an obvious way, even if this means that multiple sheets are needed. The most obvious trap that developers fall into is to try to use the several thousand rows in each sheet, in order to avoid creating more sheets. This is almost always a bad idea. The only time it is justified is when all the formulae need to refer to a single sheet for speed, and even then, it is dubious.

Large data arrays, say asset portfolios or cash flows, have a few natural dimensions that need to be mapped onto the two-dimensional sheets. Say, for instance, we have a handful of alternative portfolios, each with a few hundred assets, where each asset is described with a few dozen characteristics. The natural mapping is a handful of sheets, one per portfolio. Each sheet would have an asset per row. If the portfolios are mapped this way, then the size of one portfolio can grow without bumping into another.

Mappings become tricky when the sizes of the dimensions are similar. If an asset were described by a few hundred characteristics, then what could we do? In such cases, storage in a database may be best. Another example of this problem is output. What to do if a structure's cash flows have a few hundred time periods and a few hundred variables of interest? This will not fit on one sheet, but probably two or three. In this case, it is best to write a general output procedure that creates and writes to extra sheets if need be.

8. Develop spreadsheet formulae that are *regular along a given dimension*. For example, consider O/C stepdown date as defined in section 4.5.2. O/C stepdown can occur only if a set of conditions is met. One of these conditions is that the period exceeds a certain threshold. Suppose that we know the threshold is 36 months for every deal. Even so, a bad way to model this (in a spreadsheet) is to set O/C stepdown to FALSE for the first 36 monthly periods, and in period 37 (and onward) have formulae that check the remaining conditions. Although this is fastest, it runs the risk of later developers dragging down a modified formula and losing information implicit in the 36 initial FALSEs. Instead, the *same* formula should be used for *every* period: =And(A14>=StepPeriod,...), where Step-Period is a named cell with value 36.

9. Avoid building fancy graphical user interfaces (GUIs). Excel sheets are sufficient for input and ouput. Macro buttons are sufficient for control. Although exploiting the rich GUI classes in Excel can result in a flashy application, in the wrong hands it can increase the complexity of the model and the time to delivery, and can obscure the core computations. It is difficult to build a hardened, robust application around Excel for delivery to a trading desk for example. A better choice for the nonprofessional programmer is to build as simple and transparent an interface as possible. Exposed cells can be protected by locking with Tools→Protection.

10. Related to the previous point, a simple GUI still requires sufficient error checking. Error checking can be done in either the spreadsheet or in VBA. It involves meticulously checking the valid bounds and types of inputs. Suppose by convention, all interest rates need to be annualized in percentage points. Prior to running the model, each rate might be checked against a lower and upper bound. Note that an upper bound, say 15%, is recommended to catch erroneous typos. VBA type checking itself

	A	B	C	D	E	F	G	H	I	J	K	L	M	N	O	P	Q
1		example 1		example 2		example 3		example 4		example 5		example 6					
2		a		b		4		4.4		4.4		a					
3	FALSE	2		4		5		#N/A		#N/A		#N/A					
4	TRUE	2		4		5		5		7		#N/A					
5		3	1	3	1	3	1	3	1	3	1	3	1				
6		a	2	a	2	a	2	a	2	a	2	b	2				
7		5	3	5	3	5	3	5	3	5	3	5	3				
8		b	4	b	4	b	4	b	4	b	4	b	4	=VLOOKUP(H$2, H$5:I$12, 2, $A$3)			
9		4	5	4	5	4	5	4	5	4	5	4	5				
10		b	6	b	6	b	6	b	6	b	6	b	6	=VLOOKUP(H2, H$5:I$12, 2, $A$4)			
11		11	7	11	7	11	7	11	7	1	7	11	7				
12		d	8	d	8	d	8	d	8	d	8	d	8				
13																	

FIGURE A.1   Six Examples of VLOOKUP

is not powerful enough to check for bounds, as in other programming languages.

11. VLOOKUP and HLOOKUP are versatile Excel built-ins. One specific use is given in Section 4.12, but these functions are more flexible. VLOOKUP(k,d,c,FALSE) searches for the first instance of the *exact* value k in the first column of data range d and returns the corresponding value from column c. The type of key k can be a number or string. Only those keys in d that match the type of k are used. If the last argument is TRUE then an *inexact* match is attempted. HLOOKUP operates on a transpose of the data range.

Figure A.1 shows six examples of VLOOKUP to illustrate how the exact and inexact matches operate. Row 2 holds the key. Each data range has two columns: the keys and one column of data (always 1–8). For instance, VLOOKUP(H2, H$5:I$12, 2, $A$4) in the fourth example is looking for the key 4.4 that does not exist in the data range. However, an inexact match is requested. Thus the value 5, corresponding to key 4, is returned.

12. There are a few keyboard sequences that are very helpful in getting around an Excel spreadsheet:

- END-↓ and END-↑: jump to bottom (top) of data vector.
- CTRL-SHIFT-↓ and CTRL-SHIFT-↑: jump to bottom (top) of data vector and select vector.
- Double-click lower right-hand corner of a selected cell: will copy down that value, *in sequence*, as regulated by an *adjoining* (left or right) column.
- CTRL-SHIFT-ENTER: create an array construct from a range. This is needed for any function, including user-defined functions, that returns an array of data (e.g., MMULT, LINEST, FREQUENCY, etc.).

A.2 CODE STYLE

1. Keep variable names consistent throughout your code. For example, this book uses names like Debt.ProRataBal, where class Debt has a method ProRataBal. Capitalization is used to indicate classes and methods. Local variables are often lower case to indicate their status. Names should be meaningful, even if they are long. If it weren't for space constraints in this book, the variable names in the model should have been taken from defined Prospectus terms (e.g., Tranche.CertificatePrincipalBalance). Different naming conventions exist; use whichever you like best, but be consistent.

2. If you are initializing a data member with a parameter passed into the class, use a naming convention to make the relationship between the two variables explicit. For example, if Coup is a data member, then Coup_ is the local variable passed as a parameter to the initialization method. Don't hesitate to use other naming conventions to make the code more transparent.

3. Break long statements with line continuations to make your code more readable, e.g.,

```
Public Sub Init( _
    Coup_ As Double, _
    Maturity As Integer, _
    Freq_ As Integer, _
    InitBal As Double)
...
End Sub
```

4. Isolate input and output (I/O) functions in classes separate from computation code. I/O in VBA will require reference to range names. These names link the code to a specific application (i.e., workbook). The best way to sever this connection is to compile the computation classes into their own library (see section A.3). The I/O classes can be compiled into another library (or left interpreted). Thus the computation library can be attached to another application with no modification.

5. Use "Option Explicit" at the top of all modules and declare all variable types. By default, function parameters are passed by reference without explicitly stating so. "ByVal" arguments should be explicitly declared as such.

6. Be wary of the following:

```
Dim x, y, z As Integer
```

that is equivalent to:

```
Dim x As Variant
Dim y As Variant
Dim z As Integer
```

7. Use extensive error checking of inputs prior to core computations in model (see the previous section about this). Allowing bad data to get deep into a model and produce erroneous results is inexcusable. All the extra code written for error checking will pay dividends in the future.
8. Build extensive benchmarking/calibration within the model. Suppose a model is used to price a given portfolio, and the price is calibrated with the market. That particular invocation of the model should be captured as a benchmark that can be reexecuted. A suite of such benchmarks should be collected and executed one after another as a validity test of the model. Prior to releasing any modifications to a model, the benchmark suite must pass. In this example, the reader may object and say that the model price will likely depend on market conditions, thus re-executing a model in the future will no longer give the same price. As a result the benchmark must encapsulate market data at the original time of calibration. This feature is often called "backwards compatibility." Fundamental changes to the model must be parameterized so that older versions can run with previous assumptions.

It is highly recommended that models be built with backward compatibility. There is a wealth of knowledge in prior markets and scenarios that is captured with benchmarking. As this experience accumulates over time, users become more and more confident that a model (verified by benchmarking) is correct. There is simply no substitute for the ability to show a user that a model prices a deal from five years ago exactly the same today as it did in the past.
9. Reproducible results are important in many applications. This becomes problematic in randomized optimization techniques (section 3.2.2), stochastic analysis (Chapter 7), and other methods that use random sampling. To stabilize these methods use pseudo-random number generators (e.g., Press 1992) and start with the same seed(s). To reinitialize VBA's Rnd use the Randomize built-in. *Caution*: Read the online help pages of these functions carefully to ensure proper use. There is however a stricter definition of model stability.

Suppose we want to compute the effective interest-rate duration of a bond that is priced stochastically. The duration requires prices to be computed with neutral rates, rates up and rates down (section B.4, Appendix B). One must ensure that the same random numbers are used *for the same functions* in each price evaluation (e.g., interest rate paths are the same in each). This ensures that no extraneous error is introduced into the prices (that will subsequently be blown up by the small denominator in the duration calculation).

In contrast, suppose we want to compare the prices of two portfolios. It probably isn't necessary to ensure that random numbers are reused the same way in each valuation. Although it would avoid extraneous error, the error in this case is not being scaled and there are other, larger errors.

10. All references to the file system should be driven from a few user inputs specified in the spreadsheet interface. For example, if there is a defacto file directory in which the model expects to find various data files, the path name of that directory should be explicitly given in a named input range in the spreadsheet. If all such path names are made explicit, it will be easier for future developers to understand file management and to rearrange the data file hierarchy. If such file specifications need to be protected from user modification, those input cells can be locked.

11. The Collection class is a VBA built-in that is quite useful. It supports a list of information accessed either by index or key. Consider the following example: A new Collection object (coll) is instantiated. Two datum (3 and "abc") are attached to it with the Add method. One is given the optional key "first."

```
Dim coll As New Collection
coll.Add 3, "first"
coll.Add "abc"
```

Methods of accessing the data are now shown. The first datum is accessed by key, analogous to accessing an array. The second datum is accessed by index with the Item method. The first datum could be accessed in a similar manner, but the second datum cannot be accessed by key because it has none. Last, we (sequentially) iterate over all data in coll. After code execution, $x = 3$, $y =$ "abc," and $z =$ "3abc."

```
Dim c As Variant
Dim x As String
Dim y As Integer
Dim z As String

x = coll("first")
y = coll.Item(2)

For Each c In coll
    z = z & c
Next
```

12. When instantiating objects in a class architecture, it is important to recycle these objects after use. Without recycling objects, a computationally intensive program might slow down due to excessive memory use. To recycle an object, it is set to Nothing.

```
Dim coll As Collection
. . .
Set coll = New Collection
. . .
Set coll = Nothing
```

For every New, there should eventually be an assignment to Nothing. One can see that the following code makes this impossible. The pointer to the first object is lost forever, so the object cannot be recycled.

```
Dim coll As Collection
. . .
Set coll = New Collection
Set coll = New Collection
```

13. In certain circumstances, one would like to develop a massive spreadsheet for a computation, yet to do so would overburden Excel. For example, consider an "exposed" Monte Carlo simulation where each of thousands of paths is explicitly computed with spreadsheet formulae. Such quick-and-dirty Monte Carlos are useful in many cases.

    To alleviate the burden on Excel, the following technique can be exploited. The formulae characterizing a single path are debugged and kept on the first row of an empty sheet. The following recorded macro (Tools→Macro→Record New Macro) copies down the single path thousands of times.

```
Sub Macro1()
    Rows("1:1").Select
    Selection.Copy
    Rows("2:10000").Select
    ActiveSheet.Paste
End Sub
```

The spreadsheet is then recalculated. This minimizes the saved size of the application, decreasing the time to open and save the application. Exposed paths in a Monte Carlo facilitate visualizing worst-case paths. Distributions are easy to calculate (with the Frequency built-in) and plot (with the Chart Wizard). Quantiles can be easily estimated with

Data→Sort, etc. For example, suppose the loss of each path (row) is in column A. The following recorded macro sorts the losses. The 95% quantile of the loss distribution is now in A500.

```
Sub Macro2()
    Range("A1:A10000").Select
    Selection.Sort Key1:=Range("A1"),Order1:=xlDescending
End Sub
```

14. Avoid recomputation of user-defined spreadsheet functions. Defining your own functions for use in a spreadsheet is a great idea. It modularizes the computation and creates higher-level abstraction that helps problem solving and modeling. However, if too many of these function invocations are in the workbook it can drastically slow down calculation. The problem is that the Excel mechanism for determining if cells need to be recalculated gives up on user-defined functions. So to be on the safe side, all such functions are recalculated for any workbook change! To avoid this, have an additional Boolean argument in each function that controls its evaluation. At the top of each function, test the argument and immediately return if FALSE. The problem remains how to set this argument. Avoid anything sophisticated. For example, suppose collateral cash flows are computed, for a given asset, in a spreadsheet filled with various user-defined functions. Since all these functions are fundamentally used to re-compute cash flows, they can be enabled by a single flag. A related issue is that of hidden sheets with functions: these sheets get recalculated every time the workbook is recalculated, so what you don't see can hurt you!

15. Array ranges can be easily assigned to VBA variables if they are declared Variant. For example,

```
Dim x As Variant
x = Range("x")
```

Such an array is indexed starting at one. Note that ranges specifying row and column data vectors are input into VBA as two-dimensional arrays. The first dimension of a row vector and the second dimension of a column vector are both [1..1]. If Variant types are to be avoided, and the code fully typed, then arrays must input element by element, e.g.,

```
Dim i As Integer
Dim j As Integer
Dim x() As Double
Dim r As Range
```

```
Set r = Range("x")
For i = 1 To r.Cells.Rows.Count
    For j = 1 To r.Cells.Columns.Count
        x(i,j) = r.Cells(i,j).Value
    Next
Next
```

A.3 COMPILATION

A common problem on a trading desk is that Excel/VBA models are slow. Although Excel is flexible and facilitates application development, the underlying macros are interpreted rather than compiled. A solution to this problem is to pull out the critical kernel of the computation and compile it into a dynamically linked library (DLL).

Figure A.2 shows an image of Design Studio for Visual Basic. The tool is used for developing a VBA "project," essentially a set of modules. The code can be executed directly from Studio or via Excel. It can be interpreted or compiled. Figure A.2 shows a function in a class module of a project. The project files are displayed in the upper right pane ("Project Explorer"). Module properties are shown in the lower right pane ("Properties Window"). There are other windows available for debugging, the same as in the Excel Visual Basic Editor.

This section outlines some helpful hints for compiling a project. For detailed information, refer to online help.

1. The compiled VBA code must be organized as a set of *class modules*. There must be at least one public function inside each class. This code will be compiled into a library. Any additional code can be organized as a set of *code and class modules* to reside within the Excel application.
2. Do not declare any functions "Volatile." The compiler will generate *very slow* code for such functions.
3. The compiled code (library) will be called by interpreted code in the Excel application (in the program modules). More than one DLL can be linked to an Excel application.
4. Inside the project save your modules periodically—these options are under the "File" menu. Also save the entire project. When you are done you should have the following key files:

   - myproj.vbp   the project
   - mymain.bas   a standard code module within the project
   - myclass.cls   class module within the project

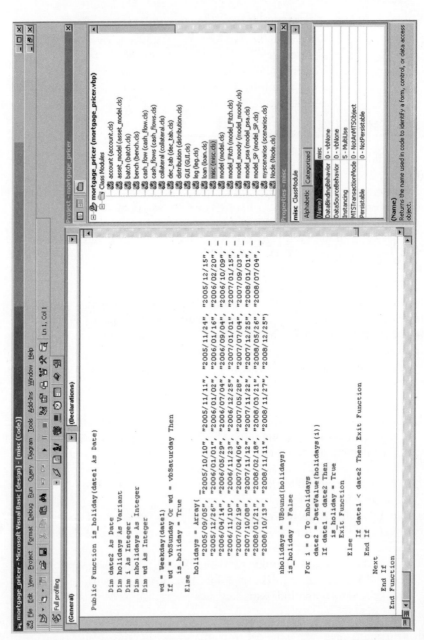

FIGURE A.2 Visual Basic Design Studio

- myproj.dll   DLL for linking to Excel and other programs
- myproj.exe   executable for running within Design Studio

5. To set up the compilation within Design Studio, the "Project" menu is critical. There are two key selections on this menu: "References" and "Properties." References are used to select libraries needed by the code you are writing. For example, if you are using Excel statistics functions you will need to link Excel. In general you can link user-defined DLLs here also.

6. Calls to Excel library built-ins, as enabled by the previously described reference, are *very* slow in compiled code. They should be avoided at all costs. Precomputing them in a table is advisable. For example, even *Min* and *Max* are slow and rewriting them achieves significant speedup.

7. A DLL has no implicit context as does a user program interpreted in Excel. The latter has the context of an Application object. For example, be careful how input and output is implemented in compiled code. All invocations of "Range," "Calculate," etc. must be preceded by the workbook and worksheet. For example, you cannot use:

```
Calculate
x = Range("myField")
```

This will fail because the Range has no context. Instead, you must use:

```
With Workbook("mybook").Worksheets("mysheet")
    .Calculate
    x = .Range("myField")
End With
```

Similarly, output using the status bar can only be accomplished by passing in the Application object from the Excel program. For example instead of:

```
Public Sub MyMethod()
    . . .
    Application.StatusBar = "program is running"
    . . .
End Sub
```

you must use the following:

```
Public Sub MyMethod(ExcelApp as Excel.Application)
    . . .
    ExcelApp.StatusBar = "program is running"
    . . .
End Sub
```

8. Project→Properties controls compilation. Under "General" one must select "ActiveX DLL" to build a DLL for linking to Excel, or "Standard EXE" to test the compiled code on its own. In the latter case, for "Startup Object" select "Sub Main." If building a DLL, for "Startup Object" select "(None)."

9. Project→Properties→Compile should be set to "full" optimization. One may also try "advanced" optimizations; they shouldn't harm the code, although in my experience (with non-numerically intensive programs, like those described in this book) they have not produced significant speedup.

10. There are essentially three ways to run your program. Each of these is explained in more detail below.

   ■ Stand-alone executable: this is an "EXE" file.
   ■ Debuggable link to Studio: this is a "VBP" file.
   ■ Fast execution in Excel: this is a "DLL" file.

11. Project→Properties→Debugging has a field "Start program." Here you can enter the path to Excel should you wish to test the compiled code running within your Excel application. When debugging your program you should execute by Run→Start in Studio. This will invoke Excel and open the application specified in "Start program."

   Immediately you should open the VBA editor in Excel and in Tools→References ensure that `myproj.vbp` is linked. Caution: Every time you recompile the project in Studio, the link in the Excel application breaks. Also, be very careful to load the VBP file rather than the DLL file. The former has symbolic information for debugging. If you accidently link the DLL file, the program will execute but cannot be traced into the DLL. If you properly link the VBP file, the library can be single-stepped.

   In any case, when running the application via Studio, if the application is interrupted by the user or by an error, it will arrive in the debugger. From there, the program can be examined, single-stepped, and so on. However, if the program is terminated, it cannot be restarted from the current Excel session. *Excel must be shut down and restarted.*

   If you are debugging in Studio as described above, you should not click on Excel to examine or change worksheets. If you do, a deadlock will likely ensue between Studio and Excel. There is usually no way to remove this deadlock except by terminating both processes with the Task Manager.

12. When creating a DLL it is critical to select "MultiUse" as the "Instancing" property of *each module*. This option is listed in the "Properties" window that can be displayed in Design Studio (Figure A.2). In fact, if

this selection is not made, the compiler will refuse to generate compiled code (although the error message won't say why).

13. When debugging the EXE in Design Studio, a `main()` should be written that sets up the inputs for the desired function. In the "Immediate" window you can type "`call main()`" that starts execution. Breakpoints can be set, and so on.

14. Once the EXE is debugged, switch the aforementioned parameters to create a DLL. Start up Excel independently and under Tools→References browser so that you can select your DLL. Be sure that the DLL is correctly selected (it should be automatically selected when future Excels are instantiated). In certain cases the selected DLL has the prefix: "(MISSING)." This might be due to the fact that the DLL had been renamed. In any case, periodically check to be sure that Excel is linking the DLL you want.

15. Once the new DLL is created and Excel is linked to it, you can run interpreted code that calls your compiled code. The debugger will not jump into the compiled code should there be a runtime bug (although the bug will be announced in an error window). Be sure that you instantiate class objects correctly before use and destroy after use.

16. If you link the DLL as described above (via the "References" menu in Excel) then there appears to be no need to use a Declare statement in the interpreted VBA code.

17. Profiling code is the process of determining bottlenecks. Commercial software products abound to help with VBA profiling. In general these products insert counters between every VBA statement and compile into a new executable. Running this executable (say in the form of a DLL) results in a data file of statement counts and timing statistics. The profiling tool displays the data to allow the developer to easily see the bottlenecks. Once a bottleneck is rewritten to lessen its impact, the process is repeated and hopefully that particular code no longer appears among the top bottlenecks (although others will take its place). After all reasonable code improvements are exploited and there are no more ideas for bottleneck removal, it is time to consider migrating bottlenecks to C++.

A.4 BLOOMBERG

A Bloomberg terminal is a great source of information on the asset-backed security (ABS) market. This section only touches upon this topic to point readers to more information on the deals analyzed in this book. IXIS Securities North America issued a series of subprime mortgage securitizations over the past few years, constituting the IXIS Real Estate Capital Trust. One can

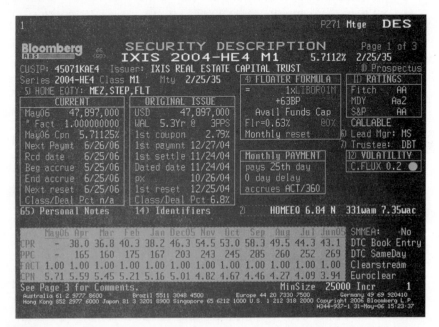

view this "shelf" with the Bloomberg keyboard command: IXIS <MTGE> <GO>. For example, 2004-HE4 can be selected from the shelf menu. The screen in Figure A.3 shows the capital structure of 2004-HE4 with current coupons and original balances and WALs. Notice that A2 has paid down. These screens were printed in May 2006.

Drilling down further, one can select M1 for example to see the details of the first mezzanine bond. There is a lot of information offered about these bonds. For instance the long description of M1 is shown in Figure A.4. This can be directly accessed by typing: 45071KAE4 <MTGE> DES. Notice the last twelve months of prepayment rates and coupons are given. There are a few more pages of description (e.g., concerning collateral). One can even access the prospectus of the deal.

Bloomberg offers limited access to its own cash flow model also. For example with the YTR calculator, the M1 bond discount margin can be estimated given user assumptions for price and prepayment speed. Zero loss is assumed in the Bloomberg model, but alternative prepayment curves can be specified. The interested reader is referred to Calabretta and Salvesen (2006) and Pratt (2006).

Bond Math

This appendix reviews the mathematics underlying the mortgage models. For an underlying's cash flows and a discount rate (yield), one would like to determine its present value or price. Alternatively, given an underlying's cash flows and its price, one would like to find the discount rate. Given an underlying's cash flows and either a price or discount rate, one would like to find the underlying's modified duration. The valuation model underlying credit default swaps (CDSs) is also given. Finally, a credit card model is reviewed.

B.1 MORTGAGE PAYMENT

Let M be the number of periods in the loan and r be the constant periodic interest rate. Let B be the initial loan balance and B_k be the balance at the *end* of period k. Let I_k and P_k be the interest and principal payments made in period k. Let $Pmt = I_k + P_k$, the total payment made in any period. Our goal is to derive a closed-form expression for constant Pmt.

In the first period:

$$I_1 = B \times r$$

$$P_1 = Pmt - I_1$$

$$B_1 = B - P_1 = B - Pmt + I_1 = B - Pmt + B \times r = B(1+r) - Pmt$$

In the second period:

$$I_2 = B_1 \times r$$

$$P_2 = Pmt - I_2$$

$$B_2 = B_1(1+r) - Pmt = [B(1+r) - Pmt](1+r) - Pmt$$
$$= B(1+r)^2 - Pmt(1+r) - Pmt$$

In the third period:

$$I_3 = B_2 \times r$$

$$P_3 = Pmt - I_3$$

$$B_3 = B_2(1+r) - Pmt = [B(1+r)^2 - Pmt(1+r) - Pmt](1+r) - Pmt$$

$$= B(1+r)^3 - Pmt(1+r)^2 - Pmt(1+r) - Pmt$$

In general, the balance remaining at the end of period k is:

$$B_k = B(1+r)^k - Pmt(1+r)^{k-1} - \cdots - Pmt(1+r) - Pmt$$

$$= B(1+r)^k - Pmt \times \sum_{j=0}^{k-1}(1+r)^j \tag{B.1}$$

The terms inside the summation are a geometric series. A geometric series $a_k = g^k$ has a closed-form summation (e.g., Weisstein 2006):

$$S_n = \sum_{j=0}^{n} g^j = \frac{1-g^{n+1}}{1-g} \tag{B.2}$$

In the case of the mortgage, $g = 1+r$ and $n = k-1$. Substitute Equation (B.2) into Equation (B.1). The remaining balance is:

$$B_k = B(1+r)^k - Pmt \times \frac{1-(1+r)^k}{1-(1+r)}$$

At maturity (after M periods) the remaining balance is zero. With this end condition, we can solve for Pmt:

$$B_M = 0 = B(1+r)^M - Pmt \times \frac{1-(1+r)^M}{1-(1+r)}$$

$$Pmt \times \frac{1-(1+r)^M}{1-(1+r)} = B(1+r)^M$$

$$Pmt = B(1+r)^M \times \frac{1-(1+r)}{1-(1+r)^M}$$

$$= \frac{Br(1+r)^M}{(1+r)^M - 1} \tag{B.3}$$

This payment is for a fixed-rate loan. For a floating-rate loan with periodic rate resets, we can use this equation with the new rate and the remaining periods to maturity.

B.2 YIELD TO PRICE

Computing price from yield for a mortgage loan or bond is relatively straight-forward once we assume a set of cash flows. The models described in Chapters 1 through 6 are deterministic; that is, instruments are priced assuming one interest rate curve or scenario. (If multiple scenarios are used, as in bond sizing, the results are aggregated into a single "deterministic" cash flow.) In Chapter 7, nondeterministic techniques are introduced, namely Monte Carlo simulation, wherein probable cash flows are generated. In the most general case, each must be discounted individually to produce a price distribution. Under simplifying assumptions, the multiple cash flows can be aggregated into a single cash flow to produce a price.

An underlying instrument has a single set of cash flows that occur on a given schedule of dates. Complications arise from the treatment of an irregular (long or short) first "period," if the price is "clean" or "dirty," and the day count convention: actual/360 or 30/360. Figure B.1 illustrates the cash flows with respect to the time line. By definition, there is a period lag between the First Pay Date ($t = 1$) and the second pay date ($t = 2$). The first period can be irregular.

The inputs to the algorithm are:

- y: annual yield
- *DayAdj*: fraction of year for each period, defined in Section 4.4 (depends on day count convention used).
- *CF*: cash flows

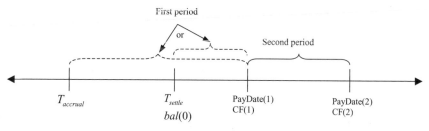

FIGURE B.1   General Cash Flow Schedule of a Liability

- M: number of periods
- Bal: balance

$YtoP(y, DayAdj, CF, M, Bal)$

$$d(t) = \begin{cases} 1 & t = 0 \\ d(t-1) \div (1 + DayAdj(t) \times y) & \text{otherwise} \end{cases}$$

$$YtoP = \frac{1}{Bal(0)} \times \sum_{t=1}^{M} CF(t) \times d(t)$$

An alternative version of this algorithm is driven from a forward interest rate curve rather than an effective yield. For each period, the forward curve is converted into a spot rate and added to an appropriate (constant) spread. This is used to compute the discount factor.

B.3 PRICE TO YIELD

We review the price-to-yield solver here. Figure B.2 summarizes the Newton-Raphson algorithm (e.g., Press 1992) in the specific context of finding a yield from a present value. Refer to the timeline in Figure B.1. The inputs are:

- PV_{target}: target present value.
- *Tolerance*: terminate when present values are within *Tolerance* (e.g., 0.01).
- *Coupon*: underlying annual coupon. For a floating-rate bond, this is the spot rate plus margin.
- *Freq*: number of periods per year.
- M: number of periods.
- *DayAdj*: fraction of year for each period (section 4.4).
- *CF*: cash flows.

The annual coupon is first converted into a periodic yield y, based on the frequency of the deal (5). This is just an initial guess so its value is not critical to the algorithm. The error is defined as difference between the target value PV_{target} and the estimated value PV (17). The algorithm loops until the error is within a certain tolerance (6). Each iteration two values are estimated (12–15) from yields (8–9) that differ by ε, a small constant (3). The values are estimated by discounting the cash flows CF. The values then are used to estimate duration DPV that, in conjunction with the error, is used to compute a yield increment Δ to direct the search (16–18). By convention the estimate

1	$PtoY(PV_{target}, Tolerance, Coupon, Freq, M, DayAdj, CF)$
2	$\Delta = 0$
3	$\varepsilon = 10^{-4}$
4	$d = d' = error = 1$
5	$y = Coupon \div Freq$
6	$while \, | error \, | > Tolerance$
7	$PV = PV' = 0$
8	$y = y - \Delta$
9	$y' = y + \varepsilon$
10	$\forall t \in [1..M]$
11	$s = DayAdj(t) \times Freq$
12	$d = d \div (1 + s \times y)$
13	$d' = d' \div (1 + s \times y')$
14	$PV = PV + CF(t) \times d$
15	$PV' = PV' + CF(t) \times d'$
16	$DPV = (PV - PV') \div \varepsilon$
17	$error = PV_{target} - PV$
18	$\Delta = error \div DPV$
19	$PtoY = (1 + y)^{Freq/2} \times 2 - 2$

FIGURE B.2 Price-to-Yield Algorithm Using Newton-Raphson

y is converted to an annualized bond-equivalent yield at the completion of the algorithm (19).

An alternative algorithm converts price to *discount margin* rather than yield. Rather than iterating over y, iterate over dm. The discount factor is computed as $d(t) = d(t - 1) \div [1 + s(t) \times (r(t) + dm)]$.

B.4 DURATION

Duration can be defined in many ways—in general, it is the sensitivity of price with respect to some other factor, for example, market rate, underlying spread, prepayment rate, correlation, recovery rate, and so on. For mortgages a major concern is market-rate price sensitivity. Theoretically, duration is represented by a partial derivative, for example, $dur = \partial P / \partial r$ for price sensitivity with respect to interest rates. Modified duration is duration normalized by price, for example, $dur = (-1/P) \times \partial P / \partial r$. If the derivative is difficult to compute, a linear approximation can often be used, called the "effective" duration.

B.4.1   Index or Interest-Rate Duration

Market interest rate sensitivity is important because market rates strongly affect mortgage value. To compute effective modified duration, shock the model up and down:

$$dur_{eff} = \frac{-1}{price(yield)} \times \frac{price(yield + \Delta) - price(yield - \Delta)}{2\Delta} \tag{B.4}$$

The meaning of *yield* + Δ above is a *parallel* shift of the underlying interest rate curve. Should the curve be flat then this is a simple increment of the market rate. Floating-rate instrument cash flows will be affected by this shift. Both floating and fixed instrument discounting will also be affected by this shift.

The yield-to-price calculation has been previously described. For our purposes, shocking the market interest rates implies that the optimal structure may change—thus, the structure must be resized for every price computation. Furthermore, when the NIM and post-NIM are sized to target yields—these targets change when the market is shocked. A reasonable assumption is that these targets change by the same shock as the market.

The structure is resized within the duration calculation because if shocked rates implied a different optimal structure, we would naturally use that structure rather than the previous, neutral-rate structure. Unfortunately, by reallocating within the duration computation, we cannot rely on alternative ways to calculate duration. To be more precise: if underlying cash flows are not a function of market rates (for example in a fixed-coupon bond) then duration can be computed directly from those cash flows. However, if the cash flows change with market rates (for example if the structure gets reallocated or if the structure has floating coupons) then duration cannot be computed from static cash flows.

In certain instances it is sufficient to compute the index duration without reallocating the structure. This approximation is easier to calculate.

B.4.2   Discount Spread Duration

Spread duration is the sensitivity of price with respect to a bond's spread. (Note that this is different from the sensitivity of price with respect to an *asset's* spread, i.e., the "delta" for synthetic structures as discussed in section 7.5.3.) Recall (from section 4.2) that a bond's "spread" is added to a base interest rate to give a yield for discounting its cash flows. For a given tranche, sensitivity of price to spread movement is important because discount spreads can change with the market every day, just like interest rates. One method

1	$SpreadDur(BEY, Freq, M, DayAdj, CF)$
2	$y = (1 + BEY/2)^{2/Freq} - 1$
3	$d = 1$
4	$PV = PV' = 0$
5	$\forall t \in [1..M]$
6	$\quad s = DayAdj(t) \times Freq$
7	$\quad d = d \div (1 + s \times y)$
8	$\quad PV = PV + CF(t) \times d$
9	$\quad PV' = PV' + DayAdj(t) \times CF(t) \times d$
10	$MacDur = PV' \div PV$
11	$SpreadDur = MacDur \div (1 + BEY \div 2)$

FIGURE B.3 Spread Duration Algorithm

of computing spread duration is to shock spreads (but not market rates) and measure the resulting prices. The advantage of this calculation is that it can account for reallocation of the liability structure (although for small Δ the structure will likely retain the same allocation).

$$dur_{spread} = \frac{-1}{price(spread)} \times \frac{price(spread + \Delta) - price(spread - \Delta)}{2\Delta} \quad \text{(B.5)}$$

The cash flows of the issued bonds are not functions of spread, which is used only for discounting. Fabozzi (1997) and others define effective duration for fixed-coupon instruments (i.e., instruments with no spread sensitivity). Thus, their definition can be used instead of the shock calculation above. This has the advantage of speed; however, reallocation of the structure will not be captured in this calculation. Figure B.3 presents this discount spread duration algorithm, based on Macaulay duration. The inputs are:

- *BEY*: the annualized bond-equivalent yield.
- *Freq*: number of periods per year.
- *M*: number of periods.
- *DayAdj*: fraction of year for each period (section 4.4).
- *CF*: cash flows (interest plus principal).

Table B.1 shows a structure with its discount spread durations. The structure was run with and without O/C step down enabled to show how duration changes drastically for the subordinate bonds if they are allowed to pay down concurrently.

TABLE B.1 Typical Deal with Discount Spread Durations

Tranche	Rating	Alloc	Bench	Margin	Coupon	Spread	Yield	w/o step down		w/ step down	
								WAL	Dur	WAL	Dur
A1	AAA	40.2%	1mL	6 bp	5.14%	6 bp	5.14%	0.80	0.78	0.80	0.78
A2	AAA	12.4%	1mL	12 bp	5.20%	12 bp	5.20%	2.00	1.89	2.00	1.89
A3	AAA	16.9%	1mL	16 bp	5.24%	16 bp	5.24%	3.00	2.75	3.50	3.15
A4	AAA	10.8%	1mL	26 bp	5.34%	26 bp	5.34%	4.35	3.84	6.73	5.58
M1	AA+	3.5%	1mL	29 bp	5.37%	29 bp	5.37%	5.35	4.61	4.95	4.26
M2	AA	3.2%	1mL	32 bp	5.40%	32 bp	5.40%	5.98	5.06	4.89	4.21
M3	AA−	1.9%	1mL	33 bp	5.41%	33 bp	5.41%	6.55	5.46	4.86	4.18
M4	A+	1.7%	1mL	40 bp	5.48%	40 bp	5.48%	7.03	5.77	4.84	4.16
M5	A	1.6%	1mL	44 bp	5.52%	44 bp	5.52%	7.55	6.11	4.83	4.14
M6	A−	1.5%	1mL	51 bp	5.59%	51 bp	5.59%	8.14	6.47	4.81	4.12
B1	BBB+	1.4%	1mL	100 bp	6.08%	100 bp	6.08%	8.82	6.75	4.80	4.05
B2	BBB	1.2%	1mL	110 bp	6.18%	110 bp	6.18%	9.59	7.15	4.80	4.04
B3	BBB−	1.0%	1mL	195 bp	7.03%	195 bp	7.03%	10.42	7.28	4.78	3.93
B4	BB+	1.0%	1mL	240 bp	7.48%	550 bp	10.58%	11.48	7.00	4.73	3.69
N1	BBB+	0.0%	FIXED		6.25%	650 bp	6.50%	0.59	0.57	0.59	0.57
N2	BBB−	0.0%	FIXED		6.75%	950 bp	9.50%	1.19	1.11	1.19	1.11
OTE	N/A	100.0%				3344 bp	33.44%	6.50	2.77	3.79	2.69

In summary:

- We can use the last set of formulae for approximating the spread duration of floating-rate instruments. Since we are mostly concerned with floating loans and tranches, this is a good approximation. There is no loss of accuracy when the allocation of the liability structure has been finalized. If spread duration for the desk's "long position" (unsecuritized portfolio of whole loans) is needed then computation by shocking the spreads is better.
- We can use the market rate shock method for approximating the effective duration of any instrument or a portfolio of instruments.
- None of these equations say anything about prepayment duration and other sensitivities.

The duration of mortgage assets is based on 30/360-day count conventions. Thus we combine cash flows from the various loans into a single cash flow and discount this as if it were a fixed security. The *aggregate* liability structure duration is also assumed to have a 30/360-day count.

For the purpose of calculating a trading desk's open risk position, compute the effective modified duration by shocking the market rate. The yield of floating components of the underlying will thus also be shocked up and down. For fixed components of the underlying (e.g., the NIM and post-NIM tranches), the underlying yields must be explicitly shocked. The resultant prices are used to compute the price-yield sensitivity as a percentage of price (i.e., the effective modified duration).

Computing asset duration entails another choice. Liability tranches have *a priori* yields, hence prices. Thus the aggregate liability structure has a concrete yield and price. A mortgage collateral portfolio has neither. Or rather, either can be taken as given, for derivation of the other. For example, assume a yield and derive a price. Note that this assumed asset yield must be explicitly shocked during the duration calculation.

Table B.2 gives empirical results for a typical deal assuming the aggregate asset yield is 5.82%. The table shows the price and yield corresponding

TABLE B.2 Experimental Results for Effective Duration of Typical Deal

	−5 bp	+0 bp	+5 bp	dur
asset price	104.7071	104.6112	104.5155	1.83
liability price	104.3447	104.2647	104.1602	1.77
asset yld	5.7646%	5.8145%	5.8644%	
liability yld	5.7738%	5.8194%	5.8737%	

to the neutral case and two shocks: ± 5 bps. The assets contain a significant percentage of hybrid adjustable-rate mortgages (ARMs), so it is understandable that their duration is a few years. If assets and liabilities were perfectly "matched," then their durations would be equal.

B.5 HAZARD RATE

To derive hazard rate consider that the market price of a credit default swap (CDS) should *equally* price the premium leg (payments to the protection seller) and the protection leg (payments from the protection seller should the credit default). Given the default and survival probabilities Q_i and P_i derived in section 7.2.3:

$$PV^T_{premium} = \sum_{t=1}^{T} P_t \times s \times D_t \tag{B.6}$$

$$PV^T_{protection} = \sum_{t=1}^{T} Q_t \times (1 - R) \times D_t \tag{B.7}$$

$$PV^T_{swap} = PV^T_{protection} - PV^T_{premium} \tag{B.8}$$

where T is the number of periods, R is the recovery rate, s is the premium coupon (credit spread), and D_t is the discount factor for period t. The premium present value weighs each coupon by the probability that the credit survives to that period. Similarly, the protection present value weighs each recovery by the probability that the credit survives up to the previous period and defaults in this period. This is a slight simplification of the "street" CDS model, where the premium leg has another term (J. P. Morgan 2001). The missing term represents a partial fee that may be paid in the period in which default occurs.

Netting the present values gives the value of the swap, which at par should be *zero*.

$$PV^T_{swap} = \sum_{t=1}^{T} Q_t \times (1 - R) \times D_t - \sum_{t=1}^{T} P_t \times s \times D_t$$

$$= \sum_{t=1}^{T} [Q_t \times (1 - R) - P_t \times s] \times D_t$$

Substituting the definition of Q_i from Equation (7.12):

$$PV_{swap}^T = \sum_{t=1}^{T} [(P_{t-1} - P_t) \times (1 - R) - P_t \times s] \times D_t$$

$$= \sum_{t=1}^{T} \left[\frac{P_t}{P_t}(P_{t-1} - P_t) \times (1 - R) - P_t \times s \right] \times D_t$$

$$= \sum_{t=1}^{T} \left[\frac{1}{P_t}(P_{t-1} - P_t) \times (1 - R) - s \right] \times P_t \times D_t$$

Simplifying a bit more:

$$PV_{swap}^T = \sum_{t=1}^{T} \left[\left(\frac{P_{t-1}}{P_t} - 1 \right) \times (1 - R) - s \right] \times P_t \times D_t \qquad \text{(B.9)}$$

Observing the cumulative survival probability from Equation (7.11):

$$P_i = \prod_{t=1}^{i} (1 - q_t)$$

$$P_{i-1} = \prod_{t=1}^{i-1} (1 - q_t)$$

$$\frac{P_{i-1}}{P_i} = \frac{\prod_{t=1}^{i-1} (1 - q_t)}{\prod_{t=1}^{i} (1 - q_t)} = \frac{1}{1 - q_i}$$

$$= 1 + h_i \qquad \text{(B.10)}$$

Substituting Equation (B.10) into Equation (B.9) gives:

$$PV_{swap}^T = \sum_{t=1}^{T} [(1 + h_t - 1) \times (1 - R) - s] \times P_t \times D_t$$

$$= \sum_{t=1}^{T} [h_t(1 - R) - s] \times P_t \times D_t$$

This can be solved for the par premium s_T:

$$PV_{swap}^T = 0 = \sum_{t=1}^{T} [h_t(1-R) - s_T] \times P_t \times D_t$$

$$\sum_{t=1}^{T} h_t(1-R) \times P_t \times D_t = s_T \sum_{t=1}^{T} P_t \times D_t$$

$$s_T = \frac{\sum_{t=1}^{T} h_t(1-R) \times P_t \times D_t}{\sum_{t=1}^{T} P_t \times D_t} \qquad (B.11)$$

For homogeneous credits and survival probabilities, the hazard rate will be constant, h:

$$s_T = \frac{\sum_{t=1}^{T} h(1-R) \times P_t \times D_t}{\sum_{t=1}^{T} P_t \times D_t} = h(1-R)$$

$$h = \frac{s_T}{1-R}$$

Thus the hazard rate for a par swap can be approximated as the spread divided by the loss severity. For a derivation of these in continuous time, see (Bank of America 2004). If the market has a certain term structure for CDS par premiums, then Equation (B.11) is "bootstrapped" to solve for hazard rates corresponding to the terms. For example, suppose a certain corporate name has CDS trading in $T = 1, 2, 3, 5, 7$, and 10 year maturities. These market spreads constitute the par premium term structure s_T. Let's rewrite Equation (B.11) as a function f of hazard rates:

$$s_1 = f(h_1)$$
$$s_2 = f(h_1, h_2)$$
$$s_3 = f(h_1, h_2, h_3)$$
$$s_5 = f(h_1, h_2, h_3, h_5)$$
$$s_7 = f(h_1, h_2, h_3, h_5, h_7)$$
$$s_{10} = f(h_1, h_2, h_3, h_5, h_7, h_{10})$$

This illustrates the bootstrap. The market spread s_1 is used to derive h_1 (say by Newton-Raphson search). The market spread s_2 and h_1 are used to derive h_2, etc. Note that tenors missing in the term structure are skipped in the bootstrap. These need to be interpolated afterwards.

B.6 STATIC CREDIT CARD MODEL

As a change of pace from mortgages, this section describes a simple credit card securitization model. A few input parameters characterize the assets (e.g., yield and default rate). These parameters are stressed according to a rating target, e.g., AAA to BBB. The higher the rating, the greater the stress. Thus, for instance, AAA yield is *lower* than BBB yield (i.e., AAA is more stressed than BBB). The stresses presented here are derived from Fitch.

A simple liability structure is assumed with three tranches: senior, mezzanine, and junior. The mezzanine and junior tranches provide the credit enhancement for the senior tranche. The senior tranche is considered to have achieved the target rating if its total credit enhancement exceeds estimated costs. The fundamental equation for modeling credit cards is:

$$\text{Excess spread} = \text{Yield} - \text{Coupon} - \text{Loss} - \text{Fees}$$

Excess spread is the yield thrown off by assets less the coupon owed to bond investors, less any realized losses, less servicing and other fees.

Let's look at the model in more detail. Table B.3 lists six input parameters driving the model. Investor WAC is the average coupon paid to bond investors. Portfolio yield is the average yield of the credit card assets. Monthly Payment Rate (MPR) regulates the speed of redemption. Default rate is the average loss rate (defaults are immediately realized as losses). Servicing rate is the cost of servicing the assets. Except for MPR, these are annual rates. Cash flows are generated on a monthly period (i.e., *Freq* = 12).

Initial levels for these parameters are taken from historical data. For example, the base level for yield and MPR in Table B.3 were the minimum historical levels seen in the late 1990s. The stress percentages came from rating agencies. Portfolio yield and MPR are stressed immediately and charge offs (defaults) are stressed linearly over six months. Industry standard is to charge off over 180 days, hence the ramp.

The recurrence equations describing the model are now given. A linear ramp is specified for all input parameters except servicing rate which is fixed. These parameters ramp from their base to stress levels. The ramp either inclines or declines. This is specified for WAC as follows, where

TABLE B.3 Credit Card Model Input Parameters and their Stress Factors (Stress Level at AA Level)

Parameter		Base Level	Stress Level	AAA	AA	A	BBB	Stress Adjust	Ramp-up Months
Investor WAC	WAC	7.2%	24.5%	240%	240%	240%	240%	Increase	6
Portfolio Yield	Yield	15.7%	11.0%	35%	30%	25%	20%	Decline	0
Monthly Payment Rate	MPR	15.7%	9.4%	45%	40%	35%	30%	Decline	0
Default Rate	DefRate	6.0%	22.5%	350%	275%	200%	150%	Increase	6
Servicing Rate	SvcRate	2.0%	2.0%						

$Ramp_{WAC} = 6.$

$$Stress(t) = \begin{cases} 0 & Ramp_{WAC} = 0 \\ \dfrac{Ramp_{WAC} - t}{Ramp_{WAC}} \times (WAC_{stress} - WAC_{base}) & otherwise \end{cases}$$

$$WAC(t) = WAC_{stress} - stress(t) \tag{B.12}$$

MPR is inclusive of principal and interest payments. Hence, the true Principal Payment Rate (*PPR*) is computed as *MPR* less yield.

$$PPR(t) = MPR(t) - Yield(t) \div Freq \tag{B.13}$$

The model assumes that an early amortization event has occurred and that stress happens on the last day of the revolving period. Purchase rate is constant for credit cards such as VISA and AMEX, leading to a constant collateral pool size during the amortization period. Principal paid to the bonds is removed from the investor's balance.

$$Collat(t) = Collat(t - 1)$$

$$Prin(t) = \frac{Bal_{invest}(0)}{Collat(0)} \times Collat(t) \times PPR(t) \tag{B.14}$$

$$Bal_{invest}(t) = \max\left[0, Bal_{invest}(t - 1) - Prin(t)\right] \tag{B.15}$$

Initially, the bonds are sold to investors and the cash proceeds are used to buy collateral. It is possible for the seller/securitizer to have a participation in the deal as equity holder. Investor and seller balances are kept separately.

$$Collat(0) = Bal_{iinvest}(0) + Bal_{iseller}(0)$$

$$Bal_{seller}(t) = Collat(t) - Bal_{invest}(t) \tag{B.16}$$

During the amortization period, investor participation in the pool drops off as excess spread is used to pay down principal. As the investors get out of the deal, the seller/securitizer increases its participation. The bonds pay down the investor's share of the coupon, servicing, and defaults, from the investor's share of the yield. This excess spread can be positive or negative. The sum of all negative excess spreads is the cumulative loss. The credit enhancement to achieve the target rating must exceed the cumulative loss. Because weighted-average-coupon (WAC) and yield are stressed in opposite directions, yield is

TABLE B.4 Cash Flows (×$1MM) of $500MM Two-Tranche Credit Card Structure at AA Stress. Sum of Excess Spread is −$31.75MM.

Month	MPR	PPR	WAC	Yield	Yield'	DefRate	Collat	Invest Bal	Seller Bal	Excess Spread
0	9.4%	8.5%	7.2%	11.0%	11.0%	6.0%	500	500.0	–	-1.75
1	9.4%	8.5%	10.1%	11.0%	15.1%	8.8%	500	457.4	42.5	-2.19
2	9.4%	8.5%	13.0%	11.0%	18.0%	11.5%	500	414.9	85.0	-2.94
3	9.4%	8.5%	15.8%	11.0%	20.8%	14.3%	500	372.4	127.5	-3.49
4	9.4%	8.5%	18.7%	11.0%	23.7%	17.0%	500	329.9	170.0	-3.85
5	9.4%	8.5%	21.6%	11.0%	26.6%	19.8%	500	287.4	212.6	-4.01
6	9.4%	8.5%	24.5%	11.0%	29.5%	22.5%	500	244.8	255.1	-3.98
7	9.4%	8.5%	24.5%	11.0%	29.5%	22.5%	500	202.3	297.6	-3.29
8	9.4%	8.5%	24.5%	11.0%	29.5%	22.5%	500	159.8	340.1	-2.60
9	9.4%	8.5%	24.5%	11.0%	29.5%	22.5%	500	117.3	382.6	-1.91
10	9.4%	8.5%	24.5%	11.0%	29.5%	22.5%	500	74.7	425.2	-1.22
11	9.4%	8.5%	24.5%	11.0%	29.5%	22.5%	500	32.2	467.7	-0.52
12	9.4%	8.5%	24.5%	11.0%	29.5%	22.5%	500	–	500.0	0.00
13	9.4%	8.5%	24.5%	11.0%	29.5%	22.5%	500	–	500.0	0.00
14	9.4%	8.5%	24.5%	11.0%	29.5%	22.5%	500	–	500.0	0.00

adjusted in case that the stressed WAC exceeds stressed yield.

$$Yield'(t) = \max[WAC(t) + 5\%, Yield(t)] \tag{B.17}$$

$$ExcessSpread(t) = Bal_{invest}(t) \times (Yield'(t)$$
$$- WAC(t) - SvcRate(t) - DefRate(t)) \div Freq \tag{B.18}$$

$$ReqCreditEnhance = \sum_t \min[0, ExcessSpread(t)] \tag{B.19}$$

The required credit enhancement can be compared to the total subordinate bond balance to determine if the structure supports the target rating. If there is not enough enhancement, then more subordinate bonds are needed.

As an example, consider a structure with $462.5MM seniors and $37.5MM mezzanine for a total of $500MM. There are no junior bonds and no seller participation. The seniors cannot be rated AAA, yet it can be rated AA, given the inputs in Table B.4. For AAA stress, the necessary credit enhancement is $43.5MM, about $6MM greater than the mezzanine tranche. For AA stress, the necessary credit enhancement is $31.75MM, so the mezzanine is sufficient. Table B.4 shows a portion of the AA cash flow.

One way to convert this static model into a dynamic model is to treat MPR and default rate as stochastic variables. For instance, changes in each of these variables can be sampled from the standard Normal distribution $N(0,1)$ scaled by an appropriate variance. The two variables can be sampled in a correlated manner. Shor (2002) suggests the values: 0.15% monthly change in default variance and 79% (monthly change in) MPR variance, with –20% correlation. These factors are negatively correlated because under economic stress, defaults increase as payment rate decreases.

References

Agarwal, N., "Update to Subprime Residential Mortgage Securitization Assumptions," Structured Finance Special Report, Moody's Investors Service, December 2, 2005.

Ahmed, S., M. Cohen and S. Libreros, "Use of Transition Matrices in Risk Management and Valuation," Fair Isaac White Paper, September 2004.

Bank of America, "*The Bank of America Guide to Advanced Correlation Products*," London, 2004.

Bear Stearns, "Across the Curve in Rates and Structured Products," Fixed Income Research, Bear Stearns, May 2, 2006.

Benninga, S., *Financial Modeling*, 2nd ed. Boston: MIT Press, 2000.

Calabretta, T., and J. Salvesen, "Mortgage Calculations," *Bloomberg Markets*, pp. 156–157, August 2006.

Carty, L., "Moody's Rating Migration and Credit Quality Correlation 1920–1996," Special Comment, Moody's Investors Service, July 1997.

Chaplin, G., *Credit Derivatives*, Hoboken, NJ: John Wiley & Sons, Ltd., December 2005.

Cifuentes, A. and B. Lancaster, Ed., *Collateralized Debt Obligations: Structures, Strategies & Innovations*, 2nd ed. Wachovia Securities, 2004.

Cifuentes, A., and G. O'Connor, "The Binomial Expansion Method Applied to CBO/CLO Analysis," Moody's Investor Service, Special Report, December 1996.

Countrywide Home Loans, "CWABS Asset-Backed Certificates Trust 2005-3," Prospectus Supplement, October 25, 2004.

Credit Suisse, "Introduction to ABS CDS and the ABX Index," *Fixed Income Research*, January 25, 2006.

Davies, P. J., "Difficulties for U.S. Auto Industry Raise Queries Over CDOs," *Financial Times*, March 23, 2006.

Drake, A., *Fundamentals of Applied Probability Theory*, New York: McGraw-Hill, 1967.

Dullmann, K., "Measuring Business Sector Concentration by an Infection Model," Deutsche Bundesbank, Discussion Paper No. 03/2006.

Dupire, B. ed., *Monte Carlo: Methodologies and Applications for Pricing and Risk Management*. London: Risk Books, 1998.

Fabozzi, F. J. and F. Modigliani, *Mortgage & Mortgage-Backed Securities Markets*. Boston: Harvard Business School Press, 1992.

Fabozzi, F. J. ed., *The Handbook of Fixed Income Securities*, 5th ed. New York: McGraw-Hill, 1997.

Fitch, "Basel II: Bottom-Line Impact on Securitization Markets," Special Report, Fitch Ratings Ltd., September 12, 2005.

Gauthier, L., "The Secrets of NIMs," UBS Warburg, April 26, 2002.

Glasserman, P., *Monte Carlo Methods in Financial Engineering*. New York: Springer, 2003.

Gottfried, B. S., *Spreadsheet Tools for Engineers*. New York: McGraw-Hill, 1996.

Hull, J. "Valuing Correlation Dependent Credit Derivatives," Presentation at IXIS Capital Markets, December 8, 2006.

ILOG, "ILOG CPLEX 8.0 User's Manual," July 2002.

Jackson, M., and M. Staunton *Advanced Modelling in Finance Using Excel and VBA*. New York: John Wiley & Sons, Ltd., 2001.

J. P. Morgan, "Par Credit Default Swap Spread Approximation from Default Probabilities," Credit Derivatives, October 24, 2001.

J. P. Morgan, "ABS Monitor: 2006 Outlook," Global Structured Finance Research, December 20, 2005.

Kornfeld, W., "U.S. Subprime Mortgage Securitization Cashflow Analytics," Moody's Investors Service, March 17, 2004.

Larson, R. J., and M. L. Marx, *An Introduction to Mathematical Statistics and its Applications*, 2nd ed. Upper Saddle River, NJ: Prentice Hall, 1986.

Lehman Brothers, "ABS Credit Default Swaps—A Primer," *Fixed Income Research*, December 9, 2005.

Lehman Brothers, "Introduction to the ABX," *Fixed Income Research*, January 18, 2006.

Li, D. X., and J. Skarabot, "Valuation and Risk Analysis of Synthetic Collateralized Debt Obligations: A Copula Function Approach," in: Gregory, J., ed., *Credit Derivatives: The Definitive Guide*, London: Risk Books, 2003.

Longstaff, F., and A. Rajan, "An Empirical Analysis of the Pricing of Collateralized Debt Obligations," presentation at IXIS Capital Markets, Fall 2006.

Lucas, D.J., L.S. Goodman, and F.J. Fabozzi, *Collateralized Debt Obligations: Structures and Analysis*, 2nd ed. Hoboken, NJ: John Wiley & Sons Inc, 2006.

Mahadevan, S., et al., *Structured Credit Insights: Instruments, Valuation and Strategies*, 2nd ed., Morgan Stanley, 2006a.

Mahadevan, S., et al., *Structured Credit Insights: Single Name Instruments & Strategies*, 2nd Ed., Morgan Stanley, 2006b.

Mansour, S., "Optimization with Dynamic Functions," *ACM SIGAPL Quote Quad*, Volume 29, Issue 3, March 1999.

MCS (Mathematics and Computer Science Division), Argonne National Laboratory, www.mcs.anl.gov, May 2006.

Molony, W., "Housing Affordability Index Hits 30-Year High," National Association of Realtors (NAR), May 1, 2003.

Morgan Stanley, "CDO Market Insights—Streetwise Correlation: Taking the ABS Road," *Fixed Income Research*, November 14, 2006.

Morgan Stanley, "Mortgage Pass-Through Certificates, Series 2004 HE2," Prospectus Supplement, March 10, 2004a.

Morgan Stanley, "NIM Trust 2004-HE2N Private Placement Memorandum," May 26 2004b.

Morgan Stanley, "Mortgage Pass-Through Certificates, Series 2004 HE4," Prospectus Supplement, Nov. 12, 2004c.

Morgan Stanley, "Mortgage Pass-Through Certificates, Series 2005 HE3," Prospectus Supplement, July 25, 2005.

NAG, *NAG Fortran Library Introductory Guide, Mark 20*, The Numerical Algorithms Group Ltd., September 2001.

Papadimitriou, C. H., and K. Steiglitz, *Combinatorial Optimization: Algorithms and Complexity*, Dover, 1998.

Pratt, R., "Analyzing MBS Collateral," *Bloomberg Markets*, pp. 152–153, August 2006.

Press, W. H., *Numerical Recipes in C*, 2nd ed. New York: Cambridge University Press, 1992, www.library.cornell.edu/nr/cbookcpdf.html.

PSA (Public Securities Association), "PSA Standard Formulas," June 29, 1993.

Schonbucher, P. J., *Credit Derivatives Pricing Models*, Hoboken, NJ: John Wiley & Sons, Ltd., 2003.

Schorin, C. and M. Mehra, *Home Equity Handbook*, 2005 edition, Morgan Stanley, February 17, 2005.

Shor, J., "Credit Card ABS: Profiling Risks and Return," Brown Brothers Harriman, May 2002.

Simon, R., "New Type of Mortgage Surges in Popularity," *Wall Street Journal*, April 19, 2006a.

Simon, R., "Lenders Push Home-Equity Deals," *Wall Street Journal*, April 27, 2006b.

Standard & Poor's, "Technical Specifications for Standard & Poor's LEVELS Engine Version 5.6," McGraw-Hill, 2003a.

Standard & Poor's, "Standard & Poor's LEVELS Version 5.6," McGraw-Hill, 2003b.

Standard & Poor's, "Cash Flow Assumptions," Residential Mortgage Group, Memorandum, McGraw-Hill, June 17, 2005a.

Standard & Poor's, "Standard & Poor's SPIRE," Technical User Guide, Version 2.0, McGraw-Hill, 2005b.

Standard & Poor's, "Standard & Poor's Announces Revised U.S. RMBS Simultaneous Second Lien Criteria," U.S. RMBS Issuer Alert, McGraw-Hill, April 7, 2006.

Stoppard, T., *Rosencrantz & Guildenstern Are Dead*, Grove Press Inc., 1967.

Strang G., *Linear Algebra and Its Applications*, 4th ed. Brooks Cole, 1995.

Tavakoli, J., *Credit Derivatives & Synthetic Structures: A Guide to Instruments and Applications*, 2nd ed., Hoboken, NJ: John Wiley & Sons, 2001.

Tavakoli, J. M., *Collateralized Debt Obligations and Structured Finance*, Hoboken, NJ: John Wiley & Sons, 2003.

Weisstein, E., *mathworld*, Wolfram Research, www.mathworld.worlfram.com, 2006.

Whetten, M., and M. Adelson, *"Credit Default Swap (CDS) Primer," Fixed Income Research*, Nomura Securities International, Inc., May 12, 2004a.

Whetten, M., and M. Adelson, *"Correlation Primer," Fixed Income Research*, Nomura Securities International, Inc., August 6, 2004b.

Whetten, M., and M. Adelson, *"Tranching Credit Risk," Fixed Income Research*, Nomura Securities International, Inc., October 8, 2004c.

Whetten, M., and M. Adelson, "*'The Bespoke [bispouk]'—a Guide to Single-Tranche Synthetic CDOs*," *Fixed Income Research*, Nomura Securities International, Inc., November 17, 2004d.

Whetten, M., and W. Jin, "CDO Equity, Correlation, and IRR," *Fixed Income Research*, Nomura Securities International, Inc., March 21, 2005.

Xie, M., and G. Witt, "Moody's Modeling Approach to Rating Structured Finance Cash Flow CDO Transactions," *Structured Finance*, Moody's Investors Service, September 26, 2005.

Zimmerman, T., "State of Subprime Credit and Correlation Modeling," UBS, January 2007.

Index